The New York Times

TAKE IT WITH YOU MONDAY CROSSWORDS

Published in the United States by St. Martin's Griffin,
an imprint of St. Martin's Publishing Group

THE NEW YORK TIMES TAKE IT WITH YOU MONDAY CROSSWORDS.
Copyright © 2022 by The New York Times Company. All rights reserved.
Printed in the United States of America. For information, address
St. Martin's Publishing Group, 120 Broadway, New York, NY 10271.

www.stmartins.com

All of the puzzles that appear in this work were originally published in
The New York Times from January 1, 2018, to November 1, 2021.
Copyright © 2018, 2019, 2020, 2021 by The New York Times Company.
All rights reserved. Reprinted by permission.

ISBN 978-1-250-84748-5

Our books may be purchased in bulk for promotional, educational, or
business use. Please contact your local bookseller or the Macmillan Corporate and
Premium Sales Department at 1-800-221-7945, extension 5442, or by email
at MacmillanSpecialMarkets@macmillan.com.

First Edition: 2022

10 9 8 7 6 5 4 3 2 1

The New York Times

TAKE IT WITH YOU MONDAY CROSSWORDS
200 Removable Puzzles

Edited by Will Shortz

ST. MARTIN'S GRIFFIN
NEW YORK

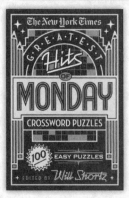
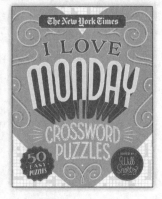

ACROSS

1. ___ Polo, traveler at the court of Kublai Khan
6. Rings of water around castles
11. Russian fighter jet
14. Come clean
15. Property defacer
16. Signature Obama legislation, for short
17. Jon Bon Jovi torch song?
19. Centerpiece of a frat party
20. Stick in one's ___
21. Province west of Que.
22. Chest muscles, for short
23. J.F.K.'s W.W. II command
26. Tiny battery size
27. Med. school subject
28. Lawyer's charge
29. Elvis Presley torch song?
32. Squid, in Italian cuisine
35. Tough puzzle
36. Bangles torch song?
40. Sudden outpouring
42. Some Canadian petroleum deposits
45. The Doors torch song?
49. "Lower your voice, please"
50. Pale blue hue
51. Horse of a certain color
52. With prudence
55. Fat used in mincemeat
56. Place
57. Match up
58. Sarcastic laugh syllable
59. The Trammps torch song?
64. Opposite of WSW
65. Letter-shaped girders
66. Diplomat
67. Norm: Abbr.
68. Drives the getaway car for, say
69. Grabs some Z's

DOWN

1. Unruly throng
2. Leatherworker's punch
3. Genetic carrier, briefly
4. Ancient Incan capital
5. "Madama Butterfly," for one
6. S.I. or GQ
7. Given out for a time
8. Hebrew for "my Lord"
9. Scottish pattern
10. Crafty
11. Speak gobbledygook
12. Glacial chamber
13. Joke writer
15. Ex-G.I.'s org.
18. Crunchy, healthful snack
22. Pablo Picasso's designer daughter
23. Army E-3: Abbr.
24. Pekoe, for one
25. Under siege
26. "Madama Butterfly" highlight
30. Server with a spigot
31. Transcript figs.
33. To boot
34. Chance upon
37. Pork cut
38. Christmas tree
39. "Inside ___ Davis" (Coen brothers film)
40. Cuts drastically, as prices
41. Pleasingly tangy
43. FedEx competitor
44. Like a wallflower
46. Onetime Dr Pepper rival
47. "Get it?"
48. Wealthy sort, informally
53. Derive via logic
54. Public outburst
57. Kim, to Kourtney or Khloé
59. A day in Spain
60. Yoga chants
61. #vanlife homes, briefly
62. "Let's ___ and say we did"
63. Kvetchers' cries

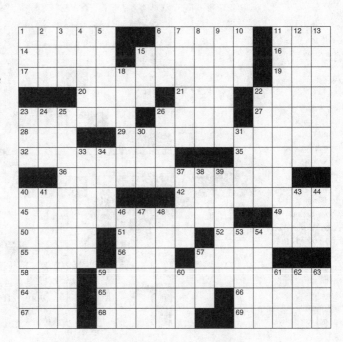

by Matthew Sewell

ACROSS

1 Pour love (on)
5 Prod
9 Antlered Yellowstone denizens
13 "Vous ___ ici" (French for "You are here")
14 Derby entry
15 ___ fide (in bad faith)
16 Cries of discovery
17 "Would you mind?"
19 Letter accompanying a college application, informally
20 "This can't be good"
21 N.F.L. team for which Joe Namath was a QB
22 Informal breakfast beverage order
25 Approximately, datewise
26 Cowboy movie setting
27 "Yes," at the altar
29 "Quiet!"
30 "Dumb" bird
31 Botches
33 Hypnotist's command
38 Expensive
39 Actor Jared of "Suicide Squad"
42 College dorm overseers, for short
45 Neckwear for a lobster eater
46 Michigan/Ontario border river
49 Skin care brand
51 "Ulysses" star, 1967
53 Like the first "d" in "Wednesday"
55 Salon job
56 Potentially alarming sight for an ocean bather
57 Cappuccino relative
59 Pizazz
60 Desertlike
61 Skiers' shelter
62 Poker table payment
63 Strong cleansers
64 Like the Amazon rain forest
65 Company heads, in brief

DOWN

1 "Holy Toledo!"
2 Board game named after a Shakespeare play
3 Container for oolong or chai
4 Figure on Superman's chest
5 Stop being strict
6 Branch of dentistry, informally
7 Fireplace residue
8 College person with a "list"
9 Smiley face or frowny face
10 Los Angeles hoopsters
11 Coffee get-together
12 Prepares for a doctor's throat examination
14 Chipper greetings
18 Holder of baseball's highest career batting average (.366)
20 Manipulate
23 In one fell ___
24 ___ Stein, Green Party candidate for president in 2012 and 2016
28 Twosome
31 Take to the skies
32 Opposite of buys
34 University of Illinois city
35 Nintendo Switch predecessor
36 Cold War weapon inits.
37 "Sure, whatever"
40 Connect with
41 Sunset shades
42 Scamp
43 Where birds of a feather flock together
44 Many a Snapchat pic
46 Santa's vehicle
47 Rich cake
48 Alternative to "net" or "org"
50 Monopoly cards
52 Tablets that run Safari
54 Rock's Jethro ___
58 "Skip to My ___"
59 Onetime teen heartthrob Efron

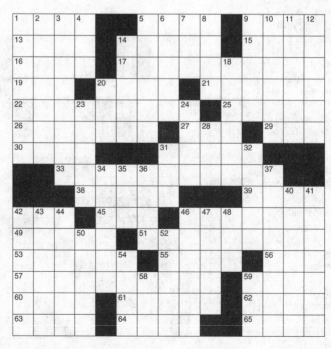

by Sam Ezersky

ACROSS

1 Big advertiser at auto races
4 Sunoco competitor
9 Distinctive smell
13 Breakfast restaurant chain
15 Quarter Pounder topper
16 Jay who preceded Jimmy Fallon
17 Singer's latest
19 "What's gotten ___ you?"
20 Poems whose titles often start "To a . . ."
21 Con's opposite
22 Alternatives to Nikes
23 Lodge member
24 Like religious institutions vis-à-vis the I.R.S.
26 King Arthur's magician
29 The lion in summer?
30 "Disgusting!"
31 What gigabytes might measure
35 Vexes
39 "We can go safely now"
42 Like food from a West African drive-through?
43 Tire material
44 In the style of
45 Envision
47 Scores two under par
49 "Excuse me?"
55 YouTube posting, casually
56 Praise highly
57 The Diamondbacks, on scoreboards
58 Vicinity
60 ___ monster (desert denizen)
61 Final words of Martin Luther King Jr.'s "I Have a Dream" speech . . . or a hint to the endings of 17-, 24-, 39- and 49-Across

64 Wartime friend
65 Actress Christina
66 Chunk of concrete
67 Loch ___ monster
68 Approved, as a contract
69 Resting place?

DOWN

1 Covet one's neighbor's wife, e.g.
2 "The Cosby Show" son
3 Volatile situation
4 Mustard in the game Clue, e.g.: Abbr.
5 Bumbling
6 Queen's crown
7 Shout at Fenway Park
8 Final word shouted before "Happy New Year!"
9 Cruet filler at an Italian restaurant
10 Jeans material
11 Not bottled, at a bar
12 Perch in a chicken house
14 Green shampoo
18 ___ Pie (frozen treat)
22 Tree toppler
25 French president's palace
26 Catcher's glove
27 Canyon effect
28 More proximate
32 East Lansing sch.
33 Gambling parlor, for short
34 Umbrella part
36 Super bargains
37 Vitamin-rich green vegetable

38 Mmes. of Madrid
40 Dresses up for a comic con, say
41 Fancy tie
46 Grab a bite
48 TV's "2 Broke ___"
49 Started
50 Napoleon, on St. Helena
51 Vexes
52 Bobby who sang "Mack the Knife"
53 Big name in vacuum cleaners
54 Sister's daughter, e.g.
59 "Right now!"
61 Payday, often: Abbr.
62 Help
63 Letters on an unfinished sched.

by Agnes Davidson and Zhouqin Burnikel

4

ACROSS

1 Ponzi schemes, e.g.
6 Agatha Christie or Maggie Smith
10 Times past noon, informally
14 "Sounds exciting . . ."
15 Iranian currency
16 Applaud
17 Cutting-edge brand?
18 2016 Best Actress Oscar winner for "La La Land"
20 Unwelcome looks
22 Somewhat
23 Encouragement for a matador
24 Half of a half step in music
26 Relieved (of)
27 Biden and Pence, informally
28 Abbr. in an office address
29 Pacific source of unusual weather
31 Stoic politician of ancient Rome
33 Places to get quick cash
36 Chess endings
37 Weight unit equal to about 2,205 pounds
40 Group of eight
43 Gym locker emanation
44 On the briny
48 "Legally ___" (Reese Witherspoon film)
50 Fix, as an election
52 Be nosy
53 "Leaving ___ Vegas"
54 "Puh-LEEZE!"
58 Like the name "Robin Banks" for a criminal
59 Make, as money
60 Grand stories
61 Enthusiastic audience response, informally
64 Bit of clowning around
66 Title of a list of errands
67 ___ Wallace, co-founder of Reader's Digest
68 Fish typically split before cooking
69 Sudden problem in a plan
70 Look for
71 Ariana Grande's fan base, mostly

DOWN

1 "Red" or "White" baseball team
2 Deep-fried Mexican dish
3 Div. for the N.F.L.'s Jets
4 Less talkative
5 Laughs through the nose
6 "Forgot About ___" (2000 rap hit)
7 Put in the cross hairs
8 Caribbean ballroom dance
9 "Seinfeld" character who wrote for the J. Peterman catalog
10 One of two in "Hamilton"
11 Go from 0 to 60, say
12 What sunning in a swimsuit leaves
13 Racer's swimwear
19 Sailor's patron
21 Start to attack
24 Home shopping inits.
25 Back in style
30 Grandmother, affectionately
32 Muscat is its capital
34 Prefix with life or wife
35 Look down on
38 Swirled
39 Jiffy
40 Administrative regions in Russia
41 Eric who sang "Layla"
42 Deep-fried Mexican dish
45 Bond film after "Skyfall"
46 Natural process illustrated by the last words of 18-, 24-, 37-, 54- and 61-Across
47 Novelist Rand
49 Inbox buildup
51 Exceed
55 "Sesame Street" character long rumored to be Bert's lover
56 Something acute or obtuse
57 Chop finely
62 Holiday drink
63 Tree with acorns
65 Successors to LPs

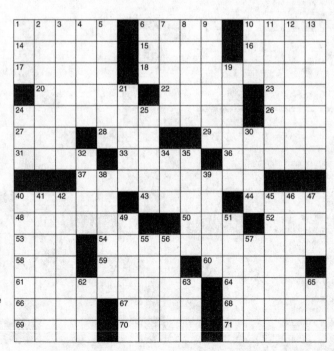

by Paolo Pasco

ACROSS

1 Scuttlebutt
7 ___ Fridays (restaurant chain)
10 Slob's creation
14 Hedy in Hollywood
15 Dessert topper from a can
17 And others, in a bibliography
18 Estrange
19 Org. for Penguins and Ducks
20 Wintry coating
22 Vice president Spiro
23 Cunning
25 Spill the beans
28 Online source for health info
30 Take a stab at
34 "Ye olde" place to browse
36 Up to, as a particular time
37 Govern
38 Goopy roofing material
39 High U.S. Navy rank
42 Farrow in films
43 Building annexes
45 Particle with a charge
46 Thief
48 Students' simulation of global diplomacy, informally
50 Arctic abode
51 "Scram!"
53 Sleepover attire, informally
55 Twisty curves
58 The "P" of PRNDL
60 Scanned lines on a pkg.
62 Diminish the work force . . . or a literal hint to the answers to the four starred clues
65 Deficiency in red blood cells
67 Ship-related
68 Searched thoroughly, with "through"
69 Fighting force
70 Raises
71 Praises highly

DOWN

1 "Galveston" singer Campbell
2 Inauguration Day vows
3 *"Crazy to run into you here!"
4 Erie Canal mule of song
5 Blue or hazel eye part
6 *Newspapers or magazines
7 Fish with a heavy net
8 Form of some shampoo
9 Amin exiled from Uganda
10 One circulating at a party
11 "Trainspotting" actor McGregor
12 Building lot
13 Spurt forcefully
16 Gave a hand
21 Brit. resource for writers
24 "You betcha!"
26 Den
27 *Contest for an areawide seat
29 Controversial chemical in plastics, for short
31 *Nonsense
32 Ballerina's bend
33 Drop running down the cheek
34 Pipe part
35 Angel's band of light
36 Sardine container
40 Like early LPs
41 Response to an online joke
44 Age reached by a septuagenarian
47 1940s–'50s jazz
49 Asian yogurt drink
50 "This ___ test"
52 German cars with a lightning bolt logo
54 Long-winded sales pitch
55 Poet ___ St. Vincent Millay
56 Rise quickly
57 Taken a dip
59 U.S. fort with very tight security
61 Scoundrels
63 Post-O.R. area
64 Stick in the microwave
66 Fire dept. responder, maybe

by Lynn Lempel

6

ACROSS
1 Possesses
4 Grape-Nuts or Apple Jacks
10 Ewe's offspring
14 Man's name that's an investment spelled backward
15 Pumpkin color
16 Revered one
17 Pot's cover
18 Traditional night for partying
20 Side of a diamond
22 Thomas ___, "Rule, Britannia" composer
23 Bowling target
24 Texas landmark to "remember"
27 Sampled
29 Curved Pillsbury item
33 Misplace
34 "The Way We ___"
35 "Yeah, right!"
39 Pie ___ mode
40 Detectives
42 Batman portrayer Kilmer
43 Deserve
45 ___-Pacific (geopolitical region)
46 Something to click online
47 Ones calling the plays
50 Teeter-totter
53 Walk with a swagger
54 Every last drop
55 Parade spoiler
58 "Piece of cake" or "easy as pie"
61 40-hour-a-week work
65 Guadalajara gold
66 Actress Falco of "Nurse Jackie"
67 "Hot" Mexican dish
68 Prefix with natal or classical
69 Clarinet or sax
70 Crossed home plate, say
71 One who might follow into a family business

DOWN
1 50%
2 Song for a diva
3 Early TV comic known for "Your Show of Shows"
4 Popular cold and flu medicine
5 "But I heard him exclaim, ___ he drove out of sight . . ."
6 Uncooked
7 One-named Irish singer
8 Ending with golden or teen
9 Makeshift shelter
10 Fleur-de-___
11 Highly capable
12 Multiplex offering
13 Mix
19 Kingdoms
21 "Anything ___?"
25 Whimper like a baby
26 Like most Bluetooth headsets
28 Underhanded
29 Tight-lipped sort
30 Part to play
31 Be confident in
32 Fixes, as shoelaces
36 Forcible removals, as of tenants
37 Pull hard
38 Civic-minded group
40 Fictional mouse ___ Little
41 Male deer
44 Mensa stats
46 Lavish praise on
48 Hangs around for
49 Gave some money under the table
50 More secure
51 Give the slip
52 Actress Kemper of "Unbreakable Kimmy Schmidt"
56 Apple on a desk
57 Pixar's "Finding ___"
59 Nabisco snack since 1912
60 It has phases that are represented by the starts of 18-, 29-, 47- and 61-Across . . . and by 1-Down
62 Was in front
63 Pickle holder
64 Bullfight cheer

by Alan Arbesfeld

ACROSS

1 Horror sequel of 2005
6 Reverberation
10 Movers' vehicles
14 Sow, as seeds
15 Clammy
16 Theater award
17 Best-selling autobiography by Priscilla Presley
19 Be the best, in slang
20 Michelle of the L.P.G.A.
21 Any singer of the 1973 #1 hit "Love Train"
22 Actor John of "Problem Child"
24 Neil who sang "Laughter in the Rain"
26 Antiriot spray
27 State capital ESE of Guadalajara
33 Like a porcupine
36 Woods nymph
37 Cartoon "devil," informally
38 Window part
39 Sanders in the Pro Football Hall of Fame
40 Jazzman Stan
41 Onetime competitor of the WB
42 Machine near the end of a car wash
43 ___ Island (amusement park site)
44 Many a 1970s remix
47 Rock's Clapton or Burdon
48 Dressed for a classic fraternity party
52 Fixes, as a photocopier
55 Front's opposite
57 Sch. in Charlottesville
58 Dove calls
59 One with credit . . . or a literal hint to 17-, 27- and 44-Across
62 Queue
63 What separates Nevada from Colorado

64 Barely visible, as a star
65 Rarely getting rain
66 Hang in the balance
67 ___ the bill (pays for something)

DOWN

1 Shoots out
2 "Kate & ___" of 1980s TV
3 Signaled with the hand
4 Singer Kamoze with the 1994 hit "Here Comes the Hotstepper"
5 "There, there"
6 Author Ferber
7 Suffragist Elizabeth ___ Stanton
8 "Lemme think . . ."
9 1990s "Saturday Night Live" character with a cape
10 Whirlpool
11 Touch
12 Stream near the Great Pyramids
13 Crystal ball user
18 Cleanser brand with a name from mythology
23 Like some sprains and tea
25 Primo
26 City hall V.I.P.s
28 High muckety-muck on Madison Avenue
29 Town ___ (colonial figure)
30 Major Calif.-to-Fla. route
31 Oscar-winning actress Blanchett
32 Rocker Osbourne
33 Tater
34 Big ___ (longtime Red Sox nickname)
35 B&Bs

39 Tennis tournament since 1900
40 Percussion in a Buddhist temple
42 Wriggler on a fishhook
43 "Iron Chef" competition
45 Brought to a halt
46 Poison ivy symptom
49 Sound part of a broadcast
50 Happening
51 Pub game
52 Home of the N.C.A.A.'s Bruins
53 Pinot ___
54 Folk singer Mitchell
55 Muffin material
56 What Ritalin helps treat, for short
60 Had a bite
61 "7 Faces of Dr. ___" (1964 film)

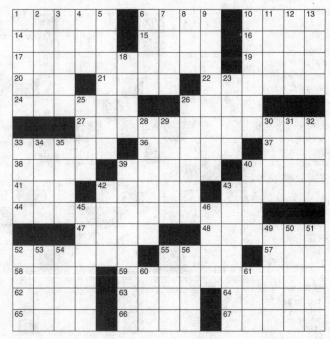

by Michael Black

ACROSS

1 Skirt bottoms
5 Ticklish Muppet
9 Gets thin on top
14 With: Fr.
15 Banquet
16 Lewis and ___ Expedition
17 GARFIELD + U = Beach V.I.P.
19 "___ at the Bat"
20 City NW of Detroit
21 "Help me, Obi-Wan Kenobi," e.g.
23 Home for Nixon and Reagan: Abbr.
24 "It's a date!"
26 MADISON + A = "Me, too!"
29 Shakespearean cries
30 Bounding main
32 Pathetic group
33 Mysterious sighting in the Himalayas
35 Some rulings on PolitiFact
38 Mortgage, e.g.
39 FILLMORE + V = Movie buff
42 Like racehorses' feet
44 Who asks "What can I help you with?" on an iPhone
45 Author Silverstein
49 Soccer blocker
51 President pro ___
53 Lab eggs
54 HARDING + P = Squeezable exercise tool
57 Actor Snipes of "White Men Can't Jump"
59 Approves
60 Famous ___ cookies
62 River of Cologne
63 Uncle Sam's land, for short
66 COOLIDGE + P = Narc's four-footed helper
68 Humdingers
69 Panache
70 Pistol sound
71 Hybrid picnic utensil
72 Philosophies
73 First half of a Senate vote

DOWN

1 Two-year mark, in a presidential term
2 Wicked look
3 Egoistic demand
4 National Mall, for a presidential inauguration
5 Six-foot bird
6 ___ years (when presidents are elected)
7 Maples formerly married to Donald Trump
8 Like the days of yore
9 Send covertly, as an email
10 Leader in a state roll call: Abbr.
11 Milan opera house
12 "You wish!"
13 Like atria
18 Onetime Pontiac muscle cars
22 What a majority of campaign spending goes toward
25 Dickens's Little ___
27 Store sign on Presidents' Day
28 Aromas
31 Gets ready to shoot
34 "Too rich for my blood"
36 QB Manning
37 Separate, as whites from colors
40 "Got it!," beatnik-style
41 ABC show on weekday mornings, with "The"
42 Absorbs
43 "Star Wars" pilot
46 There's one to honor presidents every February
47 The slightest amount
48 What hens do
49 Grave robbers
50 Word after many presidents' names
52 Bygone Ford make, briefly
55 Celebrated Chinese-born architect
56 Diving venues
58 Queen of ___ (visitor of King Solomon, in the Bible)
61 Poetry competition
64 Mink or sable
65 Query
67 Political connections

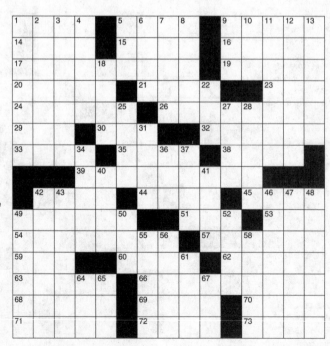

by Bruce Haight

ACROSS

1 Sound from a pound
4 Discontinued Swedish cars
9 Snapshot
14 ___ Zedong
15 ___ Vanilli, group with three #1 hits in 1989
16 Open the door for
17 Be sick
18 Drip-dry fabric
19 Preferred seat request in an airplane
20 Not dead yet!
23 Substituted (for)
24 Laceless shoe fastener
28 Horror director Craven
29 Warm winter wear
31 Baseball's Gehrig
32 Dilutes
36 ___ ex machina
37 Listens to
38 Sí : Spain :: ___ : France
39 "Fee-fi-fo-fum" sayer
40 Objectives
41 Pick up dry cleaning, go to the post office, etc.
43 ___ v. Wade
44 Author Vonnegut
45 Snakelike fish
46 Avenging spirits of Greek myth
48 With possibly even direr consequences
52 "What is life?," "Why are we here?," etc.
55 Bricklayer, e.g.
58 Slight advantage
59 Soph. and jr.
60 Bathroom unit
61 Be of ___ (avail)
62 Fannie ___ (mortgage company)
63 Full of the latest
64 Glossy finish
65 Midlength records, for short

DOWN

1 Stockpile
2 Bonnie who sang "I Can't Make You Love Me"
3 First ___ (Shakespeare volume)
4 Burns slowly
5 Simulated smooch
6 Like a poker player who's either very confident or really bluffing
7 Like-minded voting group
8 Swim's alternative
9 Mercury or Mars
10 Katherine of "27 Dresses"
11 Settlers of tied games, for short
12 Michael Jackson's "Don't Stop ___ You Get Enough"
13 Tip jar bill
21 Brings to half-mast
22 ___ the Terrible
25 Fresh from the laundry
26 Circular
27 Ejects
29 Go "1, 2, 3, 4 . . ."
30 Injury, in totspeak
32 Where ships dock
33 "Wheel of Fortune" purchases
34 Circus whip-cracker
35 Gloomy
36 Conversation
39 Enjoyed frequently as a child
41 Trick
42 Send on a detour, say
44 With enthusiasm
47 Personal heroes
48 "Well, shucks!"
49 What the first, second and fifth lines in a limerick do
50 Pocketbook part
51 Slalom curves
53 +
54 Pianist/radio host John
55 AOL alternative
56 Breakfasted or lunched
57 Wise old saying . . . like the first words of 20-, 32-, 41- and 52-Across

by Andrea Carla Michaels and Mark Diehl

ACROSS

1 Snake charmer's snake
6 Pushy
11 Coquettishly playful
14 First zodiac sign
15 Highway
16 Network of medical providers, in brief
17 Country bumpkin's counterpart
19 Oil-drilling apparatus
20 Weed-whacking tool
21 Assists
22 Prius maker
24 Following
26 From Shanghai or Mumbai, say
27 Woman having literary interests
31 Hosts for roasts
34 Carried the day
35 Corporate head, for short
36 Group choosing a 35-Across
37 Smucker's product
38 Grew ashen
40 Hit on the head
41 Ad exhortation
42 Solitary sorts
43 Pompous person
47 Usually spicy Indian dish
48 Disheveled
52 Lou on six winning World Series teams
54 Soup can painter Warhol
55 Motorists' org.
56 "How ___ doing?"
57 Know-it-all
60 Smith & Wesson product
61 Swimming phenom Ledecky
62 Fjord, e.g.
63 He hee-haws
64 Slammin' Sammy of golf
65 King on "CBS This Morning"

DOWN

1 Hidden stash
2 Hunter in the night sky
3 What fishermen want from fish but not from mosquitoes
4 Heroine of "Star Wars: The Last Jedi"
5 Attacked vigorously
6 What you might come across at a river?
7 Fierce fliers of myth
8 Diving bird of the Arctic
9 High, wide-brimmed hat
10 Brave
11 Historical account
12 Skip
13 Hindu-inspired exercise
18 "Peanuts" boy with a security blanket
23 Shaggy Tibetan beast
25 Cab company competitor
26 Elemental bit
28 Persuades
29 ___-do-well
30 Mount Olympus residents
31 Subsides
32 No longer relevant
33 Monkeys named for monks
37 Children's writer Blume
38 Looney Tunes character who says "Th-th-th-that's all, folks!"
39 Card game stake
41 Ingmar who directed "The Seventh Seal"
42 Lucky ___ (nickname for the Spirit of St. Louis pilot)
44 Taboo for PETA
45 Pats down, as a suspect
46 Pursued, as prey
49 Virile
50 Dev who starred in 2016's "Lion"
51 One of the five senses
52 Infatuated
53 Birds on Australian coins
54 Operatic solo
58 Cleaned one's plate
59 Santa ___ winds

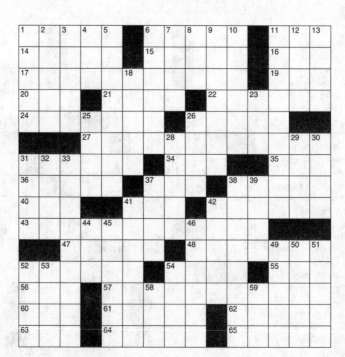

by Lynn Lempel

ACROSS

1 Parts missing from the Venus de Milo
5 Ancient Greek market
10 What hairy dogs do in the spring
14 Boyfriend
15 Toilet paper layers, e.g.
16 Architect Saarinen
17 Complain querulously
18 *Monster outsmarted by Odysseus
20 Drivers doing 90, say
22 With mouth wide open
23 Indian queen
24 Tin lizzies
26 *Rat Pack member who sang and danced
30 Parts with irises
31 Actor Morales of "La Bamba"
32 See 39-Across
35 Dawn, to Donne
36 Like clothes in the hamper
38 Servant in "Young Frankenstein"
39 With 32-Across, what the answers to the starred clues each have
40 Brief moments, briefly
41 Frighten
42 *Black face card whose face is seen in profile
45 Indy or Daytona
48 What two fives are change for
49 Cancel at Cape Canaveral
50 "Star Wars Episode IV" subtitle
54 *Comic character on a gum wrapper
57 Satanic
58 Part of a list with bullets
59 Scam
60 Swimmers' units

61 Hawaiian goose
62 "Two mints in one" sloganeer
63 Nolo contendere, e.g.

DOWN

1 Things learned in "The Alphabet Song"
2 Harvest
3 Stallion's mate
4 Hero who's neither a bird nor a plane
5 Tack on
6 Steinem who co-founded Ms. magazine
7 Classic paintings
8 Spanish king
9 Biter of Cleopatra
10 Folk legend Pete
11 Blood-related
12 Blow, as a volcano
13 Amounts in a hypodermic needle

19 Pilgrim to Mecca
21 February has the fewest of them
24 Aerosol spray
25 Start of "The Star-Spangled Banner"
26 Sport originally part of a Shinto ritual
27 Shakespeare's stream
28 Parisian mother
29 Left page in a book
32 "Heavens to Betsy!"
33 Bygone times
34 "___ Tú" (1974 song)
36 Ten: Prefix
37 Highly off-putting
38 "Allow me"
40 Handled, as a task
41 Blow, as from a volcano
42 Saint known for translating the Bible into Latin

43 Spread, as people in a search party
44 The Lone Ranger's Silver and others
45 Former Israeli P.M. Yitzhak
46 Lessen
47 Cheat
50 "When it's ___" (answer to an old riddle)
51 Squished circle
52 Prop for Sherlock Holmes
53 Two-time Oscar-nominated actress Lanchester
55 The Colonel's restaurant
56 "I am, you ___, he is"

by John R. O'Brien

12

ACROSS

1 Radical Hoffman who wrote "Steal This Book"
6 Stimulating quality
10 Huff and puff
14 John who married Pocahontas
15 On the briny
16 Opposite of "on tape"
17 *Garnish for a cocktail
19 Takes advantage of
20 The "A" of A.D.
21 Zipped along
22 Tin Man's desire
23 *Bureaucratic rigmarole
25 Place for drinks
26 *"Closer to Fine" folk-rock duo
32 How some home videos are stored
36 Disney World transport
37 53, in old Rome
38 Father, to Li'l Abner
40 Russian legislature
41 Dole out
43 Bit of land in the ocean
44 *Caution to slow down
47 Very long time
48 What the starts of the answers to the seven starred clues constitute
53 Fountain drinks
56 Letters suggesting "I'll just go ahead and throw this out"
58 Anise-flavored liqueur
59 Taiwanese computer brand
60 *DC Comics superhero with the sidekick Speedy
62 "30 Rock" star Fey
63 Shipwreck site, perhaps
64 Chili con ___
65 Circular water current
66 Exerciser's sets
67 Did a blacksmith's job on

DOWN

1 Loud, as a crowd
2 Carried
3 Flavorless
4 "Otherwise . . ."
5 Hosp. readout
6 Heated in a microwave
7 "Uh-huh"
8 Requirement
9 Cowpoke's sweetie
10 *Symbols of happiness
11 Simpson with a high I.Q.
12 So last year, as a fad
13 Sunset's direction
18 "Monday Night Football" channel
22 Victor who wrote "The Hunchback of Notre Dame"
24 Earthquake relief, e.g.
25 Small equine
27 Louvre Pyramid architect
28 Lincoln was its first successful standard-bearer, for short
29 ___ Julia, actor who played Gomez Addams
30 Tart, green fruit
31 Shutter strip
32 Neutrogena rival
33 Cairo's river
34 It's in a pickle
35 *Antique medical device used for electrotherapy
38 Lowly chess piece
39 Home of the Braves: Abbr.
42 Dove sounds
43 "Lord, is ___?": Matthew 26:22
45 Intense sorrows
46 Actress Goldie
49 "Don't Know Why" singer Jones
50 Beast of burden
51 Layer of the upper atmosphere
52 Superimposed
53 One sock, to another
54 Gastric ___
55 Supply temporarily
56 They say there's no such thing as this kind of lunch
57 Shed tears
60 Watchdog's warning
61 Cooling units, for short

by Michael Wiesenberg and Andrea Carla Michaels

ACROSS

1 Sassy
5 "Ooky" TV family name
11 "___ the Force, Luke"
14 Bell-ringing cosmetics company
15 Cash alternative
16 Pester no end
17 Site of a postrace celebration
19 Yank (on)
20 Caribou kin
21 Without ice, at the bar
22 ___ acid (protein component)
24 Snarling dog
26 Director of "Lawrence of Arabia" and "Doctor Zhivago"
29 Snoopy's comic strip
32 Neighbor of Ben & Jerry's in the freezer section
33 Tolkien language
34 Corporate boss, briefly
35 Salem or Marlboro, slangily
38 Follow one's political group
42 Bro's sibling
43 Still in the shrink-wrap
44 Body of work
45 Does in, in mob slang
47 Military forays
48 Helping hand for a low-income entrepreneur
52 Investigator, in old film noir
53 Common last option on a questionnaire
54 One-third of a hat trick
56 Lightly apply
59 Popularizer of the Chinese tunic suit
60 Classic Debussy work that translates as "Light of the Moon"
64 "I have a dream" orator, for short
65 Shot two under par on

66 Tallest active volcano in Europe
67 "Yes, captain!"
68 Does 50 in a school zone, say
69 Like Easter eggs

DOWN

1 Finish a drive?
2 Fiendish
3 Things spelunkers explore
4 Detonation producer, for short
5 Field measurement
6 Wood nymphs, in myth
7 "Keep climbing" sloganeer
8 Abbr. on toothpaste tubes
9 Max's opposite
10 Like a good surgeon's hands
11 Loosen, as shoelaces
12 Finnish bath
13 Goad
18 Deluge
23 Seattle Sounders' org.
25 Syllabus section
27 Zig or zag
28 "Same here!"
29 Dogs, cats and gerbils
30 "The Time Machine" race
31 Org. featured in 2015's "Concussion"
34 Crow's call
35 Voting or jury service, e.g.
36 About, at the start of a memo
37 Bee ___ ("Night Fever" group)
39 Cuban currency
40 Turtle in a Dr. Seuss title

41 Renaissance stringed instrument
45 Shipment to a smeltery
46 Troops
47 Sawed logs
48 "Throw ___ From the Train" (1987 Danny DeVito comedy)
49 Where the Renaissance began
50 Snatch defeat from the jaws of victory
51 Nimble
55 Puts two and two together, say
57 Name shared by two of Henry VIII's wives
58 Droplet of sweat
61 One of 200 in the Indy 500
62 What the number of birthday candles represents
63 Went first

by Andy Kravis

ACROSS

1 Arnaz of "I Love Lucy"
5 Skewered meat dishes
11 Col. Sanders's restaurant
14 Muscat's land
15 Battery terminals
16 Not feeling well
17 62-Across landmark
19 Siegfried's partner in Vegas
20 Laurence who wrote "Tristram Shandy"
21 Vietnamese holiday
22 What's thrown in a cafeteria fight
23 Blue Jays' home, for short
24 62-Across museum
26 Turn down, as an offer
29 N.B.A. coach Steve
30 62-Across bridge
32 "I know! I know!"
36 Opposite of WSW
37 Basketball venue
40 Roadside bomb, for short
41 Artoo-___ of "Star Wars"
44 62-Across school
47 Clutch
50 Toy that shoots foam darts
51 62-Across cathedral
55 ". . . or so ___ told"
56 ___ vera
57 Airport guess, for short
58 Exile
61 Family members
62 World capital that's the theme of this puzzle
64 She tasted the forbidden fruit
65 Many
66 One of three in a hat trick

67 Dôme ___ Invalides (historic church)
68 Extends, as a lease
69 Abbr. on many a cornerstone

DOWN

1 Bucks' mates
2 Let out
3 Social Security, Medicare, etc., collectively
4 Leading the pack
5 Green vegetable with tightly curled leaves
6 Suffix with differ
7 Diner seating option
8 Trade publication read along Madison Avenue
9 Ladybug or scarab
10 Ukr., e.g., once
11 Big name in Russian ballet
12 Elevator stop
13 Bonnie's partner in crime
18 Scandal-ridden company of the early 2000s
22 Pelts
24 Grand ___ (cultural trip around Europe)
25 ". . . man ___ mouse?"
26 Zoomed
27 Top-notch
28 Drink that's often iced
31 Second-largest city of Morocco, after Casablanca
33 Mythical ruler of Crete
34 List of options
35 Genesis garden
38 ___ of the above
39 "Vous êtes ici" ("You ___ here")

42 Shrek, e.g.
43 Galena or bauxite
45 Hide-out for Br'er Rabbit
46 At the point in one's life
48 Think up
49 St. Genevieve, for 62-Across
51 Like a jaybird, in an idiom
52 Shade of green
53 Shades of color
54 State formed as part of the Missouri Compromise
58 Bosom buddies, in modern lingo
59 Sing like Ella Fitzgerald
60 Clutched
62 Golf course standard
63 Strew, as seed

by Jason Mueller

ACROSS

1 Address including "www"
4 Doctors' org.
7 Small computer program
13 Biblical sister of Rachel
15 Purr-fect pet?
16 Succeed greatly
17 Get 10%–15%, say
19 Signaled, as a cab
20 *Actor in "The Bridge on the River Kwai" (1957)
22 Where Seoul and Pyongyang are: Abbr.
23 "Encore!"
27 *Actor in "Ocean's Eleven" (2001)
32 Mets' old stadium
33 In ___ straits
34 ___-de-sac
35 Gchat exchange, for short
36 All ___ (what a G rating means)
37 Freshman, sophomore, etc.
40 Here's the kicker!
41 Photos, informally
42 Unprocessed, as data
43 Part of the roof with the gutter
44 Number between dos and cuatro
46 *Actress in "Mogambo" (1953)
49 Fourth letter of "business"
51 "___ whiz!"
52 Setting for the answers to the three starred clues - appropriately enough, given their initials
58 New York home to Cornell University
61 Not meant to be thrown away
62 Tinklers on porches
63 Rower's blade
64 Scottish girl
65 Aficionado
66 Letters on a beach bottle
67 "Are we there ___?"

DOWN

1 Big name in beauty supplies
2 Genuine
3 "Go jump in the ___!"
4 What typists and archers are judged on
5 Second-largest Hawaiian island
6 Memo heading abbr.
7 Greek goddess of wisdom
8 New or full moon, e.g.
9 Light-refracting objects
10 Rapper ___ Wayne
11 Preholiday night
12 Cruz in the news
14 Enthusiastic agreement
18 Wide-eyed with excitement
21 "There's ___ in team"
24 From Columbus or Cleveland
25 Take away
26 Holiday with an egg hunt
27 Turns from a book into a movie, say
28 Sushi consisting of thin slices of fish over rice
29 University in Philadelphia
30 Regret
31 Nurse Barton
38 Old washcloth
39 Rhythmic group dance of the 2010s
40 Bigger than local or state
45 "___ Street"
46 "I thought this day would never come!"
47 Woman's palindromic nickname
48 Letters of support, for short
50 Less of a jerk
53 Greek equivalent of Cupid
54 Collect in the field
55 Auction service since 1995
56 Besides that
57 Place for baby birds
58 It goes "clink" in a drink
59 Quick expression of appreciation
60 Culturally conversant

by Erik Agard

ACROSS

1 Crudely sexual
5 Orange-yellow
10 Quick and not well thought out
14 Creative start
15 Longest river in France
16 "Sesame Street" monster
17 World's largest religious denomination
19 Matty or Felipe of major-league baseball
20 Play a role
21 Org. for the Suns and the Heat
22 Inuit homes
24 Org. looking for aliens
28 Ink problem
30 End of a business's email address
31 Tales set on Mount Olympus, e.g.
32 Say "No, thanks" to
35 Baby's starting place
37 Supporting nativist policies
43 Cow sounds
44 Device behind a deli counter
45 Dog on "The Jetsons"
49 Moon vehicle, for short
51 Supermodel Banks
52 One teaching pizza slices and S-turns
56 Make blue
57 Partner of the Father and Holy Ghost
58 Musical Yoko
61 Gas or electric: Abbr.
62 Asset for a public speaker . . . or a hint to 17-, 24-, 37- and 52-Across
66 Philosopher Descartes
67 Hole in one on a par three
68 Move text here and there
69 Avant-garde
70 Radioer's "Got it"
71 Old U.S. gas brand still seen in Canada

DOWN

1 Crossword-solving girl on "The Simpsons"
2 Cabinet dept. concerned with schools
3 Became lenient
4 Roseanne's hubby on "Roseanne"
5 Accused's line a judge might not believe
6 Artwork with tiles
7 Cartoonist Keane
8 End of an ___
9 Send, as payment
10 Property in buildings and land
11 "110%"
12 Alternative to chunky, for peanut butter
13 Purchases before hotels, in Monopoly
18 Bad throw for a QB: Abbr.

23 Stabilizing part of a ship's compass
25 Needle case
26 Still uninformed
27 Urban air pollution
28 Upper half of a bikini
29 ___ Goodman, longtime judge on "Dancing With the Stars"
33 Gymnast Biles with four Olympic gold medals
34 Offshoot of punk rock
36 ___ Fields cookies
38 Shed, as feathers
39 One of the Jackson 5
40 Winter driving hazards
41 "___ the ramparts we watched . . ."
42 Gun enthusiast's org.
45 Guarantee

46 Glided on ice
47 Satisfying until later, with "over"
48 Daisy who plays Rey in "Star Wars" films
50 Brawn
53 Make a nasty face
54 One making dove sounds
55 Channel that became Spike TV in 2003
59 Long-running CBS police drama
60 Good name for a chauffeur?
63 Ming worth millions of dollars
64 ___ McMuffin
65 Item in a caddie's bag

by David Woolf

17

ACROSS

1 Engaged in country-to-country combat
6 Dance movement
10 Story about Zeus and Hera, e.g.
14 Be dishonest with
15 Language of Bangkok
16 Salmon variety
17 Small floor covering
19 Witticism
20 Gummy gumbo vegetable
21 "Winnie-the-Pooh" baby
22 Irene of old Hollywood
23 Standard breakfast order
27 Johnny who sang "Chances Are"
29 Toward shelter, at sea
30 White as a ghost
31 Legacy student's relative, for short
33 Friendly
37 Nintendo game console
38 Lead off . . . or a hint to the circled letters
41 Aye's opposite
42 Makings of a castle at the beach
44 Gyro wrap
45 Waste maker, in a saying
47 At any time
49 Entries in the minus column
50 Passover no-no
55 Holder of unread emails
56 Savings plan for old age, in short
57 Kudrow of "Friends"
60 Cut and paste text, e.g.
61 Play H-O-R-S-E, say
64 Michelangelo's "David," for one
65 German luxury carmaker

66 Arctic people
67 Put the pedal to the metal
68 Get over a sunburn, maybe
69 Green pasta sauce

DOWN

1 Likewise
2 Sound of a watch
3 Diminishes, as patience
4 Embassy staffer
5 "Poppycock!"
6 Longtime senator Thurmond
7 Pulsate
8 French water
9 Big Bad Wolf's target
10 Steve who directed "12 Years a Slave"
11 The "Y" of Michael Jackson's "P.Y.T."
12 The "T" of Michael Jackson's "P.Y.T."
13 "High" feelings
18 Timeline periods
22 J.F.K.'s predecessor
24 Age indicator in a tree trunk
25 Actress Linney in "Kinsey"
26 Trees attacked by bark beetles
27 Cavernous openings
28 Home to 48 countries
31 Blazing
32 Blazing
34 Sneakily dangerous
35 Suffragist Carrie Chapman ___
36 Baby blues, e.g.
39 Like most businesses from 9 to 5
40 "Get ___ to a nunnery": Hamlet

43 Totally loyal
46 Sea snail with a mother-of-pearl shell
48 Annoy
49 "Shucks!"
50 Creditors' claims on property
51 Ultimately become
52 Bear patiently
53 Semiconductor device with two terminals
54 Swelter
58 Barbecue rod
59 Concerning
61 Source of maple syrup
62 Choice from a painter's palette
63 Belly dancer's gyrating body part

by Lynn Lempel

ACROSS

1 Quick drinks, as of whiskey
6 What one might be after doing 1-Across
11 "___ be my pleasure!"
14 Trunk of the body
15 Run off to the preacher
16 Neither's partner
17 Underwear for judges?
19 Ginger ___ (soft drink)
20 Singer Grande with the #1 albums "Yours Truly" and "My Everything"
21 Terminates
22 The "O" of B.Y.O.B.
24 Underwear for Frisbee enthusiasts?
28 Feeling of a person stranded in the desert
30 Silvery hair color
31 Mediocre
32 Who says "To be, or not to be: that is the question"
34 Underwear for beginners?
39 Soap operas, e.g.
40 What "I" or "me" refers to
42 Belgian diamond center
45 Fixed charge
47 Underwear for actors?
50 "Gross!"
51 One direction for an elevator
52 Romantic hopeful
54 Nasty Amin
55 Underwear for tycoons?
60 Furry sitcom alien
61 Like the moon landing, according to conspiracists

62 ___ Marie, singer of the 1985 hit "Lovergirl"
63 Director Spike
64 "Woo-hoo!"
65 English class assignment

DOWN

1 Cardinals, on scoreboards
2 Soil tiller
3 Any living thing
4 Romanov ruler
5 Opponent of stripes in billiards
6 Shore fliers
7 Relating to part of the pelvis
8 Who wrote the line "Once upon a midnight dreary . . ."
9 Rating on a Coppertone bottle, for short
10 "Indubitably!"
11 More ridiculous
12 "See, I was right!"
13 Like formal clothing
18 Worms for fishing
21 Heart health evaluation, for short
22 Extra periods, in brief
23 "Stop right there!"
25 Doorframe parts
26 Nobel Peace Prize city
27 Cereal in a party mix
29 Victory in an away game
32 "Well, I never!"
33 Notre Dame's Parseghian
35 Part of an arbor

36 Distinctive features of Mr. Spock
37 Whistle blowers
38 Whole bunch
41 Small bunch
42 It goes from about 540 to 1700
43 Casserole bit
44 Laura vis-à-vis Rob Petrie, on "The Dick Van Dyke Show"
45 Use a swizzle stick
46 Property in a will
48 Actor Milo
49 Rosy-cheeked
53 Has bills
55 Corp. money honcho
56 "How relaxing!"
57 Where clouds are
58 Genetic stuff
59 Second word of "The Star-Spangled Banner"

by Bruce Haight

ACROSS

1 Peak near Tokyo: Abbr.
7 Facts and figures
11 Guy's date
14 Stuff that may make you go "Ah-choo!"
15 Actor Wilson of "Midnight in Paris"
16 Cheer at a bullfight
17 Group preparing a ball field for a game
19 Homes on wheels, for short
20 Slippery fish
21 Like Monday crosswords, relatively speaking
22 Protection
24 Blown away
26 DuPont fiber
27 1972 platinum album by the Allman Brothers Band
31 "___ out of it!"
33 Opposite of a liability
34 Window section
36 Bit of acne
37 Globe: Abbr.
38 Locale of all the circled items in this puzzle
41 Suffix with pay
42 Running total at a bar
43 Apartment building overseer, informally
44 Gets whiter
46 Not working
48 Doesn't get near
51 Peter who compiled a book of synonyms
53 James of jazz
54 The Audi symbol has four of them
55 Fly high
57 Musical cousin of calypso
60 Ancient
61 Japanese delicacy served in thin slices
65 Hearty brew
66 Send off, as rays
67 One always making adjustments on the job?
68 ___ Moines, Iowa
69 Releases of Drake and Cardi B
70 Tune out

DOWN

1 Fuel economy measure, for short
2 Ripped
3 Ice sheet
4 Wail in grief
5 Actress Aniston, to friends
6 Seriously involved
7 E.R. figures
8 Off-kilter
9 Shirt that might have a slogan on it
10 Egypt's Sadat
11 Blue-veined Italian cheese
12 American Dance Theater founder
13 Not so much
18 "Smooth Operator" singer, 1985
23 Aboveground trains
25 Light bulb units
26 "Say it isn't so!"
27 Shoe that ties around the ankle
28 Some women with light-colored hair
29 Cop ___ (confess in return for lighter punishment)
30 Taxi
32 School grps.
33 Sparkling Italian wine
35 One living abroad, informally
39 Boot out
40 Make a choice
45 Completely covered with
47 Shape of a Silly Putty container
49 Affirmative votes
50 Sheetlike gray clouds
52 Ending with poly-
54 The Beatles' "Abbey ___"
55 Scissors sound
56 Honey Bunches of ___
58 About 2.2 pounds, for short
59 Latin love
62 Actress Thurman
63 What shoulders may do after a disappointment
64 Fury

by Julie Bérubé

ACROSS

1 Wolfish look
5 Lead-in to "di" or "da" in a Beatles song
9 Fowl raised for food
14 Commedia dell'___
15 Gas, oil or coal
16 Port St. ___, Fla.
17 End of a drinking hose
19 Rand McNally volume
20 Diving gear
21 Get going, as an old motorcycle or a new company
23 Spheres, in poetry
25 Angsty music genre
26 Rapper with the 1996 double-platinum album "Hard Core"
29 Handyman's inits.
31 What sirens do
35 Enero begins it
36 Certain red dye
38 Having a high metallic sound
39 Like some magazine perfume ads
42 Ill-tempered
43 Borden milk's cow
44 6-3 or 7-6, e.g.
45 Cy Young Award winner Hershiser
46 Faux ___
47 Tribal leaders
49 Like non-Rx drugs
51 Female friend of François
52 Party vessel with a ladle
57 "There ___ to be a law!"
61 Loud, as a crowd
62 1999 Brad Pitt movie hinted at by the beginnings of 17-, 21-, 39- and 52-Across
64 Planet demoted to "dwarf planet" in 2006
65 Woman of the Haus
66 Fishes that may shock you

67 Good ___ (repaired perfectly)
68 Appear (to be)
69 Go bananas

DOWN

1 Parts of science courses
2 "Spamalot" creator Idle
3 Caesar's rebuke to Brutus
4 Nike competitor
5 Birds ___ feather
6 Gains muscle, with "up"
7 Blue jeans pioneer Strauss
8 Trump portrayer Baldwin
9 Blood fluid
10 Not just playing for fun
11 The N.C.A.A.'s Bruins

12 Word repeated before "pants on fire"
13 Word repeated while tapping a microphone
18 Magazine of show business
22 Code breaker
24 Fellow who might be senior class president, for short
26 Rope in a Wild West show
27 Run up, as expenses
28 Peter of "The Maltese Falcon"
29 Uses a rotary phone
30 Bed-and-breakfasts
32 Licorice flavoring
33 Derive by logic
34 Alternatives to Ubers
37 Mets' former ballpark
38 Poet whose work inspired "Cats"
40 Distribute, as resources

41 Carpe ___ (seize the day: Lat.)
46 Banned pollutant, in brief
48 Cards that may be "wild" in poker
50 Lose on purpose
51 Fish tank gunk
52 "___ Was a Rollin' Stone" (Temptations hit)
53 Addresses that may be linked on the web
54 Person, place or thing
55 Murders, mob-style
56 Hide a mike on
58 Campbell who sang "By the Time I Get to Phoenix"
59 Hawaiian dance
60 Recipe measure: Abbr.
63 Vocalize on a kazoo

by Andrea Carla Michaels

ACROSS

1 Levi's material
5 Coconut tree
9 Lacks, in brief
14 The sun and the moon
15 ___ facto
16 Women's golf star Lorena
17 Holder of some precious memories
19 Transports between airport terminals
20 Position for a baseball batter
21 What sending someone to Mars would be
22 Wunderkind
26 Recede, as the tide
29 1960s–'70s Ford named for an Italian city
30 Fashion magazine spinoff
33 "Here's to you!," e.g.
38 Turn at high speed
39 "As American as apple pie," for example
40 Jokes and such
41 Popular Cartoon Network programming block
44 The "M" of NASA's LEM
46 Smartphone download
47 Temporary mental lapse
53 Squirrel's stash
54 ___ Herman (Paul Reubens character)
58 Insinuated
59 Place where no one lives anymore
62 Bring joy to
63 Actress Hatcher
64 Crucifix
65 Philadelphia N.B.A. player, informally
66 Plow pullers
67 Inquires

DOWN

1 Steve who once headed Apple
2 The "E" of Q.E.D.
3 Swedish pop quartet that won the 1974 Eurovision contest
4 Justin Timberlake's original group
5 Assign two projects, a long reading and several writing assignments, say
6 Police alert, for short
7 Baton Rouge sch.
8 Dad's partner
9 Run fast
10 Having a burning smell
11 Puppeteer Lewis
12 Request to a waiter
13 Yummy
18 German's "Oh!"
21 Prince Valiant's son
23 Item in a grate
24 ___ Hill (R&B group)
25 Chart type
26 Write on metal, say
27 Lover boy
28 Road shoulder
31 Prefix with liberal
32 Bernie Sanders, for one
34 Meditation sounds
35 Onetime electronics giant
36 Lose one's footing
37 Worker hired for the day
39 Has a lazy Sunday morning, say
41 Naval chief: Abbr.
42 Batman and Robin are a "dynamic" one
43 Einstein's birthplace
45 Where surgeons do surgery, for short
47 Wise ones
48 Bacterium that can help or hurt
49 Levy-free
50 Furious
51 Alternative to .com
52 Prefix with -hedron
55 Tries to win, as a damsel
56 Furry "Star Wars" creature
57 Kills
59 Sporty Pontiac
60 Bewitch
61 It's mined

by Hannah Slovut

22

ACROSS

1 Trudges
7 Billboard Hot 100 and others
13 Language spoken by Jesus
14 Hinged part of an airplane wing
16 "Bye Bye Birdie" song
18 Partner of his
19 Untagged, in tag
20 "Star Trek" lieutenant
21 Ore-___ (frozen taters brand)
22 Inflatable item for water fun
24 Bon ___ (clever remark)
25 Russian cottage
27 Philosopher ___-tzu
28 Humiliate
30 Super bargain
31 Internet connection faster than dial-up, for short
32 More Solomonlike
33 ___ roaming (smartphone setting)
35 "Well, shoot!"
37 What you might do if you sing 16-Across
44 500 sheets of paper
45 Most deals that sound too good to be true
46 1 1 1
47 Units of farmland
49 Before, in poetry
50 Elizabethan neck decorations
51 Florida's ___ National Forest
53 ___ four (small pastry)
54 How you might feel if you sing 16-Across
59 Prefix with center
60 Show hostility to, as a dog might a mail carrier

61 Powerful cleaner
62 Medium strength?
63 No-goodnik
64 Girl at a ball, in brief

DOWN

1 Slangy "Amen!"
2 Corporate hustle and bustle
3 "Famous" cookie name
4 Fellow
5 It has 88 keys
6 Prom, e.g.
7 Washington image seen on the back of a $50 bill
8 Aware of, informally
9 Prince ___ Khan
10 Ones whistling while they work?
11 Shocks with lasting impact

12 "Almost got it that time!"
13 Pests in the garden
15 Spay, e.g.
17 Travel aid made obsolescent by GPS
22 ___ paneer (Indian dish made with spinach)
23 Expressions of boredom
26 Ate substantially
29 One who blabs
34 "My country, ___ of thee . . ."
36 Some small batteries
37 Undergarment with straps
38 Makes back, as an investment
39 Bit of jewelry on the side of the head
40 Roofing sealant

41 Area for six of the nine baseball positions
42 Part of the head hidden on the jack of spades
43 Curvy letter
48 Long, tiring jobs
50 Right-hand page in a book
52 Big top?
53 BlackBerrys, e.g., in brief
54 Lawyer's charge
55 ___ long way
56 Possess
57 Antiquated
58 Yank's Civil War foe

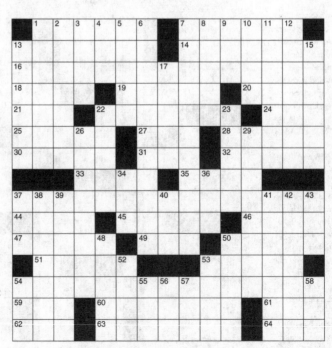

by Alex Eaton-Salners

ACROSS

1 "Meet the Press" host Chuck
5 Trippy drug
8 Iraqi city whose name, appropriately, is an anagram of ARABS
13 Dumpster emanation
14 Berry for a purple smoothie
16 Silly prank
17 Watch, as the bar
18 "Nonsense!"
20 Best
22 Home to the N.B.A.'s Heat
23 Flier from flower to flower
24 Shady places
27 Covering of a corn ear
29 Boneless cut named for a New York restaurant
34 Saucer in the sky, for short
35 ___ Alto, Calif.
36 Carrying a gun
38 Very off-color
40 Some showy blossoms, informally
43 City north of Carson City
44 Samples
46 "Later!"
48 180° from SSW
49 Jet that evades radar detection
53 The biblical wise men, by tradition
54 Slobbers
55 Corner PC key
58 Steer clear of
61 Sup
62 Hilton hotel chain . . . or what 18-, 29- and 49-Across each have
65 Actress Perlman of "Cheers"
68 National Geographic has a new one every month

69 Spot for a flowerpot
70 "Nuts!"
71 Sweetness, sourness or bitterness
72 Kim, to Khloé Kardashian, for short
73 "Don't go!"

DOWN

1 Wee one
2 Verse dedicated to someone
3 Snarky comment after "This is your big chance"
4 Archenemy of the Fantastic Four
5 Place for experimenting
6 Run a con on
7 Limp watch painter
8 Server at a coffeehouse

9 "What else?"
10 Random guess
11 Get up
12 Painful throb
15 Boise's state
19 Birds on some Australian coins
21 Item held by an actor
24 18+ ticket category
25 Alludes (to)
26 Glitch
28 Deborah of "The King and I"
30 Down with a bug
31 Cheap section in a plane
32 "So true!"
33 Dog shelter
37 Active types
39 Bug spray component
41 "What's the ___?" ("Who cares?")

42 Expressed
45 Brand that "nobody doesn't like"
47 Folklore baddie
50 Performing now
51 Honeybunch
52 Squirrels away
55 Polish, as prose
56 Baseball's "Slammin' Sammy"
57 Use four-letter words
59 State flower of Tennessee
60 Place to order a ham on rye
63 "However . . ."
64 Golfer Ernie
66 Time in history
67 "___ takers?"

by Zhouqin Burnikel

ACROSS

1 Home made of mud and thatch
4 Mob informant
7 Knight's title
10 "I do," at a wedding
13 George Bernard Shaw wanted his to read "I knew if I stayed around long enough, something like this would happen"
15 Professional's opposite
17 Motorcycle attachment
18 French ballroom dance
19 Chef Lagasse
21 Tropical tree with hot pink flowers
22 Sis's sibling
24 Spreadsheet amount shown in parentheses
26 "The ___ shall inherit the earth"
27 Gushing review
29 Inky mess
30 Dermatological sacs
31 Result of iron deficiency
33 The "k" of kHz
35 "I've got this round!" . . . or a literal hint to this puzzle's theme
40 Moonwalker Armstrong
41 Press agents, informally
43 Dresses in India
47 Roster
49 Nerd
50 Colored part of the eye
51 Thomas Edison's middle name
52 Hush-hush government org.
53 Hand tool for boring holes
55 One with only younger siblings
59 Sticker that might start "Hello . . ."
61 Danny DeVito's role in 1975's "One Flew Over the Cuckoo's Nest"
64 Minor gain in football
65 Fair way to judge something
66 "Cool!"
67 Back talk
68 U.S.'s largest union, with 3.2 million members
69 Short albums, for short

DOWN

1 "___ Just Not That Into You"
2 Longtime inits. in newswires
3 Sustain temporarily
4 5K or 10K
5 On ___ with (even with)
6 Surge of exhilaration
7 Droop
8 Muslim leaders
9 Sitarist Shankar
10 Nixes from Nixon, e.g.
11 Beginning
12 Unleashes, as havoc
14 President pro ___
16 Designer Hilfiger
20 "Pay attention out there!"
22 Undergarment usually fastened in the back
23 Kentucky senator Paul
25 Mix, as paint
28 Classic record label
29 Pie recipe directive
30 Pie recipe directive
32 B&Bs
34 Pointing in this direction: <--
36 Window ledge
37 Chronic complainer
38 Country's Reba
39 Barely makes, with "out"
42 Some Jamaican music
43 Mister, in Milan
44 Singer Grande
45 Horn-___ glasses
46 The ___ Brothers of R&B
48 Fish sometimes served smoked
51 Big name in arcade gaming
54 And others, in a bibliography
56 Copenhagener, e.g.
57 Bombeck who wrote "Housework, if you do it right, will kill you"
58 Sault ___ Marie, Mich.
60 Meas. of a country's economic output
62 Puppy's bite
63 "___ over" ("We're done")

by Gary Cee

ACROSS

1 Letters meaning "Make it snappy!"
5 Mouth-puckering
9 Sidewalk's edge
13 Nut from Australia
15 Actress Raymonde of "Lost"
16 Wall fixture for a landline
17 Gives off, as light
18 Beetle Bailey's superior
19 Abounds (with)
21 Stage prompt
22 Cremation vessel
23 Bathroom bar offering so-called "round-the-clock" protection
25 Quilting or crossword solving, e.g.
30 Spanish rice dish
31 One-percenters and such
34 Reddish
35 Start, as a meeting
38 Q-tip, for one
40 The "A" and "S" of 1-Across
41 Biblical land
44 Doing sentry duty
48 Candy suckers in the form of jewelry
51 Historical period
52 "I Like ___" (1950s campaign button)
53 Science fiction writer Asimov
55 Yearns (for)
57 Make an offer for at auction
59 Trendy, much-used lingo . . . or a hint to the starts of 16-, 23-, 35- and 48-Across
61 Barely making, with "out"

62 Postal letters, deprecatingly
63 Location
64 Temporary rain cover
65 Chip or coin thrown in the pot

DOWN

1 Excites
2 African desert
3 Squirrel's stash
4 Twinge of guilt
5 ___ Mahal
6 Amo, amas, ___ . . .
7 Like not-quite-mashed potatoes
8 George of the original "Star Trek"
9 Filming device, informally
10 Monochromatic
11 Sacred ceremonies
12 Salary before bonuses
14 Actor Billy ___ Williams
15 Model 3 electric car maker
20 An "X" might "mark the spot" on one
24 Venus's tennis doubles partner
26 Earl Grey pouch on a string
27 Needing medicine, say
28 Thousand thou
29 "At Last" singer ___ James
32 Goddess of the dawn
33 Meh
35 Stopped all that yapping
36 Presidential son Reagan
37 ___ Jones industrial average
38 Old-fashioned writers
39 Hawaiian surfing mecca

42 Mimicking
43 Rejections
45 Capital of Iran
46 College degree unit
47 Big inconvenience
49 Blue Ribbon brewery
50 Place to sweat it out
54 Ruler until 1917
55 Hole-making tool
56 Result of a serious head injury
58 ___ Direction (boy band)
60 Nada

by Ross Trudeau

ACROSS

1 Classic name for a poodle
5 Branded cotton swab
9 Much-prized golden statuette
14 Black, in poetry
15 ___ Bell
16 Tract of low-growing shrubs
17 Locale for a traditional Japanese ceremony
19 Source of pancake syrup
20 Toll units for semis
21 Israeli gun
23 Lead-in to fall
24 Slip of paper to take to the grocery
28 Louis who developed a rabies vaccine
31 High-five sound
32 Yoko who loved John
33 Places with lions and giraffes
36 Sushi bar eel
39 The Masters and others
43 Sign in a broadcast booth
44 ___ John letter
45 Part of the body that's stubbed
46 Marsh grass
48 Risky bridge play
51 Classic Austrian pastry
55 Homophone of 46-Across
56 ___-la-la (song syllables)
57 Rubs the wrong way
61 Actress Zellweger
63 Message clicked on by an online buyer . . . or a hint for 17-, 24-, 39- and 51-Across
66 Obvious
67 "Hold the ___" (deli order)
68 Build-it-yourself furniture chain
69 ___ corgi (dog breed)
70 Hunted animal
71 Pre-twentysomething

DOWN

1 Crumbly cheese
2 Mountain goat
3 Stable newborn
4 Consume
5 15 min. of college football
6 Tiny amount
7 Acquire a winter coat?
8 ___ scheme (scam)
9 Unit of electrical resistance
10 Flier that can take off from water
11 Apparel also known as clamdiggers
12 Rand McNally book
13 Scarlett's Butler
18 Tennis legend Arthur
22 Electees
25 Anise-flavored liqueur
26 Peacockish
27 Down in the mouth
28 "We have met the enemy and he is us" comic strip
29 Ever and ___
30 Green energy source that might go on top of a house
34 Rock with valuable nuggets
35 Not just a glitch
37 Old sporty Pontiacs
38 "So that's it!"
40 Fly ball catchers
41 Genealogical chart
42 Desert-dry
47 "Spring forward" letters
49 Disney clown fish
50 Draw out
51 Cupid's missile
52 Pet ___
53 Walk with heavy steps
54 Speed reader?
58 Not real
59 Gratis
60 Lee of Marvel Comics
62 Biblical verb ender
64 Clothes colorer
65 Slinky or Silly Putty

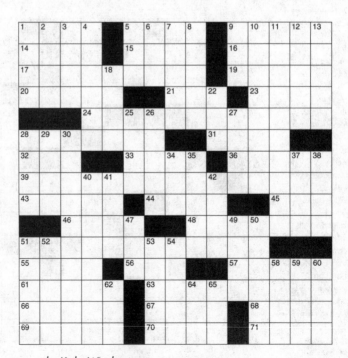

by Kathy Wienberg

ACROSS

1 Foggy mental states
6 Play a role onstage
9 Wild hog
13 Atlantic or Pacific
14 Soothing substance
15 Bullets and BBs
16 Italian food item that can be stuffed and baked
18 Doesn't stop talking
19 Common canine command
20 Militia of farmers, e.g.
22 ___ Solo of 2018's "Solo"
23 Corn unit
24 "He's so polite"
32 Sir's counterpart
33 What poi is made from
34 What a plane's hold holds
35 ___-Man (shrinking Marvel superhero)
36 Hit musical set in Argentina
38 Something the eco-conscious bring to a grocery
39 "I.e.," spelled out
42 Vaper's device
43 A-list group at an event
44 It may allow a text document to be displayed on a web page
47 Once ___ while
48 No room at the ___ (problem once in Bethlehem)
49 3, 5 or 7, but not 9
55 Guerrilla ___ Guevara
58 "Today" co-host Kotb
59 "Keep this between us" . . . or hint to this puzzle's circled letters
61 December 24 and 31, e.g.

62 One probably not with the jocks at the lunch table
63 Practices boxing
64 Watered down, as coffee
65 Verizon Fios or Comcast's Xfinity, for short
66 Striped cat

DOWN

1 Kangaroo movements
2 Berry marketed as a superfood
3 Lemon rind part
4 Consume
5 Get testy with
6 Lager alternatives
7 ___ wars (longtime advertising battle)
8 Early computer connection protocol
9 Where San Francisco and Oakland are
10 Actor Epps
11 12-hour toggle on clocks
12 Flushed, as cheeks
14 "Eureka!"
17 Its members serve six-year terms
21 Barber's powder
22 Nonkosher sandwich meat
24 "A Fish Called ___" (1988 comedy)
25 Jealous critic, informally
26 Judge's mallet
27 Writer Jong
28 Away from the office
29 Head honcho
30 Open-mouthed
31 Spiced holiday drinks
32 Seriously injure
37 Texas A&M team
40 Robber's identity-protecting headwear

41 Something carried by a singer
43 Tradesperson's vehicle
45 Sandwich with grill marks
46 Turmoil
49 [What a relief!]
50 Wander about
51 What a light bulb indicates in cartoons
52 Beehive State tribe
53 Car sticker fig.
54 Word to a dog that has just chewed the sofa
55 One who complains, complains, complains
56 Parsley, sage, rosemary or thyme
57 Website for craft vendors
60 Busy worker in April, for short

by Evan Kalish

ACROSS

1 Reamer or wrench
5 Danglers on luggage
11 Cruise amenity
14 Where icicles may hang
15 World ___ (October event)
16 Center of a poker table
17 Arm exercise at a dairy farm?
19 Engine lubricant
20 "Ben-___"
21 Fruit in a holiday gift box
22 Hawaiian coffee region
23 Any boat
25 Shoulder exercise at a cutlery store?
29 Clip, as a coupon
32 Jeers
33 Currier and ___
34 Classy articles of neckwear
37 Wrist exercise at a candy factory?
43 Highest point in an orbit
44 Region
45 Swizzle stick
49 Fame
51 Chest exercise at a vintner's?
54 Itching desire
55 Small whirlpool
56 What a relaxed soldier is at
58 One of four for a grand slam, in brief
61 Face on a fiver
62 What the exercise regimen in 17-, 25-, 37- and 51-Across is worth?
66 Traditional Father's Day gift
67 Wise sayings
68 ". . . or ___!"
69 Engine additive since 1954
70 Far from extravagant
71 Consider to be

DOWN

1 Computer crash investigator, informally
2 Where Waikiki Beach is
3 Exceed, as one's bounds
4 See 31-Down
5 "Ah, now that's clear"
6 Coffee choice before bed
7 Cape Cod resort town
8 It's thin on top of Everest
9 Hair goo
10 Serpent's warning
11 Parodies
12 Route map start
13 "Finally!"
18 Blueprint detail
22 Package for a model plane
24 Shed door feature
26 River that passes through Lake Geneva
27 1970s TV's "Welcome Back, ___"
28 Like Little Bo-Peep's sheep
29 Brief swim
30 Apple eater in Genesis
31 With 4-Down, "To Kill a Mockingbird" writer
35 Campfire treat
36 Marlboro offering, informally
38 Wyatt of Dodge City
39 Decline
40 Totalitarian control
41 Use a Singer machine
42 Result of sunning
45 Gymwear
46 Choice morsel
47 Seriously embroiled
48 King: Sp.
50 Good lookers?
52 Wetlands plant
53 Business successes
57 The "S" of CBS: Abbr.
59 Military post
60 Grocery list component
62 Beaver's project
63 Predictable reply at the altar
64 Pop
65 "And that proves it"

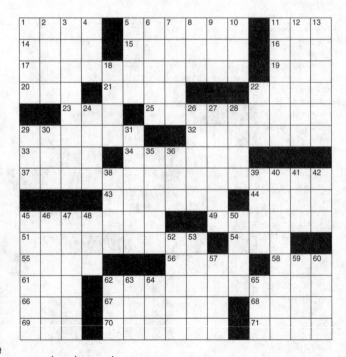

by John Lampkin

ACROSS

1 Australia's national gemstone
5 "___ Surfin'" (2008 rap song)
9 Lead-in to frost
14 Walk back and forth nervously
15 What a fisherman might bring home even if he doesn't catch any fish
16 "Later!"
17 Singer Fitzgerald
18 Yoked animals
19 Weavers' devices
20 Start of an overseas telephone number
23 Former org. for James Comey
24 Three on a sundial
25 Test in a hospital tube, for short
26 Classic game now sometimes played with "lasers"
27 Faux money
33 Wolf Blitzer's channel
34 Madam's counterpart
35 Latest dope
36 Couches
39 Dental problem fixed by braces
41 Annual award from Stockholm
44 "You said it, brother!"
46 Open ___ night (comedy club offering)
48 "Many years ___ . . ."
49 What a micromanager would like to have
54 "Yes, ma chérie"
55 "This might be of interest," on a memo
56 Fish eggs
57 Georgia's capital: Abbr.
58 Approach respectfully, in modern parlance
64 Indian yogurt dish
66 Boys' school near Windsor
67 Of all time
68 Ringo of the Beatles
69 Political competition
70 Farm structure
71 Weirdly spooky
72 Space on a schedule
73 Friend in war

DOWN

1 Oil grp.
2 ___ Alto, Calif.
3 Org. defending the Bill of Rights
4 Move so as to hear better, say
5 The Empire State Building has 102 of them
6 Like candles
7 Smart ___ (wiseacre)
8 Human ___ Project
9 Add even more criticism
10 Music genre related to punk
11 Place to see the town while painting the town red?
12 Most populous city in India
13 Symbol starting a Twitter handle
21 Palindromic bird
22 What icicles do
27 Amts. of blood
28 Musical Yoko
29 Alien
30 Fix, as an election
31 Picture holder
32 Dove's sound
37 Item on a concert stage
38 Tending to one's own well-being
40 Instagram upload, for short
42 Bigheadedness
43 [That was a funny one]
45 R&B singer with the hits "So Sick" and "Miss Independent"
47 Princess' headwear
49 Sandpaperlike
50 Bested in a hot dog contest, say
51 Stopwatches, sand clocks, etc.
52 Neither's partner
53 Mother with a 41-Across Peace Prize
59 Abbr. at the end of an abridged roster
60 Hit 2017 computer-animated film . . . or a hint to 20-, 27-, 49- and 58-Across
61 Bad, bad, bad
62 An amoeba has just one
63 Helen of ___
65 Prefix with -fecta

by Erik Agard

ACROSS

1 Host with a microphone
6 Egyptian goddess with a repetitive name
10 Three blind creatures, in a children's rhyme
14 West Coast N.F.L. player
15 Smeller
16 Black, to poets
17 Unplanned
20 Suffix with count
21 California/Nevada border lake
22 Chutzpah
23 Singer with the multiplatinum albums "19," "21" and "25"
25 "That's all ___ got"
27 Suffix with cash or cloth
28 Parliamentary agenda
32 Hold on property
33 Pitching stat
34 Memo-heading inits.
35 "___ fool!"
37 Yang's partner
39 Writer ___ Rice Burroughs
43 Chest protector
45 San Francisco's ___ Hill
47 Fish in some salads
48 Literary club feature
52 Preceder of Alamos or Angeles
53 She's a sheep
54 "I Still Believe ___" (#1 Vince Gill country song)
55 Pen name
57 Door fastener
59 Dallas sch. with a presidential library
62 Annual Time issue
65 "CHiPs" actor Estrada
66 First chip in the pot
67 Previously aired show
68 Profit's opposite
69 Old Russian ruler
70 Place for camels to rest

DOWN

1 Otherwise
2 GPS graphics
3 One leading a fight for change
4 Good listener?
5 Displayer of one's feelings
6 Possibly, but unlikely
7 Artsy Manhattan neighborhood
8 "Yeah, that seems plausible"
9 College term: Abbr.
10 Idea that spreads popularly and widely
11 Barcelona's peninsula
12 Pass along
13 Go through the door
18 Not true
19 Cyclops feature
24 "Raging Bull" star Robert
26 TV broadcast band
28 Rock-___ (jukebox brand)
29 Fabric tear
30 Like a sound that can barely be heard
31 Playground retort
36 This way
38 Pitcher's tour de force
40 N.R.A. members
41 Insect in a colony
42 Quaint college cheer
44 Ship's front
46 Park furniture
48 Orchestral work by Ravel
49 Egyptian god who's a brother of 6-Across
50 Criminals
51 "You saved me!"
52 Place to put an American flag pin
56 Poses a question
58 Skin conditioner brand
60 Island ESE of Oahu
61 Large coffee holders
63 Turner who led a slave rebellion
64 Vote in favor

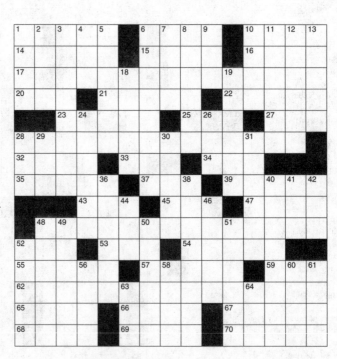

by Todd Gross

ACROSS

1 Bouquet holder
5 Leaf-gathering tool
9 Org. that distributes music royalties
14 "SportsCenter" channel
15 Better than ___
16 Hole digger's tool
17 *Annual event displaying agricultural products
19 Japanese beer brand
20 Unexpressed
21 Children's author ___ Asquith
23 Dog biter
24 ___-friendly (green)
25 *Spilling a drink or eating all the guacamole, say
27 Rhythmic pattern
30 Junior ___, 12-time Pro Bowl linebacker
31 Rock grp. with the 1977 song "Rockaria!"
32 Sun or planet
34 Socially assertive types
38 Original Beatles bassist ___ Sutcliffe
39 *Candy from a candy machine
41 Miner's haul
42 Hauling
44 Fold-up bed
45 Item in a caddie's bag
46 Bread served with vindaloo
48 Rangers or Flyers
51 *Attack from the sky
55 One might end with .org
56 Roulette playing piece
57 Envision
58 Low voice
61 A hot one might be trending
63 Narrow escape . . . or what the end of the answer to each starred clue is?

66 Met performance
67 Brother mentioned more than 70 times in Genesis
68 Nonstick cookware brand
69 Extend, as a membership
70 Peeved
71 Dreamcast console maker

DOWN

1 Word after life or bulletproof
2 "The Thin Man" dog
3 *In a daze
4 Lead on
5 Official with a whistle, informally
6 Screen siren Gardner
7 Knightley of "The Imitation Game"
8 Flubs
9 "___ and ye shall receive"
10 Add some style to
11 Monte ___ (gambling haven)
12 Parisian goodbye
13 Punishment-related
18 School founded by King Henry VI
22 Covertness
25 Request at a hair salon
26 "You folks," in Dixie
27 "___ la vie"
28 Midlevel voice
29 Middle-aged women with eyes for younger men
33 Original "Monty Python" network
35 *Vacationer's container for valuables
36 Length × width, for a rectangle

37 Appear to be
39 Pesky flier
40 Of the highest rank
43 Motivate
47 Siblings' daughters
49 It lets things slide
50 Expanses of land
51 One in a cast
52 "If there's any justice!"
53 Become edible, as a fruit
54 Ashton Kutcher TV role
59 Metal refuse
60 Widemouthed pot
62 Sound like a crow
64 Rowboat propeller
65 Take legal action

by Gary Cee

ACROSS

1 "Let's take it from the ___"
4 Kind of exam that's not written
8 Seafood often served on a toothpick
13 Clean Air Act org.
14 Anaconda, e.g.
15 Lopsided wins
16 Mess up
17 Open the door for
18 President elected with the slogan "Yes we can"
19 "Hurry up!"
22 It can get you into a lather
23 ___ Shriver, sister of J.F.K. and founder of the Special Olympics
27 Computer glitch
28 "Watch your ___!"
30 Electrical unit
31 Magical drink that gets someone smitten
35 Use shears
36 Impersonators
37 Frequently, to Frost
38 Actor/director Eastwood
39 Hamilton's bills
40 Less fortunate
42 Word on a wine label
43 Calligrapher's collection
44 Bill's "excellent adventure" partner
45 Give a hard time
47 Walk drunkenly
51 L.B.J. campaign to help the poor
54 Midrange golf club
57 Velvet-voiced Mel
58 "So that's your game!"
59 Like a diet that allows only fats and protein
60 Creative thoughts
61 Bear's home
62 Posts, as a letter
63 What children should be, and not heard, they say
64 High trains in Chicago

DOWN

1 Overflows (with)
2 The "O" of O magazine
3 Ski jacket
4 "Almost finished!"
5 Dustin Hoffman's role in "Midnight Cowboy"
6 Comparable (to)
7 "Game of Thrones" actress Headey
8 Prevent from falling, perhaps
9 English rocker Hitchcock
10 Simon & Garfunkel's "I ___ Rock"
11 Typist's stat, in brief
12 Hush-hush grp.
14 Boo-boos
20 Smoldering remains
21 Hammer's end
24 Like some Greek columns
25 Armor flaw
26 Like some promises and gas tanks
28 Painstakingly sorts (through)
29 Tykes
31 Door fastener
32 "The Magic Flute," for one
33 Planet between Mercury and Earth
34 Bugs Bunny or Wile E. Coyote
35 Muddy deposit
38 Splits in two
40 ". . . ___ the twain shall meet"
41 Cushioned footstool
43 Alternatives in case things don't work out
46 Swashbuckler's weapon
47 Wild shopping expedition
48 A+ or C−
49 Fred Mertz's wife in 1950s TV
50 "___ Hope" (soap opera)
52 Redding who sang "(Sittin' On) the Dock of the Bay"
53 Bump on a log, literally
54 Decade that spawned the slogan found at the starts of 19-, 31-, 40- and 51-Across
55 Cubes in a freezer
56 Competed in a marathon

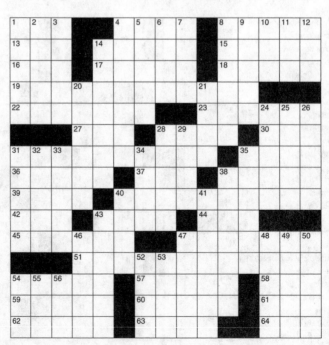

by Andrea Carla Michaels and Mark Diehl

ACROSS

1 Pear variety
5 Fiction's opposite
9 Peruvian animal
14 Toledo's home
15 Carpet layer's measurement
16 Common golf shirts
17 Leave a lasting legacy . . . or do worse at school
20 Drug giant ___ Lilly
21 English school on the Thames
22 The Gershwins' "Of ___ I Sing"
23 Succeed on the gridiron . . . or invite a slap in the face
26 Word after Near, Middle or Far
27 Waders with curved bills
28 Gunky roofing stuff
30 Diplomat's forte
31 Cannabis variety used for rope
35 Times Sq. squad
38 Sound of annoyance
39 Score in baseball . . . or ruin some hose
41 Part of Adam from which Eve was fashioned
43 "SportsNation" station
45 Shoe with holes
46 Helper
47 Curling surface
49 One of the Baltic States
51 Femme fatale
54 Be lucky in Scrabble . . . or come up short memorywise
58 Gel-producing succulent
59 Starting point for a horse race
60 Have dinner
61 Start of a mixed message, as illustrated by 17-, 23-, 39- and 54-Across

66 Excessive
67 Vichyssoise vegetable
68 Drop that might run down the face
69 Land with pyramids
70 "Roseanne" actress Gilbert
71 Jason's fleece-seeking ship

DOWN

1 Spongy ground
2 "Well, whaddya know!"
3 Trusty companions
4 Most hip
5 Devoted follower
6 Zodiac ram
7 ¢
8 Chevy model named for a Western lake
9 Carole King's "Tapestry" and "Music"
10 Small chance to win big bucks
11 Hawaiian hello
12 Group's basic customs
13 Up to now
18 Clean (off)
19 The "I" of M.I.T.: Abbr.
23 Barack's opponent in 2012
24 Demean
25 Arthur with a namesake stadium
29 TV journalist Curry
32 List shortener: Abbr.
33 Damage somewhat
34 One giving you the aye?
36 Nongovernmentally owned ship decked out for war
37 Brought to ruin
39 Health products chain
40 Sch. near Hollywood
42 A pelican has a big one
44 Chimed in on the conversation
46 U.S. city with the world's busiest airport
48 Margin
50 Under the covers
51 Unclear
52 Sing-___ (hootenanny feature)
53 Temperamental
55 Lou with more than 70 albums
56 Out on a naval deployment
57 Big name in grills
62 Bit of fishery equipment
63 Stephanie Clifford ___ Stormy Daniels
64 Jokester
65 Letters suggesting a sellout

by Lynn Lempel

34

ACROSS

1 Mattress cover
6 Desert beast
11 "Born in the ___"
14 Deserves
15 Cockamamie
16 Catch cold?
17 Meat entree in Ukraine
19 "Weekend Update" show, for short
20 Carne asada holder
21 Low-fat
22 Practice piece at a conservatory
24 Travel about
26 Back of a boat
28 Meat entree in Austria
33 Have a hunch
34 Pewter component
35 Excellent, informally
36 Pound sound
37 Brand that "nobody doesn't like"
41 Greek "H"
42 Home to the majority of earthlings
44 ___ Air (affluent neighborhood of Los Angeles)
45 Bold type
47 Meat entree in New Zealand
51 Emmy winner Christine
52 Christmas carol
53 Freshwater polyp
55 Jam ingredient?
57 Alan who wrote the book "If I Understood You, Would I Have This Look on My Face?"
61 Sound elicited by a punch in the gut
62 Meat entree in the United Kingdom
65 Olive of cartoons
66 Disney World park

67 Be in accord
68 Small dog
69 Pro in taking dictation
70 Landowners' papers

DOWN

1 Religious offshoot
2 "That's funny!"
3 California politico Garcetti
4 Concert bonuses
5 Sound of disapproval
6 The movie industry
7 "My Way" lyricist Paul
8 Thing attached to a sloop's boom
9 Direction from Mo. to Me.
10 River embankments
11 Person not getting credit for a brave act
12 Hourglass contents
13 Up to the task
18 Panache
23 Mouse catcher
25 Easiest numbers to dial on a rotary phone
27 Adjust the pitch of
28 Chapter's counterpart
29 Pop-up that results in the batter being called out even if the ball isn't caught
30 Public bathroom compartment
31 No longer on the plate
32 Symbol on the Texas state flag
33 Bygone Swedish car
38 Assist in a crime
39 Trust

40 Cutting-___ (pioneering)
43 From a distance
46 Like a prison fugitive
48 Moby Dick and others
49 Counting everything
50 Separator of a.m. and p.m.
53 Owl's sound
54 Dimwit
56 Thick Japanese noodle
58 Traditional knowledge
59 Ran out of juice
60 Pub pints
63 Choose, with "for"
64 Reprimand to a dog

by Peter Gordon

35

ACROSS

1 Writing on a book jacket
6 Leveling wedge
10 Be on the mend
14 Total, as expenses
15 Mario who wrote "The Godfather"
16 Farmland measure
17 Part of a book that's rarely read straight through
18 Shortly
19 Brand of beans
20 Ring result, for short
21 Actor Cameron + actor Fairbanks = actor ___
24 Is the right size
25 Temporary support for a bone fracture
26 Infuse with bubbles
29 Black tea variety
31 Comedian Carell + comedian Short = comedian ___
33 Bluesy woodwind
36 Curly cabbage
37 Where a mole shouldn't be, in brief
38 Place that's buzzing
39 Hog's home
40 Singer Brown + singer Swift = singer ___
44 Elaine of "Seinfeld"
45 Provides funding for
46 Drug for insomniacs
49 Assign stars to
50 Basketball player Walton + basketball player Westbrook = basketball player ___
53 ___-mo replay
56 Frenzied way to go
57 Flapjack franchise, briefly
58 =
60 Two-wheeler

61 Commotion
62 Cuban dance
63 Got a perfect score on
64 Thumbs-up votes
65 Full of attitude

DOWN

1 One whose car has a bonnet and tyres
2 Blockhead
3 "Erase" on a computer
4 Traveling salesperson's assignment: Abbr.
5 Flying toy that's open-ended
6 Practices pugilism
7 Object of an ogler
8 Polo competitor
9 Relative of a snowboard
10 Try to get a better deal
11 Reason for a food recall
12 Early Indus Valley inhabitant
13 Bare minimum
22 Unit in an online order cart
23 Atop
24 Top choice, informally
26 Raises a question
27 Coup d'___
28 Bank (on)
29 Gets nosy
30 Greek H's
32 Pinnacle
33 Barn adjunct
34 Openly declare
35 Gen ___ (post-baby boomers)
38 Jekyll's counterpart

40 Loudly razz
41 Retirement income, for some
42 Bluish green
43 Stag's pride
44 Swindled
46 Addis ___, Ethiopia
47 Copycat
48 Chap
49 Seized vehicles
51 Loafer or pump
52 Drink at an ice cream shop
53 Simplest arithmetic problems
54 Hands-on science classes
55 Neutrogena competitor
59 Sine ___ non

by Susan Gelfand

ACROSS

1 Big name in banking
6 Tempest
11 Something to download
14 "The Fox and the Grapes" author
15 Ancient Asia Minor region
16 Subject for "Dunkirk" or "Apocalypse Now"
17 Defenseless target
19 Hawaii's Mauna ___
20 Pitching stat
21 Transmits
22 Hall-of-Fame Broncos QB John
24 Artsy Big Apple neighborhood
25 "Crazy Rich ___" (hit 2018 movie)
26 Directive that's in force until canceled
31 Eagles' nests
32 Puerto ___
33 Just a touch
36 Lobbying org. for seniors
37 Pioneer in email
38 Wild's opposite
39 "'Sup, ___?"
40 New Age energy field
42 Part of an urn that can turn
44 Notice when getting fired
47 Scarf down
49 Big parts of donkeys
50 Birds that honk
51 Justice Sotomayor
53 Furry foot
56 Meadow
57 Repeated comical reference
60 Like most things in "Ripley's Believe It or Not!"
61 Words said just before dinner
62 Stan's buddy of old comedies

63 Pre-C.I.A. spy org.
64 "Holy cow! This could be bad!"
65 With ___ in sight

DOWN

1 Lawyer's assignment
2 Prince, to a throne
3 "The Thin Man" dog
4 One in need of drying out
5 Unit of a TV series
6 Agree to join
7 Newsman Chuck
8 Burden
9 Ocasek of the Cars
10 Muddles through with what one has
11 Middle school years, notably
12 Song of praise
13 Says "Dear God . . ."
18 Sodas not much seen nowadays
23 It can be white or boldfaced
24 Small scissor cut
25 Path of a Hail Mary pass
26 Bygone Swedish auto
27 Bit of weeping
28 Images on Kansas City Chiefs' helmets
29 A pun can induce one
30 Resource extracted from Alaska's North Slope
34 Roman god of love
35 Wagers
37 NPR's Shapiro
38 Much of a salon worker's income
40 Peanut or pollen reaction, possibly
41 Hawaiian instrument, for short

42 Land on the Strait of Gibraltar
43 Model of excellence
45 Small batteries
46 Ones who are said to grant three wishes
47 Eskimo home
48 Must-haves
51 Crackle and Pop's buddy
52 Fairy tale beginning
53 Tree : Christmas :: ___ : Festivus
54 Similar (to)
55 Dandelion, for one
58 Spoon-bending Geller
59 Singer and former "American Idol" judge, familiarly

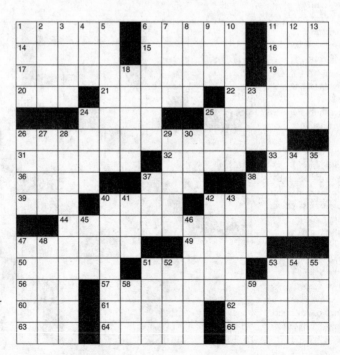

by Trent H. Evans

ACROSS

1 Sticker that says who you are
6 Part of the body that crunches work
9 Dreadlocks wearer, informally
14 The "F" of R.A.F.
15 Kitten's sound
16 Use as a dinner table
17 Zero-tariff policy
19 Back's opposite
20 Shaggy grazer
21 Orders (around)
23 Swanky
24 Beginning blossoms
25 With 39-Down, last words in many an old movie
27 Six-sided game piece
28 With 45-Across, savory topping found in tubs . . . and the circled squares?
31 Complete lack of wind, as at sea
33 Feeling good to wear, say
34 Languages
35 Iced tea brand in a bottle
36 When repeated, gets specific, as an informer
37 "Where there's ___, there's hope"
40 Guinness world record holder for longest live weather report
42 Alternative to an S.U.V.
43 "Cat on a Hot Tin Roof" actor
45 See 28-Across
46 Pen filler
47 ExxonMobil product
48 Work's opposite
49 Bowled over
51 Messiah
53 Only three-letter zodiac sign
56 "Well, obviously!"

58 Device to remove water from a ship
60 Aged fairy tale character
61 "We're number ___!"
62 Worth
63 Secondary building
64 Marry
65 Wide-mouthed jugs

DOWN

1 Far from certain
2 ___ the Explorer
3 Journey
4 Crackerjack
5 "Start working!"
6 Accumulate
7 Where flowers and oysters grow
8 Sugar, e.g.
9 Wearer of stripes on a court, informally
10 Grp. making after-work plans?
11 Moved out of the way
12 Throat part
13 "O Canada," for Canada
18 Was a passenger
22 Retrieves, as baseballs
24 Happened to
26 Last part of U.R.I.'s URL
28 Includes in an email
29 Slangy ending for "any"
30 Began, as a voyage
31 Mosque toppers
32 Waldorf salad ingredient
34 Acknowledges applause, maybe
36 Bursting stars

38 Org. overseeing airports
39 See 25-Across
41 Oil ___ (gulf sight)
42 "Oh, puh-leeze!"
43 Human rights advocate Jagger
44 Like brand-new clothing
45 Trudge
48 Stacked
50 Sand ridge
52 Grape or watermelon plant
53 Item in a tackle box
54 Mideast bigwig
55 Chooses, with "for"
57 Bit of voodoo
59 Where parishioners sit

by Jacob Stulberg

ACROSS

1 Shoot out, as 14-Across
5 Peach stones
9 Demanding that people do this and do that
14 Volcanic rock
15 Uncork, as a bottle
16 Livid
17 At the lower side of the pH scale
18 Maple or oak
19 Stepping on the baseline when serving in tennis, e.g.
20 Holder of wires along a street
23 Gloom's partner
24 Actor Efron of "The Greatest Showman"
25 Subway scurrier
28 Like one end of a battery: Abbr.
31 Aggressive defensive soccer maneuver
34 Midterm or final
36 That, in Tijuana
37 Eco-conscious Dr. Seuss character
38 Red facial spots
39 Transmits
42 Toward sunrise
43 ___-wip (dessert topping)
45 "Black gold"
46 Nickname for John Wayne, with "the"
47 Series of funny outtakes
51 Smidgen
52 Fashion designer's monogram
53 Have another birthday
54 Golf ball props
56 Toy in a 2017 craze
62 Cricket's sound
64 Pairs
65 College in New Rochelle, N.Y.
66 Pavarotti, voicewise
67 Inner: Prefix
68 Some natural hairdos, for short
69 Horned safari animal

70 Student body overseer
71 Use the items found at the ends of the answers to 20-, 31-, 47- and 56-Across

DOWN

1 Part of a bed's base
2 Tempo
3 Wicked
4 Walked through water
5 Things filled by a highway crew
6 "On my honor!"
7 Adolescent
8 Something that's impossible to do with one's eyes open, per an urban legend
9 Dual-purpose bit of eyewear
10 Of the mouth

11 Hot dog topper
12 The Cards, on a scoreboard
13 Up until now
21 Like one end of a battery: Abbr.
22 Consoling touch
26 Anchorage's home
27 Communicated via iMessage or WhatsApp
28 In the area
29 Gets all A's, say
30 James ___, portrayer of Tony Soprano on "The Sopranos"
32 Benefactor
33 Like mixed doubles tennis, in college
35 "Love ___ " (Beatles hit)
40 Fizzy, sugarless beverage

41 Takes a night to think over
44 Apple tablet with an attachable keyboard
48 Omelet or quiche ingredient
49 Like clarinets and oboes
50 Hawaiian garland
55 Quick smell
57 Hotel amenity with a cord
58 Adjust, as a piano
59 "Me neither"
60 Grandson of Adam and Eve
61 What talcum powder may prevent
62 Middle: Abbr.
63 The laugh of someone who's up to no good

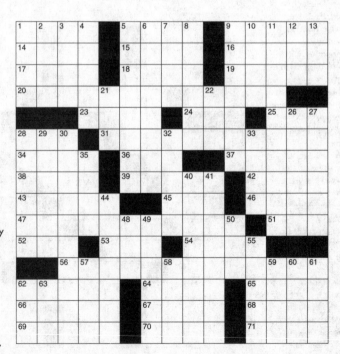

by Caitlin Reid

ACROSS

1 Just one year, for Venus and Serena Williams
7 Small plumbing problem
11 ___-Caps (candy)
14 It gets beaten at a party
15 McEntire with a twang in her voice
16 Long, long time
17 Remove, as from a belt
18 Popular program usually shown back to back with 34-/36-Across
20 Strong brews
22 Speaker's place
23 Host of 18-Across
27 One of four on a fork
28 Anger
29 Some hospital pics
30 Ham and lamb
31 Immigrant's class, for short
32 Money that may go in a slot
33 Purchase at Citgo
34 With 36-Across, popular program usually shown back to back with 18-Across
36 See 34-Across
40 Engine cooler
41 Lose vibrancy, as from exposure to sunlight
42 H.S. proficiency exam
43 Vegas hot spot, with "the"
46 One-liner
47 Smelting refuse
48 Uzbekistan and Kazakhstan's ___ Sea
49 Co-host of 34-/36-Across
51 "You can stop explaining the joke to us"
53 Peter, Paul and Mary, e.g.
54 Co-host of 34-/36-Across
56 Notices
60 "Who am ___ say?"
61 Actress ___ Flynn Boyle
62 Kathmandu native
63 Cookbook amt.
64 "___ Eyes" (Eagles hit)
65 It shakes things up

DOWN

1 Kwik-E-Mart clerk on "The Simpsons"
2 Alcohol that's transparent
3 Accompanier of a letter inside an env.
4 Samsung product
5 At an angle
6 Movie for which Tatum O'Neal won an Oscar
7 Nickname for Erving in the old N.B.A.
8 ___ Pieces
9 Onetime Apple product
10 One of the Three Bears
11 Country below Hungary
12 "Stop, I beg you!"
13 Banded gems
19 Precollege exam that offers college credit
21 Sans ___ (font type)
23 Not many
24 Like green, green vegetation
25 Writer ___ Stanley Gardner
26 Big storage item
30 Mother with a foal
32 Applaud
33 Aunt or uncle, sometimes
35 Does one's taxes online
36 Like light from a far-off star
37 Unattractive fruit
38 "Awesome!"
39 Perimeter
41 "Ain't we got ___?"
43 Ditch for cutting timber
44 Pays for everyone
45 Convertible, in slang
46 From Doha, e.g.
47 Quaint store
49 Golfer Singh who won the 2000 Masters
50 More sagacious
52 Always bumping one's head on doorways, say
55 Topeka's home: Abbr.
57 "Are you?" response
58 "Strange Magic" band, in brief
59 Ma'am's counterpart

by Michael Black

ACROSS

1 West Coast law force, for short
5 Insurer whose name rhymes with "quack"
10 Q-tip, e.g.
14 Regions
16 Where the Dolphins play
17 Prey for cats
18 Characters in a play, formally
21 Unit of corn
22 Loopy from drugs
23 Some herding dogs
24 Monarch renowned for his wealth
28 N.Y.C. subway inits.
29 Down Under hoppers, informally
30 Overlook rudely
33 Ice cream treat
36 Veer, as a ship
37 Miracle-___ (garden brand)
38 With 39-Across, doomsayer's assertion . . . or a phonetic hint to 18-, 24-, 51- and 61-Across
39 See 38-Across
42 Santa ___ winds
43 "How stupid of me!"
46 More tidy
47 Trail mix
49 Japanese noodle
50 61, in old Rome
51 College team from the land of Lincoln
57 How TV series DVDs may be sold
59 DNA sequence
60 Gen ___ (millennial forerunner)
61 Yom Kippur War clash
65 Response from a greatly amused texter

66 Better aligned
67 Goes way, way up
68 Bellow
69 Comic Bruce with a foul mouth
70 Big Board inits.

DOWN

1 Stows, as cargo
2 Pianist Claudio
3 Gem strung on a necklace
4 Beaver's construction
5 Mexican friend
6 Popular Friday feast
7 Once around the track
8 Soul: Fr.
9 Ringling Brothers offering, once
10 Round-the-campfire treats
11 Going off script
12 Smoothie "superfruit"
13 "Subjects" of a queen, not a king
15 Like the climate of the African desert
19 Like some auto windows
20 "Like father, like ___"
25 Beach washer
26 Breath-taking snake
27 Specification on an airline ticket
31 Desire
32 Physics Nobelist Niels
33 Without a date
34 "You might think so, but . . ."
35 Grave, as injuries
39 Queued
40 Strictly platonic
41 Hammer's target
43 Bit of an ellipsis

44 Japanese sash
45 Do a surfing maneuver
48 Glock, for one
49 Jewish village of old
52 Dr. Scholl's padding
53 Architect Frank
54 No, in pig Latin
55 Comes closer
56 "And Still ___" (Angelou volume)
57 With competence
58 Uncreative bar order, with "the"
62 Metal before refinement
63 When said three times, a Beach Boys hit
64 Charged particle

by Chuck Deodene

ACROSS

1 Something up one's sleeve?
6 To's opposite
10 Fool
14 Fashion designer Geoffrey
15 Four-star review
16 "Lovely" Beatles girl
17 Anode or cathode
20 Onetime leader of Iran
21 Former Disney C.E.O. Michael
22 Antlered animal
23 Land for O'Connor or O'Casey
25 Unspoken but understood
27 Iconic San Francisco bridge
33 Chanel of perfume fame
34 Response to "Who wants to go?"
35 In order that one might
37 Jewel
38 Where to find the ends of 17-, 27-, 50- and 65-Across
41 Vinyl records, for short
44 Hester of "The Scarlet Letter"
46 "Water Under the Bridge" singer, 2016
48 Frozen dessert franchise
50 Steinbeck novel set in Monterey
53 Admission of perjury
55 Daytime store window sign
56 Candy from a dispenser
57 Urbana-Champaign students
61 Rock music boosters
65 Letting others occupy the spotlight
68 Roman poet who wrote "Ars Amatoria"
69 Hat's edge
70 Pioneering name in video games
71 Garfield and Odie, for two
72 Subdue through electric shock
73 1800s president nicknamed "His Accidency"

DOWN

1 ___ and flows
2 Jacob's first wife, in the Bible
3 Software version for testing
4 Discreetly, informally
5 Tiny
6 Cooking in a pan with oil
7 "Confound it!"
8 Place to cook a turkey
9 Only
10 The first "T" of TNT
11 Relative of alcopop
12 Like tilted type
13 Address, as a listener
18 Bridle strap
19 Action star originally known as Laurence Tureaud
24 Team race
26 Make a scene?
27 Band's booking
28 "You ___ me one"
29 Rap rock band with the 7x platinum album "Significant Other"
30 "Quaking" tree
31 Excessively
32 Distinctive feature of Mr. Spock
36 Look that might "shoot daggers"
39 Abbr. ending a company name
40 Genetic stuff
42 West Bank-based grp.
43 Make clothing
45 Ingredient in a manhattan
47 China's Ming or Manchu
48 Pinnacle
49 Synonym for both "adhere" and "split"
51 Undistinguished
52 "Beowulf," e.g.
54 Loud noise
58 Pride parade inits.
59 Actress ___ Flynn Boyle
60 Long-legged wader
62 Offering now discontinued by most discount carriers
63 Cut (down)
64 Keep the sauce from congealing, say
66 Passports et al.
67 Kit ___ bar

by Jacob Stulberg

ACROSS

1 Night demon
8 Japanese dog
13 Romantically daydreaming of, with "over"
14 Not the main wager
17 Brandy fruit
18 French novelist ___ France
19 Perfume, as in a religious ceremony
20 Neither Dem. nor Rep.
21 "Mamma ___!"
22 Cable material that transmits data using light
27 Read, as a bar code
30 Western tribe member
31 Candied Thanksgiving dish
32 Dog with a wrinkly face
33 Transportation in the Old West
35 Stand around the mall?
39 "Really?!"
42 Alternative to a convertible or station wagon
43 ___ beaver
44 ___ G BIV (mnemonic)
45 Wrestler Flair
47 ___ system (GPS device)
48 Pleads
49 Legendary jazz saxophonist
54 King topper
55 Former Gov. Cuomo's constituency: Abbr.
56 Dough raiser
60 Question ending many a riddle
63 State symbol of Massachusetts
65 Container typically with a pull tab
66 Answers

67 With 68-Across, still feeling like a teenager, say . . . or a hint to the answers with shading
68 See 67-Across

DOWN

1 Apple computer
2 "Huh-uh"
3 Food that's husked
4 Togetherness
5 Curl target, informally
6 Card game made by Mattel
7 ___ Friday (main role on "Dragnet"): Abbr.
8 Yoga posture
9 In a gentle manner
10 Suffragist ___ B. Wells
11 Vietnamese New Year
12 Manhattan Project weapon, informally
15 Peace Nobelist Wiesel
16 Rip
20 Planets like Neptune and Uranus
23 Ballerina's skirt
24 "May ___ your coat?"
25 Eastern ascetic
26 "You can count on me"
27 Mineral springs
28 Goal of cancer research
29 Elderly
33 Drive-in chain featuring carhops
34 Tarzan creator ___ Rice Burroughs
36 Fairy tale fiend
37 Pollution from car emissions, in part

38 Unfortunate things to leave locked in a car
40 Tall tale
41 Hindu divinity
46 Scammer
48 Classic VW
49 Movie with an iconic theme that starts with two alternating notes
50 Eight: Sp.
51 Intoxicating
52 Making up stories
53 Forest or mountain maiden of myth
57 Opera solo
58 One with a crystal ball
59 Try out
61 "___ Te Ching"
62 Prefix with pressure or puncture
63 Mesozoic, for one
64 Call from a tennis official

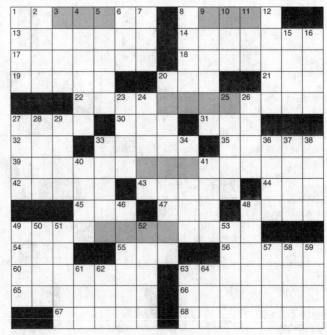

by Amanda Chung and Karl Ni

ACROSS

1 Base after third base
5 Flows back
9 1, 8, 27, 64, etc.
14 The "U" of B.T.U.
15 1982 movie inspired by Pong
16 Yoga posture
17 *Capricious
19 French "thank you"
20 ". . . man ___ mouse?"
21 Jokester's jokes
22 *Forgivable
23 ___ McDonald (clown)
25 Additionally
27 Gas brand whose logo has a blue oval
28 "Desserts" made from wet dirt
30 Pupu ___
32 Isaac's elder son
33 Gas brand whose logo has a red triangle
35 What free apps often come with
36 *Warlike
38 Little rapscallion
41 Glass that makes a rainbow
42 Website for crowdsourced reviews
46 Church activity
48 Clothing
51 "Will do!"
52 "The War of the Worlds" villains, briefly
54 Sitting Bull's people
55 *Jolly
57 Meriting a "D," say
59 Figure in the form 123-45-6789, e.g.: Abbr.
60 "___ ears!" ("Listening!")
61 *Gloomy
63 Portions (out)

64 Vaper's device
65 Italy's shape
66 "You ___ right!"
67 Composer John with six Emmys
68 Tiny hill builders

DOWN

1 "Just play along, please"
2 Burdensome
3 "Hamilton" composer
4 List-ending abbr.
5 Brokerage with an asterisk in its name
6 Clink on the drink
7 Toot one's own horn
8 Weekly parody source, briefly
9 Arrived
10 Online discussion forum

11 Professional coffee server
12 Fully surrounded (by)
13 Ones under a captain's command
18 ___ fruit (wrinkly citrus)
22 Europe's longest river
24 Kwik-E-Mart minder on "The Simpsons"
26 Kia model
29 What actors memorize
31 Alternative to Hotmail
34 "___ Not Unusual" (Tom Jones standard)
36 Car speed meas.
37 Shakespearean sprite
38 Site of a 1945 Allied victory in the Pacific
39 Amino acid vis-à-vis a protein, e.g.

40 Public's opposite
42 Tibetan beast
43 Beachfront property woe
44 "How about we forgo that"
45 Etymological origins of the answers to the five starred clues
47 Subway entrances
49 What oxen pull, in England
50 Catherine who married Henry VIII
53 The final frontier, per "Star Trek"
56 Additionally
58 Big name in elevators
61 Prepare, as a dinner table
62 Org. for the Sixers and Spurs

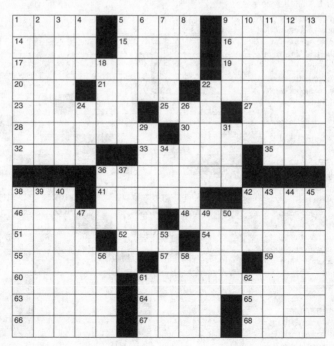

by Alex Eaton-Salners

44

ACROSS
1 Snatch
5 Mil. schools
10 Irritably impatient
15 Actress Dunham who wrote "Not That Kind of Girl"
16 What a designated driver should be
17 Where "I dos" are exchanged
18 Leave out
19 Children's publisher whose name includes a black-and-white animal
21 Home of Pago Pago
23 Moo goo ___ pan
24 Wonderland girl
25 Foul-smelling swamp plant whose name includes a black-and-white animal
28 Sent to the canvas, in brief
30 What "I do" means
31 Tavern
32 On, as a horse
34 Some small batteries
35 Volcanic residue
37 Samberg of "Brooklyn Nine-Nine"
38 Areas for pedestrians whose name includes a black-and-white animal
43 Hoedown seat
44 Schumer of "I Feel Pretty"
45 Relative of dynamite
46 Small sugar serving
49 Bread for a Reuben sandwich
50 Deg. from Wharton
53 Sharpshooter's asset
54 Restaurant chain whose name includes a black-and-white animal
58 Opposite of o'er
60 Sick
61 Line at an airport
62 Men's fancy duds whose name includes a black-and-white animal

65 Wait
66 Brand of blenders
67 High points
68 High cards
69 German steel city
70 Sheriff's group
71 Flip, as a coin

DOWN
1 Shiny photo
2 New version of an old film
3 Strong dislike
4 Relay race handoff
5 Nile biter
6 Mountain lion
7 Britcom of the 1990s, informally
8 E.M.T. procedure with electric paddles, for short
9 ___ Lanka
10 iPad, e.g.
11 Elite race in "The Time Machine"

12 Item hung on Christmas Eve
13 Accept a bet
14 100 in a century: Abbr.
20 Repeatedly scolds
22 "Allahu ___" (Muslim cry)
26 Spanish house
27 Sounds at spas
29 Susan of "L.A. Law"
33 Deliver a diatribe
34 Whom Cain slew in Genesis
35 Triceps locale
36 Sushi sauce
38 Buffoonery
39 Listings on the periodic table
40 ___ Crunch (cereal)
41 River of the underworld
42 Ham-handed
43 Drag queen's wrap
47 Economic improvement

48 When doubled, a dolphinfish
49 Depends (on)
50 Where Guadalajara is
51 Where less-played tunes can be found on old records
52 Levy, as taxes
55 Dance club that might have a rotating mirrored ball
56 Homecoming attendees, for short
57 Morocco's capital
59 James who wrote "A Death in the Family"
62 Poet who wrote "Once upon a midnight dreary . . ."
63 Midday snooze
64 Mao ___-tung

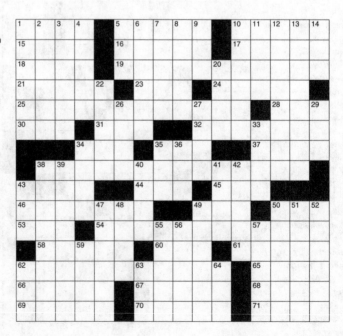

by Peter Gordon

ACROSS

1 Pulsate, as with pain
6 What a red traffic light means
10 Container for soup or cereal
14 ___ acid (protein builder)
15 "Very funny!"
16 Eye layer
17 Chocolaty candy on a stick
19 500 sheets of paper
20 Realtors' showings
21 Endless, in poetry
23 Guard at an entrance
26 Length × width, for a rectangle
27 Desertlike
28 Breakfast cereal with a naval officer on its box
33 Put through a blast furnace, say
35 Dissolute sort
36 Rope-a-dope boxer
37 ___-relief
38 Two marks in "résumés"
41 Easy-to-chew food
42 It ends with diciembre
43 Danny who co-starred in "White Christmas"
44 Make red-faced
46 Brittle, spicy cookie
50 Besides
51 Hilarious person
52 Plan going forward, as for peace
54 As originally placed
57 Constantly rising things in gentrifying neighborhoods
58 Where Hartford is: Abbr.
59 Broadcast news snippets . . . or an apt description for 17-, 28- and 46-Across?
64 Grand-scale production
65 ___ Krabappel, teacher on "The Simpsons"

66 Love, love, love
67 Meyers of late-night
68 Most mammals have four of them
69 Core belief

DOWN

1 Tit for ___
2 Care provider, briefly
3 2016 Olympics host, informally
4 Hush-hush, slangily
5 ___ buddy
6 "For Your Eyes Only" singer Easton
7 Water spigots
8 "Look what I found!"
9 Slice from a book?
10 The "B" of F.B.I.
11 On top of
12 Withdraw gradually (from)
13 Unfunny, as a joke

18 Apple desktop
22 Mother canonized in 2016
23 Long-winded sort
24 Italian designer Giorgio
25 Attaches using string
26 Unknown author, for short
29 Fuss in front of the mirror
30 Incendiary weapon used in the Vietnam War
31 Category for a minor-league team
32 Rap, by another name
34 "Grab this!"
39 Amusement park ride that goes around and around
40 Growth under the skin

45 Unflattering angle of one's face
47 Christmas stealer in a Dr. Seuss book
48 Stadiums
49 Duck's habitat
53 Hitter's turn to hit
54 Helps reduce the swelling of, say
55 Slangy refusal
56 Foul mood
57 Step on a ladder
60 Poem of praise
61 2,000 pounds
62 Before, poetically
63 "On your mark, get ___ . . ."

by Roland Huget

46

ACROSS

1 Walk in the kiddie pool
5 Org. for the Los Angeles Sparks and New York Liberty
9 Minor fight
14 Affordable German car
15 Garden worker
16 "Star Trek" lieutenant who speaks Swahili
17 Drops dead
19 Tilts
20 Declare something completely finished
22 Cain or Abel, to Adam and Eve
23 Tiny
24 "___ we can" (2008 campaign slogan)
25 Self-proclaimed greatest boxer
28 One-named soccer great
31 Sis's sibling
33 Expression of disgust in Valley Girl-speak
39 Give the glad eye
40 Grp. to call to get a tow
41 Site with a "Shop by category" button
42 Have surgery
47 Not worth a ___
48 One-named singer with the 1985 hit "Smooth Operator"
49 Concorde, e.g., for short
50 Ingested
53 Org. with the longtime leader Wayne LaPierre
55 QB's mistake: Abbr.
57 Show up for negotiations . . . or a hint for 20-, 33- and 42-Across
63 ___ Gay (W.W. II plane)
64 Act all hoity-toity
66 Indian princes
67 Felipe ___, first Dominican manager in M.L.B. history
68 Small construction unit?
69 Lose in a staring contest
70 Littlest in a litter
71 Sexual appetite

DOWN

1 Moo goo gai pan pan
2 Residents of a 1968 movie "planet"
3 Mosquito repellent brand
4 ___ Island, immigrants' landing spot, once
5 Comment after an amazing fact is stated
6 ___ Scotia
7 Meat in a burger
8 → or ←
9 Chumps
10 Spiced tea from the East
11 Like some noses and egg yolks
12 Bandleader Shaw
13 Histories
18 Listerine competitor
21 McEntire known as "The Queen of Country"
25 Eagerly expectant
26 Italian body of water
27 Inuit shelter: Var.
29 Pinocchio, notably
30 Les ___-Unis
32 Request from a dentist
34 Clothing department with jackets and ties
35 [LOL]
36 Japanese sashes
37 Clods
38 No, in Moscow
43 "You wouldn't believe it if I told you"
44 Currency unit usually worth a little more than a dollar
45 Delete from a manuscript
46 Longtime "S.N.L." cast member Thompson
50 Sour
51 Like music with traditional harmony
52 Smiley face with hearts for eyes, e.g.
54 Equal to face value
56 Pre-Little League game
58 Panache
59 Giant in streaming video
60 School attended by princes William and Harry
61 In ___ of (replacing)
62 Units of work in physics
65 Drunkard

by Kathy Bloomer

ACROSS

1 Jack who starred on "Dragnet"
5 Percussion in a pagoda
9 Serves as a lookout for, say
14 Mata ___ (W.W. I spy)
15 Actress Perlman of "Cheers"
16 Tennis star Djokovic
17 Vaping device, informally
18 Skeptical comeback
19 Where pasta originated
20 "Green" 1986 film?
23 Word before Ghost or Grail
24 Not strict, as security
25 Defiant challenge to a bully
28 Singer McCartney
30 Resort with springs
33 Seller of TV spots, informally
34 Subject most familiar to a portrait painter
35 Roseanne who's not on "The Conners"
36 "Fluid" 2017 film?
39 Capital of 19-Across
40 Enter a pool headfirst
41 Streamer of "Game of Thrones"
42 Rink surface
43 "O.K. by me"
44 "Whoa there!"
45 Ginger ___ (soft drink)
46 Light source that needs occasional replacement
47 "Noted" 1965 film?
55 Black ___ spider
56 Carl who composed "Carmina Burana"
57 Greek sandwich
58 Sheep-related
59 Teeming
60 Chew on like a beaver
61 Frighten off
62 Apple device with earbuds
63 Hankerings

DOWN

1 Sharpen
2 To ___ his own
3 Cracker topping spread with a knife
4 Grand pooh-bah
5 Car part between the headlights
6 "Yippee!"
7 ". . . and ___ the twain shall meet"
8 Feline: Sp.
9 Neither vegetable nor mineral, in a guessing game
10 Cosmetic injection
11 Welsh "John"
12 Story
13 Vodka in a blue bottle
21 Energy, informally
22 Trivial entertainment
25 Prefix with lineal
26 Like a committee formed for a special purpose
27 Krispy ___ doughnuts
28 Minor annoyance
29 Soothing plant extract
30 Withheld the publication of
31 Alternative to Ragú
32 Symbol on a one-way street sign
34 What planets do on their axes
35 Pram
37 Word of parting in Paris
38 Engulf, old-style
43 Blossom
44 Breathed heavily
45 In unison
46 Terrific, on Broadway
47 Lacking depth, informally
48 Hill : ants :: ___ : bees
49 Revise, as text
50 "Me neither," formally
51 Reason to call a plumber
52 "Auld Lang ___"
53 Longtime rival of Saudi Arabia
54 Anthropomorphic figures in many "Far Side" cartoons

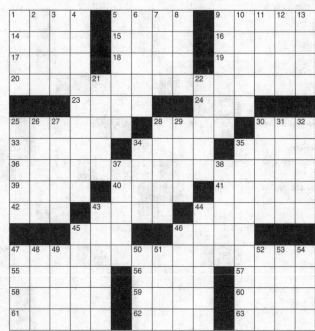

by Jim Hilger

ACROSS

1 Aware, in a modern way
5 Idris ____, People's 2018 Sexiest Man Alive
9 Abyss
14 "Man, I'm sorry to hear!"
15 Nursery rhyme word repeated before "go away"
16 "Social contract" philosopher John
17 Dachshund
19 Totally wipe out
20 Plant, as seeds
21 Our sun
22 Dress in Delhi
23 Copies of movies submitted to critics prior to release
28 ____ mark (#)
30 "Mazel ____!"
31 Witnessed
32 Partner at a table for two
35 Mideast grp. once headed by Yasir Arafat
36 Otherworldly
37 Big argument
38 Levin or Gershwin
40 The "L" of LSAT
41 Hawaiian necklace
42 Times when everything goes perfectly
45 Ambulance crew, for short
47 Words exchanged at an altar
48 Fellas
49 Genetically engineered, highly selective medical treatment
53 Modern food concerns, for short
54 Night before a holiday
55 Sack
58 Sing like Dean Martin
60 The secret geeky part of you . . . or a hint to 17-, 23-, 32-, 42- and 49-Across
63 Trailblazing Daniel
64 Modest poker holding
65 Et ____ (and others)
66 Jewish observance
67 Conveniences at many cash-only businesses
68 "Don't go!"

DOWN

1 Really impresses
2 Columbus's home
3 Was in the loop
4 Really, really long time
5 One might lead to an unearned run
6 Soup scoop
7 Book jacket bit
8 Director Lee of "Life of Pi"
9 Cloudless
10 Stockpiles
11 Running around during recess, e.g.
12 Bit of Winter Olympics equipment
13 Opera presenter, with "the"
18 Artist M. C. ____
22 Extreme
23 Nine-digit ID
24 When you'll likely reach your destination, for short
25 Away
26 Transportation problems caused by 27-Down, say
27 Winter precipitations
28 Plea from a fugitive
29 Announcer's cry after a successful field goal attempt
32 Handed (out)
33 Spring birds
34 Nickname for a 12-time N.B.A. All-Star
39 Attorney in court, e.g.
43 Neither's partner
44 Was really into
46 Olympic gold-medal gymnast Biles
50 Dead duck
51 Jean material
52 Camper enthusiasts, informally
55 Alternative to suspenders
56 Tune from "Turandot"
57 Greeting Down Under
58 "____ Evening News"
59 Fish eggs
60 Brewery output, for short
61 D.C. ballplayer
62 "Illmatic" rapper

by Evan Kalish

ACROSS

1 Expressions of amazement
6 Amaze
9 Illegal motions by pitchers
14 Houston player
15 Great Dane, e.g.
16 Notable happening
17 Great Dane of animated cartoons
19 Happen again
20 Immensely long stretches
21 Broke bread
22 Limited in number
23 Escalator feature
24 Result of overnight condensation
26 Lipton offerings
28 "Bus Stop" dramatist William
29 Nut often squirreled away
31 Basic trig ratio
33 Invitation request, in brief
37 Sound on a dairy farm
38 "Impossible for me!"
41 Harmful cigarette stuff
42 Equestrian's sport
44 Umpteen
45 Lessen
47 Fee payer, often
49 Londoner, e.g., informally
50 Words on returned mail
55 Vegetarian's no-no
58 Aviator Earhart
59 Cozy lodging
60 Ricelike pasta
61 Bring home, as a runner
62 Couple's ballet dance
64 Turn aside
65 Number replaced by "hup" by a drill sergeant
66 Resort island near Naples
67 Key Watergate evidence
68 72, maybe, on a golf course
69 Twin Mary-Kate or Ashley

DOWN

1 Oxygen and nitrogen
2 Racecourse near Windsor Castle
3 Implement for a Neanderthal
4 Thrive
5 Break down in tears
6 Make larger
7 Swain
8 Conscious self, to Freud
9 Explorer who lent his name to a strait off Alaska
10 Member of a Marvel superhero team
11 French play about a storied Spanish soldier
12 Gridiron legend Rockne
13 Spread here and there
18 Thanksgiving dishes
22 Made to pay as punishment
25 Dingbat
27 TV journalist Curry
29 Intensify, with "up"
30 Dove's sound
31 Fright
32 Knighted actor McKellen
34 Some down-ballot electees, informally
35 Big tub
36 Lead-in to occupy
39 From alpha to ___
40 Rowboat mover
43 Summary of key points
46 Like a probability curve with two peaks
48 New Orleans footballers
49 Flex
50 "Blue Ribbon" brew
51 Nebraska's largest city
52 Establish
53 Princess mourned in 1997
54 Indy racer Al or Bobby
56 Sky-blue
57 Snake venom, e.g.
62 Champagne-opening sound
63 Environment-related prefix

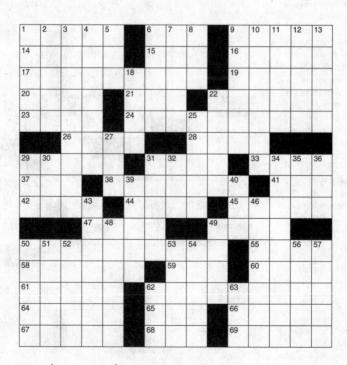

by Lynn Lempel

ACROSS

1 Shoestrings
6 Cook in oil
9 Brewing giant originally based in Milwaukee
14 Roofing alternative to shingles
15 Whopper (but not the Burger King kind)
16 Hawaiian greeting
17 Extremely inexpensive
19 Things sometimes hidden behind paintings
20 Extinguish, as a fire
21 Cost of a bank transaction that's not with one's own bank
22 Confucian philosophy
24 Bottom-up, as a political movement
26 Runs away to marry
29 Like some winter highways
30 Perfect test grade
31 New Testament trio
33 Pop a fly?
37 "Now things are getting interesting" . . . or a hint to the first words of 17-, 24-, 45- and 57-Across
40 Gilbert of "Roseanne" and "The Conners"
41 Knots
42 Ship of 1492
43 High degree
44 Bub
45 Amateurish
51 GPS lines: Abbr.
52 Going from gig to gig
53 Texas city seen in many westerns
56 Hatred
57 Bars that kids go to?
60 Get a feeling
61 Iraq War danger, in brief
62 One of the Hawaiian Islands

63 Parts of a forest
64 "Here's something interesting," in brief
65 Got some Z's

DOWN

1 Timothy Leary's drug
2 "The Greatest" in the ring
3 One who doesn't travel to work alone
4 "___, Brute!"
5 Religious offshoot
6 ___-de-lis
7 Cowboy's rope
8 Informal affirmative
9 Danish or cream puff
10 Avis competitor
11 Highly successful, in theaterspeak
12 One of 500 in a ream
13 Zaps with a police gun

18 Harleys, in slang
21 PC character set
22 Milk dispensers
23 Leader of the pack
25 Sounds of resignation
27 Stage after larva
28 Bilingualism subj.
31 Sacred peak in Greek myth: Abbr.
32 Had one's fill
33 Equipment often transported on a car's roof
34 Was a maverick
35 Chipped in at a poker game
36 Old Russian royals
38 None of the above
39 Computer's "brain," for short
43 Clouds of smoke
44 What the Titanic had a disastrous encounter with

45 Give a lift
46 Beneath
47 "Goosebumps" writer R. L. ___
48 One of four purchased for a Monopoly property
49 Sticky
50 We, on a candy heart
54 Fraternal group
55 "You're on!"
57 Alternative to Skippy or Peter Pan
58 Big mouth
59 Cambridge sch. for budding engineers

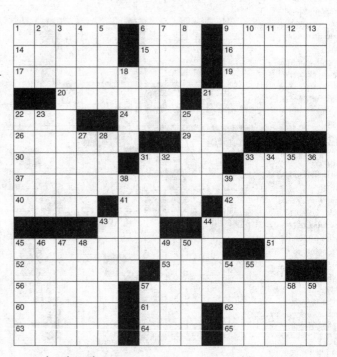

by Alex Eylar

ACROSS

1 Baseball's record-setting Ripken
4 Catches a touchdown pass, e.g.
10 Not much
14 Lead-in to carte or mode
15 Tel Aviv's land
16 Helen of ___ (mythical beauty)
17 Flier that may carry rabies
18 Small bird of prey
20 French girlfriend
22 Ginger ___ (soft drink)
23 Seaweed, e.g.
24 Something falling down, in a children's song
28 Lucy of 2000's "Charlie's Angels"
29 Summons, as strength
33 Put the kibosh on
36 Actor Efron of "High School Musical"
37 Sign by a fire escape
38 "Mazel ___!"
39 Commandeers . . . or a friendly hello to the people starting 18-, 24-, 51- and 62-Across?
42 Inits. on an airport uniform
43 ___ out a living (barely gets by)
45 Moonshine container
46 Carriage named for an English county
48 Careful reading
50 Farrow of "Hannah and Her Sisters"
51 Dorothy's footwear in "The Wizard of Oz"
57 White-faced
60 Bit of cookware
61 Biz bigwig
62 What follows Thanksgiving
66 "What ___?!" (cry of surprise)
67 Volcanic flow
68 From not long ago
69 Was in charge of
70 In a dead heat
71 No longer shrink-wrapped
72 First Republican prez

DOWN

1 Group of schemers
2 Mission where Davy Crockett was killed
3 Don Juan sort
4 Bro's sibling
5 Network for political junkies
6 Big name in toothbrushes
7 Pinker in the middle, say
8 Always, in poetry
9 ___-mo (replay option)
10 Olympics competitor
11 Toot one's own horn
12 Sioux City's state
13 Young 'un
19 Goes back and forth, as a tail
21 Revise copy
25 "That's gotta hurt!"
26 Big name in desktops
27 Teals and mallards
30 Start of a newsboy's cry
31 Move skyward
32 Obedience school command
33 "Watch your ___!"
34 Soft drink choice
35 Muslim woman's head cover
36 Make a sharp turn back
40 Bastille Day's month
41 Kind of pump
44 "I'm up for doing the job!"
47 Like thumped watermelons making a deep sound
49 Like ships on the ocean floor
52 Pizazz
53 Filled with cargo
54 Harebrained
55 2007's Record of the Year by Amy Winehouse
56 Big public display
57 Up to the task
58 Czech or Croat
59 "Girls Just Want to ___ Fun"
63 Jimi Hendrix's do, informally
64 Sen.'s counterpart
65 Paycheck stub abbr.

by Brian Thomas and Andrea Carla Michaels

52

ACROSS

1 Kiss, in Spanish
5 Cooper of hard rock
10 "That was a bear!"
14 Reclined
15 Snake poison
16 Shovel's creation
17 Dog in "The Thin Man"
18 First ex-wife of Donald Trump
19 One of the Great Lakes
20 Features of some eco-friendly vehicles
23 Give the go-ahead
24 Comes to understand
26 ___ the chips fall where they may
28 City near Scottsdale
30 Dry region covering most of Botswana
36 Swamp
37 Similar
38 Battery for a remote
39 It may or may not correspond with one's birth sex
44 More crafty
45 "Delicious!"
46 Former attorney general Jeff
51 Involving warships
55 Getting picked up by the side of the road . . . or what 20-, 30- and 39-Across are literally doing?
57 Partly open, as a door
59 One way to commute
60 Jane Austen title woman
61 Broad valley
62 Clement C. ___, writer of "A Visit From St. Nicholas"
63 One twixt 12 and 20

64 Birds that hoot
65 In a pouty mood
66 George H. W. Bush had four

DOWN

1 Bored feeling, with "the"
2 Course you're almost guaranteed to get a good grade in
3 Not get involved while something's happening
4 Really cookin'
5 Rah-rah
6 Pry bar, e.g.
7 Silly
8 Dance done in a line
9 One might end "Sent from my iPhone"
10 Asthmatic noises
11 Taboo alternative to beef
12 Manning with a good throwing arm
13 Tiny
21 Furniture giant founded in Sweden
22 Time after dark, in commercials
25 Apply, as pesticides
27 Them ___ hills
29 Info on an airline website
30 Falls (over)
31 Woody Allen comedy that won Best Picture
32 Mahershala ___, co-star of 2018's "Green Book"
33 Cleanse (of)
34 Eisenhower, informally

35 Say it isn't so
36 Some fourth down scores: Abbr.
40 Wishes
41 Once, back in the day
42 Sandwich fish
43 Ottoman inns
47 Parts of a Cold War arsenal, for short
48 Words to a josher
49 Actor Williamson
50 Sarcastic comments
52 Alternative to YouTube
53 Some jingle writers
54 Favors one side
56 ___ Poupon mustard
57 Hullabaloo
58 Scary part of a T. rex

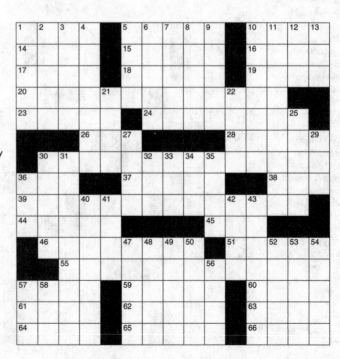

by Brendan Emmett Quigley

ACROSS

1. ___ San Lucas (Baja resort city)
5. Chew the fat
8. Maze runner in an experiment
14. Brewery products
15. Pitcher's stat
16. "Uncle!"
17. Five-time N.B.A. championship-winning coach with the Lakers and the Heat
19. Cable channel with many science shows, familiarly
20. "Ready, ___, fire!"
21. Ballad, e.g.
23. Circus enclosure
24. Garfield, to Jon Arbuckle
27. Notable statistic for Jeff Bezos or Bill Gates
29. Opening number?
30. Prosciutto, e.g.
32. Physicians, for short
33. Obtain
34. Mountain overlooking Tokyo
37. Casino floor V.I.P.
40. Make tiny criticisms
43. Ruler of old Russia
44. Broadcast
45. ___ tai (cocktail)
46. Bygone monthly for the 12-to-20 set
50. "The A-Team" actor with a mohawk
51. Road hazards that need filling
54. "Be patient!"
56. "Your turn," on a walkie-talkie
57. Appear to be
59. Surface of a sty
60. Peeved
62. Dessert loaf
66. Cheap cigar, slangily
67. CBS forensics franchise
68. Midwife's delivery
69. Sailor
70. "I know what you're thinking" feeling, for short
71. First word in a fairy tale

DOWN

1. Salary limit
2. ___ carte
3. Software trial runs
4. Duel overseer in "Hamlet"
5. Do stuff?
6. Warlike Greek god
7. Musket attachment
8. Width's counterpart
9. Santa ___ winds
10. Proceeding from low to high
11. America's largest firearm manufacturer
12. Secret ___ (007, for one)
13. Egyptian god usually pictured with the head of an ibis
18. Apple computer
22. Neighbor of Homer on "The Simpsons"
24. "___ and Circumstance"
25. Break off a relationship
26. Yanks (on)
28. Drift, as an aroma
31. Hi-___ screen
35. Singer with the 1961 hit "Big Bad John"
36. Comforting words
38. Place to shower and brush one's teeth
39. Cookie with creme in the middle
40. Never, in Nuremberg
41. Tehran's land
42. Eartha who sang "C'est Si Bon"
44. Perfect attendance spoiler
47. Yankees legend ___ Howard
48. Originally named
49. Egyptian pyramid, e.g.
51. John, Paul and John Paul
52. Undeveloped seed
53. Four: Prefix
55. High-performance engine
58. Dishevel, as the hair
61. Work ___ sweat
63. Extra 15% or so for a waiter
64. Simple as ___
65. Henna, for one

by Andrew Kingsley

54

ACROSS

1 Become narrower
6 "Come to ___"
10 Kindergarten fundamentals
14 "Well, isn't that something!"
15 Genesis garden
16 Opening for a coin
17 Facial feature that can be eliminated by cosmetic surgery
19 Trigonometric ratio
20 "For sure!"
21 "___ put it another way . . ."
22 Rather, informally
23 Disney World attraction
26 Walk over
29 Continuously
30 Easy win
31 ___ good example
32 Weaponize
35 Increase, with "up"
36 Friend of Archie and Betty in the comics
39 "Little piggy"
40 Chum
41 Fashion monthly founded in France
42 Congers and others
43 "___ ed Euridice" (Gluck opera)
45 The 20 in 20 Questions
48 Speak briefly
51 Where the belly button is
52 German auto import
53 Try to win through romance
56 Metropolitan ___
57 "Gross" title for this puzzle
60 Hit the tarmac, e.g.
61 Skin problem
62 Titleholder
63 This, in Tijuana
64 Wagers
65 Hangman's loop

DOWN

1 Having everything in its place
2 Natural salve
3 Asset
4 Flow out, as the tide
5 Insert a new cartridge
6 Marmalade ingredient
7 For one purpose only
8 Architect I. M. ___
9 Actress Miller or Blyth
10 Transfer (to)
11 Romantic setups
12 Weeklong vacation rental, maybe
13 Prepare, as mussels
18 Therefore
22 Work, as dough
23 It helps to know where you're going
24 Joint between the hip and ankle
25 Letter after theta
26 Snare
27 Capital of Italia
28 Professional work
31 "Steady as ___ goes"
33 Part in a movie
34 Filthy state
36 "The Family Circus" boy
37 Peter Fonda title character
38 Give off light, as a firefly
42 Suffix with lion or shepherd
44 Marriott rival
45 Seriously overcharges
46 Pakistani language
47 Incandescent lamp inventor
48 Old, as bread
49 Surrounding lights
50 "There ___ a dry eye in the house"
53 Tippler's favorite radio station?
54 Bills exchanged for a five
55 Menacing fairy tale figure
57 Tiny amount to apply
58 Rink surface
59 A couple

by Craig Stowe

ACROSS

1 Turkish bigwig
6 Norway's capital
10 Luke, to Darth Vader ("Star Wars" spoiler)
13 Released from bondage
14 Bounce, as off a billiard cushion
15 Israeli gun
16 Regal
18 Bellum's opposite
19 "___ Te Ching"
20 Brother of Cain
21 Nothing more than
22 Yosemite and Yellowstone
27 Mike who was a three-time N.L. M.V.P. with the Phillies
29 Close
30 Big piles
31 Make a quick drawing of
35 Address in a browser, for short
36 What a bald tire lacks
38 Ending with neutr- or Filip-
39 "The View," for one
42 Flower in a pond
44 Finished, as a cake
45 Heading on a personal bio
47 Something promised in a court oath
51 Hot-rod engine, informally
52 Love, in Latin
53 Prefix with friendly
56 "A Nightmare on ___ Street"
57 Cause championed by the figures named at the ends of 16-, 22- and 47-Across
61 Travel on Alaska or Hawaiian
62 ___ Beckham Jr., three-time Pro Bowler for the New York Giants
63 Pageant crown
64 Many Ph.D. candidates
65 Fish trying to find Nemo in "Finding Nemo"
66 In a foxy way

DOWN

1 Dismissive sound
2 Opera solo
3 Roman Catholic-affiliated university in New Jersey
4 Playboy founder, for short
5 Ruckus
6 Like bourbon barrels
7 Country once known as Ceylon
8 Actor Chaney of "The Phantom of the Opera"
9 Texter's "Holy cow!"
10 "Terrific!"
11 Missouri's ___ Mountains
12 Puts the kibosh on
14 Early North American explorer John
17 Bug spray from S. C. Johnson
21 Podcaster Maron
23 Box on a concert stage
24 "___ the season . . ."
25 Green building certification, for short
26 Bit of butter
27 Close
28 Actor Michael of "Juno"
31 Stitch
32 Go to bed, informally
33 "E pluribus ___"
34 Prepare for a photo
36 One of the Huxtable kids on 1980s–'90s TV
37 Australian winner of 11 Grand Slam tournaments
40 Native New Zealander
41 U.S.C. or U.C.L.A.: Abbr.
42 Funny Costello
43 Openly gay
45 Island with a lagoon
46 "It's c-c-cold!"
47 Pilferage
48 Very, slangily
49 More than 60 awards for "Saturday Night Live"
50 One of the Brontë sisters
54 ___-Alt-Del
55 Start of "The Star-Spangled Banner"
57 Fish caught off the New England coast
58 Wedding affirmation
59 Word before "a bird," "a plane" and "Superman!"
60 Baseball's Hodges

by Sean Biggins

ACROSS

1 Joint that a sock covers
6 Small recess
11 Karl Marx's "___ Kapital"
14 Country star Tucker
15 Theater worker
16 Month with Columbus Day: Abbr.
17 Giving away unwanted items rather than trashing them
19 Second letter after epsilon
20 Rage
21 Luau dance
22 Absorbs, as gravy on a plate
24 Broccoli ___
26 Clark of the Daily Planet
28 Obsessive to a fault
29 The Supremes' "___! In the Name of Love"
30 Extra job in the gig economy
33 Gin's partner in a classic drink
35 Look at, in the Bible
36 Put in more ammunition
39 Greeting in Tel Aviv
42 Lessens, as pain
44 Alternatives to Nikes
46 Dramatically end a speech, in a way
51 Result of a traffic ticket
52 Many, many, many, many, many moons
53 Hanker (for)
54 Ex-senator Bayh
55 "Hold your horses"
58 Tear to bits
60 Mind's I?
61 Reaction to an overshare
62 Crowdfunding site . . . or a hint to the beginnings of 17-, 30- and 46-Across

65 Goal
66 Inventor Howe
67 Prefix between tri- and penta-
68 Martial arts master Bruce
69 What a star on the American flag represents
70 Slightly off

DOWN

1 Initially
2 Holden Caulfield, for "The Catcher in the Rye"
3 Patella
4 Chemical compound with the formula NaOH
5 Made for ___ other
6 Centers of atoms
7 Components of archipelagoes

8 Second letter after upsilon
9 Roosters' mates
10 Therefore
11 "Crime ___ pay"
12 Real
13 Alternative to a paper clip
18 Hardy-har-hars
23 Previous incarnation
25 Disorder resulting in seizures
27 Bagful carried by a caddie
31 When repeated, a sneaky laugh
32 Mil. branch with B-52s
34 Paint layer
37 Wood for a baseball bat
38 Profound
40 Classic typewriter brand

41 Bosses
43 Look smugly upon
45 Madrid matrons
46 Insurance type that often accompanies medical
47 Dormmate, e.g.
48 Punctual
49 Existing: Lat.
50 Coin with Lincoln on it
56 Barely makes, with "out"
57 Pinball fail
59 Facts and figures
63 Spying org.
64 Band with the 1993 hit "Everybody Hurts"

by Thomas van Geel

ACROSS

1 Two of a kind
5 Buildings near barns
10 Stinging insect
14 Bone alongside the radius
15 Jack in a deck of cards
16 Camera setting for amateur photographers
17 Paranoiac's headgear
19 Walked (on)
20 Up, in baseball
21 Straps for an equestrian
22 Soak (up)
25 Present en masse
28 Pen pal's plea
30 Like a Monday crossword, typically
31 Actress Chlumsky of "Veep"
32 Part of the eye
33 In the past
36 "This means trouble, my friend"
41 Motor oil product
42 Hero fighter pilots
43 Partner of "go seek"
44 Celebrity
45 Keeps under surveillance
48 Blueberries and fatty fish, nutritionists say
51 Visitors from outer space, for short
52 Without toppings
53 Walled city WNW of Madrid
55 Watermelon waste
56 Dirt . . . or what 17-, 25-, 36- and 48-Across all have?
61 Gives a tattoo to
62 ___ and true
63 Not spicy
64 Soup to go with sushi
65 Delicious
66 Potato, informally

DOWN

1 "___ 'er there!"
2 "The Greatest" boxer
3 Lodging for the night
4 Tennis great Nadal, to fans
5 One who's always looking for a lift?
6 What a worker who oversleeps will be
7 Christine of "The Blacklist"
8 Eggs in a lab
9 Cry between "ready" and "go!"
10 Diluted, as a drink
11 ___ Goldfinger (Bond villain)
12 Something skipped across a pond
13 Racing vehicles for Anakin Skywalker
18 Nebraska native tribe
21 Martini & ___ (brand of sparkling wine)
22 Rocks from side to side
23 "To be, ___ to be"
24 Photo of Marilyn Monroe, once
26 Last emperor of the Julio-Claudian dynasty
27 Not foul, as a baseball hit
29 Toxic part of cigarettes
32 Uncertainties
33 Licoricelike flavoring
34 Title character who never arrives in a Beckett play
35 Jesse of the Berlin Olympics
37 "___ good in the neighborhood" (restaurant slogan)
38 Volunteer's words
39 Spongy toy material
40 First word of every "Friends" episode title
44 Declared
45 The first "S" in U.S.S.R.
46 Onetime alias of Sean Combs
47 ___ of Wight
48 Thin Russian pancakes
49 Places in order of preference
50 Desert stop for camels
52 ___ and proper
54 Prepares to shoot
56 Cousin in the Addams family
57 Arms-loving grp.
58 Little bite
59 Bug mostly seen in winter
60 Peculiar

by Ali Gascoigne

ACROSS

1 Closes
6 Like the voice of someone who's stuffed up
11 [Guests must provide their drinks]
15 Went after
16 Sheep-related
17 Where the first presidential caucuses are held
18 "Crossing my fingers!"
19 Squiggly mark in "piñata"
20 Earl ___ tea
21 2001 Tom Cruise thriller
23 Some rides from the airport, nowadays
24 Leave out
25 James who sang "At Last"
27 Nickname for former N.B.A. star Darryl Dawkins
35 "Star Wars" princess
36 Maya who designed the Vietnam Veterans Memorial
37 Diamond pattern
38 Suffix with different or confident
39 "Chill out!"
42 Connected PC system
43 Ready to assemble, as a home
45 Reef predator
46 Flowy hair
47 Amy Adams or Emma Stone, hairwise
51 Keep it ___ (be honest)
52 Sound from a ghost
53 "What a shame"
56 Kind of ice cream suggested by the starts of 21-, 27- and 47-Across
62 Swear
63 Largest city in South Florida
64 Japanese dog breed
65 "Look how great I did!"
66 Shenanigan
67 Enticed
68 Kill, as a dragon
69 Sits for a photo
70 Venue often named for its sponsor

DOWN

1 Makeshift knife
2 Funny (or sarcastic) joke response
3 Japanese noodle type
4 Pudding ingredient
5 Patron for sailors
6 Friendly response to "Do you mind?"
7 Hertz rival
8 ___ Road, route for Marco Polo
9 "Still . . ."
10 Director Spike
11 Beginning of the universe
12 Days of ___
13 One with a debt
14 Large inlets
22 Rapper ___ Wayne
23 Maneuver upon missing a GPS instruction
26 Take out of the freezer
27 Video excerpts
28 Symbol on a valentine
29 Floating fuel carrier
30 Race official
31 Rear-___ (auto accident)
32 "The Times They Are a-Changin'" singer
33 African antelope
34 Opera singer Fleming
39 Made the sound of a crow
40 Group that inspired "Mamma Mia!"
41 The first modern one was held in Athens in 1896
44 Off in the distance
46 Nickname
48 Pacific weather phenomenon
49 Unfortunate crowd reaction to a performer
50 [I don't know the words to this part]
53 College entrance exams
54 Egg-shaped
55 Mr. Pibb or Dr Pepper
57 Has a nosh
58 French female friend
59 Ocean motion
60 Heaps
61 Nickname for grandma
63 It may include the words "You are here"

by Howard Barkin

ACROSS

1 Fortuneteller's deck
6 Flabbergasted
10 Material for a rock climber's harness
14 Collective bargaining side
15 ___ Hari (W.W. I spy)
16 Follow orders
17 "Sleep well!"
19 Actress Hathaway of "The Devil Wears Prada"
20 Australia's unofficial national bird
21 Work from Keats or Shelley
22 Nut used to make marzipan
24 Content that has already been shared, as on a Reddit forum
27 Coastal county of England
28 Billy Idol hit that starts "Hey little sister, what have you done?"
32 Bullfighters' entrance march
35 Stroke gently
36 Crankcase fluid
37 Sidestep
38 ___ Enterprise
39 Secret ___ (metaphoric key to success)
41 Pal of Harry and Hermione
42 Corporate money V.I.P.
43 Henrik ___, "Hedda Gabler" playwright
44 Vegetarian spaghetti topper
49 Chicken holders
50 Bears witness (to)
54 Austin Powers, vis-à-vis James Bond
56 ___-Caps (candy)
57 Stocking stuffer?
58 Elderly
59 Graduation garb . . . or what the compound answers to 17-, 28- and 44-Across represent?

63 Birch or beech
64 Astronaut Shepard
65 Elements of a roll call
66 Minute or hour marker on a clock
67 Fey of comedy
68 iPhone maker

DOWN

1 One doing piano repair
2 Japanese cartoon art genre
3 Assemble, as equipment
4 Cry of delight
5 Big bang maker
6 Surrounded by
7 $15/hour, maybe
8 Biblical verb suffix
9 Collection of figures for a statistical analysis
10 Meandered
11 Very annoying
12 Quaker William
13 Took a gander at
18 "Me? Never!"
23 '60s hallucinogenic
25 "Never in the field of human conflict was so much ___ by so many to so few": Churchill
26 Slipper or sandal
27 Females in wool
29 British racing town that lent its name to a kind of salt
30 Pleasant
31 Country/pop singer Campbell
32 Request at a hair salon, informally
33 Last name of a trio of baseball brothers
34 Protection at the beach
38 Crafts in a "close encounter of the third kind"
39 Riverbank deposit

40 Partner of ready and willing
42 "Monkey see, monkey do" type
45 Like some sweatshirts and cobras
46 Item of fishing gear
47 Fruit that's peeled
48 Zillions
51 Crush with the foot, with "on"
52 Low-tech hair dryer
53 Touch, taste or sight
54 Hiker's route
55 Home of the Taj Mahal
56 Length of a bridge
60 Rumble in the Jungle champ
61 Crime lab material
62 Space between two teeth, e.g.

by Leslie Rogers and Andrea Carla Michaels

60

ACROSS

1 The Cardinals, on scoreboards
4 Egyptian cobra
7 Bracelet trinket
12 Little Red Riding ___
14 "Do ___ others . . ."
15 Former Chicago mayor Richard
16 To a sickening degree
18 Steal, informally
19 Proceeding well
21 PC key
22 Harness strap
23 Netflix's "Bill ___ Saves the World"
24 Rainy
27 "Definitely so"
29 Falls behind
31 Good name for a gemologist
33 Barely make, with "out"
35 Hungarian composer Franz
39 Place to bring aluminum cans
43 Paris subway
44 Peter and Gordon, e.g.
45 100% positive
46 English actor Idris
49 Poseidon's domain
51 Jack-in-the-___
52 Help wanted sign?
55 Twilight time
57 On the ___ vive
59 No longer in contention
65 Grammarian's concern
66 Race suggested by 19-, 39- and 59-Across?
67 Fashion
68 Like a thermometer that's put in the mouth
69 Prima donna
70 Liability's opposite
71 0, in World Cup scores
72 Break a hunger strike

DOWN

1 Kind of carpet
2 Big fuss
3 Comedian Love who co-hosts "The Real"
4 Once again
5 Step between two floors
6 ___ horse (gymnastics apparatus)
7 Music format popular in the 1990s
8 Goldie of "Snatched"
9 Straighten
10 ___ all (email button)
11 "As if!"
13 "S.N.L." alum Carvey
14 Pittsburgh-based N.Y.S.E. company
17 Hideous
20 "Mamma ___!"
24 Fishhook squirmer
25 Sword for an Olympian
26 "The ability to step on a man's toes without messing up the shine on his shoes," per Harry Truman
28 Compete in a slalom
30 Seven "deadly" things
32 Instrument for a Muse
34 Conclusion
36 Ticket leftover
37 Any digit in a googol after the first one
38 Big dinosaur, for short
40 Sudden loss of courage
41 Fellow told to "hop on the bus" in Paul Simon's "50 Ways to Leave Your Lover"
42 Like the three branches of the U.S. government
47 "Close ___ no cigar"
48 Actor Kutcher
50 Uncle's wife
52 Composer known as the "March King"
53 Removes from office
54 Doesn't leave
56 Gymnast Strug
58 Like many TV broadcasts
60 Look at with lust
61 Iranian currency
62 Nastase of tennis
63 ___ Scotia
64 Pesky insect

by Peter Gordon

ACROSS

1 Birthday cake part
6 Bundle up
10 Bother
14 Bayer brand
15 Bar mitzvah dance
16 Between ports
17 Blocked, as sound
18 Bills with George Washington's face
19 Bakery item with fruit
20 Bach masterpiece, informally
22 Bad actors
23 Break audibly
24 Big workers' group
26 Brought out to show, informally
29 Backstreet Boys member ___ Dorough
31 Bustle
32 Betty White co-star on "The Golden Girls"
36 "Blemished" fruit
38 Ban alcoholic beverages
39 Bed of roses, so to speak
40 Benadryl might treat them
42 Bear in a hit 2012 comedy
43 Bit of color
44 Brooding sorts
47 Bestows 10%, say, in church
50 Bread in Southern cuisine
51 Brainstorm
52 Bit of advice to the insecure
58 Breathe rapidly
59 Border mountain between Europe and Asia
60 Blurt out, perhaps
61 "Begone!"
62 Bring to anger
63 Ballot listing

64 British city after which the Big Apple is named
65 Baffled exclamations
66 Brecht contemporary in German literature

DOWN

1 Baby sheep
2 Bill Clinton vis-à-vis Georgetown and 54-Down
3 Beast of the Himalayas
4 "But still . . ."
5 Brand-new-looking
6 Beat badly
7 Barrett of gossip
8 Battle god for the Greeks
9 Buy the farm, so to speak
10 Brainiac in a certain high school competition
11 Biblical father of Jacob
12 Bomb architect Enrico
13 Borgnine's "big" role in "From Here to Eternity"
21 "Brilliant, dude!"
25 Balsam ___ (tree)
26 Besmear, as a canvas
27 Border
28 Beauty mark
29 Betting strategy that reduces risk
30 Boaters' implements
32 Beer ___ (frat party item)
33 Bad blood
34 Buyer of drugs, e.g.
35 Beaujolais and other wines
37 "Bother you at all?"
38 Brooklyn-born Supreme Court justice

41 Bolo ___ (Western wear)
44 Baseball's Gehrig
45 Blitz
46 Brand of chocolate
47 Boozed up
48 Boise's state
49 Barbershop quartet voice
50 Battery's + and −
53 Buffalo's lake
54 Bulldogs' school in the Ivy League
55 Brief announcements from pilots?
56 Badminton do-overs
57 Bingo card's middle square

by Ellis Hay

ACROSS

1 Cause of an infant's crying
6 Back talk
10 The first "N" of CNN
14 Chicago air hub
15 Voice below soprano
16 Lena of Hollywood
17 Zombies
19 Eat fancily
20 Like bread and newlyweds, maybe
21 Pudding ingredient from the cassava root
23 "Dallas" matriarch
25 Had a role in a movie or play
26 Like a concert album
31 Fragrance
32 One-named Grammy winner for "Soldier of Love"
33 Hip-hop's ___ Wayne
36 ChapStick product
40 Recipient of a Medal of Honor or Purple Heart
42 Spike who won a 2018 Oscar
43 Where Santa lands
45 Bard of ___ (Shakespeare)
46 Like a stolen object, when it's not where it's not supposed to be
50 Perfect grade
53 Wear away, as soil
54 In a crass way
56 Freestyle skiing jumps
61 Purchase before popping the question
62 Supposedly unknown but actually well-known fact
64 Beat narrowly, with "out"
65 What clocks keep
66 Who lives at the North Pole, in reality
67 No. 1 ___ (tournament favorite)
68 Variety of poker
69 Establish, as a university chair

DOWN

1 Indianapolis footballer
2 Separator of Indiana and Pennsylvania
3 Volcano's spew
4 Colored part of the eye
5 Tallest player on a basketball team, typically
6 Equestrian's seat
7 Ginger ___ (soft drink)
8 Measure after the governor's signature
9 Soft drink
10 "Not gonna happen!"
11 Poet T. S. ___
12 Facial reaction to pain
13 Golfer Sam with a record 82 P.G.A. Tour wins
18 Neuter, as a male horse
22 One finishing a road
24 Driver's licenses and passports, for short
26 Toilet paper unit
27 Falco of "The Sopranos"
28 Deal (with)
29 Spherical body
30 Ore-___ (brand of tater tots)
33 Jeans maker Strauss
34 Remove wrinkles from
35 What "L" stands for in pant sizes
37 Got up
38 "Skip to My ___"
39 Interminably expensive project
41 Possesses
44 Only four-term prez
46 Wasn't exact with, as facts
47 Made a ghostly sound
48 Middle-of-the-month day
49 Tranquil
50 Land measures
51 Pack of lions
52 Sudden move in fencing
55 Land parcels
57 Symbol on a computer screen
58 Former Yankee slugger, familiarly
59 Jay who preceded Jimmy Fallon
60 Ratatouille, e.g.
63 Relative of an ostrich

by Trent H. Evans

ACROSS

1 Preceder of Kitts, Lucia and Vincent in country names
6 Inexpensive sneakers brand
10 ___ tea
14 Sleeping problem
15 Showy peacock feature
16 ___-Lago (former presidential retreat)
17 Clearly visible
19 Overly proper
20 Belt out a tune
21 Mother sheep
22 Major event in golf or tennis
24 Iran's capital
26 Like two-week-old bread
27 Uncle in patriotic posters
28 Hoity-toity
31 Sgts.' superiors
34 Holders for emergency supplies
36 Fey of "Baby Mama"
37 Alternative to Chicago's Midway
39 Reagan ___ (1981–89)
40 Particulars, in slang
41 Follower of Lovers' or Lois
42 Eating outing
44 "Not impressed"
45 Sets lofty goals
47 Preceder of com or org
49 Sharp, as pain
50 Unauthorized drawings of favorite characters
53 Bits of parsley
55 "That was stupid of me!"
56 What an emoji depicts
58 Lena of "Chocolat"
59 What egotists use instead of "I"
62 Affectionate, as a farewell
63 Force from office
64 Funny DeGeneres
65 "Terrible" years for kids
66 Chinese lap dog, informally
67 What strawberries have on the outside that most fruits have on the inside

DOWN

1 Gullible sorts
2 High-level H.S. English subject
3 Totally silly
4 Sounds from a stable
5 Light brown
6 Neighborhood to get kimchi and bibimbap, informally
7 Simplicity
8 Go "pfft"
9 Detectives
10 Ill-mannered
11 Latin motto for a go-getter
12 Lake that feeds the Niagara River
13 "___ the torpedoes . . . !"
18 Sentiment from a Latino lover
23 Melancholy
25 Rant and rave
26 "Cosmos" co-creator Carl
28 Conifer that loses its needles in the autumn
29 Poker stake
30 ___ browns (side dish)
31 1970 hit for the Kinks
32 Person from Bangkok
33 Country completely surrounded by Italy
35 Light, light brown
38 Takes back, as an offer
40 Popular rodent control brand
42 Break at the Indy 500
43 Boise's state
46 Greeting from Grandma
48 Husk-wrapped food item
50 Strong suit
51 Esther of "Good Times"
52 Hauled to the impound lot, say
53 Pillowy
54 Ground breaker
55 Office furniture
57 Scout groups
60 Shade
61 "That's correct" . . . or a hint to the ends of 17-, 28-, 45- and 59-Across, in different languages

by Zhouqin Burnikel

ACROSS

1 After-bath powder
5 Mexican "dollar"
9 "Holy moly!"
14 "Young Frankenstein" assistant
15 ___ and crafts
16 Corporate giant in a 2001 bankruptcy
17 Tito Puente's specialty
20 China's Mao ___-tung
21 Fleming who created James Bond
22 "Wishing won't make ___"
23 Material that's spotted at a fashion show?
28 Matterhorn or Mont Blanc
29 Golfer's goal
30 Slippery fishes
33 "___ favor, señor"
34 Mothers, informally
38 ___ Lingus (carrier to Dublin)
40 Big name in newswires
41 Area of a basketball court near the basket
42 Lead-in to "la-la"
43 Candy that's not in-dispensable?
44 Like the hooves of wild horses
45 Kind of tide
46 What children should be (but not heard), they say
48 Dove's sound
50 12 on a grandfather clock
51 Rocket's takeoff point
56 "Right away!"
59 So-so
60 Sound from a goat
61 Court case, e.g.
67 Get a grip on
68 What you might use to get a grip on something
69 Prime draft category

70 "Hair" dos
71 Composer Satie
72 Corvette Stingray feature

DOWN

1 "Shop ___ You Drop" (old game show)
2 Turkish title
3 Mega Millions jackpot
4 Invigorating, as autumn air
5 Mushy baby food
6 Before, in poetry
7 Take it all off
8 Felix's partner on "The Odd Couple"
9 "Affirmative"
10 Kind of inspection
11 Habeas corpus, e.g.
12 Arboretums : trees :: ___ : animals
13 The "A" in A.D.
18 Kind of tide
19 Prefix with cycle
23 Drink, like a cat or dog
24 Gets hitched in haste
25 San ___ (San Francisco suburb)
26 Sketches
27 Bird's home
31 Wall covering that's washable with soap and water
32 Neighbor of Croatia
35 Speed abbr.
36 Person who sponges
37 "Same here"
39 Like a dangerous raccoon
41 Roman moon goddess
47 Texas city on the Rio Grande
49 "I guess the joke's ___"
52 Diamond head?

53 Chutzpah
54 Group singing hymns
55 Gal of "Wonder Woman"
56 Bit of pond growth
57 Medieval drudge
58 Food thickener
62 Old records . . . or a hint for this puzzle's seven longest answers
63 Long-running CBS forensic series
64 Hair-raising cry
65 Prefix with conservative
66 Dental problem that braces can fix

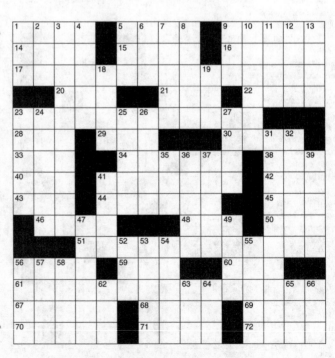

by Kevin Christian and Andrea Carla Michaels

ACROSS

1 Part of a jacket where a hands-free mic is attached
6 Powder for a gymnast
10 Part of a constellation
14 Michelle with the 2018 hit memoir "Becoming"
15 Gymnast Korbut
16 Columbus's home
17 The end
18 Unruly crowds
19 Nevada casino city
20 Tea set?
23 ___ Paulo, Brazil
24 Five cards of the same suit, in poker
25 Tune you just can't get out of your head
29 On fire
30 Suffragist ___ B. Wells
33 Rice or wheat
34 Slowly swivel sideways, as a camera
35 Unknown author, for short
36 G-string?
40 French assents
41 Bit of financial planning for old age, in brief
42 "The Little Mermaid" princess
43 Cory Booker or Cory Gardner: Abbr.
44 Spanish article
45 All together, as a crowd
47 Like many people after eating beans
49 Main squeeze, modernly
50 Beeline?
57 Earsplitting
58 Peter Fonda title role of 1997
59 ". . . and sometimes y" preceder
60 Org. fighting for immigrants' rights
61 Lack of practice, metaphorically
62 Touches down on the tarmac
63 Corridor
64 Receives
65 Olympic sleds

DOWN

1 Apartment in an old warehouse district, say
2 Not much
3 Breathe like a tired runner
4 Give off
5 Band's closing number
6 Drum with a repetitive name
7 Tons and tons
8 Rainbow symbol of pride
9 Chess move involving the king and rook
10 Out of ___ (discombobulated)
11 "Here's what you have to realize . . ."
12 Slangy negative contraction
13 Tree anchor
21 What cigarette filters are supposed to block
22 Egyptian boy king
25 Certain frozen waffles
26 Squabble
27 1980 Scorsese/De Niro classic
28 What many of the founding fathers wore
31 Old Venetian rulers
32 An obtuse one is more than 90°
34 Links org.
35 Home of the Taj Mahal
37 Supreme Court justice nicknamed "The Notorious R.B.G."
38 Shade similar to slate
39 N.B.A. souvenir
44 Thumb drive port, for short
45 ___ Field, onetime home of the Brooklyn Dodgers
46 Catch red-handed
48 Paula who once judged on "American Idol"
50 When tripled, "and so on and so forth"
51 ___ Raton, Fla.
52 Common email sign-off word
53 Lover
54 Microsoft search engine
55 Be an omen of
56 Kiss

by Joel Fagliano

ACROSS

1 Hit with a deft comeback
5 Greek T
8 Stuns, as with a phaser
12 Land unit
13 Subculture wearing a lot of black
15 Lighted sign by a stairwell
16 Chip dip, for short
17 Words on a pair of desk trays
18 Erotic
19 Comedian who co-starred in "Ride Along" and "The Upside"
22 Gloomy
25 Establishment that might have a rainbow flag in the window
29 "You may disagree," to texters
30 Wind instrument named after a Greek god
34 Regret
35 Eye of ___ (part of a witch's brew)
37 Big to-do
38 "W" column in the standings
39 Gelatin substitute made from seaweed
40 Playful furry creature
41 Loathe
42 Anonymous woman
44 Initially
46 Trackside transactions
47 "Deadpool" actor Reynolds
48 Tom turkey or billy goat
50 Jack who played Sgt. Friday on "Dragnet"
53 Heterogeneous
56 Something a horse kicks with
59 Bitter beer
60 Marked, as a box
61 Big commotion
62 Rowboat propeller
63 Changing from time to time
65 "Mona Lisa" painter
67 Causing white knuckles, say
68 Leading
69 Medicinal amounts
70 Harass endlessly

DOWN

1 Zig's opposite
2 Critical hosp. ward
3 Second Amendment-supporting grp.
4 Geico spokeslizard
5 Author Morrison
6 Lots and lots
7 "Not gonna happen!"
8 Having a kick, as food
9 Lumberjack's tool
10 Photos, informally
11 Hog's home
13 Words from Woodsy Owl before "don't pollute!"
14 Gathering just for guys
20 Mind-reading ability, for short
21 "Insecure" actress Issa ___
22 Rap star Nicki
23 Greek letter shaped like a horseshoe
24 ___ Atkinson, portrayer of Mr. Bean
26 Prickly bush
27 Mothers of cousins
28 Stopwatch button
31 Do, re, mi, etc.
32 Middle of a poker table
33 Start of a rumor
36 Kind of musical clef
38 Complained
43 Road sign that hints at what can be found three times in this puzzle's grid
45 Lavish praise upon
48 Pepperidge Farm cookie with a geographical name
49 Wards off, as danger
51 Hair color that can be "dirty" or "platinum"
52 Lighthouse light
53 Bowie or Beckham
54 Smell, taste or touch
55 Eight things on an octagon
56 Assailed
57 Pocatello's state
58 Obtain money illegally
64 Supporting vote
66 "___ the Walrus" (Beatles song)

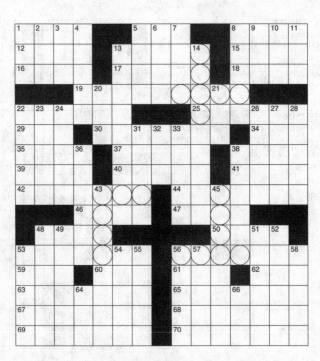

by Tracy Gray and Jeff Chen

ACROSS

1 Filming device, for short
4 Men's Health or Women's Health, for short
7 Sticks (to)
14 Mined rocks
15 Years that one has lived
16 Presidents and prime ministers
17 Gun advocacy grp.
18 It flows from the Himalayas to the Bay of Bengal
20 Piece of sports equipment with strings
22 First-___ (best)
23 Back-to-school mo.
24 Relaxation
28 Greek goddess of the hunt
30 Reference point during a piano lesson
33 Coke or 7Up
34 Bring into the company
35 Summer zodiac sign
36 "If memory serves . . ."
40 Nada
43 Black gemstone
44 Bulletin board fastener
47 Firm, as pasta
49 Fully illustrated, as a novel
52 Work of Shakespeare
53 "Norma ___" (1979 film)
54 German article
55 Where heads of the Pacific are found?
60 $ $ $
63 PBS-funding org.
64 Singer Flack with the 1973 hit "Killing Me Softly With His Song"
65 Serve that nicks the net
66 Paving goo
67 Reached the golf course standard
68 CPR sites
69 Tax org. undergoing some "reform" in this puzzle's circled squares

DOWN

1 Iran-___ (1980s scandal)
2 Behind in payments, after "in"
3 Did intentionally
4 O. Henry's "The Gift of the ___"
5 Court great Andre
6 Blues and rock, for two
7 Actor Guinness
8 Schoolroom assignment
9 Relative of a rabbit
10 Revised, as copy
11 Gun, as an engine
12 "But I heard him exclaim, ___ he drove out of sight . . ."
13 Byelorussia, e.g.: Abbr.
19 Cumberland ___
21 "Boy, do I ___ drink!"
25 Nothing's opposite
26 "Didn't I tell you?"
27 Green: Prefix
29 Worker with a trowel
30 Prop you might drop
31 Savings for the golden years, for short
32 Airline whose name is a Greek letter
34 Evil spell
37 QB miscue: Abbr.
38 Loaf that might have seeds
39 Place to pin a pink ribbon
40 Stick in the microwave
41 Sick
42 Holding hands or kissing on the street, for short
45 Italian red wine
46 Actor Greg of "Little Miss Sunshine"
48 Hole for a lace
49 Use mouthwash
50 Rob who directed "The Princess Bride"
51 Evergreens with fragrant wood
53 Big outdoor gear retailer
56 Senior party?
57 Mex. title that's an anagram of 58-Down
58 Old Russian title that's an anagram of 57-Down
59 Old Concordes, in brief
60 Hosp. V.I.P.s
61 Awed reaction
62 Certain Wall St. acquisition, for short

by Patrick Blindauer and Samuel A. Donaldson

68

ACROSS

1 Turn away, as one's gaze
6 Bird's beak
10 Varieties
14 "Toy Story" studio
15 "Point taken"
16 Ne, on the periodic table
17 Tennis with dad?
19 With 8-Down, dessert brand that "nobody doesn't like"
20 Messy meal for pigs
21 Motorists' org.
22 "Not in a million years!"
23 Losing tennis player's prayer?
26 In a trite way
30 Exam for a future atty.
31 Wonderland girl
32 "___ making myself clear?"
33 Guzzle down
37 Dislike for tennis?
41 Sharp as a tack
42 ExxonMobil business
43 Jargon
44 Famous ___ (cookie brand)
46 Things for cleaning dishes
48 "Wow, no wonder you're playing such great tennis!"?
52 Overdo, as a stage role
53 Assistance
54 "Good heavens!"
58 Letter-shaped beam
59 Lose every set of a tennis match 6-0?
62 Ship of 1492
63 "___ be over soon"
64 Take home from the shelter, say
65 And others: Abbr.
66 "Porgy and ___"
67 Soda in an old blind taste test

DOWN

1 Smartphone downloads
2 Relative of a cello
3 Big fair
4 Speak with a gravelly voice
5 First "T" in TNT
6 Problem with more than one marriage?
7 Ayatollah's faith
8 See 19-Across
9 "___ Miz"
10 Arcade game instruction before playing
11 Depart
12 Locale for Pyongyang and Seoul
13 Snide remarks
18 Hammer's target
22 Org. for the Suns and the Heat
23 Tickled-pink feeling
24 Ticklish Muppet
25 "You wish!"
26 With 28-Down, part of a golf course
27 ___ vera
28 See 26-Down
29 "Pretend nothing just happened"
32 Home to the world's busiest airport: Abbr.
34 Like Christmas decorations and some juries
35 Egg on
36 Sporty Pontiacs introduced in the '60s
38 Boggy wasteland
39 Italian city you might be "leaning" toward visiting?
40 Congeal, as blood
45 Something with a "You are here" arrow
46 Listings on a résumé
47 Mani-___ (spa offering)
48 Complain annoyingly
49 Nun's wear
50 Kitchen appliance brand
51 "Let" and "Fault," from a chair umpire
54 Quaint, as a shoppe
55 Circular kind of earring
56 Some postseason awardees, for short
57 Hairy Himalayan humanoid
59 Little lie
60 Gobbled up
61 Catch a few Z's

by Bruce Haight

ACROSS

1 Where pumpkins grow
6 Count in Lemony Snicket books
10 Apex
14 Snoozer's sound
15 Prefix with -technology and -second
16 Greek earth goddess
17 Firefighter Red
18 Class stars
20 Misplaced
21 Suzuki with the M.L.B. record for hits in a single season (262)
22 To date
23 "The A-Team" actor with a mohawk
24 Initials meaning "I've heard enough"
25 Thread holder
27 ___ Lanka
28 Peter ___, Nixon impeachment hearings chairman
32 General vibe
33 "Toy Story" boy
35 Serta competitor
37 Hop to it . . . or what to do to the various eggs in this puzzle's shaded squares?
41 Hot drink sometimes served with a marshmallow
42 Explorer Ericson
44 Neighbor of Ghana
47 Cuban-born Grammy winner Jon
50 Little fellow
52 Go halfsies on
54 Disney dwarf with the shortest name
55 Pinocchio's undoing
56 One of the Kardashians
57 Spicy Korean side dish
61 Clark of the Daily Planet
62 Triangular Swiss chocolate bar
64 Coffee drink sometimes served with milk "art"
65 "Buy one, get one free" event
66 The "A" of U.S.A.: Abbr.
67 PC key above shift
68 Patella's joint
69 Polling expert Silver
70 Monopoly cards

DOWN

1 Biblical book of poems
2 181-square-mile country in the Pyrenees
3 Honoring, as at a wedding
4 Lit ___ (coll. course)
5 "On ___ Majesty's Secret Service"
6 Using LSD
7 Where mascara goes
8 Adamantly against
9 Number of Teenage Mutant Ninja Turtles
10 Get older
11 Words starting a request
12 Shooting star
13 SoCal area bordering the neighborhoods of El Sereno and Boyle Heights
19 Uno + uno
21 Texter's "if you ask me"
24 "___ see it my way"
26 Alexander who directed "Nebraska" and "Sideways"
29 Asimov or Newton
30 Japanese electronics giant
31 Sturdy wood
34 Interior design
36 Light purple
38 Includes when sending an email
39 ___ v. Wade
40 "The best a man can get" sloganeer
43 Blacked out
44 "Naughty, naughty"
45 Buckeye
46 Play the slots, e.g.
48 Stick like glue
49 Emphatic agreement
51 Discourages
53 Scrape (by)
58 Tehran's land
59 N.Y.C.'s home to Matisse's "The Dance"
60 Tech news site
61 "Citizen ___"
63 Ang who directed "Brokeback Mountain"
64 Pioneered

by Andrew Kingsley

ACROSS

1 Poseidon's domain
4 Mortar accompanier
10 Swirl of smoke
14 Well-suited
15 Noah's landing place
16 Tennis's Kournikova
17 ___ for tat
18 Lone Star State baseball player
20 State whose license plates say "Famous Potatoes"
22 "That was a close one!"
23 "It's a mouse!"
24 Not national, as an airline
27 Fad
29 Gave off, as radiation
30 "Secret" person who writes a love note
32 What Marcie calls Peppermint Patty in "Peanuts"
33 Take unfair advantage of
35 What you might drape a dress or shirt on in a closet
40 Got ready to be operated on
41 Loud noise
43 Foreign ___ (international matters)
46 Fidgety
49 Hands out cards
50 Young gallant in "Romeo and Juliet"
51 Noah's craft
52 Drifter
55 Lumberjacks
56 Sandwich chain whose name is French for "ready to eat"
60 Time in history
61 Actress Hatcher of "Desperate Housewives"
62 Sailor's affirmative
63 Singer ___ King Cole

64 River of the underworld
65 See 59-Down
66 "What's the ___?" (pessimist's cry)

DOWN

1 Works like "Animal Farm" and "Gulliver's Travels"
2 Rapid spread of a disease
3 "Way to go, sister!"
4 Tushie
5 Bard's "before"
6 "Wailing" instrument
7 Fish by dragging a net
8 Place for mascara
9 Raison d'___
10 Pallid
11 Out of neutral, as a car
12 "Gesundheit!" elicitor

13 "Sex and the City" star Sarah Jessica ___
19 "You've got to be kidding me!"
21 Top 10 song
25 Lower in position
26 Ones selling commercial time, informally
28 Boxing venue
30 Cling (to)
31 ___ than a doornail
34 Egyptian cobra
36 October's birthstone
37 Country singer Yearwood
38 Where to find "Cut" and "Paste"
39 Coastal resort areas
42 Someone who was literally born yesterday
43 Makes a screenplay out of

44 Search (out)
45 Flimflam
47 Frightens
48 Men's formal attire, informally
50 "A blessing that is of no advantage to us excepting when we part with it," according to Ambrose Bierce
53 Minnesota representative Ilhan ___
54 1990s Indiana governor Evan
57 Box office purchases, for short
58 Pod of whales
59 With 65-Across, what the last words of 18-, 35- and 56-Across are to each other

by Peter Gordon

ACROSS

1 Drink, as water from a dish
4 Bits of broken glass
10 Locks in a barn?
14 Top card
15 How café may be served
16 ___ out (barely manages)
17 "Lady Chatterley's Lover" novelist
19 "Nervous" reactions
20 Goes down, as the sun
21 Change from the norm
23 Bart and Lisa's dad
27 King Arthur's home
30 Cigar residue
31 Flamenco cheer
32 Blow, as a volcano
35 Newspaper opinion piece
39 Early railroad tycoon whose nickname is a hint to the starts of 17-, 23-, 51- and 62-Across
43 James of jazz
44 Lauder of cosmetics
45 18 or so, for a typical first-year college student
46 "You don't mean me?!"
49 Made certain
51 Real-life lawman who lent his name to a 1950s–'60s TV western
56 Pilots
57 ___ car salesman
61 Appear
62 Utah senator who once ran for president
66 "Star Trek: T.N.G." counselor
67 Captivate
68 Noah's vessel
69 Europe's highest volcano
70 Getting up
71 "The Bells" poet

DOWN

1 Young chaps
2 Pain in a tooth or the heart
3 Hit repeatedly, as with snowballs
4 Viewed
5 Ben-___ (Charlton Heston role)
6 Pub offering
7 Time off, informally
8 Cuts into small cubes
9 Sugar substitute
10 Nerves of steel, e.g.
11 Actor Claude of old TV
12 Classic brand of candy wafers
13 German industrial city
18 Arthur of tennis fame
22 Gchats, e.g.
24 Bread spread
25 Time starting at dawn, to poets
26 Practice piece for a pianist
27 Secret message
28 Came down to earth
29 Vegetarian's no-no
33 Bedwear, briefly
34 Solution strength
36 Early talk show host Jack
37 Precipice
38 Like Easter eggs, colorwise
40 Abba song or musical
41 Department store department with shirts and slacks
42 Kiss: Sp.
47 Grain in Cheerios
48 Chemical cousin
50 "E pluribus ___"
51 Moisten, as a turkey
52 Deflect
53 Attach with a string, say
54 Singer Lopez
55 Form of the Spanish for "to be"
58 Become unhinged
59 Architect Saarinen
60 Comic actor Dick Van ___
63 "That's overly explicit," in textspeak
64 "Dianetics" author L. ___ Hubbard
65 Alternative to .com or .net

by Gary Larson

ACROSS

1 Wide open, as the mouth
6 Treaties
11 "What ___ I say?"
14 "Whoa, ease up!"
15 Stan's co-star in over 100 early film comedies
16 Made-up story
17 *Government's credit limit
19 Hubbub
20 Like many infield grounders
21 Lester Holt and Anderson Cooper
23 Issa ___ of HBO's "Insecure"
24 Smith or Scialfa of rock
27 Vienna's home: Abbr.
28 *Beanbag juggled with the feet
32 Massage intensely
36 Put on a black coat?
37 Guarantee
38 Great Plains tribe
39 "Start the music!" . . . or what one could do to the finish of the answer to each starred clue
41 Vaping device, informally
42 Full-time resident of a college community
44 "___ you through?"
45 Belles at balls, informally
46 *Symbol for "O.K."
48 "The ___ & Stimpy Show"
49 Labor organizer Chávez
52 Resort with mineral waters
55 Like a gift from above
58 Reproductive part of a flower
60 18+, e.g., in order to be able to vote

61 *Much-visited site in Jerusalem
64 Sleuth, in slang
65 Bury, as ashes
66 Girl Scout cookie with a geographical name
67 Cry of fright
68 Barely warm
69 "E" on a gas gauge

DOWN

1 Intense devotion
2 Actress Davis of "The Accidental Tourist"
3 Edward who wrote "Who's Afraid of Virginia Woolf?"
4 Trail
5 Onetime police officer
6 Dish made from taro root
7 None's opposite

8 Medical facility
9 Fork prong
10 Motorized two-wheelers
11 *Seafood topping that may be red or white
12 Assistant
13 Illuminating gas
18 Org. concerned with ecosystems
22 Figured (out)
25 Language in Bangkok
26 Served raw, as steak
29 McKinnon of "S.N.L."
30 Place for a baby to sleep
31 Beer barrels
32 Military program for coll. students
33 "Alternatively . . . ," in texts

34 *Part of a ship just above the hold
35 Practices épée, e.g.
36 Not us
40 Ticks off
43 "No surprise to me!"
47 Develops a glitch
50 First full month of Major League Baseball, often: Abbr.
51 Get the suds out
52 Post office purchase
53 Person in a cockpit
54 Ease, as fears
55 Concert proceeds
56 Double-curved molding
57 State bird of Hawaii
59 Did a backstroke, say
62 Prefix with -state
63 Conclusion

by Gary Cee

ACROSS

1. ___-dandy
4. Tramps
9. Wild guess
13. "___ we having fun yet?"
14. Humdinger
15. BMW rival
16. What M.B.A.s enter upon graduation
19. On bended ___
20. Yoko who loved John Lennon
21. Spelling contest
22. Verbatim
27. Allows to expire
30. Slap the cuffs on
31. Prefix with -friendly
32. Extra energy
35. Upper floor of a barn
38. Canadian team in the N.B.A.
41. How music can be stored
42. Cause one's bedmate to use earplugs, say
43. "Moby-Dick" setting
44. Gluttonous type
46. Make a mess, as hot grease on a surface
48. Tale that might feature a haunted house
52. Christmas ___ (Dec. 24)
53. ___ constrictor
54. "Hey! Over here!"
58. Kind of test . . . and a hint to a word hidden three times each in 16-, 22-, 38- and 48-Across
63. "What a pity . . ."
64. Like a haunted house
65. Roof repair material
66. R&B singer with the 2006 #1 hit "So Sick"
67. Mascara misadventure
68. "I wonder . . ."

DOWN

1. Beanstalk climber in a children's story
2. Golf club that's not a wood
3. Simple
4. "Game of Thrones" airer
5. Opposite of 'neath
6. Sheep's plaint
7. No longer having in stock
8. Old office worker who took dictation
9. ___ Paulo, Brazil
10. Increase in engine power
11. Chicago's ___ Planetarium
12. Waited
17. Seats for parishioners
18. Frayed, as clothing
23. Stuff oneself with, briefly
24. Prison disturbances
25. Exorcism target
26. Poet Whitman
27. Actor Jared
28. Supply-and-demand subj.
29. Ceremonial pre-Olympic event
33. "Cheers!," in Berlin
34. A Marx brother
36. Complimentary
37. Pre-1917 ruler
39. Scent
40. Fruit that flavors liqueurs
45. Desert crossed by the ancient Silk Road
47. Spell-checker find
48. Virile one
49. Small egg
50. Word after "on the" and "learn the"
51. Site of 1690s witch trials
55. Jedi foe
56. Grifter's game
57. A U.S. senator's is six years
59. Chinese menu general
60. Poet's "before"
61. Org. where one needs a security clearance to work
62. That lady there

by Bruce Haight

ACROSS

1. 33⅓ r.p.m. records
4. Cher or Adele, musically
8. Allude (to)
13. Annoy
14. Building for bovines
15. Mogadishu native
16. *Chief source of support
18. Self-centeredness
19. ___ fixe (preoccupation)
20. General Mills puffed corn cereal
21. Distances in Britain
22. *Chapel Hill athlete
24. Pyromaniacs' pleasures
25. Monogram for Long John Silver's creator
26. Cut (off)
27. Outbuilding for storage
30. Quarrel
33. Yankee great Yogi
35. Park or Madison, on an N.Y.C. map
36. Bouncy youngster in Pooh's crowd
37. Praise after a proper response to the end of the answer to each starred clue
39. Kesey who wrote "One Flew Over the Cuckoo's Nest"
40. Vow sworn at the altar
41. Round Mongolian tents
42. Wary
44. Spot for a teacher's apple or Apple
46. Virtuous conduct, in Confucianism
47. Dot follower in a website address
48. Pass, as a law
50. *"Why?"
54. Saudi city where Muhammad is buried
56. One running for office, informally
57. Noteworthy periods
58. First king of the Franks (A.D. 481)
59. *Tend an absent resident's property
61. M.L.B. division that includes the Astros
62. Prefix with -tasse meaning "half"
63. Word before "blastoff"
64. Uptight
65. Harmonious, after "in"
66. Originally named

DOWN

1. Outer boundary
2. Devil's fashion choice, in a Meryl Streep film
3. Person on a slippery slope
4. Midsection muscles, briefly
5. Potato treats for Hanukkah
6. Backpacker's path
7. Black, banded gemstone
8. Radioer's "Got it"
9. Is melodramatic
10. *Equitable treatment
11. Otherwise
12. Edges, as of craters
15. Athlete getting part-time pay
17. India's first P.M.
23. Plaintive poem
24. Fiestas and Fusions
26. Resulted in
28. ___ and anon
29. Reject as false
30. Extremely dry
31. Went as a passenger
32. *Soft bedding material
33. Title character in a Sacha Baron Cohen mockumentary
34. Radiant
38. One rejected by a group
43. Roast host
45. Butchers' tools
47. Op-ed offering
49. Plant seed with a licoricelike flavor
50. Poppycock
51. "Citizen Kane" star Welles
52. State that's the largest U.S. producer of lobsters
53. Beauty mogul Lauder
54. Exam for a wannabe doc
55. Her: Fr.
56. Degrees after M.A.s
60. Error indicator in a quotation

by Lynn Lempel

ACROSS

1 Stitches
5 Old workplace sitcom with Danny DeVito as a dispatcher
9 Flashy effect
14 Honolulu's island
15 "Terrible" Russian despot
16 Many a New Year's resolution prescribes getting into it
17 Not strict adherence to what really happened, say
20 Convenience at a business that doesn't take credit cards
21 Confirmed the flavor of
22 Biblical garden
23 Surefire winner
25 Bewhiskered river swimmer
27 Touched down
29 "Be that as it may . . ."
33 When a fresh factory crew arrives
38 Singer Yoko
39 Elusive Tupperware components, often
40 Air quality watchdog created by the Nixon admin.
41 Norway's capital
42 Web address
43 Archipelago forming the southernmost part of the continental U.S.
47 Gloomy pal of Winnie-the-Pooh
49 Auditioner's goal
50 Newborn horses
53 Run for a long football pass
57 Singer Edith known as "The Little Sparrow"
60 Disappear
62 "Despicable Me" character voiced by Steve Carell
63 Member of an N.F.L. team transplanted to Los Angeles in 2017
66 "Could you, would you, with ___?" (Dr. Seuss line)

67 Black-and-white Nabisco cookie
68 Medics
69 Annual awards . . . like the one actor Shalhoub won in 2018
70 Fret (over)
71 Poker buy-in

DOWN

1 Fizzy drinks
2 Our planet
3 Company that makes Frisbees
4 Redundant word in front of "total"
5 Passenger ship in a 1912 calamity
6 Hertz rival
7 Hobbyist's knife brand
8 Cove
9 PC panic button
10 Upbeat
11 Touch down
12 Church recess
13 Someone who is not yet 20
18 Leaning
19 Canine collar dangler
24 Lummoxes
26 WSW's opposite
28 Letter you don't pronounce in "jeopardy" and "leopard"
30 Garden waterer
31 "It's ___ a matter of time"
32 Pursues romantically
33 Swivel around
34 Add to the payroll
35 Without really thinking
36 Mo. for fools and showers
37 Hair removal cream brand
41 Approved
43 To and ___
44 Order to party crashers

45 Annual Westminster event
46 Hawaiian greeting
48 Time of lackluster performance
51 Largest city and former capital of Nigeria
52 Derisive laugh sound
54 Prod
55 Standing upright
56 Where the endings of 17-, 33-, 43- and 63-Across are often found
57 Exam for sophs. or jrs.
58 "Othello" villain
59 In a little while
61 Drink that can cause brain freeze
64 "___ never too late to learn"
65 Abbr. on old vitamin bottles

by Brad Wilber

ACROSS

1 Benchwarmer
6 Shut loudly
10 Calendar units: Abbr.
13 Dried plums
15 Part of a brain or a 59-Down
16 Cry at a fireworks show
17 Beach outing, say
19 Hit CBS forensics series
20 Movie filming locale
21 Merchandise
22 TV studio alert
24 Ice cream drink
25 Engender, as suspicion
26 High point of winter?
29 Sound of ice cream hitting the floor
31 On easy street
35 Raw metals
36 + or – particle
37 Stick in one's ___
39 Financially afloat again
44 Adds to the payroll
45 Comics' goals
46 Mother of Calcutta
49 Nota ___
50 Mobile app's clientele
51 Sweeping stories
53 Cry at a fireworks show
56 Instagram upload, informally
57 Traffic helicopter, e.g.
60 "Four score and seven years ___ . . ."
61 Landlord's due
62 Partner of "signed" and "delivered" in a Stevie Wonder hit
63 Anderson Cooper's channel
64 Utters
65 Wear down

DOWN

1 Coppertone stats, for short
2 Mötley ___
3 Peewee
4 Prefix meaning "one"
5 Most widely spoken native language of India, after Hindi
6 Toboggan, e.g.
7 L's meaning, in box scores
8 Aladdin's monkey sidekick
9 Hanukkah display
10 Asian gambling mecca
11 Refuge in the desert
12 Suffix in many English county names
14 Like a thief's loot
18 Like a thief's loot, slangily
23 "Beats me!"
24 Dutch artist known for his "impossible" drawings
25 Gore and Capone, for two
26 "I think," in textspeak
27 Low-___ diet
28 Brainchild
29 Drinks not meant to be savored
30 Phnom ___ (capital of Cambodia)
32 Fork prong
33 RuPaul's purview
34 A pop
38 Calendar units: Abbr.
40 Pieholes
41 Savings plan, for short
42 Votes into office
43 Gaelic spirit who wails to foretell a death in the family
46 Rapper Shakur
47 Provide one's digital John Hancock
48 Military info-gathering
49 Recycling receptacle
51 ___-weeny (small)
52 Very bad, with "the"
53 Nobel Peace Prize city
54 Ratified, for short
55 Jekyll's bad side
58 Senate assent
59 Place for a stud or a ring

by Erik Agard and Yacob Yonas

ACROSS

1 Talks with a gravelly voice
6 Fastener with a twist
11 Brevity is said to be the soul of it
14 Sir John of London
15 Not get caught by, as a pursuer
16 Patient's insurance option, for short
17 "Affliction" suffered by Fab Four devotees
19 "The Simpsons" storekeeper
20 ___ stage left
21 Prefix with -air or -afternoon
22 Big person on the small screen
24 Prince Charles's onetime partner, affectionately
26 Removes from nursing, as a foal
27 "Affliction" suffered by bracketologists
32 Child, legally speaking
35 Villain's retreat
36 Quartet minus one
37 Has left the office
38 Triage locales, for short
39 Enjoy the taste of
40 Move like a butterfly
41 Green stone popular in Chinese craftwork
42 Woods who voiced Cinderella
43 "Affliction" suffered by clothes lovers
46 Track-and-field competitions
47 Insinuates
51 Person with a chrome dome
52 Cow's sound
54 "Gone With the Wind" plantation
55 Atty.'s org.
56 "Affliction" suffered by the winter-weary
59 Big part of a T. rex
60 What diamonds and straight-A students do
61 Gown
62 Commercials
63 Japanese port of 2+ million
64 "Same here"

DOWN

1 One in revolt
2 Amazon Echo persona
3 Reserved in manner
4 Spewing naughty language, as a child
5 Weekly show with a cold open, for short
6 Vehicle that can jackknife
7 Attired
8 Go for elected office
9 Tussle between wiki page modifiers
10 Bobbed and ___
11 "Well, I never!"
12 Fill with zeal
13 P.G.A. ___
18 Kuwaiti leader
23 Mail addressed to the North Pole
25 Missile aimed at a bull's-eye
28 Off drugs
29 The fourth letter of "circle," but not the first
30 Scrooge
31 Achy
32 Make peeved
33 Capital of Pakistan
34 Peace-and-quiet ordinances
39 Small, medium or large
41 Brooklyn's St. ___ College
44 "Quite correct"
45 Wide-eyed
48 Placed money in the bank
49 "Am not!" comeback
50 Ankle bones
51 ___ California
52 Stole fur
53 Prime draft status
57 Narrow waterway
58 Agcy. overseeing Rx's

by Ross Trudeau

ACROSS

1 Many flat screens
6 "Red, white and blue" land, for short
11 Zero, in soccer scores
14 Quintet followed by ". . . and sometimes Y"
15 Absolute minimum
16 Rocks sent to a refinery
17 Devil-may-care
19 Piece of lawn
20 Actor Guinness of "Star Wars"
21 Fashion line?
22 Summer romance, perhaps
24 Town crier's cry
28 Diamond great Ripken
31 Gives a red card, in short
32 Lerner's partner on Broadway
33 Carne ___ (burrito filler)
35 Broadband letters
36 Touch
39 Bar request . . . or hint to the letters in the circles
43 German auto sold mainly in Europe
44 Reaction to a body blow
45 Latches (onto)
46 Élan
48 Offering from Hertz or National
50 Message-spewing program
51 Rock drummer whose last name is the same as his band
55 Gift recipient
56 Eggs for fertilization
57 Petri dish medium
61 Hour after midnight
62 Accessing, as a password-restricted website
66 Race, as an engine
67 Pick up the tab for
68 Be of use
69 Slice of time
70 Dark wood
71 Midler of "Beaches"

DOWN

1 ___ funny (genuinely humorous)
2 "You're on!"
3 Goodyear product
4 Give personal assurance (for)
5 Total
6 Belly aches?
7 Run-down
8 Crew blade
9 The Seminoles of the A.C.C.
10 Charge to get cash from a bank, say
11 "Absolutely, positively not!"
12 Humor with a twist
13 Overhang
18 Basketball's O'Neal, informally
23 Permissible
25 Dutch cheese town
26 Disney snow queen
27 Wrestling maneuver
28 G.I. garb, for short
29 "Hurry!," on an order
30 Body of water between France and Switzerland
34 Of the highest quality
35 ___ Jam records
37 Falsetto-voiced Muppet
38 For fear that
40 Wee bit
41 Lunchtime, often
42 Fairy tale villain
47 Gracefully thin
48 Cause for a dental filling
49 Computer science pioneer Turing
51 Love to pieces
52 Recluse
53 Paul who played Crocodile Dundee
54 Easily fooled
58 Flying pest
59 Going ___ (fighting)
60 Part in a movie
63 Space ball
64 Nat ___ Wild (cable channel)
65 Yammer

by Damon Gulczynski

ACROSS

1 Al who created Li'l Abner
5 Chatting online, in brief
10 Almost any offer that's too good to be true
14 Doozy
15 "I swear!"
16 Robe in old Rome
17 The "A" of U.A.E.
18 *Basketball position for Magic Johnson or Steph Curry
20 *Level on the military wage scale
22 Player in front of a net
23 What sailors and beachgoers breathe
24 Uncouth person
25 Colorado summer hrs.
26 *Alternative to a brush when coating the side of a house
30 Things coiled on the sides of houses
33 With 44-Across, onetime British slapstick comic
34 Single-stranded genetic molecule
35 ___ and crafts
36 Consumer products giant, for short . . . or a hint to the answers to the eight starred clues
37 Tylenol target
38 "You got it now?"
39 Toyota hybrid
40 North Pole resident
41 *The Beach Boys or Backstreet Boys
43 Amusement
44 See 33-Across
45 Marx's collaborator on "The Communist Manifesto"
49 ___ Field, former home of the Seattle Mariners
52 *Shade akin to olive
54 *Sorority types who go out a lot
56 Eugene O'Neill's "___ Christie"

57 Help with a crime
58 Letter-shaped fastener
59 "Veni, ___, vici"
60 Hellmann's product, informally
61 Daytime or Primetime awards
62 Holler

DOWN

1 Applauds
2 Enveloping glows, old-style
3 ___ del Rey, Calif.
4 *Darts and snooker
5 Somewhat
6 An emoji may suggest it
7 1970s tennis champ Nastase
8 Writer Anaïs
9 Dig into work
10 E. B. White's "___ Little"
11 Unwanted stocking stuffer

12 Prefix with -cultural
13 Prepared, as dinner or a bed
19 Foolish, informally
21 Frees (of)
24 Marching halftime crews
26 Fence in
27 Mom's mom, for short
28 The "U" of I.C.U.
29 Mom's mom
30 Lock securer
31 ___ O's (breakfast cereal)
32 One of 12 in Alcoholics Anonymous
33 Oksana ___, 1994 Olympic skating wonder
36 What may precede Chapter 1 in a novel
37 *Roast accompaniment prepared with drippings
39 $$$$, on Yelp

40 Like choir music
42 Run-down area
43 Lavish meals
46 Counting-off word
47 1980s tennis champ Ivan
48 Creature that leaves a slimy trail
49 What an email filter filters
50 Rhyme scheme for Robert Frost's "Stopping by Woods on a Snowy Evening"
51 Glenn of the Eagles
52 School event with a king and a queen
53 "For Better or for Worse" mom
55 Company that pioneered the U.P.C. bar code

by Ned White

ACROSS

1 Cow's newborn
5 Upbeat, as an outlook
9 SWAT team actions
14 Singer India____
15 Aunt Bee's charge on "The Andy Griffith Show"
16 Disney attraction in Florida
17 Trendy terms
19 Ragú rival
20 Palestinian territory bordering Israel
21 Busybody, from the Yiddish
23 ____ Dhabi, part of the United Arab Emirates
24 Most unspoiled
26 First host of "America's Funniest Home Videos"
28 "Haste makes waste" and similar sayings
30 "Venerable" monk of the Middle Ages
31 "Able ____ I ere I saw Elba"
32 Ship's wastewater
35 State led by Lenin, in brief
36 Magical powder in "Peter Pan"
39 "I do solemnly swear . . . ," e.g.
42 Browned bread
43 "Fee, fi, fo, ____"
46 Stick back in the microwave
49 Going from two lanes to one
51 Style of collarless shirt
54 ____ Pieces (candy)
55 Nonkosher meat
56 Say "Nyah, nyah," say
58 Snow queen in "Frozen"
59 To any degree
61 Timesavers . . . or the starts of 17-, 26-, 36- and 51-Across?
64 Scalawag
65 Peace Nobelist Wiesel
66 Length × width, for a rectangle
67 Opening golf shot
68 Pepsi, for one
69 Hang in the balance

DOWN

1 Taxi
2 Peppery salad green
3 Chameleons, e.g.
4 Some Moroccan headwear
5 Aussie marsupial, in brief
6 Grand Ole ____
7 Lesser-played half of a 45
8 Like some straightforward questions
9 Meal
10 Its showers bring May flowers: Abbr.
11 Periods with the largest glaciers
12 Places for pooped pooches
13 Having a heavier build
18 Sushi bar condiment
22 Atlanta-based channel
24 Sound effect on "Batman"
25 Candy bar packaged in twos
27 Touch geographically
29 Open with a letter opener
33 Prefix with -cache
34 Cheese from the Netherlands
36 "Glad that's over!"
37 Addict
38 Word before map or smarts
39 Apple production site
40 Aquarium accessory
41 Biblical group bearing gifts
43 Opening, as after an earthquake
44 Like leftovers
45 British sports cars of old
47 "Crouching Tiger, Hidden Dragon" director
48 ____ Aviv
50 Tablet alternative
52 Trig ratio
53 Mexican artist Frida
57 Hard labor
60 Sentiment on a candy heart
62 Stephen of "The Crying Game"
63 Unhappy

by Ed Sessa

ACROSS

1 Mushroom part
4 ___ Xing (road sign)
8 Managed to avoid
14 South America's Carnaval city, informally
15 Not doing anything
16 Baltimore bird
17 Psychic ability, in brief
18 Yard event to clear out the attic
20 Manage to avoid
22 Big coffee holder
23 Applaud
24 Louisiana's avian nickname
28 Giant in health insurance
29 Mortal dangers
33 "Phooey!"
35 Commotions
38 Provide with continuing funds
39 Athlete who said "Silence is golden when you can't think of a good answer"
40 Strong-smelling cheese made in England
42 Investment for the golden yrs.
43 Cook's workspace
45 Enroll for another year of duty
46 Work by Wordsworth or Whitman
47 Coughed (up)
49 Ledger entry on the minus side
51 One barely in the water?
56 German carmaker
59 ___ Paulo, Brazil
60 Big name in mattresses
61 Fairy tale question whose answer is spelled out in the starts of 18-, 24-, 40- and 51-Across
65 Fast asleep
66 Mythical beauty who lent her name to a continent
67 Oil producers' grp.
68 "___ to Joy"
69 Singer/songwriter Crow
70 Shipped
71 Gave a meal to

DOWN

1 Slimeball
2 Supermarket section
3 China's is around 1.4 billion
4 Without stopping en route
5 Part of a campus URL
6 "Slippery" tree
7 Co-founder of Rome with Romulus
8 Run off with a boxer, maybe?
9 Gold waiting to be discovered
10 Recognize, as differences
11 Objective for a soccer player
12 Fitzgerald of jazz
13 Profound
19 The "A" of MoMA
21 Conks out
25 Med school subj.
26 Low point
27 Juliet Capulet or Holden Caulfield, agewise
30 Impossible to mess up
31 Set of traditional beliefs
32 Got one's kicks at the pool?
33 Hoarse voice
34 Voice above tenor
36 Grand ___ Opry
37 Prepare for a hard test
40 Search for
41 Coup for a newspaper freelancer
44 Someone dropping by
46 Something that might spring a leak
48 Dreary
50 Cut in half
52 Vote that cancels out a yea
53 Unacceptable actions
54 Musical practice piece
55 Given a PG-13, say
56 Bowls over
57 Thumbs-down response
58 Show gumption
62 Someone not likely to show off intelligence?
63 "Great" hominid
64 Word on a restroom door

by Lynn Lempel

82

ACROSS

1 Major uncertainty
6 Canvas for a tattoo
10 Mae who said "I used to be Snow White, but I drifted"
14 "You ___ Beautiful" (Joe Cocker hit)
15 Mexican entree in a shell
16 Large fair, informally
17 Athlete with a mitt
19 Bridle strap
20 Poker stake
21 Bill Clinton's was in the 1990s
22 ___ Haute, Ind.
23 One going for a stroll among urban greenery
26 "Quit wasting time!"
30 Abba of Israel
31 Even a little
32 ___-haw
33 Plumbing woe
37 Official hearing a case
41 Fish that wriggle
42 What's dropped off a cigarette
43 Words of empathy
44 Weights that may be "short" or "long"
46 Tevye's occupation in "Fiddler on the Roof"
48 Herbie Hancock or Chick Corea
52 "Later, amigo!"
53 Employ
54 Bleats
58 William with a state named after him
59 Place where 17-, 23-, 37- and 48-Across might be found
62 Sheltered from the wind
63 Parks in civil rights history
64 Language family of Africa
65 Loch ___ monster
66 "That's enough!"
67 Adventurous journey

DOWN

1 "Ali ___ and the 40 Thieves"
2 Land with an ayatollah
3 Hanukkah "moolah"
4 ___ of Capri
5 Dandyish dresser
6 Van Gogh's "The ___ Night"
7 Boat you might shoot rapids in
8 What a "neat" drink doesn't come with
9 Word paired with "neither"
10 "How fortunate for us!"
11 Apply, as force
12 Former vice president Agnew
13 Printer cartridge contents
18 Meadows
22 Airport screening org.
23 Tug on
24 Turn sharply
25 Skeptic's sarcastic comment
26 Racehorse's starting point
27 Raison d'___
28 Pin the ___ on the donkey
29 Bomb testing areas
32 "Come again?"
34 Semihard Dutch cheese
35 City that's home to the Taj Mahal
36 Sharp-witted
38 "Is it O.K., mom?"
39 Peak near Olympus
40 Leave at the altar
45 Special ___ (military missions)
46 Event that's an "Oops!"
47 "Ah, makes sense"
48 Where Honda and Mazda are headquartered
49 Grammy-winning singer of "Hello"
50 Fan publications, informally
51 Bonkers
54 Lover boy
55 Youngest of the Brontë sisters
56 Things passed in Congress
57 "___ your piehole!"
59 Surgery sites, for short
60 Word after waste and want
61 Cookout, briefly

by Bruce Haight

ACROSS

1 Group in a play
5 Plasterwork backing
9 Bracelet securer
14 Arthur with a stadium named after him
15 Feeling fluish, in a way
16 "___ me" ("Go along with it")
17 ___ the Man (old baseball nickname)
18 Be overrun (with)
19 "E" on a gas gauge
20 Pre-snap powwow
22 Garden munchkin
24 "How was ___ know?"
25 2012 Best Picture winner set in Iran
27 Kind of toy that moves when you turn a key
31 Semiaquatic salamanders
33 Flowers on trellises
35 Bill in a tip jar
36 Slangy "sweetheart"
37 Horace, as a poet
38 Barrister's headgear
39 Scrub vigorously
41 Manipulate
42 Littlest ones in litters
44 Contagious viral infection
45 Cross ___ with
47 Side-to-side nautical movement
48 Plural "is"
49 First appearance, as of symptoms
50 Toronto N.H.L. team, for short
53 Common ankle injury
55 Biggest bear in "Goldilocks and the Three Bears"
57 "V for Vendetta" actor Stephen
58 Grind, as teeth
60 Withstands
62 Gemstone measure

65 Chopped down
67 3:1 or 4:1, e.g.
68 Superior beef grade
69 They're mined and refined
70 Large, scholarly book
71 "For ___ waves of grain" (line in "America the Beautiful")
72 Water swirl
73 Elderly

DOWN

1 Redeem, as a savings bond
2 Uncommonly perceptive
3 Air-punching pugilist
4 Manage, as a bar
5 "Ciao"
6 Unreturned tennis serve
7 2006 Matt Damon spy film
8 Song sung on Sunday
9 Place with beakers and Bunsen burners
10 Measure of light's brightness
11 Electric guitar accessory
12 Drunkard
13 Jimmy (open)
21 Lecturer's implement with a light at the end
23 Is indebted to
26 Fills, as tile joints
28 Popular yoga pose . . . or a literal hint to the ends of 3-, 7-, 9- and 21-Down
29 The "U" in I.C.U.
30 Cribbage scorekeepers

32 Letter after sigma
34 Nap south of the border
39 Pampering places
40 Bus. concern
43 Persian Gulf country, for short
46 Actress Kendrick
51 What "woof" or "meow" may mean
52 Talked back to with 'tude
54 Best effort, informally
56 Colorful flower with a "face"
59 Pump or oxford
61 Smidgen
62 Helper during taxing times, for short?
63 Triceps location
64 Poke fun at
66 Marry

by Tracy Gray

84

ACROSS

1 Sharp's counterpart, in music
5 "Livin' la Vida ___"
9 Stories with many chapters
14 Like rain forest vegetation
15 "Ars Amatoria" poet
16 Story that lets you off the hook
17 Theatrical honor
19 Mountaineering spike
20 Person to exchange letters with overseas
21 Fortune 500 listings: Abbr.
23 Jane Austen novel
24 "Star Wars" role for Alec Guinness
27 Put into operation
30 They: Fr.
31 Zig or zag
32 Lauder with beauty products
35 Little extra attention, as from a repairer, for short
38 Where education is pursued doggedly?
42 "Mad ___" (Mel Gibson film)
43 "It's a ___ shame"
44 Approximately
45 "You stink!"
46 Sent out, as rays
49 Delivery people?
54 Foundry detritus
55 Environmental prefix
56 Inventor's quest
60 Chicken raised for cooking
62 "Hush, you!"
64 Big-time football venue
65 Honey-based drink
66 Start to deteriorate, as a cord
67 Put back to zero, say
68 A and Z, in the alphabet
69 Chop down

DOWN

1 Theatrical failure
2 Auto maintenance job, informally
3 X ___ xylophone
4 Where stray animals are taken
5 Darkish, as the interior of a restaurant
6 Sperm targets
7 Approximately
8 Supplemental item
9 Weaken
10 "Futurama" figures
11 U.S. base in 28-Down, informally
12 Detonation of 7/16/45
13 Egyptian peninsula
18 Rhyme scheme of Robert Frost's "Stopping by Woods on a Snowy Evening"
22 Irving Berlin's "Blue ___"
25 Teeny-___
26 Certain utility: Abbr.
27 Quark's place
28 Havana's home
29 Image in the "Jurassic Park" logo, informally
33 Biol., for one
34 Guiding principle
35 Legal wrong
36 Misplace
37 Lump of soil
39 Stylized "W" for Microsoft Word, e.g.
40 Wear away
41 Something extremely cool, paradoxically
45 Past
47 Two-wheelers
48 Baghdad's land
49 One of five for composer John Williams
50 Sound loudly, as a trumpet
51 Registers awe
52 "___, All Ye Faithful"
53 Singer/songwriter Leonard
57 Dublin's land
58 Actress Patricia of "Hud"
59 "Bye for now," in a text
61 Singer ___ King Cole
63 Deserving to get gonged

by Jeffrey Wechsler

ACROSS

1. Greek philosopher who was a student of Socrates
6. Disparaging remark
10. Some bake sale groups, for short
14. ___ box (computer prompt)
15. With 52-Down, home of the Leaning Tower
16. French river to the English Channel
17. Parish leader
18. "Yeah, sure"
19. Fill to excess
20. Took in takeout, say
21. *Seesaw
24. What a spin doctor might be called on to take care of
26. Hair stiffener
27. Prepare to be published
28. Coin that's been legal tender since New Year's Day in 2002
30. *Bring forward for display
33. Island near Java
36. Bandmate of McCartney, Lennon and Harrison
38. Tech school on the Hudson, for short
39. Harbinger
40. Falafel sauce
42. Noun-forming suffix
43. Singer DiFranco
44. Birds symbolizing peace
45. Component of natural gas
47. *British hitmaker on Iggy Azalea's "Black Widow"
49. "It's c-c-c-cold!"
50. "Cubist" Rubik
51. Science class, for short
53. Mathematician once pictured on Swiss money
57. *1970 war film about the attack on Pearl Harbor

61. Genesis woman
62. Genesis man
63. Forum garment
64. "The Handmaid's Tale" author Margaret
66. ___ Field (home to the Mets)
67. Stuntman Knievel
68. Freshens, as a stamp pad
69. White Monopoly bills
70. Depend (on)
71. *Clarinetist Shaw . . . or, when said aloud, the only two consonants in the answers to the starred clues

DOWN

1. Michelangelo masterpiece
2. Like sneakers but not slippers
3. PC key
4. *"Sadly, you're right"
5. Fairy tale meanie
6. Desire to harm
7. Defame in print
8. Computer operator
9. *Vermin-hunting dog
10. Stickie
11. *Pasta-serving cafe
12. The "a" of a.m.
13. Palm reader, e.g.
14. Lacking brightness
22. Part of the psyche
23. Febreze target
25. Ivy League school in Philly
29. *Plumbing company whose jingle says "away go troubles down the drain"
30. Suede shade
31. Second word of fairy tales
32. Fork prong
33. Wild pig
34. Prefix with -potent or -present
35. *Say again
36. Pronoun for a ship

37. "___ the season to be jolly"
41. Actress Gardner
42. No ___ traffic
44. Word of warning
46. *Trick-or-___ (kid on Halloween)
48. One of the Three Musketeers
49. Halloween shout
51. Doughnut-shaped roll
52. See 15-Across
54. Téa of "Madam Secretary"
55. Bring to mind
56. Only M.L.B. team that Johnny Bench played for (1967–83)
57. Part of a Chipotle order
58. Chief Norse god
59. Wander
60. ___ avis
65. Jokester

by Peter Gordon

ACROSS

1 Groups of actors in plays
6 Protective wear for lobster eaters
10 Summa cum ___
15 Outdo
16 Soothing ointment ingredient
17 Neighbor of Hertfordshire
18 Start of a nursery rhyme on a farm
21 Outer part of a crater
22 Feel sorry about
23 Indent key on a keyboard
24 Sport with kicking and boxing, for short
25 Claim without evidence
27 Superlatively kind
29 Bow-tie-wearing cub in Jellystone Park
34 "You're telling me!"
37 Stitch's human pal, in film
38 Singer Minaj
42 Cookie that's 29% cream
43 Pass along
45 ___ fides
46 Clock sound
47 Grow fond of
48 Skyline-obscuring pollution
49 Bring up in a Q. and A.
50 Spanish for "south"
51 Falsehood
53 Palindromic kitchen brand
54 1963 musical that was Dick Van Dyke's film debut
59 What dogs do when they're hungry
61 Former attorney general Holder
62 Photo-sharing app, colloquially
65 Place for driving lessons (the golf kind)
66 The "sun" in sunny-side-up eggs
67 N.B.A. phenom Jayson
68 Didn't venture out for dinner
69 Competitive advantage
70 Put into law
71 Actress Thompson of "Sorry to Bother You"
72 Bucks and does
73 Students sit at them

DOWN

1 Fearsome snake
2 Nin of erotica
3 Bursting at the ___
4 Bathroom fixture
5 Bird that "His eye is on," in a hymn
6 Term of endearment
7 Sick
8 Snaky scarf
9 Result of a religious schism
10 The "L" of L.G.B.T.Q.
11 Volcanic detritus
12 "I'm at your disposal"
13 Judges to be
14 Person living abroad, informally
19 Modern prefix with -correct
20 "Citizen ___"
26 Virtual volume
28 Places infants sleep
30 Having trouble seeing in the morning, perhaps
31 Sound from a piggery
32 Adjective after "Ye" in many a pub's name
33 Suck-up
34 Littlest bit
35 ___ Kringle (Santa Claus)
36 Pork dish of Southern cuisine
39 "How goes it?," in Spanish
40 Fort ___, home of the U.S. Bullion Depository
41 "Othello" villain
43 What's left of a ticket after it's been used
44 Pinot ___
50 One-named queen of Tejano music
52 Made revisions to
55 Some spiritual advisers
56 Gradually disappear, as support
57 Nonsense
58 Nonsensical
59 "Tarnation!"
60 Apt rhyme for "evaluate"
63 Hide, as shirttails, with "in"
64 Quantities: Abbr.

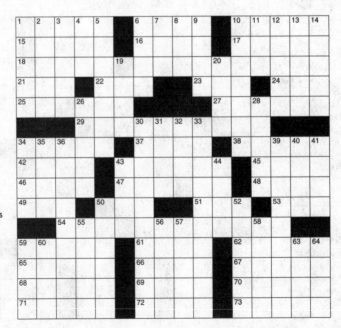

by Erik Agard

ACROSS

1 Place to get a mud bath
4 "Got it now!"
7 Airport about 13 miles from the Loop
12 Perfect scores for divers
14 "Good heavens!"
15 Polite palindromic term of address
16 Spice holder
17 *Arthur Carlson portrayer on "WKRP in Cincinnati"
19 Ancient Chinese book of divination
21 Prefix with -angle or -cycle
22 Extremely fun, as a party
23 *Job for a model
26 Website for some custom-designed jewelry
27 Use steel wool on
28 Hacks with an axe
30 Pro-____ (some golf tourneys)
33 Dead set against
34 Street sign with an arrow
37 Country between Togo and Nigeria
39 Sheepskin boot brand
41 Assault or kidnapping
42 Producer Rhimes who created "Grey's Anatomy" and "Scandal"
44 Coupe or sedan
46 National park freebie
47 Showers with flowers and chocolates, maybe
48 Native New Zealander
50 Inflatable transport
52 *2000 stop-motion animated comedy hit
57 Deep anger
58 Colorful pond fish
59 Bust out of jail
60 Summer Olympics contest whose participants do the ends of the answers to the starred clues

64 Sugar bowl invaders
65 Acquire, as debts
66 Helps
67 Traditional wearer of plaid
68 Fitness program popularized in the 1990s
69 Bit of clothing often worn with shorts
70 DeskJet printers and others

DOWN

1 Peel off
2 Popular cobbler fruit
3 Dried chili in Mexican food
4 In the past
5 Belly laugh syllable
6 Toss in
7 Hyatt alternative
8 Mecca pilgrimage
9 *Late-night Cartoon Network programming block
10 Harold who directed "Caddyshack"
11 Opposite of full
13 Comic sketches
14 Goads
18 Company that makes Bug B Gon
20 "Sorry, pal"
24 Member of the largest Rwandan ethnic group
25 A folder is needed for this
26 Still-life vessel
29 Stage comebacks?
30 Muscles strengthened by belly dancing, for short
31 "I'm not impressed"
32 *Winter barrier
35 Org. for physicians
36 "Uh-huh"

38 How some exciting N.B.A. games are won
40 Avocado dip, informally
43 Noted British racecourse
45 Substitutes for coins
49 Ancient Peruvians
50 Hit the ball out of the park
51 Staples Center, for one
53 Component of a drum kit
54 Cowhands' home
55 "Give me five!"
56 Tree houses
58 Corn syrup brand
61 Soaking spot
62 Make up a cover story, say
63 Laudatory poem

by Zhouqin Burnikel

88

ACROSS

1 Jazz quartet, e.g.
6 Abbr. about alcohol on a party invitation
10 Like logs that have been cut
14 The Hunter constellation
15 Des Moines's state
16 "If you ask me . . . ," in a text
17 Very soft loaves of bread?
19 Cheer (for)
20 Heavens
21 Japanese noodle dish
22 Thickheaded
23 18-wheeler
25 Went off, as a timer
26 Neckwear with the letters A, B, C, D, etc.?
31 Nissan rival
32 Desire
33 Flow back, as the tide
36 Infield covers
37 Bit of voodoo
38 Step between floors
40 Kerfuffle
41 Cold, cold drink
43 Attends
44 Indigo, henna, etc.?
46 Didn't take part
49 Quite an accomplishment
50 Dweeb
51 Wacky
53 Opposite of none
56 Fairy tale villain
57 "You haven't aged a bit" and "I love that jacket you're wearing"?
60 Small plateau
61 "Your turn," on a walkie-talkie
62 Ball of yarn
63 Actress Amanda
64 Salon job, briefly
65 Customary

DOWN

1 Extra bed in a hotel room
2 Metal-containing rocks
3 Relative of a weasel
4 Where to take a car for repairs
5 See 6-Down
6 Golf score of 5-Down under par
7 Toy on a string
8 Actor Wilson of "Midnight in Paris"
9 Some humanities degs.
10 Ambulance sounds
11 Surrounded by
12 TV's "___ Line Is It Anyway?"
13 Eminent
18 Cuban ballroom dance
22 Sprite Zero Sugar, for one
24 Enjoys the flattery, say
25 Awful racket
26 Lead-in to girl or boy
27 Washing machine unit
28 Arsonist, in brief
29 Stereotypical material for a professor's jacket
30 Government levy
33 Like falling off a log
34 What hungry fish do
35 Warner ___
37 Rooster's mate
39 Popular lecture series
42 Pet asking for milk, purr-haps?
43 Garbo of silent films
44 Upset with
45 State as fact
46 Beat handily
47 "Oh, shucks!"
48 Opposite of verbose
51 Peacenik
52 One providing great service?
54 In ___ of (replacing)
55 "Star Wars" princess
57 Soak (up)
58 S.E.C. school in Baton Rouge
59 TV show that originally included John Belushi and Jane Curtin, for short

by Dan Schoenholz

ACROSS

1 Design details, informally
6 Archaeologist's treasure
11 "Nova" airer
14 Major manufacturer of soda can materials
15 Justice Kagan
16 Fe, on the periodic table
17 Adjudicator of an attempt at a physical feat, say
20 Early birds?
21 Eldest of the von Trapp children
22 What polytheists believe in
23 "Let's do it!"
25 Hole ___ (golf feat)
27 Vocalist who doesn't tour
32 Cosmopolitan or People, for short
35 1960s vice president Humphrey
36 L.A.'s ___ Arts District
37 Pepsi-___
38 Genre for Puccini and Ponchielli
39 Rear end
40 Macho
41 Rowboat propellers
42 Fumbles
43 Nickname of King Edward VII
44 Channel for lovers of old films
45 One versed in shorthand
47 Standing straight
49 Elton John musical based on a work by Verdi
50 Deep blue dye
51 Throw, as an anchor
54 Mention as an example
58 "To be totally clear" . . . or why to bring in a 17-, 27- or 45-Across?
61 Whale found in every one of the world's oceans
62 Gold or platinum
63 Like most notebook paper
64 "___, humbug!"
65 Impolitely overlooks
66 Amble (along)

DOWN

1 Wise one
2 What goes into a socket
3 Juul, e.g., briefly
4 Takes under advisement
5 The "S" of S.F.
6 Pine secretions
7 "What ___ would you like?"
8 Births between Cancer and Virgo
9 Airborne
10 Half-___ (coffee order)
11 June observance commemorating the Stonewall Riots
12 Drag neckwear
13 Sketch show with celebrity hosts, for short
16 Green "X" for Microsoft Excel, e.g.
18 T. S. ___, poet who wrote "The Love Song of J. Alfred Prufrock"
19 Assistant to Dr. Frankenstein
24 Oscar winner Sorvino
26 Prefix with -liberal
27 Aim for the basket
28 Rapper Shakur
29 Nietzsche's ideal man
30 Put away, as ashes
31 "Nuh-uh!"
33 "Kate & ___" (1980s TV show)
34 More gleeful
37 Dish of thinly sliced raw meat
39 Fellow members of a church
40 Quaff made with honey
42 "Yadda, yadda, yadda . . .": Abbr.
43 Bramble
45 Who "I" refers to
46 Auctioneers' mallets
48 Moreno of "West Side Story"
50 Atmosphere
52 Question to a betrayer
53 Monomaniacal captain of literature
55 Charged particles
56 Christmas purchase that's quickly thrown out
57 Small whirlpool
58 Nine-to-five activity
59 Yogi's sounds while meditating
60 Dutch ___ disease

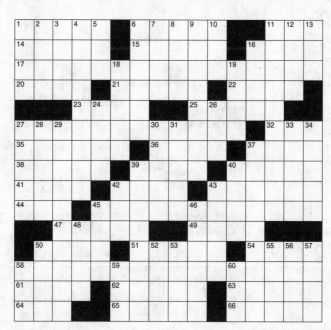

by Amanda Rafkin and Ross Trudeau

ACROSS

1 Lion's hair
5 Film reel
10 "The King and I" setting
14 One who might be caught off base
15 Squabble
16 Sharp side of a blade
17 One who yaks, yaks, yaks . . .
19 Passion
20 Big Band ___
21 Finish line ribbon
22 Prevent from happening
24 12th grader
26 Supreme Court justice ___ Bader Ginsburg
27 . . . yaks, yaks, yaks . . .
33 Product Pittsburgh is famous for
36 One fighting the status quo
37 The "G" of L.G.B.T.Q.+
38 Old-time N.B.A. great Chamberlain
39 Hellos and goodbyes, in Italy
40 Lose one's footing
41 Sheryl Crow's "___ I Wanna Do"
42 Museo in Madrid
43 Fashion
44 . . . yaks, yaks, yaks . . .
47 Guns, as an engine
48 "Whatever you want!"
52 African nation whose name consists of three U.S. state postal abbreviations
55 Wine holder
57 Museum curator's deg.
58 Makes the most of
59 . . . yaks, yaks, yaks
62 [Ah, me!]
63 Otherworldly
64 Place to order bagels and lox
65 "No problemo"
66 Long, tedious trip
67 Puts two and two together

DOWN

1 Aussie pals
2 On the ball
3 Christopher who directed the "Dark Knight" trilogy
4 Member of a benevolent order
5 Vegas casino named for an African locale
6 Comedian's visual
7 Eye amorously
8 Sí : Spanish :: ___ : French
9 Professors' addresses
10 "Oh yeah? You and what army?"
11 What a light bulb represents in the comics
12 Culture medium in a lab
13 Disappear, as snow

18 Island with a reef
23 Web programming inits.
25 "Yeah, sure!"
26 Make again, as hotel plans
28 Brambles
29 Some hippie neckwear
30 Like a fairy tale duckling
31 Horse's "fly swatter"
32 Bumped-up publicity
33 Q-tip tip
34 Cash register drawer
35 Jazzy Fitzgerald
39 Small fissures
40 Cherry throwaway
42 Expression of relief
43 Something stuck through a vampire's heart

45 Extremely lowbrow
46 Marching synchronously
49 Plant deeply
50 "Too rich for my blood"
51 Cabs
52 Creative inspiration
53 Home to more than 4.5 billion
54 Turkey drumsticks
55 Baseball Hall-of-Famer Yastrzemski
56 End in ___ (be deadlocked)
60 Little chuckle
61 Abbr. on a food label

by Andrea Carla Michaels

ACROSS

1 Den
5 Some HP products
8 Wardrobe supplies for Batman
13 ___ vera
14 "Like I told you!"
15 Player at Baltimore's Camden Yards
16 Bash some tobacco holders?
18 Name on a 24-Across container
19 Bash some small trucks?
21 Something a prospector stakes
24 NaCl
25 "O.K., got it"
26 $
28 Functions
30 Went on horseback
31 Small town
34 Winner's two-finger gesture
38 Ace's value, at times
39 Bash a laundry room brand?
41 Down Under hopper
42 Rachel Maddow's channel
44 Bills with Alexander Hamilton
45 Actionable misdeed
46 Diamond Head's island
48 Some hearty steaks
50 Strikebreaking worker
53 Slices of time
56 Calf-roping rope
57 Bash an Alex Haley classic?
60 Peter of "Lawrence of Arabia"
61 Bash a bug repellent brand?
65 Prepared for planting
66 Tibetan beast of burden
67 Lake ___ (what separates Ohio and Ontario)
68 Monica in the International Tennis Hall of Fame
69 Sophs. in two years
70 Disavow

DOWN

1 You need to sit down for this
2 Brownie ___ mode
3 Particle that's positive or negative
4 Chameleon or iguana
5 Biggest of the Three Bears
6 Game on an 8 × 8 board
7 Malia Obama's sister
8 Gator's cousin
9 Action accompanied by a "Mwah!"
10 White House V.I.P.
11 Marry on the cheap, say
12 Have a feeling
15 Skips over
17 Woman whose name is an anagram of MIRA
20 Connect to an electrical outlet
21 Data holder put into a drive
22 Water birds with haunting cries
23 John who arrived on the Mayflower
27 Slugging stat
29 Adam's madam
32 Improvement, as in the economy
33 GPS suggestion: Abbr.
35 Clubs at a country club
36 Vice-presidential family of the 1990s
37 "That's just wrong!"
39 Classic TV brand
40 Cause of a Mar. clock change
43 Bill Clinton's 1996 opponent
45 Like some bagels and newlyweds
47 Chopped
49 Nonkosher sandwiches, for short
50 Features of peacock tails
51 Adorable sort
52 Island with a lagoon
54 Fast-food chain with a cowboy hat logo
55 Type of clean energy
58 Bullring cheers
59 Acorn-producing trees
62 Mined find
63 Telltale evidence of a shark
64 "Sisters" co-star Tina

by Lynn Lempel

ACROSS

1 Choose
4 Prominent items in sports bars
7 "___ Pepper's Lonely Hearts Club Band"
10 Spring jauntily
13 Painful injury, in totspeak
14 "Say again?"
15 Place for ferns and pine needles
17 Opposite of departure: Abbr.
18 Basketball one-pointers: Abbr.
19 Bathroom towel support
20 The "L" of N.F.L.
22 Philosopher who wrote "Disobedience is the true foundation of liberty"
25 Skillful handling of a situation
26 This very instant
27 Filmmaker Rob
29 Church bell sounds
32 Bird: Prefix
33 Poetic tributes
37 Leaning Tower city
38 Trickles slowly
40 iPhone voice
41 Abbr. at the top of an office memo
42 Unordained
43 Middle part of an insect's body
45 Transports for tots
48 Ginger ___
49 Stories in installments
52 Often-lost camera part
56 "Right," slangily
57 Start of the Lord's Prayer
58 Election Day in the U.S.: Abbr.
59 Sauvignon blanc, e.g.

60 Some Down answers in this puzzle
64 Corner key on a keyboard
65 Remove from power
66 Snack for Bugs Bunny
67 To the ___ degree
68 Home of the Empire State Bldg.
69 Golf peg

DOWN

$\sqrt{1}$
2 Products pioneered by IBM
3 Prefix with -hedron
$\sqrt{4}$
5 Orchestra's concertmaster, usually
6 Peaceful
7 Makes love to, à la Austin Powers
8 Experts
$\sqrt{9}$
10 Sound of failure
11 ___ I.R.A.
12 Flame thrower?
13 Outdated
$\sqrt{16}$
21 Most deodorants, once
23 With 35-Down, literary period known for flowery poetry
24 Ram's mate
$\sqrt{25}$
28 "Straight Outta Compton" rapper, 1988
29 Many an I.R.S. employee
30 Chart-topper
31 "To be or not to be . . . ," e.g.
34 Person who calls "Action!"

35 See 23-Down
$\sqrt{36}$
39 Acorn producers
44 Solo in the "Star Wars" saga
46 Betrays, as to the cops
47 Talk trashed?
$\sqrt{49}$
50 Be
51 Style of house or dressing
53 Put up, as a house
54 Hertz rental
55 Little brother, stereotypically
57 Bit of horse feed
61 The Trojans of the Pac-12 Conf.
62 Issa of HBO's "Insecure"
63 Valuable rock

by Keiran King

ACROSS

1 Kings, queens and jacks
6 Refuse to obey
10 State of confusion
14 To no ___
15 Stackable cookie
16 Moviemaker Preminger
17 Carpet woven in Iran
19 "See what I ___ ?"
20 Fury
21 First responder, for short
22 Send off on a different course
24 Key to the left of "Q"
25 Tattered threads
27 Ho-hum feeling
29 Opposed to, in dialect
31 Tangy condiment
34 Reveal slightly
36 "You ___ kiddin'!"
37 August 1 birth, astrologically
38 One of two in the larynx
42 Network to keep an "eye" on
45 Go by sea
46 Vessel with a silent "ch" in its name
50 Where planes land on an aircraft carrier
54 Duo
55 Specialized military group
56 Beach hill
58 Player for money
59 Cups, saucers and a pot, say
62 Preschooler
63 Winter hrs. in Me.
64 Bogus
65 Survive elimination . . . or what one may do to the ends of 17-, 31-, 38- and 50-Across?

68 Long-lasting hair wave, informally
69 Eye part covered by the cornea
70 Overact
71 West Point team
72 Chic
73 More disrespectful

DOWN

1 LIKE EVERY LETTER IN THIS CLUE
2 C-worthy
3 Melted cheese over toast
4 Criticize, in slang
5 More crafty
6 "Stay!"
7 Slip up
8 Nasty, long-running dispute
9 Name before Berra or Bear
10 Never a dull ___
11 Endless
12 Eminence
13 Prince, but not a princess
18 Southeast Asian housemaid
23 Clergy's changing room
26 Temporarily conked out
28 Wedding vow
30 Black Friday's mo.
32 One might say "One, two, testing, testing" into it
33 Numero ___ (top dog)
35 Light eats
39 Pet said to have nine lives
40 Word after first or financial

41 Fist bump
42 Freon initials
43 Empty talk
44 One way to pitch
47 Massachusetts vacation area
48 Shaggy
49 Horse in a harness race
51 Award from the Recording Academy
52 Overly precious
53 One nautical mile per hour
57 Old anesthetic
60 Send out, as waves
61 Root in Polynesian cuisine
64 Day ___ (getaway)
66 Family members
67 Bird that can run up to 30 m.p.h.

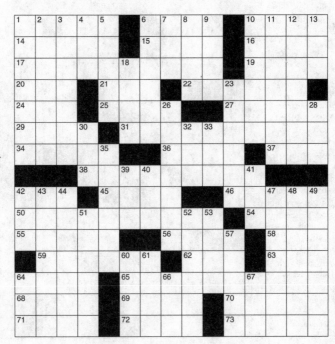

by Gary Cee

94

ACROSS

1 "Monday Night Football" airer
5 Letters on a rush order
9 "The west wind whispered, / And touched the eyelids of spring: / Her eyes, Primroses," for a classic example
14 Entice
15 Scantily dressed nightclub entertainer
17 Is highly versed about something
19 Chow chows and chihuahuas
20 The "E" of E.S.L.: Abbr.
21 Org. for which Edward Snowden once worked
22 Trevor of "The Daily Show"
24 Kirsten of "Spider-Man"
26 Major athletic event along the Thames
31 Puts frosting on
32 Besmirch, as a reputation
33 Alternative to Google Sheets
35 Devotee
36 Bases loaded . . . or a hint to the contents of 17-, 26-, 44- and 56-Across
39 Attempt
40 Jong who wrote "Fear of Flying"
42 Neither's partner
43 Revolutionary Revere
44 Bob Dylan album that he called "the closest I ever got to the sound I hear in my mind"
48 The "P" of R.S.V.P.
49 Furniture giant with a blue-and-yellow logo
50 401(k) alternative
53 Financial services corp. with an orange lion logo
54 Partner of ready and willing

56 Romantic getaway for a married couple
62 Thanksgiving-related race
63 Just
64 Newspaper opinion pieces
65 Cravings
66 Connection point

DOWN

1 Antlered animal
2 What planets orbit
3 In favor of
4 Ones taking paternity leave for the first time
5 Wide-eyed with excitement
6 Daughters' counterparts
7 Add years
8 Wannabe
9 Positions one's toes off the surfboard
10 Singer DiFranco

11 A blue compass, for the browser Safari
12 Dolls seen near Barbies
13 ___ Major (constellation)
16 Disco singer Summer
18 Manhattan neighborhood next to TriBeCa
22 Like a diet that prohibits bread and pasta
23 Low-scoring soccer win
24 Lack the courage to
25 Counterpart of "pls," in a text
26 "To ___!" ("L'chaim!")
27 To the ___ degree
28 Mo. before April
29 Component of gasoline
30 Poet Pablo who won a Nobel in Literature
34 Lovett of country music

36 Marks left by swimsuits
37 Long, long time
38 Spherical shape
41 Robber chaser, in a children's game
43 ___ Go (2016 fad)
45 Hunky-dory
46 Number of days it took Phileas Fogg to go around the world
47 Flower near a pad
50 What ":" stands for in an analogy
51 Continue one's military service
52 Farm measure
54 Of uncertain origin: Abbr.
55 Wagers
57 Green-lit
58 Valuable rock
59 Musician Yoko
60 Longtime
61 12/31, briefly

by Joe Deeney

ACROSS

1 Hollywood trophy
6 Paleo diet restriction, informally
10 Tiebreaker periods, for short
13 Pinterest posting
14 Skater Harding
15 Minor criticism
16 Look (at)
18 "As I see things . . . ," in a text
19 Pronoun for a yacht
20 Facts and figures
21 Cook under a hot flame
23 Singer with the 2018 #1 hit "Thank U, Next"
26 Giant in test prep
29 Fallback option
30 Sir ___ Newton
31 All there mentally
33 Chutzpah
36 Reno's home: Abbr.
37 "Address" for Springsteen's band
40 Viscous substance
41 Black-tie affair
43 Sneaker named for a cat
44 Like argon or neon
46 The Hunter constellation
48 Evil-repelling charm
49 Locale for London's Royal Opera House
53 What a crying emoji means
54 Roald who created Willy Wonka
55 Little mischief-maker
58 Senator Cruz
59 Safe . . . or how the last words of 16-, 23- and 49-Across are made?
63 Swellhead's problem
64 Mind-boggling designs
65 Barnyard honker
66 Droop, as an old couch
67 Ready for picking
68 Wander off

DOWN

1 Chooses, with "for"
2 Ousted Iranian ruler
3 Soft drink in a red can
4 Snacked on
5 Monaco Grand Prix, e.g.
6 Late-night host O'Brien
7 In addition
8 Bread for a Reuben sandwich
9 10-time Grammy winner Streisand
10 Alternative to a bialy
11 Lacking courage
12 Didn't ask before taking
14 "See ya!," for a Brit
17 Pick up, as yards in football
22 Tolled, as bells
23 Pie ___ mode
24 Sleeper's breathing problem
25 Sheer delight
26 Checker after reaching the other side of the board
27 On the ocean
28 Salivating animal in a classic conditioning study
31 Attacked by hornets
32 Elbow's place
34 Folk tales
35 Trent ___, former Senate majority leader
38 Feature of a cheetah's coat
39 Problems with glitchy livestreams
42 Carpet measurement
45 Mother Teresa, for one
47 Opposite of alfresco
48 Condition treated with Ritalin, in brief
49 References, as prior court decisions
50 Luxury Swiss watch
51 Love to death
52 Vessel in which to shoot the rapids
55 Composer Stravinsky
56 Flat-topped hill
57 Gazelles, for cheetahs
60 News inits. since 1958
61 Light touch
62 "What's ___ to like?"

by Zhouqin Burnikel

ACROSS

1 Facial hair generally banned in the military
6 Joint between the ankle and hip
10 Distinctive bunny features
14 Impressive display
15 Brother of Cain
16 On
17 Rock band with the 2001 #1 hit "How You Remind Me"
19 Spanish artist Francisco ___
20 Pain
21 Not at home
22 Edgar ___ Poe
23 Classic Christmas song with the lyric "City sidewalks, busy sidewalks, / Dressed in holiday style"
26 Sportscaster Bob
30 Discrimination
31 First U.S. multimillionaire John Jacob ___
32 Golf pegs
34 Dove sounds
38 Million-selling albums
41 All's opposite
42 Loads and loads
43 Largest island in the Philippines
44 Some C.E.O.s' degs.
46 Engines
47 Old New York song publishing locale
52 "The game is ___" (Sherlock Holmes declaration)
53 State east of Miss.
54 "Return of the ___" (Episode VI of "Star Wars")
58 Grain-grinding facility
59 Genre for Slayer and Iron Maiden . . . or a hint to 17-, 23-, 38- and 47-Across
62 Elegant ballet bend
63 One of 10 or fewer, maybe, in a checkout lane
64 Silly

65 Hearty draughts
66 "Gone With the Wind" plantation
67 Find a new purpose for

DOWN

1 See 2-Down
2 With 1-Down, player of the Hulk in 2003's "Hulk"
3 One of two in the McDonald's logo
4 Leaf-gathering tool
5 Easter egg coloring
6 Afghanistan's capital
7 Pro hoops network
8 Common Market letters
9 Antlered animal
10 Earner of at least 21 merit badges
11 Island with a lagoon
12 Prince or princess
13 Wing-to-wing measures
18 ___ Lane, lover of Superman
22 Lawyer's org.
23 Dress in Delhi
24 Roger of "At the Movies"
25 What bread dough and the morning sun do
26 Quaker's ___ Crunch cereal
27 Norway's capital
28 Ollie's partner in old comedy
29 Carvings of Pacific Northwest tribes
32 Oklahoma's second-largest city
33 Comedian Philips
35 Rice-shaped pasta
36 Ammonia has a strong one
37 Identifiers on tax returns: Abbr.

39 Indian flatbread
40 Be too sweet, possibly
45 One of Dracula's forms
46 Not just a snack
47 Home of the Rays and Buccaneers
48 Peabody Award-winning journalist Gwen
49 "That's the truth!"
50 "See ya!"
51 Peruvian pack animal
54 Big month for weddings
55 Biblical son of Isaac
56 Rackets
57 Drink brand with a polar bear in its logo
59 Sch. about a mile from Harvard
60 When to expect someone, for short
61 Bygone Russian space station

by Trent H. Evans

ACROSS

1 Fallout from a volcano
4 Where the heart is
9 Foundation
14 Vietnamese bowlful
15 Southwestern plant with swordlike leaves
16 Skilled (at)
17 *Hustler with a cue stick
19 Japanese beer brand
20 March 17 honoree, informally
21 Regrets
23 Truckload
24 *Showy basketball two-pointer
28 Way one positions one's legs
31 "___ sure about that?"
32 Many book-marks, for short
33 Where a cat may be picked up
37 Make a mess of
39 Newsstand purchase, for short
40 *Riot dispersal weapon
42 On the ___ (fleeing)
43 Arabian Peninsula resident
45 Little Red Riding ___
46 Money in Mexico
47 Completely flat surface
49 Comes up
51 *1960s–'70s teen idol with the hit "Julie, Do Ya Love Me"
55 Everyone
56 Walkway
57 Chefs
61 Ministore at a mall
64 Research institute . . . or, when read as a direction, a hint to the ends of the answers to the starred clues
66 Japanese mushroom
67 "___, meenie . . ."
68 Lawyer's charge
69 Dance version of a song, maybe
70 Definitely not look forward to
71 Stitch up

DOWN

1 Downloadable programs
2 Photographed
3 Circular earring
4 ___ fibrosis
5 "Say again?"
6 Digital birthday greeting
7 Rugby formation
8 George of the original "Star Trek"
9 What makes a ewe turn?
10 Commercials
11 Water creatures that hatch on land
12 Protection sold at an Apple Store
13 Reek
18 Things that are mowed
22 Wily
25 Protected Hawaiian bird
26 Arcing tennis hits
27 Simon & Garfunkel, e.g.
28 Competition between two heavyweights
29 Gym equipment with springs
30 Rapid green growth in a lake or pond
34 "That feels so-o-o good!"
35 Expert
36 Lead-in to maniac
38 Certain insurers, for short
40 Minuscule
41 One with a first-person narrative?
44 Capture
46 ___ grigio (wine)
48 Paranormal ability, for short
50 Arranged, as billiard balls in a triangle
51 Worker with an apron
52 Loathed
53 Old anesthetic
54 760-mile river that starts in Switzerland
58 Bumbling sorts
59 Take a ___ (protest, in a way)
60 Make biased
62 Winter Olympics item
63 General Mills cereal since 1937
65 Actress Vardalos

by Evan Kalish

98

ACROSS

1. Shape, as clay
5. Brother of Cain
9. Alpha's opposite
14. Cookie that's often pulled apart
15. ___ someone to tears
16. Song snippet
17. Containers for leftovers
19. Singer Shore or Washington
20. Charms
21. "I'm finished after this"
23. Tooth in the back of the mouth
24. Mexican moolah
25. Prominent position from which to pontificate
31. Island state of Australia
35. Jerry's gal pal on "Seinfeld"
36. James who wrote "A Death in the Family"
37. Old Renault
39. Slender shorebird
40. Capital of Angola
42. Got back to
44. In a diagonal position (to)
46. Upright, as a box
47. Annoy with endless talk
52. Bit of acting-out in a parlor game
55. Peter of the "Pink Panther" films
57. Sponsorship
58. Savings repository for a kid
60. Thin and bony
61. Excited about
62. One of the Great Lakes
63. Mournful poem
64. "Untouchable" Eliot
65. Gave the once-over

DOWN

1. Internet hookup device
2. University of Maine town
3. Permissible
4. Accepted doctrine
5. Mon., for Monday
6. Fancy items of neckwear
7. Unit of work
8. Stahl of "60 Minutes"
9. King Cole was a "merry" one
10. Comment made when itching to leave a dull party
11. Rubik with a famous cube
12. Composer ___ Carlo Menotti
13. Painful throb
18. ___ Linda, California birthplace of Richard Nixon
22. Speak ill of
24. Protester's sign, e.g.
26. Not tied, as sneakers
27. Falsehood
28. Santa Monica landmark
29. Memo opener
30. Watch, as a bar
31. Powder in a medicine cabinet
32. Spanish water
33. What an usher ushers you to
34. Helping a protégé
38. ___ Arbor, Mich.
41. Ming or Qing, in Chinese history
43. With tongue in cheek
45. Nearest target for a bowler
48. Playwright Edward who wrote "Who's Afraid of Virginia Woolf?"
49. Arctic explorer Robert
50. Nickname for Schwarzenegger
51. Clucked in disapproval
52. Home for a pet bird
53. Get better
54. Fever and chills
55. Ones ranked above cpls.
56. Things bigheaded people have
59. Suffix with nectar- or serpent-

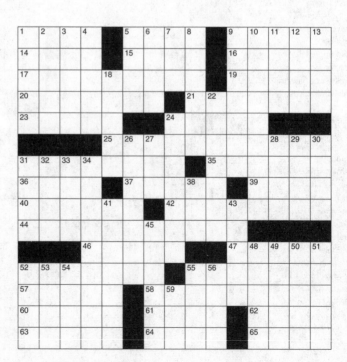

by Alan Arbesfeld

ACROSS

1 Very bottom
6 [OMG!]
10 Super Mario Bros. console, for short
13 ___ trump (bridge bid)
14 Killer whales
16 Be ___ loss for words
17 Reason to raid the fridge
19 Biol. or chem.
20 What a pun rarely evokes
21 Restrained, as a dog
23 "Shucks!," only stronger
25 Iranian currency
27 Easy camera setting
28 Regret
29 No longer astray
32 Tony winner Menzel
34 In pieces
35 Batter's grip-enhancing goo
38 Encourages
42 Romanced, in a way
44 "Keen!"
45 1986 Keith Haring antidrug mural
50 Muscles used in pull-ups, informally
51 Greeting in Granada
52 Bitter part of an orange
53 "Oh, man!"
54 The "A" of D.J.I.A.
57 Tore into
59 T. ___ (fearsome dino)
60 Gab
64 3-D medical test
65 John depicted in the biopic "Rocketman"
66 Tiny pond plants
67 Conscription org.
68 Garage sale caveat
69 Wanting others' attention and approval

DOWN

1 1, 2, 3, 4, 5, etc.: Abbr.
2 ___ Arbor, Mich.
3 Poker player's request
4 Like an ancient Andean civilization
5 Streaming media device
6 Like Mary Shelley's "Frankenstein"
7 Guggenheim holdings
8 Distinctively shelled bivalves
9 Walk nervously back and forth
10 New Hampshire's second-largest city
11 And so on, and so on, for short
12 Assented
15 Reggae relative
18 Taj Mahal city
22 French philosopher Jean-Paul
23 Insipid one
24 Car with a four-ring logo
26 Letters before an alias
29 Hand-dyeing technique
30 40 winks
31 Prominent part of an elephant
33 Part of many a showcase on "The Price Is Right"
36 Singer/songwriter DiFranco
37 Abides by, as rules
39 Throw a monkey wrench into
40 Singer Redding
41 Bite between meals
43 Hwy. infraction after a night at the bar, maybe
45 Bracelet items
46 NASA's Spirit and Opportunity
47 De Tocqueville who wrote "Democracy in America"
48 City often considered the birthplace of democracy
49 F.D.R.'s fireside event
53 ___ King, morning TV personality
55 "Yes, captain!"
56 Big bash
58 Actress Cannon
61 Japanese pond fish
62 Two-timing sort
63 Word after skeleton or answer

by Daniel Mauer

ACROSS

1 Process of childbirth
6 Mountains seen in "The Sound of Music"
10 Adjusts lengthwise, as a skirt
14 Manage to dodge
15 "I'll ___" ("Try me")
16 Impulse
17 Hurt in the bullring
18 Scrabble or Monopoly
20 Be obligated to
21 Set on fire
23 Curly and Shemp's fellow Stooge
24 Syncopated Latin dances
26 Rational selves, to Freud
28 Place to set a baby or a napkin
31 Nigerian princes offering you money, probably
32 Craving companionship
34 Assn. like Oxfam or Doctors Without Borders
35 Degs. for entrepreneurs
36 ___ milk (source of Roquefort cheese)
37 Pretend
39 High cry at doggie day care
40 High point
41 High point
42 Fearsome figure of folklore
43 Flat tire's need
44 Prepare to take, as a test
46 Helps with a heist
48 Piper's son who stole a pig in a nursery rhyme
49 Tennis great Roddick
50 Morse code O's have three of them
52 Grp. of medical providers
53 Othello, e.g.
55 Cotton gin inventor Whitney
56 Learns about through books
60 Flowed out, as the tide
62 All tidied up
63 Painful to the touch
64 Vestige
65 Many an Eastern European
66 Sean Penn and Guy Ritchie, to Madonna
67 Puts into categories

DOWN

1 Kids' construction bricks
2 Statement of affirmation
3 Smallest possible amount
4 Beethoven's "___ to Joy"
5 W.W. I fighter pilot who is Snoopy's fantasy opponent
6 Shortened word, for short
7 Classic actor who played Mr. Potter in "It's a Wonderful Life"
8 School grp. for moms and dads
9 Church talks
10 Colossal
11 Distinctive stretch of time
12 Film studio with a roaring lion
13 "Get it?"
19 Spoonful of medicine, e.g.
22 Letters on some American naval vessels
25 Ready to take home, as groceries
27 Flip out
28 Reduce one's standards, as illustrated, respectively, in 3-, 5-, 7-, 40- and 28-Down
29 City that's home to Iowa State
30 Boll weevil, to a cotton farmer
33 World ___ of Poker
35 "Sheesh!"
37 Observe Ramadan
38 Prefix with -plasm
40 Businesses like the Kit Kat Klub in a hit musical
42 Pointless
45 Candied Thanksgiving servings
46 Hullabaloo
47 Opt for
51 French fries and coleslaw, often
52 Modern viewing for couch potatoes
54 Change for a five, say
56 Many I.C.U. workers
57 Long-bodied fish
58 High bond rating
59 Disease that causes a skin rash
61 Male buddy

by Lynn Lempel

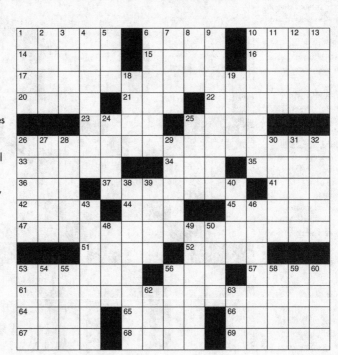

101

ACROSS

1 The Mayflower had three of them
6 Rocker Lofgren
10 Story of heroes
14 Hawaiian greeting
15 Grp. with many Mideast members
16 Outpouring from a volcano
17 Sweet citrus fruits from Southern California
20 Winter Olympics need
21 Tack on
22 Most frigid
23 ___-bodied
25 Abba of Israel
26 Only N.F.L. team that doesn't have a logo on its helmets
33 Tied, as shoes
34 Be under the weather
35 "___ till you drop"
36 W.W. II zone that D.D.E. commanded
37 Completely enchanted
41 The Cyclones of the Big 12 Conf.
42 Pimply outbreak
44 Like some batteries and baseball leagues
45 Did something
47 Some chickens
51 Angry driver's signal
52 Lover boy
53 "Quaking" trees
56 Nightly "NewsHour" presenter
57 Queen in Disney's "Frozen"
61 Hit 1980s cop show
64 Dutch town with a cheese named after it
65 Light and open
66 Deity of Islam
67 Store department with jackets and ties
68 Shaggy beasts
69 Come from behind, in scoring

DOWN

1 Dallas N.B.A. team, informally
2 Actor Alda
3 Like Lindbergh's 1927 flight to Paris
4 Crowd activity at a stadium
5 ___ Rafael, Calif.
6 "Who knows?!"
7 Apple tablet
8 Sign before Virgo
9 Write quickly and none too carefully
10 Weather phenomena from the Pacific
11 "Doctor Jones, you're needed at the front desk," e.g.
12 Currier and ___
13 Group of actors
18 Dial on a telephone
19 Rent-___ (Hertz or Avis)
24 Hotel units
25 Polish, as text
26 Unambiguous
27 Gate fastener
28 Cheap, in commercial names
29 Birth-related
30 "___ Christmas" (holiday song)
31 Edged (out)
32 Taters
38 Chief support
39 "Can ___ you a question?"
40 Zilch
43 Actor who played Andy Bernard on "The Office"
46 ___ De Vil, "101 Dalmatians" role
48 Earth's longest time divisions, geologically
49 Homes for nuns
50 Hatchlings' home
53 *cough, cough*
54 Point of view, as in an argument
55 Blueprint
56 Employee's reserved parking space, for one
58 Brief down period
59 Circus animal with flippers
60 Wan
62 Small inlet
63 What a priest, a minister and a rabbi might walk into

by Ellis Hay

102

ACROSS
1. ___ hostel (inexpensive accommodations)
6. Err
10. McEntire of country music
14. Links legend Palmer, familiarly
15. Actor Epps of "House"
16. Wicked
17. Recurring Tyler Perry movie role
18. Miller ___ (low-calorie beer)
19. Hair on a horse or a lion
20. *Trilogy set in Middle-earth, with "The"
23. A.M.A. members
24. Candlemaker's supply
25. Nag, nag, nag
29. Unite
31. Banned insecticide
34. Early April zodiac sign
35. [Just like that, it's gone!]
36. Otherworldly glow
37. *Container for a Kellogg's cereal
40. Folk singer and protester Joan
41. Singer/songwriter Redding
42. Author Zora ___ Hurston
43. Cunning
44. Muscle pain
45. Is of use to
46. Wine barrel wood
47. One more than bi-
48. *Reputed place at the North Pole
56. "The ___ thickens"
57. Words before and after "or not" in a Shakespeare quote
58. Choreographer Alvin
60. Wander about
61. Bell-ringing makeup company
62. Harsh light
63. Once around the sun
64. Marsh plant
65. What the answer to each of the starred clues has

DOWN
1. Orange root vegetable
2. Kind of test whose answers can't be erased
3. Computer command to go back
4. Arena section
5. Physical expression of frustration, in modern lingo
6. Plays a round
7. Leave off, as the last letter in this clu
8. Words at a swearing-in ceremony
9. Amenity at most hotels and airports
10. Altered version of a song
11. "Dear ___ Hansen" (Broadway hit)
12. Google alternative
13. Pub offerings
21. Hockey Hall-of-Famer Bobby
22. Published
25. Nasty comments
26. Typeface alternative to Helvetica
27. Unpredictable, in an unwanted way
28. "Unbelievable!"
29. Animated lead singer of the Pussycats
30. "My bad!"
31. Largest city in the United Arab Emirates
32. Wryly humorous
33. What the I.R.S. collects
35. The white stuff in an orange
36. Riding the waves
38. Jon Bon Jovi or Simon Le Bon
39. Make a mental image of
44. Grp. to call for a tow
45. Biblical boat
46. Furry swimmer
47. Poll finding, perhaps
48. Lively for one's age
49. Spiky plant with soothing juice
50. Celestial explosion
51. Created a tapestry
52. Slender woodwind
53. Ending with Capitol or Faith
54. Name of many Norwegian kings
55. ___ Noël (boss of 65-Across, in France)
59. Positive response

by Howard Barkin and Kevin Christian

ACROSS

1 New World natives noted for their pyramids and calendar
7 Amazon or eBay
13 Intriguingly foreign
14 Companion of Io, Ganymede and Callisto among Jupiter's moons
15 Pitcher between a starter and a closer
18 Biblical birthright seller
19 Biblical boat captain
20 TV warrior princess
21 Snow day activity
24 No longer slumbering
27 State religion of Iran
31 Fix, as an election
32 John of "Full House"
37 Female sheep
38 Bu$ine$$ execs
40 Iridescent birthstone
41 Declare
42 Metalworker's tool
45 Chow down
46 Note between fa and la
47 Popular apple variety
53 Prom rental
54 El ___ (Pacific Ocean phenomenon)
55 School grp. that might hold a walkathon
57 Play a game during Hanukkah . . . with a hint to 15-, 21-, 42- and 47-Across
62 Russian czar known as "the Great"
63 Tolkien's Lord of Rivendell
64 Six-line stanza
65 Afternoon nap

DOWN

1 Joke that goes viral on the internet
2 x or y, on a graph
3 "Star Wars" character who could this clue have written?
4 When twilight begins
5 Zilch
6 Nativity ___
7 Indian megacity of 28+ million
8 "Yes, mon ami"
9 Ferocious dinos
10 Sheltered shoreline spot
11 Business sign that's flipped in the morning
12 NPR's ___ Liasson
16 Cone's retinal counterpart
17 Big part of an elephant
22 Guitar pioneer ___ Paul
23 Insult, slangily
24 St. Louis landmark
25 What'll help you see the sites?
26 Bug-eyed
28 Blue jeans pioneer Strauss
29 Missing G.I.
30 Whine like a baby
33 One of 38 for Madonna, a Billboard record
34 Do an impression of
35 Fannie ___
36 What the vengeful seek to settle
39 Lose, as fur
41 Comic strip "___ and Janis"
43 "You hate to see it"
44 "Why ___ even bother?"
47 Cash in India
48 Turnpike turnoffs
49 Falsehood
50 Politically unaffiliated: Abbr.
51 Some prom hairstyles
52 Insert for a blocked blood vessel
53 Cough syrup qtys.
56 Hawkeye's player on "M*A*S*H"
58 Bit of equipment in fishing and basketball
59 Uno + due
60 QB Manning
61 Wrath

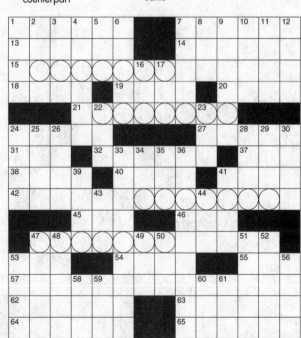

by Timothy Polin

ACROSS

1 ___ Wednesday
4 Doing battle
9 Item in a humidor
14 Hotel amenity down the hall
15 1940s–'60s singer Frankie
16 Win by ___
17 Butter substitute
19 Hereditary background
20 What locomotives and irons may give off
21 Critical, as a situation
23 One getting mostly A's in school
27 Killer whale
30 King Kong, for one
31 China's Mao ___ -tung
32 Campus bigwig
33 Rainbow shapes
35 Obliterate
39 Beavers' construction
40 Winning time after time . . . or where you might find 17-, 23-, 51- or 62-Across
42 Small inlet
43 Asparagus unit
45 Sharpen, as skills
46 Performs like Lil Wayne or Lil' Kim
47 Baseball stat
49 Suffix with ball-
50 "Or ___!" (end of an ultimatum)
51 Shiny kitchen wrap
56 Signifies
57 Obsolescent phone features
61 Rumble in the Jungle setting
62 Wallet alternative
66 Fragrant chemical compound
67 Standard Windows typeface
68 Feather stole

69 Outbuildings with garden tools
70 Gem in an oyster
71 Aardvark's morsel

DOWN

1 Goals
2 "Shoo, kitty!"
3 On earth
4 Fort where Davy Crockett died
5 Driveway surface
6 Nintendo console
7 Newswoman Curry
8 Swamp plants
9 Merry-go-round
10 Properly arranged
11 Chuck Berry's "Johnny B. ___"
12 Actor Sean of "The Lord of the Rings"
13 Change, as a clock

18 Illustrator Wilson famous for his macabre cartoons
22 Six-time N.L. home run champ Mel
24 Indian bread
25 What the "O" of O magazine stands for
26 Place for a Ping-Pong table
27 6:1 or 7:1, e.g., at a racetrack
28 Harvest
29 Arrived
34 What "ibn" and "ben" mean, in names
36 Asia's shrunken ___ Sea
37 Doesn't guzzle
38 Simplicity
40 Spacecrafts circling the earth

41 Jay formerly of late-night TV
44 Like Brink's trucks
46 Excavation find
48 Suffix with serpent-
51 Woodworking tools
52 What a dog-walker holds
53 Bring together
54 Chart often with insets of Alaska and Hawaii
55 Peaceful, picturesque scene
58 Jessica of "Fantastic Four"
59 King of the jungle
60 Small quarrel
63 Metal from a mine
64 Vardalos of "My Big Fat Greek Wedding"
65 Serving of corn

by Gary Larson

ACROSS

1 Leave empty
7 Fellow
11 One of 17-, 18-, 37-, 60- or 62-Across
14 Saudi ___
15 Director Kazan
16 "Pick a card, ___ card"
17 JULY
18 MAY
20 Pistol, slangily
21 Upper-body garment that's not tucked in
23 Surfeit
24 Source of solar energy
25 Trap
26 Zipped . . . or ripped
27 Like the waistband on underwear
30 ___ rule (typically)
32 The "p" of r.p.m.
33 Like driftwood or a has-been
35 Ill-tempered, as a baby
37 FEBRUARY
40 Rascal
43 Lessen
47 Gear tooth
48 Brain test, for short
51 More protected by a tree's leaves
52 The "A" in DNA
54 Beat poet Ginsberg
56 Fall behind
57 Post-W.W. II alliance
58 ___ Gorbachev, former first lady of the Soviet Union
59 Hi-___ monitor
60 APRIL
62 JUNE
65 Termite look-alike
66 Mark left by a whip
67 Be successful in the end
68 Director Spike
69 Breyers competitor
70 Miserly

DOWN

1 Spelling of a word that's not the usual: Abbr.
2 Salad green
3 Beach huts
4 Not much
5 Make a knot
6 Part of Manhattan where the United Nations is located
7 Actress Davis
8 Upstate New York city south of the Finger Lakes
9 Nephews' counterparts
10 Part of a cigarette rating
11 Runs, as a horse
12 Puts up with
13 Genre of the Edgar Awards
19 Actor's representative: Abbr.
22 Rough, as an 11-Across
24 Stitch
28 Phony
29 Home of Arizona State University
31 SAG-___ (Hollywood union)
34 Woodrow Wilson was the only U.S. president to have one
36 Not new
38 Noes' opposites
39 Alcoholic drink that's often flavored with fruit
40 Event ending in -gate
41 Illegal import from Colombia
42 Shake up
44 Airplane wing feature
45 Shell-less marine invertebrate
46 Unit of energy
49 Made, as an income
50 "With pleasure"
53 ___ Pérignon
55 Top 10s, e.g.
59 Hindu queen
61 Be in debt
63 "Let's ___!" (cry after grace)
64 Hog's home

by Tess Davison and Kathy Lowden

ACROSS

1 Suitable for sinking one's teeth into
6 Mountain lion
10 Speaker's platform
14 Letter before beta
15 401(k) alternatives
16 Latch ___ (grip)
17 Plumber's tool
19 Dermatological sac
20 One catching morays
21 Three-time All-Star pitcher Robb ___
23 Cry from a crib
24 Vacation relaxation destination
26 Reaches adulthood
29 Apportion
32 Moo goo ___ pan (Chinese chicken dish)
33 Check for fit
34 KLM is a "royal" one
37 Overdid it onstage
38 Defeated
42 Too much on one's plate
46 Instrument for Billy Joel
49 Snake in "Raiders of the Lost Ark"
50 Zeus : Greek :: Jupiter : ___
51 "Oops, missed the deadline"
54 Big name in ice cream
55 Statute
56 D.C. insider
57 Small, like Santa's helpers
60 Bread spread
62 Cramped spot for a plane passenger . . . or a hint to something hidden in 17-, 26-, 34-, 42- and 51-Across
66 Where a cashier puts money
67 Mani-___ (salon combo)
68 Cow in classic Borden ads
69 Two-for-one event
70 Yemeni port
71 Car company with so-called "Gigafactories"

DOWN

1 Treasure hunter's aid
2 ___ Lilly & Co.
3 Draw interest from
4 "With this ring, I ___ wed"
5 Two-masted sailing vessel
6 Polish dumpling
7 Funerary receptacle
8 Newsman Robert, former PBS partner of Jim Lehrer
9 Contents of a funerary receptacle
10 Disney dwarf with the shortest name
11 "Nevertheless . . ."
12 "The deal went through!"
13 Storyteller's segue
18 ___ room (game site)
22 Far
24 One-named hitmaker born in Nigeria
25 Desirable, as a job
27 Spoil
28 San Joaquin Valley city
30 One-eighth portion
31 Business district in downtown Chicago
35 Commotion
36 Company behind the Watson project
39 Docility
40 "Omigosh!"
41 Gainsay
43 Added up, as a score
44 Passenger-screening org.
45 Chose to join
46 Their prospects are up in the air
47 Home of Milano and Firenze
48 In addition
52 ___-Loompa (Willy Wonka worker)
53 Building wing
58 Pedal pushers
59 ___ of Capri
61 World Cup cheer
63 1950s presidential monogram
64 Be under the weather
65 Wimbledon service?

by Alan Arbesfeld

ACROSS

1 Strive for an epic effect
6 Poker or snooker
10 Plays a role
14 Savory food quality
15 "Hear, hear!"
16 Had on
17 The Devil
18 Richly adorn
19 Black gem with bands
20 Cinnamon-and-sugar cookie
23 Yang's counterpart
24 Hurdle for a coll. senior, maybe
25 Beats by ___ (headphones brand)
26 Hurdle for a H.S. senior, maybe
29 "Saturday Night Live" segment
32 Mate for a mama
35 ___ Baba, crier of "Open sesame!"
36 Pooh's pessimistic pal
37 Retail giant with a famous catalog, once
39 ___ Antonio, Tex.
41 Finger or toe
42 W.W. I's Red Baron, e.g.
44 After-tax amount
46 Zilch
47 Televised activity with Ping-Pong balls
50 Very: Sp.
51 Result no longer allowed on "Jeopardy!"
52 Reggae relative
53 School lunch sandwich, for short
56 Comprehend . . . or what 20-, 29- and 47-Across do, finally
60 Explorer Ponce de ___
62 Computer cable
63 Lake into which Michigan's "thumb" juts
64 Born and ___
65 Opera solo
66 Big name in online satire, with "The"
67 Jolts
68 Smell really bad
69 Rat Pack member ___ Davis Jr.

DOWN

1 Dress (up)
2 Neighbor of a Saudi
3 Drive home, as a runner on third base
4 Apple computer
5 Chinese tree with fan-shaped leaves
6 Collections of funny outtakes
7 In the thick of
8 Tune
9 Sign, as a check
10 Army no-show
11 Kind of wagon for pioneers
12 Attempt
13 One cause of an "R" rating
21 Humorous Bombeck
22 Deceived with a fake-out, in hockey
27 Bitter-tasting
28 Letter before iota
29 A diamond that has one is moderately expensive
30 Ross of the Supremes
31 Watching closely
32 The first one begins "Blessed is the man that walketh not in the counsel of the ungodly"
33 Quintet to which "y" is often added
34 One attending a shindig
38 Writer F. ___ Fitzgerald
40 "1984" language
43 Back-and-forth changes to a Wikipedia page
45 ___ torch
48 Bring back, as a worker
49 Chips with melted cheese
53 Jewish festival usually in March
54 Ride for a Quidditch player
55 Female donkey
57 Finishes
58 Great Lake bordered by Ohio
59 "Yellowfin" fish
60 J.F.K.'s successor
61 Time in history

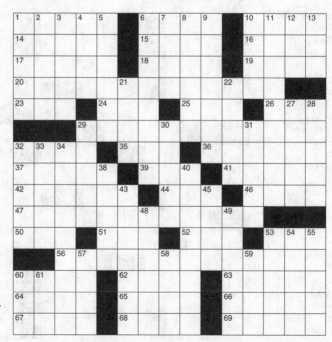

by Evan Kalish

108

ACROSS

1 iPhone downloads
5 Breakfast, lunch and dinner
10 The "A" in A&E
14 Stumble
15 Lit, as a lantern
16 Season to be full of cheer
17 Gaucho's weapon
18 *Sinister genius in a series of Sax Rohmer novels
20 With, en français
21 Luau garland
22 Los Angeles hoopster
23 *Quick-tempered, gun-toting, rabbit-hating toon
27 "You betcha!"
28 Taxis
29 Illuminated sign in a studio
31 Exchange of negative commercials
34 Choose
35 "Stupid is as stupid ___" (line from "Forrest Gump")
38 *Dudley Do-Right's enemy in old TV cartoons
42 You can usually see right through it
43 Electric ___
44 Brought about
45 Cyberbusiness, briefly
47 "Right away!"
49 Owns
51 *Chief pirate in Neverland
56 Part of an old Apple commercial tagline
58 1600 Pennsylvania ___ (D.C. address)
59 Letter in a Viking inscription
60 Archetypically villainous features possessed by the answers to the starred clues
63 James with a jazzy voice
64 Foes of elves, in Tolkien
65 Tennis star ___ Osaka
66 Lots and lots
67 Track or swimming competition
68 Typical middle schooler, agewise
69 Ending with ticker or masking

DOWN

1 Held in check
2 Utah city of more than 100,000
3 Stacks
4 Total ditz
5 Fill-in-the-blanks story
6 White-plumed herons
7 Title role for Jude Law in a 2004 remake
8 Reed who sang "Walk on the Wild Side"
9 Certain bachelor, in personals
10 Tolstoy's "___ Karenina"
11 Nutty/marshmallowy ice cream flavor
12 [Giggle]
13 Commit a fine-dining faux pas
19 ___ mater
24 Mother in a stable family?
25 Freshman, a year later, informally
26 Opposed to
30 Warning that's pure bluster
31 Egyptian cobra
32 Substance coiled in a double helix
33 Culinary concoction much used in French cuisine
34 Avian hooter
36 Body shop approx.
37 "___ nuff!"
39 Sci-fi princess helping lead the Rebel Alliance
40 Squeal of pain
41 Impulsive people tend to lack one
46 Bank no.
47 Cry from a person in peril
48 Connects (with)
49 Sign in the bleachers at a football game
50 Love, to Leonardo
52 High-altitude Western lake
53 "Get ___ here!"
54 Winning
55 "The Family Circus" cartoonist Bil
57 Discreet "Hey!"
61 Insect found in "Antarctica" . . . but not Antarctica
62 Cornfield cry

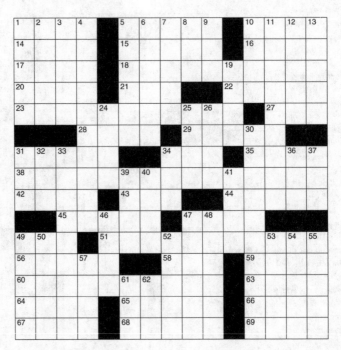

by Timothy Polin

ACROSS

1 Crumbly cheese in a Greek salad
5 ___ Xtra (Dr Pepper alternative)
9 World faith founded in Persia
14 Fatty ingredient in pie crust
15 Raison d'___
16 Warning
17 App customer
18 Prized blackjack cards
19 Old-school "Cool!"
20 Theme song for "Rocky III"
23 ___ Hawkins of "Li'l Abner"
24 Red wine choice, for short
25 Combat sport fought in a cage: Abbr.
28 Height of excellence, metaphorically
33 Company nicknamed "Big Blue"
36 Paper for jotting notes on
37 Lowly laborers
38 Feature of a 95° day in Phoenix, but not Miami
41 Not outsourced
43 Singer Mann
44 "No seats remaining" sign
45 "Mom" on a bicep, e.g.
46 Hangover remedy in which one continues drinking
51 Surgery sites, briefly
52 Cry of discovery
53 Wanders
57 Classic horror tale by W.W. Jacobs
62 Wiener topper that's "sauer"
64 Common downtown street name
65 Killer whale
66 Like some whiskey barrels
67 ___ Domini

68 Need for a cash-strapped car buyer
69 "Peace out!"
70 Slumps
71 Burden

DOWN

1 Chimney pipes
2 Course that's a cakewalk
3 Out on a limb, literally
4 Deft
5 Bog fuel
6 Poison ivy reaction
7 Glided effortlessly (through)
8 Favoritest friend
9 Gun noise
10 Sheltered, at sea
11 "I know you think this is a ludicrous idea, but . . ."
12 The "A" of MoMA
13 "Who am ___ judge?"
21 "Bah!"

22 Drop-___ (unexpected visitors)
26 High-I.Q. bunch
27 Real estate or money in the bank
29 Fuel economy authority, for short
30 Athletic club?
31 Speed limit letters, abroad
32 Prefix with classical
33 State known for its potatoes
34 Br'er Rabbit's hideaway
35 "Oops, sorry!"
39 "On ___ Majesty's Secret Service"
40 Help-wanted inits.
41 Fury
42 Doze (off)
44 Doo-wop rock band that performed in the movie "Grease"

47 Mom, pop and the kids, say
48 Supreme Court justice Clarence
49 Suffix with direct or deposit
50 Leave the band to make it big on one's own
54 Cook's garment
55 Chinese region dubbed the "Vegas of Asia"
56 Feathered Tchaikovsky dancers
58 ___ Lewis and the News
59 Periodic Sicilian erupter
60 Piece between a bishop and a queen
61 Son of Seth
62 Flattens in boxing, for short
63 Issa of HBO's "Insecure"

by Michael Schlossberg

ACROSS

1 Cost for a radio or TV commercial
6 Mafia enforcer, e.g.
10 Bra size specification
14 Glacier climber's tool
15 What Tarzan swings on
16 College in New Rochelle, N.Y.
17 Suitable for moviemaking?
19 Hauls with effort
20 ___ Taylor (clothing chain)
21 Geometric calculation
22 Impressionist Claude
23 Movie munchkin, maybe?
26 Sharply punched
29 Speedster Bolt
30 One of the 40 in "the back 40"
31 Big name in kitchen wrap
33 Ump's call for a batter
36 ___-Town (the Windy City)
37 Movie clip where the grips, boom operator and gaffer all appear?
39 HBO rival
40 Party item that has a tap
41 Caustic
42 Menial laborer
43 Image on a valentine
45 Like wetlands
47 Finalize the music for the movie?
51 "There, there . . ."
52 Bangs on the head?
53 Tasseled hat
56 Make headway
57 Redo of a movie scene?
60 Style of skirt that reaches just below the knees
61 Opposed
62 Chairlift rider, perhaps
63 Author Waugh
64 ___ Picture (Oscars category)
65 Midsection of the body

DOWN

1 Japanese consumer electronics brand
2 Rodent control brand
3 Plant with fronds
4 Dine on
5 What to do after you breathe in
6 Appliance with a screen and a remote
7 Part of a drum kit
8 Card game with Draw Two cards
9 Understand
10 Mississippi port city with an Air Force base
11 Add up the number of people present
12 Felix of "The Odd Couple"
13 Fettuccine or farfalle
18 Low-humidity
22 Had in mind
23 Civil War prez
24 Move suddenly and unsteadily
25 Jacob's biblical twin
26 "J" in a deck of cards
27 Feel sore
28 Optimist's perspective
31 Mattress brand
32 Sounds at a nursery viewing window
34 "Someone made a boo-boo!"
35 Broadway award
37 White stuff on a blackboard
38 Few and far between
42 ___ Check (T.S.A. convenience)
44 Big name in athletic shoes
45 Drudgery, in older usage
46 Put in handcuffs
47 Letter before tau
48 Cybercommerce
49 Closes
50 Go by taxi, in slang
53 Ump's call for a batted ball
54 Barely makes it, with "by"
55 Digit in binary code
57 Small amount of cream
58 Digit in binary code
59 W.B.A. result, in brief

by Bruce Haight

ACROSS

1 Young dog or seal
4 Ire
9 Bakery fixtures
14 Communication system for the deaf, for short
15 Second-largest city in Oklahoma
16 High-quality black tea
17 Author of the memoir "Spoken from the Heart" (2010)
19 Supreme Court justice Kagan
20 In ___ (as found)
21 Busy buzzer
22 Shape of a rainbow
23 Author of the memoir "First Lady from Plains" (1984)
29 Attempt
30 "I apologize!"
31 "Shogun" or "The Lord of the Rings"
33 Attend, as an event
35 Inits. in some church names
36 Author of the memoir "Becoming" (2018)
40 Sly animal
41 Internet forum overseers, informally
42 Swiss peaks
43 Kind of seat in a fighter jet
46 Sign of a B'way success
47 Author of the memoir "Living History" (2003)
52 Even a single one
53 Bagel topper
54 Egg cell
56 Gerontologist's study
59 Author of the memoir "The Times of My Life" (1978)
61 Geico mascot
62 Wash
63 Mag. number
64 "What ___!" ("It's so sloppy!")
65 Symbol of Christianity
66 Actor Billy ___ Williams

DOWN

1 Buddies
2 Former competitor of Southwest
3 Demoted planet
4 One day ___ time
5 Rough and textured, as fabric
6 Sticky
7 German steel city
8 "Go team!"
9 "La Traviata" and "Carmen"
10 Alternative to shoelaces
11 Barely make, with "out"
12 Opposite of oui
13 Mediterranean or Adriatic
18 Suitable for the country
22 Sound before someone says "Gesundheit!"
24 Prefix with angel or enemy
25 Jots down
26 Disney's "Lady and the ___"
27 Humorist Bombeck and others
28 Bread for a Reuben sandwich
31 Texter's pictograph
32 Dot in a 31-Down
33 See 34-Down
34 With 33-Down, the U.S. flag, affectionately
37 Prestigious Atlanta university
38 Farm building
39 Many
40 Sound of disgust
44 Chain-rattling sounds
45 Argentine partner dances
46 Generous portions of pie
48 Cloudless
49 Game of chance whose results are often televised
50 Egg-shaped
51 One taking vitals, perhaps
55 Commercial goods: Abbr.
56 Turkish title
57 "Columbia, the ___ of the Ocean"
58 What's dispensed from the middle of many a soda dispenser
59 Network on the telly
60 "Affirmative"

by Sally Hoelscher

ACROSS

1 Like show horses' hooves
5 Twisted person
10 ___ constrictor
13 One of the 12 tribes of Israel
14 At full speed, in nautical lingo
15 Back of a horse
16 Persia, nowadays
17 Jules who wrote "Journey to the Center of the Earth"
18 Mars' counterpart, in Greek myth
19 Cop's canine companion
21 What a door swings on
22 Where many draftees were sent in the '60s
23 Workers with a daily grind?
25 Opposite of a purebred
29 Sets of points, in math
30 W.W. II German sub
31 Failing grades
33 Crosby, Stills, ___ & Young
37 Where roots take hold
38 Ancient Greek meeting place
39 Arts-and-crafts supply
40 Menial worker
41 Wise one
42 Unmitigated
43 Make turbulent
45 Toss back tequila, perhaps
47 Direct clashes
51 Like the hours shortly after midnight
52 Swimming (in)
53 Starts shooting
58 Antidrug agent, informally
59 What a pet may be transported in
60 Weaving machine
61 Device for recording shows

62 Many a waiter around Hollywood
63 Tiny bit
64 Consumed
65 Ones anxious to take driver's ed, typically
66 Like venison that's been sitting awhile

DOWN

1 ___ of the tongue
2 Odysseus, in the "Odyssey"
3 Track shape
4 Having a meal under the stars, e.g.
5 "Hel-l-lp!"
6 Chatted on the internet, for short
7 Tree with edible pods
8 Ninth-century English monarch known as "the Great"

9 Telephone button that doesn't have letters
10 Singed
11 Letter after phi, chi, psi . . .
12 Church recesses
15 Activity depicted in a famous 2/23/1945 photograph . . . and in three of this puzzle's answers
20 Supermarket vehicle
21 Juice drink brand with a hyphen in its name
24 Civil rights activist Parks
25 Dishevel
26 Instrument with a brief solo in Beethoven's Fifth
27 Black: Fr.
28 What a law that hasn't been repealed still has

32 Typical London weather
34 ___ sax
35 Tallow source
36 That woman's
38 "Yeah, I'm real sure!"
42 Puts to work
44 "Nice one!"
46 Ones named in deeds
47 Orange or grape drink brand
48 Be in store for
49 Do the honors with the turkey
50 Flurry
54 Boys' school near Windsor
55 Tiny bit
56 Place on a Clue board
57 Award shaped like a winged woman
59 Tabby

by Jacob Stulberg

ACROSS

1 Airer of "48 Hours" and "60 Minutes"
4 Inscribe, as on a trophy
8 Bottom half of a 45
13 Clue for the clueless
15 Actress Loughlin of "Full House"
16 10:1, e.g.
17 Website with a "Buy It Now" option
18 Not give ___ (not care)
19 "A Doll's House" playwright Henrik
20 Butane-filled item for smokers
23 "___ the land of the free . . ."
24 Clumsy
27 Exercises that work the glutes, quads and abs
32 Russian refusal
34 "Krazy ___"
35 "At Wit's End" humorist Bombeck
36 With 44-Across, N.B.A. player once married to a Kardashian
37 "Who am ___ judge?"
38 Kind of rock for which New Hampshire is known
41 Con's opposite
42 "The Godfather" crowd
44 See 36-Across
45 Communication means for the deaf, for short
46 Stiffly formal
47 Star of Broadway's "Fiddler on the Roof"
50 Tilted, as printed letters
52 To the ___ degree
53 "Forget about it!" . . . or a clue to the starts of 20-, 27- and 47-Across
59 Airport bummer
62 Indication that it's time to take out the trash

63 Old Russian ruler
64 Final Greek letter
65 Singer of "Let It Go" in Disney's "Frozen"
66 Bingo-like casino game
67 Runway walker
68 Applied Clairol to, perhaps
69 Crunchy, as carrots

DOWN

1 At the home of: Fr.
2 Benjamin Netanyahu's nickname
3 "Get real, for heaven's sake!"
4 Airline that doesn't schedule flights on Shabbat
5 Actress Spelling of "Beverly Hills 90210"
6 Handhold for a rock climber

7 Genre for Cardi B and Nicki Minaj
8 Lawyer's document
9 Teenage witch of TV
10 "___ Superman!"
11 Casino cube
12 Long, long time
14 Kind of personality a go-getter has
21 Brand of taco shells and salsas
22 Profs' aides
25 Someone who might say "There, there"
26 Funeral vehicle
27 Pinch pennies
28 Resident of Doha
29 ___ Tolkien, author of "The Lord of the Rings"
30 Actress Thurman
31 Bruce Wayne's home, for one
33 One living under a bridge, in fairy tales

36 Greg ___, three-time Tour de France winner
39 Wedding vow
40 Male turkey
43 "Somehow it all gets done"
47 Clearasil target, in slang
48 Went "Hello . . . ello . . . llo . . . lo . . ."
49 Keep on the shelves
51 True-blue
54 How thumbs are twiddled
55 Middle of the face
56 May or June gown wearer
57 Mom's mom
58 Get taller
59 ___ Pérignon
60 Rock music subgenre
61 Was in first place

by Andrea Carla Michaels

ACROSS

1 Tavern
4 Fabled loser to a tortoise
8 Go searching for food
14 Flabbergast
15 German auto make
16 Ways to travel
17 Young fellow
18 What you should take dubious advice with
20 "If I'm wrong, I'll eat ___!"
22 School support grp.
23 Every family has one
24 Dry, as a desert
26 "That's not true!"
29 What a complete fool lacks
32 G.M. car no longer sold new
33 Tennis umpire's call
34 Offered for breeding, as a derby winner
38 Letter between oh and cue
39 Toilet paper layer
40 College application fig.
41 Red ___ beet
42 Passover celebrations
44 Dove's sound
45 Squeaks (by)
46 Shylock's harsh demand, in "The Merchant of Venice"
49 Leaked, as an old faucet
51 Government disaster org.
52 Greek war god
53 "Right you ___!"
55 Colorado skiing mecca
58 What "it" may hit you like
62 Before, in poetry
63 Concert gear handler
64 Brand of basketballs
65 Classic symphonic rock group, for short
66 Claim to be true
67 Odds' counterpart
68 Documentarian Burns

DOWN

1 ChapStick, e.g.
2 What a robber hopes to get?
3 How robbers can get caught
4 Immobilize with rope, in a way
5 Month after Mar.
6 Harvest
7 Snobbish sort
8 To and ___
9 "Ouch!"
10 Steals cattle
11 Maker of the game Centipede
12 Cosmetic goop
13 Toward sunrise: Sp.
19 ___ the Great of children's literature
21 Paths of falling stars
25 Gets all pretty
27 Quickly and loudly detach
28 "The Thin Man" dog
29 Klutz's cry
30 1997 title role for Peter Fonda
31 Funny Tina
35 Glimpse furtively
36 Baking soda has lots of them
37 Sprint
39 Skull, for Hamlet when he says "Alas, poor Yorick!"
40 When repeated, infant's sound
43 Any one of nine "Star Wars" films
44 Obsolescent laptop component
45 Things that suffered a 20th-century blight
47 Close by
48 Eats royally
49 Bit on a baby's bib
50 Kidney-related
52 Gillette razor option
54 M.B.A. class subj.
56 Mystery writer Stanley Gardner
57 One of the noble gases
59 ___ Newton (cookie)
60 Q: Why is a flower like the letter A? A: Because a ___ goes after it
61 Joke (around)

by John Lampkin

ACROSS

1 What cats clean themselves with
5 Had on
9 Feeling of anxiety
14 ___ vera gel
15 Highest point
16 "Congrats!"
17 Junk pile
19 Firm hand?
20 Bones of the foot
21 University sports org.
23 Destiny
24 Darth Vader's name as a boy
25 Triple Crown winner of 1977
28 Drummer Ringo
30 "Have a ___" (request in a waiting room)
31 Winnie-the-___
33 Little rascal
35 Singer ___ Davis Jr.
39 "I'm deeply indebted" . . . or a hint to the ends of 17-, 25-, 51- and 64-Across
43 British W.W. II weapons
44 "Uh-huh!"
45 Coup d'___
46 "If I may interject . . ."
49 Undercoat used in sculpture
51 Power source for an electric vehicle
55 Dark loaf
58 Very light brown
59 "Heads will ___!"
60 Folklore monsters
62 Reminders of past fights
64 Easter event in Vatican City
66 Courtroom proceeding
67 And others, in a list
68 Pimples
69 Actress Field with Oscars
70 Word after club, cream or caustic
71 Illuminating gas

DOWN

1 Macaroni or rigatoni
2 ___ Highway (nearly 1,400-mile route that runs through Whitehorse, Yukon Territory)
3 Disquieting
4 Caribbean and Caspian
5 When repeated, a trombone sound
6 A warm welcome
7 Blink or flinch, say
8 Americans living abroad, informally
9 Org. with a canine registry
10 Texas, Louisiana, Mississippi, Alabama and Florida
11 Perfect
12 Rich German cake
13 Out of alignment
18 Leaning Tower city
22 Pub pintful
26 Ireland, in poetry
27 Toward sunrise
29 Bernard Malamud novel about a baseball phenom
31 Detectives, informally
32 Mel who played at the Polo Grounds
34 "You'll ___ for this!"
36 The Indianapolis 500, for one
37 Sport also known as cage fighting, in brief
38 Nonetheless
40 Tennis legend Arthur
41 Notepaper that's usually yellow
42 Intl. group of oil producers
47 Mess up
48 Nearsighted people
50 Scandinavian drinking cry
51 One-ups
52 Capital of Ghana
53 Appalachian ___
54 Philosopher who tutored Aristotle
56 Kind of question you have a 50% chance of guessing correctly
57 German industrial city
61 F.B.I. agent, in old slang
63 ___ as a fox
65 In the style of, in cookery

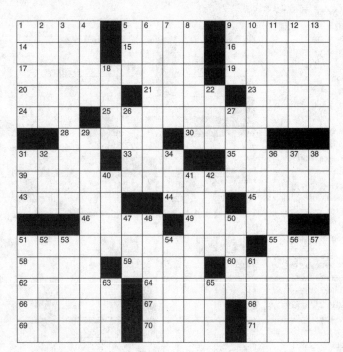

by Gary Cee

ACROSS

1 Run ___ (go wild)
5 Channel for renovators and remodelers
9 Flat-bottomed boat
14 Sleep-inducing pill?
15 Smallest Great Lake by volume
16 Japanese watch brand
17 Website for craftspeople
18 "___ No Mountain High Enough"
19 African animal that charges
20 What a last true believer might believe in
23 Pantry pests
24 "To thine ___ self be true"
25 "Don't clap yet"
33 Get rid of, as pencil marks
34 Took a chair
35 Bogus
36 Georgia's capital: Abbr.
37 Founder of the McDonald's empire
41 Tar Heels' sch.
42 Cuisine featuring drunken noodles
44 Home of Montreal: Abbr.
45 Teeming throng
47 "There was no choice but for me to say yes!"
51 Smog-monitoring org.
52 Medieval worker
53 It "cannot stand" per 1-Down . . . or a hint to 20-, 25- and 47-Across
59 Poles or Czechs
60 Dress that ends above the knee
61 Israeli submachine guns
63 [So funny!]
64 Head: Fr.
65 What may descend before the moon?
66 What tree rings represent
67 Put in a plane's overhead compartment, say
68 Ball that might attract a cat

DOWN

1 President Lincoln, informally
2 Closet pest that loves wool
3 Approximately
4 Features of touch-tone phones and A.T.M.'s
5 Physical well-being
6 Dolphins Hall-of-Fame QB Bob
7 Metal food containers
8 Docs for dogs
9 Illegible writing
10 Big cheeses
11 Egyptian goddess of life
12 Parking ticket penalty
13 Rock's ___ Fighters
21 Input, as data
22 Acknowledge as true
25 ___ bar (Hershey toffee confection)
26 Lead-in to -dontist
27 1980s–'90s NBC legal drama
28 Popped the question
29 Four, on many a golf hole
30 Swahili for "freedom"
31 Smooths the surface of, as wood
32 Show host
38 Light blue shades
39 Brynner of stage and screen
40 Dear: Fr.
43 Freeze, as a pond
46 Not on the clock
48 Grand works
49 Really digs
50 Go over again, as notes
53 Opposite of aweather, to a sailor
54 [So funny!]
55 CPR experts
56 Insects, berries and worms, for a robin
57 Old Testament book next alphabetically after Ezekiel
58 Designer Christian
59 Where pigs wallow
62 Center of the solar system

by Ed Sessa

ACROSS

1 Swiss peaks
5 Cracked open, as a door
9 DO something
14 Fabric for a winter coat
15 Sport with mallets
16 God, to Muslims
17 It's against the rules
18 Cocktail often served with a celery stick
20 Alternative to FaceTime or Google Hangouts
22 "Gil Blas" author Alain-René ___
23 Says "Our Father, who art in heaven . . . ," e.g.
25 Largest city in Switzerland
29 Yellowstone attraction
31 One of 100 in D.C.
32 ___ chi (martial art)
33 Pilgrimage to Mecca
34 Horse with a reddish coat
36 Incline
38 Thus
39 Eyes up and down
41 Adele, voicewise
42 Sign of the Ram
44 A son of Isaac
45 Utah national park
46 Film director Spike
47 Month with Earth Day: Abbr.
49 Many a marathon winner
51 Layers of rock
53 Greek sandwiches
54 Minor accident
56 From Holland
60 All settled up
64 Event on Black Friday or Cyber Monday
65 Typographic flourish
66 Actress Moreno or Hayworth
67 Enemy alliance in W.W. II
68 "Bad, Bad ___ Brown" (1973 #1 hit)
69 Ten C-notes
70 Little bites

DOWN

1 Grain bristles
2 "Here's the thing . . ."
3 My Little ___ (Hasbro toy)
4 Sandwich that might spill onto your hands
5 Police dispatch, for short
6 Pirate flag
7 Plants that yield a soothing gel
8 Aussie jumpers
9 Weapons in classic sci-fi
10 Fudd who hunts "wabbits"
11 Lead-in to carte or king
12 It goes back and forth on a street or up and down in an elevator shaft
13 "___ will be done . . ."
19 Groggy state
21 Triage centers, for short
24 Prefix with -naut
26 Home of Milano and Firenze
27 Ohio city that's home to the Pro Football Hall of Fame
28 Make a pass at
29 Setting for much of "La Bohème"
30 More jittery
31 Very cheap wine, in slang
33 Gets better, as a wound
35 Weatherman Roker and others
37 Revolving tray on a dinner table
40 Litigant
43 Hit the spot
48 Opposite of future
50 Silent sign of approval
52 Prenatal procedure, informally
53 California governor Newsom
55 Submarine sandwich
57 Conveyance preceding Uber and Lyft
58 Video segment
59 Gas company with toy trucks
60 Immigrants' class subj.
61 Geese's flying formation
62 Make a boo-boo
63 Keep pestering

by Lee Taylor

118

ACROSS

1 Rights org.
5 "It was 20 years ___ today . . ." (Beatles lyric)
8 Separately
13 Minnesota's "crazy" state bird
14 Roosters' mates
16 New ___, India's capital
17 Another name for [see shaded squares]
19 Souped-up engine sound
20 "19," "21" and "25" singer
21 Rod and ___ (fishing equipment)
23 The "M" of MSG
24 Give a quick greeting
26 Another name for [see shaded squares]
28 Refrigerated
30 Praiseful poem
32 Rug rat
33 Fawn's mother
34 "u r 2 funny!"
35 Macho guy
38 "We were just talking about you!"
43 What a radar gun measures
44 Rowing tool
45 Blackjack card worth one or 11 points
46 Homophone of 44-Across
47 Org. with the Suns and the Heat
48 Competed
49 Another name for [see shaded squares]
53 Nature photographer Adams
55 "And . . . it's gone!"
56 City about 280 miles NW of München
58 Pass, as a law
61 French place of education
63 Another name for [see shaded squares]
65 Incurred, as expenses
66 Distinguishing features of Mr. Spock
67 Place of banishment for Napoleon
68 "___, what is the meaning of life?" (modern query)
69 Holder of peas
70 Derrière

DOWN

1 ___ mater
2 Thick string
3 Toss and turn, say
4 Naked
5 "Gotcha!"
6 Throw in the trash
7 First word in a fairy tale
8 Word often ending in -ly: Abbr.
9 "If I may . . ."
10 Emotionally detached
11 French wine valley
12 East ___ (U.N. member since 2002)
15 Silverstein who wrote and illustrated "The Giving Tree"
18 King: Sp.
22 Certain Protestant
25 Virtual reality chamber in the "Star Trek" universe
27 Like many intramural sports
28 Successors to LPs
29 Klutz's cry
31 John who sang "Candle in the Wind"
36 Single and ready to mingle
37 "Good going!"
39 2005 sci-fi movie starring Charlize Theron
40 Actress Russell of "Felicity" and "The Americans"
41 Hot pepper
42 Played the first card
48 Thin wood finish
49 "Madama Butterfly," for one
50 Train that makes every stop
51 Lorna ___ (Nabisco cookie)
52 Southern Japanese port city
54 "Oh yeah? ___ who!"
57 Long jump
59 Havana's home
60 Skier's way up a mountain
62 Org. that cleans up oil spills
64 Drug to trip on

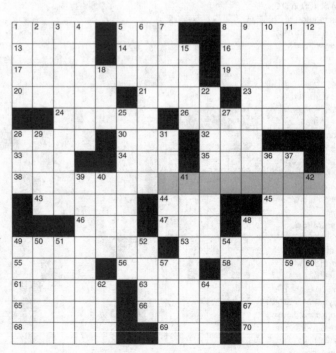

by Andrea Carla Michaels and Brian Thomas

ACROSS

1 Minute bits of water
6 What to do on the Sabbath, per the Bible
10 Fake
14 Large Starbucks order
15 Opera solo
16 Jay formerly of late-night
17 "Don't worry, everything will be fine!"
18 ___ pickle
19 Brainstorm
20 Heavens
21 Kind of economics, disparagingly
24 Restaurant handout
25 Team pulling a plow
26 Make more aerodynamic
30 "Ugh!"
33 Oktoberfest vessel
34 Nice poker holdings
35 "Thar ___ blows!"
36 Goofs up
37 Despises
39 "Enough already!"
40 Mindless card game for two
41 Room with a sink and medicine cabinet
42 Raise with ropes and pulleys
43 "Me day" destination
44 Theatrical show featuring traditional Irish music
47 Pre-Communist Russian ruler
49 Very long stretches of time
50 Ballpark illuminators
54 "Now I've got it!"
57 Regarding
58 Vegetable in Creole cooking
59 Poppy product
61 See romantically
62 Sizable bodies of water
63 Soup scoop
64 Opposite of "heel"
65 Part of Miss America's attire
66 Massive body of water

DOWN

1 Devices issued with some TV subscription packages
2 Really smell
3 Apt rhyme for "lonely"
4 School grp.
5 Four by four?
6 Element discovered by Marie and Pierre Curie
7 Guitarist Clapton
8 Material for ties or fine sheets
9 Big servings at a beer hall
10 Command to a base runner racing a throw
11 Committed to the pursuit of pleasure
12 All over again
13 Haunted house sound
22 Single-stranded genetic material
23 Old flames
24 Some diagnostic scans, for short
26 "___ in!" ("Get ready for a wild ride!")
27 Warm-colored pottery material
28 Spinning woodworking device
29 Winter sports surface
31 Selected
32 Didn't spoil, as food
33 Stitches
37 Reason for Rogaine
38 Rugged off-road ride, for short
39 Lead-in to "of Liberty" or "of Anarchy"
41 Oscar-winning Pitt
42 Chewbacca's companion in "Star Wars"
45 Go over again and again
46 Preceder of com, org or edu
48 Deschanel of "New Girl"
50 Cultural flashes in the pan
51 Future atty.'s exam
52 International retailer founded in Sweden
53 Mardi ___
54 Helper
55 Luau performance
56 "You said it!"
60 Source of campaign funds, for short

by Evan Kalish

120

ACROSS

1 Once around the track
4 Orange-nosed Muppet
8 Bump against in a crowd
14 Hospital dept. for the neediest cases
15 Document showing ownership
16 Loose, as shoelaces
17 *Something to "take me out to," in an old song
19 Hershey's coconut candy bar
20 "Sounds right to me"
21 Close buddy, in a modern coinage
22 Weight watcher's plan
23 *The presidency, e.g.
29 Desert refuges
31 Crushing defeat
32 Strip in a window blind
33 Trains like Chicago's
35 Estate in "Gone With the Wind"
37 George Gershwin's brother/partner
38 *Unpleasant tidings
42 *Means of locating one from the herd
44 Thrilla in Manila victor
45 Great ___ of China
47 Neither's partner
48 Where a nuthatch hatches
50 Circle
52 Not watertight
56 *Drama department production
59 Falco with Emmys for two different series
60 "Well, what have we here?!"
61 Flicks that sometimes end in weddings
63 Prohibit
66 "Wow!" . . . and a hint to both halves of the answers to the starred clues
67 Guarantee

68 TV talent show winner
69 Brian who coined the term "ambient music"
70 Performed some hip-hop
71 Big Board inits.
72 Trifling amount

DOWN

1 Sexual appetite
2 Maine's national park
3 Rhythmic heartbeats
4 Uptight
5 Dog strap
6 Account of one's earlier days
7 Keats's tribute to an urn, e.g.
8 Giant-sized TV, as in a stadium
9 Like a two-position electrical switch
10 Fills tightly
11 Its symbol is Sn
12 Was the front-runner
13 Some mag. workers
18 Triangular sail
24 Comprehended
25 1950s Communist-bashing grp. in Congress
26 Nastase of 1970s tennis
27 Astronomer Sagan
28 Latin list lopper, in brief
30 Whole lot
34 Gulped down
36 G.I. who's way off base
38 Prohibits
39 Knighted actor Guinness
40 Bowl or plate
41 Swill for swine
43 Kind of birth with a rear-first delivery
46 Texter's guffaw

49 Get ready for production, as a factory
51 Satirical work, like "Bored of the Rings"
53 Homes made of sun-dried bricks
54 "Madama Butterfly" dress
55 Response to "Who, me?"
57 Airport for a Bull or a Bear
58 Toys on strings
62 Spy on the inside
63 Boat propeller
64 ___ Today
65 Cough syrup amt.
66 Recycling container

by Lynn Lempel

ACROSS

1 Q-tip, e.g.
5 Largest continent
9 "___ your engines" (Indianapolis 500 directive)
14 Barbed-___ fence
15 Church recess
16 What bad headaches do
17 Thin variety of pasta
19 Home to Brigham Young University
20 End of a hangman's rope
21 Brand with the redundant slogan "Kills bugs dead"
23 Sign of things to come
24 Competitor of Home Depot and Lowe's
27 Outer layer of the eyeball
31 Pastures
32 ___ d'état
33 Trio traveling to Bethlehem
36 Religious doctrine
40 "Don't worry, it's not your fault"
43 Rolls's partner in autodom
44 Pigeon coop
45 Make, as a salary
46 ___ browns (breakfast side dish)
48 Things in eyeglass frames
50 Talk show host who won a season of "Celebrity Apprentice"
55 Bert of "The Wizard of Oz"
56 Stage item
57 King with a golden touch
62 "Horse around" or "rain cats and dogs"
64 Sudden insight . . . with a hint to 17-, 24-, 40- and 50-Across
66 More together mentally
67 Spiritual leader often pictured sitting cross-legged
68 Big seller of unassembled furniture
69 Lock of hair
70 CPR specialists
71 Small salamander

DOWN

1 Former ugly duckling, in story
2 One who tipples too much
3 Mythical ship sailed by Jason
4 Contents of an apiary
5 "That sure hits the spot!"
6 Next-best bowling frame to a strike
7 Basketball great ___ Thomas
8 Trapeze performer
9 Popular gas additive
10 Quickly raises, as windows
11 Doughnut shop attraction
12 Land ___ (British luxury vehicle)
13 Hearty steak
18 Big name in jets
22 Rapper/record executive Dr. ___
25 Arrived
26 Bit of baby talk
27 Surgery reminder
28 Fashion designer Chanel
29 Ethel's neighbor/pal, on 1950s TV
30 Odysseus and King Arthur, for two
34 Alaska's largest city
35 Classic muscle car
37 Transcript figs.
38 Measly
39 St. ___ (common church name)
41 College V.I.P.
42 Satan's domain
47 Drink slowly
49 Muppet with a falsetto
50 Most important invitees
51 Something used to catch speeders
52 What stars and bootblacks both do
53 So dull
54 Separately
58 Poker player's declaration
59 Hockey feint
60 Over again
61 "Now!," in the E.R.
63 "___ Doubtfire"
65 Juilliard field: Abbr.

by Ed Sessa

122

ACROSS

1 Kids around
6 Just about every character on "Brooklyn Nine-Nine"
9 Actress Christina
14 Created for a particular purpose, as a committee
15 Big fuss
16 Like the gases neon and argon, but not oxygen and hydrogen
17 Features of most hotel doors
19 City that's the setting for several van Gogh paintings
20 Denouement
21 Last words of a threat
23 Designer Gucci
24 Gibberish
26 Spins, as a baton
29 Flying insect with a narrow waist
30 Costa ___
31 Not do takeout at a restaurant
34 All the rage
37 What the starts of the answers to 17-, 24-, 48- and 60-Across do, punnily?
41 Mini-albums, for short
42 Like streakers
43 What you might build a winter fort with
44 Avid
46 Pickled green garnishes
48 Medical impostors, informally
53 "For ___ us a child is born . . ."
54 Muscular
55 Actress Kravitz of "Big Little Lies"
58 Singer of the 2015 #1 hit "Hello"
60 Bar with country music

62 More decisive
63 Ma that might baa
64 Knight stick?
65 Hermann who wrote "Siddhartha"
66 Fire truck's color
67 Olympians' blades

DOWN

1 Wisecrack
2 Home for Adam and Eve
3 What dogs do in the spring
4 Apex
5 Group of fish
6 Spy sent by Moses into Canaan
7 Three-time Pro Bowler ___ Beckham Jr.
8 Sheriff's group
9 Narrow inlet
10 Shabbily dressed
11 Film about food?

12 Belief system
13 "There, there"
18 Spheres
22 Dickens's "The Mystery of ___ Drood"
24 Steffi of tennis fame
25 Yin's partner
26 "Can't argue with that"
27 Puff of smoke
28 Performers in a rink
31 Animal at Yellowstone National Park
32 Beverage for a darts player, perhaps
33 Small amount
35 Frankenstein's assistant in "Young Frankenstein"
36 Basilica benches
38 Brief race, in brief
39 Things wizards wave
40 Mailing letters?

45 Places to take French classes
46 Bop on the head
47 Popular pattern for socks and sweaters
48 Suppress
49 Excessive, as influence
50 Catchall category
51 Actor Russell or director Cameron
52 Muscular
55 Certain basketball defense
56 "___ bitten, twice shy"
57 Just manages, with "out"
59 Before, in verse
61 Spigot

by Emily Carroll

ACROSS

1 Chapel recess
5 Not keep a secret
9 Egyptian "boy king"
12 Pirate's plunder
14 Follow closely, as a spy might a mark
15 Hot dog holders
16 Mattress giant
17 Like many missed field goals
18 The Phantom in "The Phantom of the Opera"
19 Places where rouge goes
21 Crash into from the back
23 Greeting in Rio
24 "Oh yeah? ___ who?"
26 Drew up, as plans
28 Brand of foam darts
30 Strikes (out)
32 "Them's fightin' words!"
33 Loving term for one caring for a sick child
35 High heels and others
37 World Cup cheer
38 Last line of a spreadsheet (as suggested by the shaded squares?)
41 Letter addenda, for short
44 Synthetic fabric
45 Horse's disapproving vote?
49 "In that case, sure"
51 Fasten
53 The East, to the West
54 "Hamilton" writer Lin-Manuel ___
56 Muscles that are targets of planking, informally
58 TV journalist Curry
59 Car opposite the locomotive
61 Late, as in making payments
63 Et ___ (and others: Lat.)
64 Gumbo vegetable
66 Decorated anew
67 What's left of a cigarette
68 Kind of roast
69 "Funny Girl" role for which Barbra Streisand won an Oscar
70 Network with an eye logo
71 Many craft brews, for short
72 Pricey seating option

DOWN

1 Leave hurriedly and secretively
2 Amy of "Parks and Recreation"
3 What a pitcher might have after a long game
4 Suffix with kitchen
5 "Oh, also . . . ," in a text
6 Den
7 Lent support to
8 More like tired eyes
9 Complete a double play, in baseball slang
10 Less than perfect
11 [Shame on you!]
13 Shaggy beasts of 53-Across
15 Strengthens, with "up"
20 "___ sells" (advertising catchphrase)
22 Betrays, in a way
25 Flavorful
27 Beats by ___ (audio brand)
29 Watch chain
31 "Drat!"
34 Rita of "West Side Story"
36 ___ vincit amor
39 ___ chicken (Indian dish)
40 "Well, aren't ___ pair!"
41 Certain lap dog, familiarly
42 Group that meets on the slopes
43 Narrow waterways
46 Adamant refusal
47 Enlivening, with "up"
48 Color manually
50 Hard thing to break
52 ___ and flow
55 Invite to one's penthouse, say
57 Peon
60 Funny Bombeck
62 Make well
63 "Black-ish" network
65 Coll.-level classes

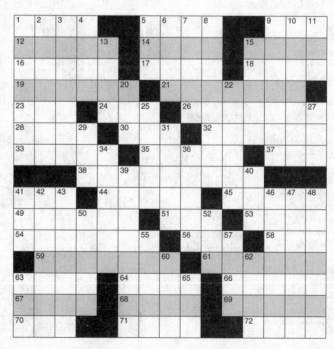

by Ross Trudeau

124

ACROSS

1 Shakespeare, for one
5 Product of Chevron or Shell
8 Many an electoral chart, in brief
13 State that's said to be "high in the middle"
14 Con's opposite
15 Take a deep breath
16 Where Army recruits go to start training
18 One placing a phone call
19 Houston-based food service giant
20 Three goals by the same player
22 Actor Wilson
25 Part of a Halloween costume
26 Shell game
30 Norway's capital
34 "___ the land of the free . . ."
35 Prefix with -vore or -scient
36 Made snide verbal attacks
38 Ostentatiously ornamented
40 ___ Arbor, Mich.
42 Shade akin to army green
43 "Finally!"
45 Avocado dip, informally
47 Antidiscrimination inits.
48 What snakes and lizards do periodically with their skin
49 British heavy metal band named for a torture device
52 What trees do in the wind
54 Coordinate, informally
55 All tuckered out
59 Go deeply (into)
63 ___ borealis
64 Game whose tokens have included the starts of 16-, 20-, 26-, 49- and 55-Across

67 Apache and Sioux, for two
68 Beetles, e.g., for short
69 It leads the orchestra in tuning
70 ___ Park, Colo.
71 Word before lion, level or legs
72 Square ones won't fit into round holes

DOWN

1 Short hairstyles
2 Greeting to a "matey"
3 Rivers, in Mexico
4 Company doing business mostly online
5 4.0 is a superb one, in brief
6 Cost an ___ and a leg
7 Student who's no longer a frosh
8 Cups and quarts
9 Controversial cosmetics ingredient
10 Its capital is Bamako
11 Trump impersonator Baldwin
12 Become more attentive, with "up"
15 Pet collar attachments
17 Some rodeo riders
21 "What ___?" (end of a riddle)
23 Stately tree
24 "99 Red Balloons" singer
26 Some fraternity party getups
27 Actor Ledger
28 Cry made while chest-thumping
29 Rock Starr?
31 Observed secretly
32 Flood blocker
33 Ancient theater

37 Slangy turndown of a request for help
39 Expectant papas
41 Convent residents
44 Bejeweled bands
46 Senator Klobuchar
50 Loaf with seeds
51 Cold treat on a stick
53 Tangle behind a computer, maybe
55 Calendar info
56 "___ is not to reason why . . ."
57 Stick-to-itiveness
58 License bureaus, for short
60 Part of an ear or brain
61 Certain YouTube posting
62 Seeing things?
65 Be indebted to
66 Secretive government org.

by Christina Iverson

ACROSS

1 Jab with a knife
5 Word after monkey or handle
9 Social class in India
14 Grammy winner India.___
15 Suffix with period or class
16 ___ : first :: omega : last
17 2011 film co-starring Owen Wilson and Rachel McAdams
20 "I'll wait to hear from you online"
21 Luau dish
22 Anger
23 Nat ___ (cable channel)
24 "You ___ be kidding!"
25 Football scores, for short
26 App introduced in 2010 to locate a missing Apple product
30 Prominent part of Dumbo
31 Ambulance workers, in brief
32 Lollygagged
35 "The ___ From Ipanema" (1964 hit)
37 Business operations, informally
40 Large, flat-topped hill
41 Environmentally conscious
43 The whole nine yards
45 33⅓ or 45: Abbr.
46 Mr. Spock player
50 Hurricane's center
52 Down with the flu, say
53 Opposite of WSW
54 Restroom, for short
55 ___ Lilly (pharmaceutical giant)
56 So-so
60 Decided otherwise . . . or a hint to the four sets of circled letters
63 Ancient land that lent its name to an order of architecture
64 Fe, chemically
65 "An apple ___ keeps . . ."
66 A little off mentally
67 Tenth of a dime
68 What just happened?

DOWN

1 Identical
2 Remove, as fat
3 Musical set in ancient Egypt
4 Not harmful
5 Title house owner in a 2000 Martin Lawrence comedy
6 It's gotta hurt
7 Cousin of a mouse
8 Goof
9 Building pictured on the back of a $50 bill
10 Pie ___ mode
11 Sugar-free lemon-lime soda
12 Place for a bronze medalist
13 Makes more bearable
18 ___ la Cité (bit of land in the Seine)
19 Quick snack
24 Place an "X" in the wrong spot on, say
26 So-so
27 Not pertinent
28 Abbr. on a pay stub
29 War zone for Rambo, informally
30 Silly Putty container
33 Annual TV award for athletes
34 Hoover ___
36 Director Spike or singer Brenda
38 "___ be my pleasure!"
39 Happening that's no big whoop
42 Small bouquet
44 Fan mags
47 "Blue" or "White" river
48 Like vinegar
49 Broadway belter Ethel
50 11th-century Spanish hero
51 "Hurray!"
56 In a little while, in poetry
57 Assistant
58 Chew (on), beaver-style
59 Ice cream brand
61 Small point to pick
62 About which someone might say "Get the lead out!"

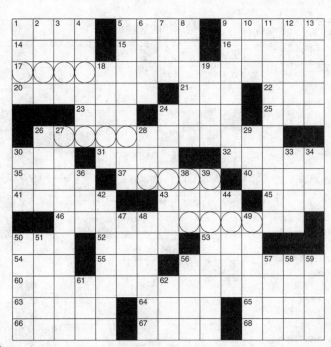

by Andrea Carla Michaels and Victor Barocas

ACROSS

1 Place underneath one's seat, say
5 "Dancing Queen" group
9 Barely open, as a door
13 "Ingredient" in molten chocolate cake
14 Decorated parade vehicle
15 Aloe ___
16 Pinnacle
17 Cuban dance
18 Sign for the superstitious
19 Message on a giant foam finger
22 Chem. or biol.
23 ___ of the tongue
24 Falsehood
27 Big jerk
30 "The Addams Family" cousin
32 Prayer endings
34 To the ___ degree
35 1999 rom-com with Freddie Prinze Jr. and Rachael Leigh Cook
39 Release, as a new album
41 Less than 90°, as an angle
42 "Livin' la ___ Loca"
43 "Anything Goes" song
46 Big California paper, for short
47 Go in
48 Orangutan, e.g.
49 Homophone of 24-Across
50 ___ Fridays
51 Target of a scratch
55 Grp. that might give you a hand on the shoulder?
57 Kellogg's Frosted Flakes slogan
63 Equestrian's "Stop!"
65 Turned white
66 ___-pads (hygiene product)
67 Lug along
68 Lesser of two ___
69 Norway's capital
70 Latch ___ (seize)
71 Not-safe-for-work transmission
72 Some whiskeys

DOWN

1 Cole ___
2 Alternative to glue
3 Above
4 Grows, as the moon
5 Grad
6 Woefully underperforms
7 Site of a biblical tower
8 Company that launched Pong
9 Stratford-upon-___
10 Award-winning sports journalist who went from ESPN to The Atlantic
11 Exist
12 Went for office
14 Signature accessory of Carmen Miranda
20 TV drama with spinoffs set in Los Angeles and New Orleans
21 Down Under gemstone
25 24 hours from now
26 Subject of a will
27 "Still . . ."
28 Well-muscled
29 "Don't hesitate to say what you want"
31 Silicon Valley industry
33 Cable channel that brought the world "Beavis and Butt-Head"
36 Take to court
37 Intro to boy or girl
38 Animals with spots
40 ___-K (early learning)
44 Lake with a namesake canal
45 Prickly ___ (variety of cactus)
52 Goes tap-tap-tap on a keyboard
53 Yearn for
54 DNA shape
56 Knight's protection
58 Angel's headwear
59 Hanukkah coins
60 "No sweat!"
61 Spinning part of a car
62 Spanish uncles
63 "Which person?"
64 ___ Solo of "Star Wars"

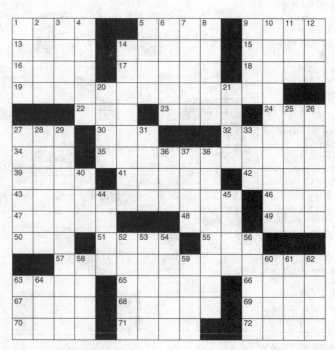

by Erik Agard

ACROSS

1 Color
4 Uninvited "guest" at a campsite
8 How great minds think, it's said
13 Finales
15 ___ of Capri
16 Money in Mexico
17 Enticing weblinks that suck people in
19 Card deck that includes The Sun, The Moon and The World
20 Pre-Olympian gods, in Greek myth
21 Collision sound
23 Chicken ___ king
24 Japanese cartoon art
25 Teen magazine founded in 1965
28 Kylo ___, Darth Vader's grandson
29 ___-friendly (green)
31 Police informer
32 Narrow advantage
34 Only three-letter sign of the zodiac
36 Like tabloid headlines
37 Hazard of being outside in the cold for a long time
40 Boys and men
42 Half-___ (latte option)
43 Map symbol for a capital, often
47 Furniture part that might leave a mark on a floor
49 Whistleblower?
51 1970s–'80s band with the hit "Don't Bring Me Down," in brief
52 Place for a blast offshore
54 Range that separates Europe from Asia
56 "I'll take that as ___"
57 Money in Japan
58 Come to light

59 Force back
62 Footwear that extends a little above the foot
64 Collection of treasure
65 "Anna and the King of ___"
66 Uncle's wife
67 Colorado resort
68 Votes in favor
69 Twinings product

DOWN

1 Unit of land that anagrams, coincidentally, to THE ACRE
2 Like some notebook paper
3 Making text adjustments
4 Handouts to lobster eaters
5 That: Sp.

6 "Get out of jail" story
7 Changes a name on, as a Facebook photo
8 Fitting
9 Pasture
10 Tel Aviv resident
11 Its mascot is a pitcher with a smiling face
12 Subject of a will
14 Swindle
18 Thigh/shin separator
22 Prudential competitor
25 "Little piggies"
26 Runaway victory
27 Makes yawn
30 Within reach
33 Key just above D
35 Non-Rx, for short
38 Depend (on)
39 Brother of TV's Lisa and Maggie
40 Bellyaching types

41 Genre for the Nigerian singer Wizkid
44 Detach, as a page
45 No longer available
46 ___ Stone (aid in deciphering Egyptian hieroglyphics)
47 Ancient Greek city-state
48 Be lenient
50 Be quietly angry
53 "Little Orphan ___"
55 Singer McEntire
58 Blighted trees
60 New Year's ___
61 Spy novelist Deighton
63 "The Jungle Book" python

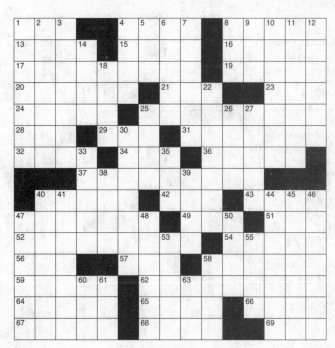

by Kyle Dolan

128

ACROSS

1 Londoner, e.g., informally
5 Get an A, B, C or D
9 Audibly expresses shock
14 "I do solemnly swear . . . ," e.g.
15 Like a billionaire
16 Rushed toward
17 Mystery-solving Great Dane of cartoons
19 Yoga pose
20 City where the "Gangnam Style" video was filmed
21 Architect Sir Christopher ___
23 Cribbage scoring piece
24 Logo art that changes almost daily
28 Place to buy a drink
31 Talk drunkenly
32 Fiction's opposite
33 50%
36 Thin as ___
39 Bobby of N.H.L. fame
40 Some household helpers . . . or an oral hint to 17-, 24-, 51- and 63-Across
42 Non-___ (label on some foods)
43 What salmon swim upstream to do
45 "I ___ a dream . . ."
46 Amount for the washer or dryer
47 Teller's partner in magic
49 Make better
51 Stir-fry ingredients, often
55 At least 35 years, for a U.S. president
56 Threesome
57 Car with a "T" logo
61 Plenty o'
63 Can't-miss
66 "Sauer" hot dog topping
67 From Bangkok, say
68 Lady ___, a.k.a. the First Lady of Song
69 Balm
70 Fermented rice wine
71 Cherished

DOWN

1 Office head
2 Marathon, e.g.
3 "Am ___ late?"
4 Something going through one's head
5 Poke one's nose (into)
6 Lend a hand
7 Angry expression
8 Beachfront
9 Breakfast mixtures with rolled oats
10 Some smallish batteries
11 Flower named for its resemblance to a winged beast
12 Group of experts
13 "All the world's a ___": Shak.
18 Ill-defined lump
22 Magazine heads, for short
25 Hawaiian honeymoon destination
26 Visual representation of data
27 "Give us this day ___ daily bread"
28 Money execs
29 Org. looking out for seniors' interests
30 Reusable material in a junkyard
34 A.L. West team, on scoreboards
35 TV's "Hawaii ___"
37 Popular Apple product
38 Vein of ore
40 Mark up, as a textbook
41 Nevada city
44 The third "w" in www
46 Hit with a beam of light
48 Counterpart of "neither"
50 URL starter
51 Pitching blunders
52 Ancient Greek gathering spot
53 Carefully sorts (through)
54 Commotion, in slang
58 Shoe part that's usually the first to wear out
59 Kinks song set "down in old Soho"
60 Many miles away
62 Jeep Grand Cherokee, for one
64 Sturdy tree
65 Tell whoppers

by Olivia Mitra Framke

ACROSS

1 Nothin'
5 Hula ___
9 [Um . . . I'm standing right here]
13 Team members that can pull more than their weight on the field?
14 Confess (to)
16 Volcanic output
17 Lines at the office?
19 Ran away from
20 Sandwich shop
21 Willing to accept danger
23 Attachment to a fishing rod
25 Before, to poets
26 Tidbit from Friskies
30 Typical physique for a middle-aged guy
34 Baseball hitter's stat, for short
35 Brief role in a film
37 "___ welcome"
38 Core muscles, in brief
39 Fugitive who, phonetically, is "hiding" in certain letters in 17-, 21-, 52- and 61-Across
41 Only four-term prez
42 Sphere or cube
44 "The Hate U Give" heroine
45 Black History Mo.
46 Sound system
48 Like a big dog's lick
50 ___ de cologne
51 Fly high
52 Lowest acceptable offers, in stock market lingo
58 Rice-shaped pasta
60 Orson Welles's "Citizen ___"
61 President between John Tyler and Zachary Taylor
64 Furniture retailer founded in Sweden

65 Disney's "Little Mermaid"
66 Actress Swenson of "Benson"
67 Small salamander
68 Handicrafts e-tailer
69 Tidy

DOWN

1 Wordlessly express approval
2 Removed from the schedule, as a TV show
3 Clichéd place to be marooned
4 Percussive piece of jewelry for an Indian dancer
5 "You wish!"
6 Stench
7 Hyatt alternative
8 Pizzas, e.g.
9 Fettuccine sauce
10 Angel's wear
11 Like 2, 4, 6, 8 . . .
12 Have it ___ (be assured of success)
15 Uttered a noise of disapproval
18 Place to insert a stud
22 It's bound to be of use to a churchgoer
24 Pastures
26 Lowbrow
27 Head of a monastery
28 Some chain theaters
29 Parts of udders
31 Neutral area between hostile forces
32 "___ in the court!"
33 Annual Louisville event
36 Gem with a play of colors
40 Love god
43 "Once again . . ."

47 Kind of board with letters printed on it
49 Flat, rectangular brooch
52 Comparable (to)
53 Japanese beverage often served hot
54 Was sure of
55 "___ to elaborate?"
56 Send off, as rays
57 Goes steady with
59 Gymnast Korbut
62 Wily
63 Krazy ___ (comics character)

by Sid Sivakumar

130

ACROSS

1 Part of a constellation
5 Facing the pitcher
10 Top Olympic medal
14 Parasitic insects that suck
15 Digestive aid brand
16 Song for a diva
17 Prefix with knock or lock
18 Position sought every six years
20 Close guy friend
22 In his Webby Lifetime Achievement Award acceptance speech (which is limited to five words), he said "Please don't recount this vote"
23 What unagi is, at a sushi bar
24 2014 film in which David Oyelowo played Martin Luther King Jr.
26 Home theater feature, maybe
31 "To thine ___ self be true"
32 Chinese-born architect who won a 43-Across
33 Well-behaved
35 Odometer button
37 Vietnamese New Year
38 Row of bushes
39 What to leave a phone message after
40 Got out of bed
42 Home heating option
43 Annual award for architects
47 Coat of paint
48 Chaney of silent films
49 Far ___ (a long distance away)
52 Safest course of action
56 Pop-up store opportunity for bargain hunters
59 Vogue competitor
60 Savings plans for old age, in brief
61 :
62 Cape Canaveral org.
63 Erotic
64 Newspaper pieces collected in the book "The Last Word"
65 "How do you like ___ apples?"

DOWN

1 Close with a bang
2 Funny Fey
3 Intermission preceder
4 Director Rob
5 Son of David in the Old Testament
6 One starting college, typically
7 Prohibit
8 Santa ___ winds
9 Wrecks beyond repair
10 Dashboard dial that goes from "E" to "F"
11 Cookie since 1912
12 Polygraph flunker
13 See socially
19 Red Muppet on "Sesame Street"
21 Kind of badge for a scout
24 One expressing contempt
25 Newspaper worker
26 Clean with a broom
27 Al ___, four-time Indianapolis 500 winner
28 Slow on the ___
29 Product for one pulling an all-nighter
30 Motherless calf
31 Heavenly sphere
34 Dover's state: Abbr.
36 Cause of seizures
38 Long lunches?
41 Lymphocyte-producing organs
44 Like most centers in basketball
45 Louisiana music typically featuring an accordion
46 Purpose
49 Thrift shop caveat
50 Taxi charge
51 Big-screen film format
52 Rorschach image
53 Lackluster
54 "If all ___ fails . . ."
55 Sports squad
57 Have a bawl
58 Ring master?

by Peter Gordon

ACROSS

1 Rafael on the tennis court
6 Mineral easily split into layers
10 Reached base feet-first
14 Michelle who wrote "Becoming"
15 Gem found in the Outback
16 Daly with a Tony for "Gypsy"
17 Like the ocean and most potato chips
18 Pianist Cliburn plays basketball defense?
20 Building extension
21 Spoken
23 Garb
24 TV host Behar takes mass transit?
26 Trash-loving grouch of children's TV
27 They bring tears to chefs' eyes
28 Young seal
30 "___ Pepper's Lonely Hearts Club Band"
31 Unstraighten, as a wire
32 Illinois city on the Illinois River
35 Actress Rogers flips out?
39 "That's enough!"
40 Kelly seen live in the morning
43 Hair goop
46 Martial arts level
47 Damsel
49 Battle site where Davy Crockett died
51 Singer Dylan has fun in the snow?
53 Change somewhat
55 "It's a shame . . ."
56 Bit of legislation
57 Businessman Gates gets out of the poker game?
59 Zola who wrote "J'Accuse . . . !"
61 "So that's how it is"
62 Fury
63 Printer powder
64 "___ of the d'Urbervilles"
65 Perfect world
66 Watermelon throwaways

DOWN

1 Rhinoplasty, informally
2 Mollusk with an iridescent inner shell
3 Wasting time
4 Quantity: Abbr.
5 Stores for future use
6 Date night staple
7 Apple tablets
8 Soup container
9 Bit of seaweed
10 Game recap figures
11 Words to songs
12 Dressed like RuPaul
13 Gobi or Mojave
19 Perfect world
22 Much-anticipated parts of Super Bowl broadcasts
25 "The Kiss" sculptor
28 Get in place for the camera
29 Large coffee vessel
32 Lowly laborer
33 Muff one
34 Month of many unhappy returns?
36 Fall asleep while watching TV, perhaps
37 "Today" show rival, for short
38 Spot for a football coach
41 Went by bicycle
42 a), b), c) and d), on a multiple-choice test
43 Stratagem
44 Fictional 6-year-old at the Plaza Hotel
45 Soup-serving utensils
47 Entrepreneur's deg.
48 Listings in a calculation of one's net worth
50 "And ___ to go before I sleep": Robert Frost
51 Award earned by a scout
52 Elizabeth of the "Avengers" series
54 Time long gone
58 Boy in knickers, perhaps
60 Bartender on "The Simpsons"

by Lynn Lempel

ACROSS

1 One-named singer with the hit "Dark Lady"
5 Regions
10 Little 'uns
14 The "R" of the Supreme Court's R.B.G.
15 Tropical fruit
16 Rude sound at the dinner table
17 Palo ___, Calif.
18 Milk source on a dairy cow
19 Asterisk
20 Flower of the tree Prunus mume
23 Bread bag closer
24 "How ya ___?"
25 Money back on a purchase
27 Month with no federal holidays
30 Hairstyle option
32 What cold weather may bring
33 Bringer of cold weather
36 See 8-Down
37 ___-hole (place to secrete oneself)
38 Word before whiz
39 Winged beast on the Welsh flag
42 Lindsay of "The Parent Trap"
44 Forms a mass of small bubbles
45 Place to store canned goods
46 "Take that!"
48 Nickname for grandma
49 Make a mistake
50 Game piece on which 20-, 33- or 39-Across might be pictured
56 One-named singer with the hit "Orinoco Flow"
58 Hairstyle option
59 Word between File and View on a menu bar
60 Gourmand's passion
61 The Little Mermaid
62 ___ mater
63 Small earring
64 "Gimme a C . . . !" and "Go team!"
65 Dee ___, director of "Bessie" and "Mudbound"

DOWN

1 "Oh, no!"
2 Main body of a ship
3 "___, Brute?"
4 Diamond shape, in geometry
5 Trinket worn for luck
6 Gas detected by home test kits
7 Gets discontinued
8 With 36-Across, in the distant past
9 Alpha Kappa Alpha, for one
10 Basic cable channel that's part of WarnerMedia Entertainment
11 "Awesome!"
12 Personality facet
13 Unrestrained shopping trip
21 Superlative
22 Work well together
26 Texter's "Oh, just remembered . . ."
27 Miles away
28 Impulse
29 Comment made with a pat on the back
30 Commotions
31 Bird whose head doesn't make a sound?
33 Close
34 Close
35 When tripled, a liar's mantra
37 "The Princess Diaries" actress Anne
40 Rainless
41 Travel all over the place
42 A.P. ___ (high school English course, for short)
43 Rampaging
45 Receptors for solar energy
46 Complaints
47 ". . . well, never mind then"
48 "To Kill a Mockingbird" or "The Maltese Falcon"
51 "Take this!"
52 One corner on a Monopoly board
53 Inactive
54 Garnish for a Corona
55 Scheduling guesses that might be updated in midair, for short
57 Subtract's opposite

by Erik Agard

ACROSS

1 Ogden who wrote "Farewell, farewell, you old rhinoceros, / I'll stare at something less prepoceros"
5 Largest continent
9 Responses to jokes
14 Female friend from France
15 Delivery vehicles
16 Make into law
17 Exact
20 Pale, as a face
21 First thing to do before changing clothes
22 UPS competitor
23 Weapon of mass destruction, informally
25 The Trojans of the N.C.A.A.
26 Girl's name that sounds like two letters of the alphabet
27 ___ Romeo (Italian auto)
28 "Cat ___ your tongue?"
30 Tows
31 Abandoned and helpless
35 Cheerios grain
36 Roman numeral X
37 Where someone who goes next is standing
45 Military vehicles
46 Hawaiian wreath
47 Google's red, yellow, green and blue "G," e.g.
48 Some canine sounds
49 Debtor's note
51 Put into office
52 Frat member
53 "They rooked me!"
56 Something that goes in a garage
57 Classic Michael J. Fox movie
60 Go off, as a volcano

61 Bat mitzvah dance
62 "Dancing Queen" group
63 Like good gossip
64 Twinkler in the night sky
65 ___ in show (canine award)

DOWN

1 Tusked marine mammal
2 Easy to get along with
3 Broadcast ender
4 Sneaky laugh sound
5 Stratford-upon-___
6 Makeup of a beach
7 As a matter of fact
8 What remains after a fire
9 Borders of skirts
10 "I'll take that as ___"
11 Dust buster

12 Like the ideal poker straight
13 Choices of hairdos
18 Place to take a bath
19 Key above a tilde
24 Welcome ___ (item at the entrance to a home)
26 Blunder
28 Pesky insect
29 Bus driver on "The Simpsons"
30 Hill on a beach
32 Charged particles
33 Suffix with Smurf
34 Where Samson slew the Philistines
37 Auto with a prancing horse logo
38 Tap the screen on a camera app, say
39 Special ___

40 Annual vaccination
41 Rapper ___ Kim
42 It goes "clink" in a drink
43 Dieting strategy that may lead to ketosis
44 Beseech
45 Made quick boxing punches
49 ___ Jima
50 Declarations at inaugurations
51 Professor's email address ending
53 ___-bitty
54 Sister and wife of Zeus
55 At a distance
58 Metric meas. of speed
59 Part inserted to close a cereal box

by Alex Eaton-Salners

ACROSS

1 Singer Bareilles who wrote and composed the music for Broadway's "Waitress"
5 Loses one's footing
10 Varsity letter earner, say
14 With 64-Down, shrinking body of water in Asia
15 Painter Matisse
16 Big name in running shoes
17 Diminutive Jedi master
18 It may include a backpack, boots and a water bottle
20 Slightly off
22 Gyllenhaal of "Brokeback Mountain"
23 Decompose
24 Japanese verse with 17 syllables
27 AOL alternative
29 Get a pet from the pound, e.g.
30 Word before chill or chimes
33 Busy worker in Apr.
36 Item compared to in "Who Wore It Best?"
38 Tony the Frosted Flakes mascot, e.g.
39 Expensive, as a product line
41 Seven Dwarfs' cry as off to work they go
43 Protection against kitchen splatters
44 Put on, as a play
46 Gratuity
47 Look closely (at)
48 Wipe the board clean
50 "Let's ___!" ("Dig in!")
52 Supermodel and longtime "Project Runway" host
56 Place for a mud bath
58 Appearance
60 "Swell!"
61 Toyota Prius and Honda Insight
65 Not fooled by

66 Fashion monthly with more than 40 international editions
67 "Well, golly!"
68 Luau instruments, for short
69 Like the part of a swimming pool with the diving board
70 "Gotta go!"
71 One of a set of four on a London taxi

DOWN

1 Doctor's request during a physical
2 Scent
3 Half-diameters
4 Juneau is its capital
5 "Quiet!"
6 Luau garland
7 Some office printers
8 Trojan War king
9 What things do in quicksand
10 Boozer's binge
11 Like some FedEx or DHL service
12 "Gotta go!"
13 Go-___ (kid's racer)
19 Thing of beauty
21 Out of the blue
25 X-rated stuff
26 Some newspaper essays
28 Big gulp from a bottle
31 Classic soda brand
32 What prices do in bear markets
33 English fellow
34 Prop for Santa Claus or Frosty the Snowman
35 Pleasant
37 Puppeteer Lewis
38 Connects (with)

40 Dance at a Jewish wedding
42 "Omigosh!"
45 Like many members of Gen Z, now
49 Barely make, as a living
51 Texter's "I didn't need to know that"
52 Actress Anne of "Wag the Dog"
53 Tall and lean
54 Speak
55 Glacier National Park sighting
56 Backyard building
57 1960s TV's "Gomer ___, U.S.M.C"
59 Vows exchanged at the altar
62 Dem.'s counterpart
63 Spanish king
64 See 14-Across

by Alan Arbesfeld

ACROSS

1 Home of Pago Pago
6 Muscles that get "crunched" in crunches
9 [Oh, well]
13 Things that go off when there's danger
16 Other: Sp.
17 Where to go for a fill-up
18 Mets' venue before Citi Field
19 Regarding
20 ___ San Lucas (Mexican resort city)
21 Member of a tough crowd, say
22 Firm place to plant your feet
24 "That sounds fun to me!"
28 "Auld ___ Syne"
29 Tuesday, in Toulouse
30 Ancient carver of stone heads in Mesoamerica
33 Move on a pogo stick
36 Viewing options popularized in the 1990s
39 ___ card (smartphone insert)
40 Beefcakes
41 Doesn't win
42 H₂O, south of the border
44 "So's your mama!," for one
45 Cash or stock, e.g.
50 Child's counterpart
51 Witty remark
52 "I'll get right ___"
56 Christmas carol
57 The terrible twos, e.g. (one hopes!) . . . or the start of 17-, 22-, 36- or 45-Across?

59 Protected, at sea
60 Floral garland
61 "Money ___ everything"
62 Opposite NNW
63 Halves of quarts

DOWN

1 Long story
2 "What a shame!"
3 What a sail is tied to
4 Approximately
5 Quantity: Abbr.
6 "I was with my girlfriend all evening," e.g.
7 Donation to the Red Cross
8 Info in a data breach: Abbr.
9 "Leaving already?"
10 "That seemed right to me, too"
11 Like most vegetation
12 Keep everything for oneself
14 Breakfast sizzler
15 And others: Abbr.
21 "Charming" jewelry?
22 What a skinny-dipper lacks
23 Kind of club for singers
24 Little rapscallions
25 Home of Timbuktu
26 Theatrical sort
27 Takes too much, in brief
30 Buckeyes' sch.
31 12, for ⅓, ¼ and ⅙: Abbr.
32 "The Marvelous ___ Maisel"
34 On top of
35 Surreptitious sound during an exam

37 Slightly
38 Word repeated in "Waste ___, want ___"
43 Throat
44 Give back to
45 Hawaiian porch
46 "Golden" things in the Bible
47 Light blue shades
48 Actress Essman of "Curb Your Enthusiasm"
49 Takes a chair
52 "Huh, funny running into you!"
53 Indian flatbread
54 "That true?"
55 Bills with Alexander Hamilton on them
57 Attys.' degrees
58 Drug also known as angel dust

by Eric Bornstein

136

3 ACROSS

1 Bay of Pigs locale
5 Constricting snakes
9 Actor who's the opposite of subtle
12 "Moby-Dick" captain
13 Large group on the move
14 Drink such as Pepsi
15 Justice's garb
16 Designation on many a driver's license
18 Bashful
19 Holder for coffee or beer
20 Attics
21 Farm building with a loft
23 Giant . . . with four of the five letters of "giant"
24 Bright, sunny area of a house
27 Setting at the prime meridian, for short
30 Pealed
31 "No more seats," in brief
32 Uncritically enthusiastic, colloquially
34 Confess (to)
36 Fruit in Newton cookies
38 Leather for fine gloves
39 Disdainful looks
41 Seoul automaker
43 Kind of ball that's supersoft
44 President after F.D.R.
45 Launch vehicle for many NASA missions
48 Miley who played Hannah Montana
49 ___ scale (rater of mineral hardness)
50 Insects that may emerge after 17 years
53 Play-___ (toy clay)
54 Boat that sailed while it rained for 40 days and nights
57 Ringlet on a salon floor
59 Bit of evidence for Sherlock
60 Author Rice who created the vampire Lestat
61 Pro Football Hall-of-Fame QB John
62 Like pie, it's said
63 "Gangnam Style" musician
64 Salon colorings
65 Dedicated poems

DOWN

1 Autos
2 "This doesn't look good . . ."
3 Wee one's sun protection
4 "Honest" president
5 Tennis champ Bjorn
6 Dot follower in a nonprofit's web address
7 In slow tempo
8 One of 100 on the Hill
9 Sharpen
10 Oodles
11 Destination of the rover Perseverance
13 Hunting dogs
14 ___ on the cob
17 Serious stage plays
19 Hosp. scan
22 Bicker
23 Groups of three
24 Next year's soph
25 Things to be mowed
26 Doggie's sound
27 Colorful dish with olives and feta cheese
28 Mother: Sp.
29 Larceny
33 Intuitive feeling
35 "Yes, proceed!," quaintly
37 Graduates of basic training, informally
40 Machine-gunned from the air
42 Weapons storehouse
46 In profusion, as plant growth
47 "This is so-o-o amazing!"
48 What you can't have and eat, too, it's said
50 Applaud
51 Charged particles
52 Big Apple school inits.
53 "Buenos ___"
55 Sly stratagem
56 Typically lost items that are "found" in the starts of 16-, 24-, 45- and 57-Across
58 Wonderment
59 Corporate biggie

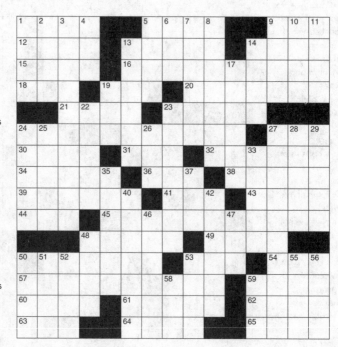

by Lynn Lempel

ACROSS

1 Goes a-courting
5 Buddies
9 Off-the-cuff remark
14 Em, to Dorothy, in "The Wizard of Oz"
15 Openly acknowledge
16 Garlic-flavored mayonnaise
17 "In ___ of flowers . . ."
18 Greets from across the way, say
20 Lollygags
22 That is to say, in Latin
23 Casually browse online
26 Word before taught or effacing
30 "Tiny" Dickens boy
31 Drop of golden sun
32 Skin care product
33 Extremes of the earth
35 Time of lament
36 Spends moolah
39 Little VW
40 Displays of huffiness
41 Fruit-filled pastries
42 Illusionist Geller
43 Modern term of endearment
46 ___ ID
47 Demonstrates some sleight of hand
51 Should arrive any minute now
53 Ice cream serving
54 Property along the ocean . . . or a hint to the starts of 18-, 23-, 36- and 47-Across
59 Dance at Jewish weddings
60 Hanukkah potato treat
61 Again
62 Shooting star, some might think
63 Lock of hair
64 ___ lily
65 Greek peak in Thessaly

DOWN

1 Financial ctr. in Manhattan
2 "Most definitely, monsieur!"
3 Feature of a Las Vegas "bandit"
4 Things, collectively
5 Dog's foot
6 Director DuVernay of "Selma"
7 The ___ Spoonful (1960s pop group)
8 Stockholm native
9 Companion of "oohs"
10 Low-calorie drinks
11 Ha-ha, online
12 Sick
13 Info in a Who's Who listing
19 Cry between "Ready" and "Go!"
21 Leisurely walks
24 Actress Berry
25 Centers of hurricanes
27 Extremities
28 Jacob's first wife, in the Bible
29 Cook in oil
32 Elements of a strategy
33 "Stupid" segments on old David Letterman shows
34 "We need help!"
35 Mixes with a spoon, say
36 Caspian and Caribbean
37 Reply in a roll call
38 E pluribus ___
39 Air-conditioning meas.
43 Needs for playing Quidditch
44 Is gaga over
45 Madrid's land, to locals
47 File shareable on a PC or Mac
48 Psychic glows
49 Sierra ___ (African country)
50 Sound preceding "Gesundheit!"
52 The Beatles' "___ Leaving Home"
54 Sandwich inits.
55 Put a ring on it!
56 Gobbled up
57 Less than zero: Abbr.
58 What it takes to tango

by Alan Massengill and Andrea Carla Michaels

ACROSS

1 State of irritability
5 Oaf
9 Undercoat of an oil painting
14 Cabernet, e.g.
15 Opening stake
16 "Oh, no, not ___!"
17 Stress between you and your former lover?
19 Carried
20 "In excelsis ___"
21 One of a pair of Old Testament books with female names
23 Place for a baseball team's insignia
24 Canada's Prince ___ Island
26 Thing your former lover said about you?
29 Straight up on a compass
32 The Beatles' "___ Leaving Home"
33 Historian's concern
36 "QB VII" author Leon
38 Halved
41 Former lover's text, e.g.?
44 What alumni do on important anniversaries
45 Write with a chisel on stone
46 Cold summer treats
47 Something Santa makes (and checks twice)
49 Aptitude
51 Former lovers' stances in photos?
54 Absolutely everything
58 See 27-Down
59 Juneau's home
62 Singer Grande, informally
63 Busy, as a restroom
66 Current lover who seems suspiciously preoccupied?

68 Chef's item for preparing apples
69 Panache
70 Author unknown, for short
71 Arrogant look
72 Things janitors keep on rings
73 Wagers

DOWN

1 Neighbor of a Norwegian
2 Vetoed
3 Dragging behind
4 Prop for a golf ball
5 Percussion instrument in a marching band
6 Hop ___ (get to work)
7 Texter's transition
8 Actress Zellweger
9 Gift of ___
10 Latin "I"
11 Like "Yeah, that'll ever happen"
12 Mideast's ___ Peninsula
13 End of a lunch hour, maybe
18 Emperor just before the Year of the Four Emperors
22 Prescriptions, for short
25 Villain in Shakespeare's "The Tempest"
27 With 58-Across, 1980s fad that "sprouted"
28 Soup legumes
30 Factual
31 Clues
33 The "p" of b.p.s.
34 It can chop a tree down . . . and then chop a tree up
35 Three-dimensional art
37 Ailing

39 Tale of ___
40 Come-___ (enticements)
42 Target of a cleanup
43 Fraidy-cats
48 Throat soother
50 Money to tide you over
51 Long stories
52 Arc lamp gas
53 Aerodynamic
55 Augusta's home
56 "Believe It ___!"
57 Yield and Right Turn Only, e.g.
60 Connector of a pair of wheels
61 Fix, as a dog
64 "Get it?"
65 Go wrong
67 Smidgen

by David Alfred Bywaters

ACROSS

1 Criticize, in slang
4 Something computers cannot write to or erase
9 Bottomless pit
14 "We ___ the World"
15 Nice smell
16 Like some handwriting . . . or tipplers
17 Up to, informally
18 Traveled in the front passenger seat
20 ___ at the wheel
22 Lye, chemically
23 Rainbow's shape
24 "Heavens to ___!"
26 Two-part
28 Captain of the 2012 and 2016 U.S. women's Olympic gymnastics teams
31 Degs. for C.E.O.s
35 Chap
36 Pants part that might need patching
37 Join a conference call, say
39 Silly
41 Monopoly properties you can't put houses on, in brief
43 End of a lasso
44 Screen ___ Guild
46 Rating between excellent and fair
48 Cry in a soccer stadium
49 Watermelon part that's spit out
50 Main ingredient in a protein shake, maybe
53 Great Lake with the shortest name
55 Mommy's sister
56 Kind of connection port on a PC
59 Overly fussy, say
61 Hit Broadway musical set partly in Paris, for short
64 What you might do to pass on an Interstate . . . or a phonetic hint to the starts of 18-, 28- and 50-Across

67 Letters before an assumed name
68 Sudden forward thrust
69 "___ could've told you that!"
70 ___ center
71 Choice words?
72 Believer in Jah, informally
73 Pack animal of Tibet

DOWN

1 Facts and figures
2 Part of the eye
3 Stamp on a milk carton
4 One tending a house during the owner's absence
5 Stops by
6 Towel holder
7 Eclipse or a black cat, some say

8 Ancient fortification overlooking the Dead Sea
9 Hi in HI
10 Spam spewer
11 Some quiet exercise
12 Appendage on a cowboy's boot
13 Align, informally
19 Elvis's "___ Dog"
21 Always, to a poet
25 Belgian river to the North Sea
27 "Hilarious!," in a text
28 Assumed name
29 Knight's weapon
30 Join the flow of traffic
32 Cocktail with tomato juice
33 Seating request on an airplane
34 Mocking smile
38 World's largest island nation
40 Lymph ___

42 Tofu bean
45 Hogs
47 Luxurious
51 Doctor, ideally
52 Lbs. and ozs.
54 Wild party, in slang
56 Sch. whose home football games used to include a live bear on the field
57 Avoid
58 Extracurricular activity for a musician
60 Molten flow
62 International furniture chain
63 "The Suite Life of ___ & Cody" (bygone teen sitcom)
65 Amnesty International, e.g., in brief
66 Super ___ (1990s game console)

by Anne Marie Crinnion

ACROSS

1 Something that may be bitten or busted
4 No laughing ___
10 "___-voom!"
14 DuVernay who directed "Selma"
15 Printing goofs
16 "___ go bragh!"
17 Entranceway to London's Hyde Park
19 Brainy sort
20 Starting stake
21 Summer coolers, for short
22 Eye makeup
23 "Yee-___!"
25 Kids' game that usually ends in a draw
28 Eternal
31 Ranter's emotion
32 "No lie!"
33 Designer Oscar ___ Renta
34 Go "boo-hoo-hoo!"
37 Singer Yoko
38 North Carolinian
40 Safe Drinking Water Act enforcer, for short
41 Japanese moolah
42 Actress Jessica
43 Speaks impertinently to
45 Classic pie crust ingredient
46 "The birds and the bees"
47 Popular food fish that's actually a flounder
51 Thanksgiving side dish
52 How the surprised are taken
53 Miracle on ___ (1980 Winter Olympics upset)
55 Greek cheese
58 Ending for "right to" or "put to"
59 How tall Barbie is . . . or what the ends of 17-, 25-, 38- and 47-Across are?
62 Connecting point
63 Joseph who wrote "Heart of Darkness"
64 Roth ___ (investment)
65 "S.N.L." bit
66 Artists' stands
67 What prevents a coffee cup from spilling

DOWN

1 Dalai ___
2 Any of several Russian czars
3 Temple on Athens's Acropolis
4 Blanc who voiced Bugs Bunny, Daffy Duck and Porky Pig
5 Geometry calculation
6 Political or religious pamphlets
7 Some ankle bones
8 And so on: Abbr.
9 When repeated, very enthused
10 Home to St. Mark's Basilica
11 "There ___ enough hours in the day . . ."
12 "Black-capped" or "yellow-throated" songbird
13 ___ the Giant (legendary 7'4" wrestler)
18 "If ___ Street Could Talk," 2018 film for which Regina King won an Oscar
22 California soccer club
24 Where Jericho and Bethlehem are located
26 First Nations tribe
27 Author Gay
28 "___, matey!"
29 Disappeared
30 Alternative to an elevator
33 UPS alternative
34 Staple of Asian cooking
35 German auto
36 Sunbathe
39 Start over
44 Aides, collectively
45 Old-fashioned keepsake
46 Like passwords, one hopes
47 Playing surfaces for croquet
48 Some downloadable reading
49 Tuesday, in Tours
50 Civic club whose motto is "We Serve"
54 And others: Abbr.
56 Singer Amos
57 Slightly
59 King beater
60 Pet with which you might form a tight bond
61 Drawbacks to a free app

by Gareth Bain

ACROSS

1 Insect that builds a paper nest
5 Takes a breather
10 Fig. of total economic output
13 Mayberry boy of 1960s TV
14 Make legal
15 Logs, for a fire
16 Riddled (with)
17 Lamented Princess of Wales
18 Sin often associated with green
19 Major-league team from the Motor City
22 Frozen H_2O
23 Female deer
24 Not quite right
27 Start of a tennis rally
29 "Hold your horses!"
32 Variety
34 Prefix often associated with green
35 "You there!"
36 Ballot for candidates of more than one party
40 One that gives a hoot?
42 Humor
43 Container at a beer bash
44 Number of minutes on hold before getting a customer representative
47 Greek I's
51 Two-___ sword
52 Precollege exam
54 Genetic material
55 Comes out ahead in either case . . . as exemplified by 19-, 29-, 36- and 44-Across?
60 Sources of much spam
62 Helper in conning
63 Nuptial exchange
64 At no cost
65 Stage before metamorphosis
66 Gambling mecca north of Carson City
67 Gave a meal to
68 Helpers
69 Genesis garden

DOWN

1 "People are saying . . ."
2 Each
3 Kitchen gizmo for flour
4 Equal
5 SiriusXM medium
6 Best of the best
7 Part of a window blind
8 Morrison who wrote "Beloved"
9 Gala giveaways
10 Item with cross hairs
11 Home of Carson City: Abbr.
12 Two-___ toilet paper
15 Physicist Enrico after whom element #100 is named
20 Three-time Pro Bowler ___ Beckham Jr.
21 Dine
25 "Nevertheless, ___ persisted"
26 Porker's quarters
28 Big shot, for short
29 Italian for "seven"
30 French for "here"
31 Tick-___
33 Green-fleshed fruit
36 How a person might feel after being passed over for a promotion
37 "Tiny" Dickens boy
38 Singer Urban
39 A narcissist has a big one
40 Be in debt
41 Lump of chewing gum
45 What good movie trailers do
46 Gridiron scores, for short
48 Sent to another team
49 "Can I get a volunteer? Somebody . . . ?"
50 Jeans brand popular in the 1980s
52 Do, as a crossword
53 Book of maps
56 Mallorca, e.g.
57 Bangkok native
58 Something "in the hand" that's "worth two in the bush"
59 Something an informant might wear
60 Very close pal, informally
61 Mine cart Contents

by John Guzzetta

ACROSS

1 Musical pieces for one instrument
6 Enthusiastic
10 Shoot out
14 Literary heroine who cries "Curiouser and curiouser!"
15 Apex predator of the ocean
16 Bear whose bed is too soft, in a children's story
17 Time to watch boxing on TV
19 Vases
20 To the greatest extent
21 "Hmm, I'm intrigued . . ."
23 .
24 Like getting a $2 bill in change
25 Gulped
28 Modern request to attend
30 One rushing in to save the day
33 Mess up
37 "___ your price!"
38 One of the housewives on "Desperate Housewives"
39 Tears out of the ground
41 Ingratiates
43 Noggin
44 ___ at hand
46 It's on the plus side
47 It makes your pupils constrict
50 Hawaiian kind of porch
51 Floral wreath
52 Stay in touch?
56 Venusians and Martians, in brief
57 Motion accompanying the words "There, there"
60 Martial art with a belt system
62 Carry
64 "Precisely!"
67 Greek counterpart of Cupid
68 Citrus fruit that won't win any beauty contests?
69 First-stringers
70 Snakes spawned by Medusa's blood, in Greek myth
71 Requests
72 Carried

DOWN

1 Less risky
2 Tony who played for 15 seasons with the Minnesota Twins
3 Large hybrid cat
4 Brownish-yellow
5 Goes down, as the sun on the horizon
6 Kind of pond in a Japanese garden
7 Small work unit
8 Sound in a long, empty hallway
9 Alliance HQ'd in Brussels
10 Bird in Liberty Mutual ads
11 Annual New Orleans celebration
12 Paradoxical response to a door knock
13 Pepsi Challenge, for one
18 Witness to the first rainbow in the Bible
22 Rooster's mate
26 Glittery addition to a Christmas tree
27 Info on an airport monitor, for short
29 Emanations to be picked up
30 Repeated question from an owl?
31 Come out
32 When doubled, a popular number puzzle
33 Foamy drink invented in Taiwan
34 Ones "standing by" in an infomercial
35 Railroad station
36 Cuban line dance
40 Explosive stuff
42 Slangy pronoun
45 Be sick
48 Au courant
49 Walk in the woods
52 ___-Lay (corn chip maker)
53 Enthusiastic
54 ___ Hunt, role for Tom Cruise in "Mission: Impossible"
55 "I've got this"
58 Water color
59 Harbor boats
61 Horse developed in the desert
63 Curve in the road
65 Kind
66 "My country, ___ of thee . . ."

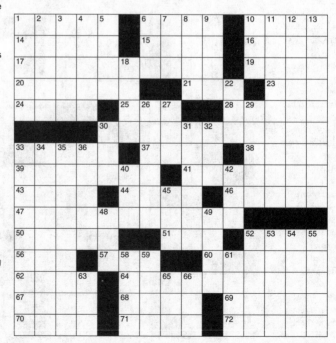

by Daniel Larsen and The Wave Learning Festival Crossword Class

ACROSS

1 "Aida" composer
6 "Do it now!"
10 "Play It as It Lays" author Didion
14 Embellish
15 Note to a staffer
16 "___ us a son is given"
17 Celebrations with hula dancing
18 Support the pasture entrance?
20 Calorie-counting regimen
22 Patron
23 Movies, informally
24 Check someone's parent to make sure she's of drinking age?
27 Pong game company
29 ___ loss for words
30 Russian space station until 2001
31 Liza Minnelli musical set in Berlin
33 Peaty places
35 Church official
37 Was introduced to the doctor?
42 Swirling currents
43 Lift on a ski slope
45 Small, lobsterlike crustacean
48 "Life Is Good" rapper
51 Thurman on the big screen
52 Derby entrant
53 Do some trawling at sea?
55 Gobbled up or down
56 Capital of Latvia
59 Sort
60 Criticize Sega's hedgehog design?
63 Annoying summer swarms
66 And all the rest, in brief
67 Actress Reid of the "American Pie" films
68 Not important
69 "___ we forget"
70 Truant G.I.'s infraction
71 Big health insurer

DOWN

1 Kilmer who played Batman
2 End of a college web address
3 Driver's furious fit
4 Priestly Gaul or Celt
5 Pants line that's partly hidden
6 Loudening device, informally
7 Blood fluid
8 "Famous" cookie guy
9 Head of the Holy See
10 Container for cider or ale
11 Equal in rank
12 Apparel
13 Dead end sign
19 Language of the Quran
21 "That's personal stuff I didn't need to hear"
24 Taxi
25 Itsy-bitsy bit
26 Corsage flower
28 Not stated directly
31 Brand of small planes
32 Radio journalist Shapiro
34 Frets (over)
36 Corrosive cleaner
38 Venomous vipers
39 Smartphone precursor, for short
40 Plentiful
41 Partner of rank and serial number
44 Dirty rotten scoundrel
45 Small place of worship
46 Turn on an axis
47 Large sports venues
49 "Don't ___!"
50 Scarlet letter, e.g.
53 Capital near the only one of the Seven Wonders of the Ancient World that's still largely intact
54 Redheaded orphan of Broadway
57 Smidgen
58 Bite like a beaver
61 Computer key not pressed alone
62 Ripken who played a record 2,632 consecutive major-league games
64 2,000 pounds
65 Mexican Mrs.: Abbr

by Lynn Lempel

ACROSS

1 Access code to use an A.T.M.
4 Inventor's goal
10 Banking org. founded during the Great Depression
14 Opposite of WNW
15 Dickens's "___ Twist"
16 Actress Garr of "Tootsie"
17 Unedited film
19 Degs. for entrepreneurs
20 Marie Curie's research partner and husband
21 In accordance with
23 Dress in India
24 East Coast rival of Caltech
26 Sam who directed the "Evil Dead" series
29 Off-the-wall concepts
33 Worker for a feudal lord
34 In a sorry state
35 Director Lee
38 "Gross! Nobody wants to hear that!"
39 ___ Majesty the Queen
40 One-named singer with the 2014 hit "Chandelier"
41 Beer brand whose popularity didn't drop during the 2020 pandemic, surprisingly
43 "Dead ___ Society"
45 Committed accounting fraud
49 Bind tightly
50 Newsroom figs.
51 Equipment in Monopoly and Yahtzee
53 Like Galileo, by birth
55 Make calm
57 Uptight sort
59 Shade of brown

62 "East of ___" (Steinbeck novel)
63 Supreme Court justice Stephen
64 Friend in France
65 "No thanks"
66 Extends, as a subscription
67 "Golly!"

DOWN

1 People in police "walks"
2 Book after Song of Solomon
3 What a revolution may usher in
4 Rich's opposite
5 ___ vera
6 Relative of a chickadee
7 "Little" girl in "Uncle Tom's Cabin"
8 Nullify
9 Number between dos and cuatro
10 Md. home to the U.S. Cyber Command
11 Gets intel from after a mission
12 $$$ put away for old age
13 Opposite of trans, in gender studies
18 Bit of embellishment
22 Before
24 Travelers to Bethlehem, in Matthew
25 "I Like ___" (1950s political slogan)
27 Hawaii surfing destination
28 Majorca, e.g.: Sp.
30 Kind of center with exercise machines
31 "Fine, stay angry!"
32 Nerd

35 No. on a bank statement
36 Koh-i-___ diamond
37 Band hangers-on
39 Tools for tilling
42 Gestures of approval
43 Goal after a master's, for short
44 Gomorrah's sister city
46 Professor's goal
47 Army knapsack
48 Devious plot
52 Spooky
54 Dict. tag
55 Dish from a crockpot
56 Not mine alone
57 Vim
58 Nutrition fig.
60 Kylo ___, Jedi-in-training seduced to the dark side
61 Bill, the Science Guy

by Evan Mahnken

ACROSS

1 Winning a blue ribbon
5 San ___ (California city, informally)
9 Trite
14 State as fact
15 Toy that hurts when you step on it barefoot
16 Defendant's excuse
17 Some deep voices
19 Kind of snack chip
20 Letter container: Abbr.
21 Have debts
22 When a plane is due to leave, for short
24 Sweetie
25 Her: Fr.
27 Parts of gas stoves
29 Like movies with considerable sex or violence
31 "___ a stinker?" (Bugs Bunny catchphrase)
32 Friendship
33 Kind of cherry
34 Electrical adapter letters
38 "Dee-lish!"
39 Mash-up
42 Paris street
43 One who's well-versed in the arts?
45 Stout and porter
46 Protein builder, informally
48 Sharp or sour in taste
50 Fireplace log holders
51 Where touchdowns are scored
54 Prefix with business or culture
55 Seoul-based automaker
56 Pretty ___ picture
57 "Dude"
58 College in Cedar Rapids, Iowa
61 They were released from Pandora's box
63 "That was fortunate"
66 Special Forces headgear
67 One of several on a superhighway
68 Analogy phrase
69 "Get Yer ___ Out!" (Rolling Stones live album)
70 School founded by Henry VI
71 Auto license issuers, for short

DOWN

1 Sweetie
2 Actress ___ Rachel Wood
3 Be in jail
4 Prefix with cycle
5 With 50-Down, place that this puzzle grid represents
6 Descartes who said "I think, therefore I am"
7 Grow older
8 Some facial jewelry
9 One holding people up
10 Pie ___ mode
11 Limited kind of market
12 Despise
13 Detroit pro team
18 "See? What'd I say!"
23 Polynesian kingdom
26 Tennis do-over
27 Brand of Irish cream liqueur
28 ___ Fáil (ancient crowning stone)
29 Skatepark feature
30 Bullets and such
33 United States symbol
35 "You did it all wrong!," e.g.
36 Hill on a beach
37 Corp. V.I.P.'s
40 Important pipes
41 Actress Robbie of "I, Tonya"
44 Cartoon "devil," informally
47 Damage in appearance
49 The U.S. has East and West ones
50 See 5-Down
51 Barely make it
52 Skin care brand since 1911
53 Milk and cheese products, collectively
57 Lead singer for U2
59 Airing
60 Self-identities
62 Meadow
64 Feedbag tidbit
65 Placed so as not to be found

by Joe Hansen

146

ACROSS

1 President George or George W.
5 Egypt's capital
10 "Casablanca" pianist
13 Start the poker pot
14 Catkin-producing tree
15 What an oenologist is an expert on
16 Anger, in the comics
18 ___ and crafts
19 Broadcast time
20 Ill-tempered
22 Harper who wrote "To Kill a Mockingbird"
23 Scores in baseball
25 Bit of sunshine
26 Refrain syllables in "Deck the Halls"
27 Burden too heavily
32 Honda model with a palindromic name
35 Uttered
36 Just sitting around
37 Letter after phi, chi and psi
38 Channel for Erin Burnett and Don Lemon
39 Make catty remarks from the side
40 Trig, calc, etc.
41 Lose color
42 Voice above baritone
43 Love, jealousy and anger
45 Classic distress call
46 Setting for TV's "Cheers"
47 German car once owned by General Motors
49 Intervening space
52 Peas and peanuts, for two
56 Perfect example
58 Presidential office shape
59 Nervousness, in the comics
61 Arm or leg
62 Country singer Steve
63 Norway's capital
64 Ginger ___
65 White-plumed wader
66 Many souvenir shirts

DOWN

1 ___ metabolism (energy expended at rest)
2 Remove a knot from
3 Mall unit
4 Group of buffalo
5 Prickly plant
6 Basketball great Iverson
7 Wedding words
8 Extend one's tour of duty
9 Arranged alphabetically, e.g.
10 In answer to the request "Talk dirty to me," she sometimes says "The carpet needs vacuuming"
11 Pantry-raiding bugs
12 See-through material
15 Odor, in the comics
17 Percussion instrument made from a gourd
21 Droopy part of a basset hound
24 No-goodnik
26 Idea, in the comics
28 Trellis-climbing plant
29 Chief Norse god
30 Big name in dog food
31 Cousin of an elk
32 Easy ___, easy go
33 Mosque leader
34 Presidential bill-killer
35 Read the U.P.C. of
39 Calm and impassive
41 Observe through a crystal ball, say
44 "Take me as ___"
45 Group of seven
48 Portrait painter Rembrandt ___
49 Bird in a gaggle
50 Enough
51 Money in Mexico
52 Name spelled out in a Kinks hit
53 Like Satan
54 Minecraft or Fortnite
55 Pirate's plunder
57 Gait slower than a gallop
60 Blunder

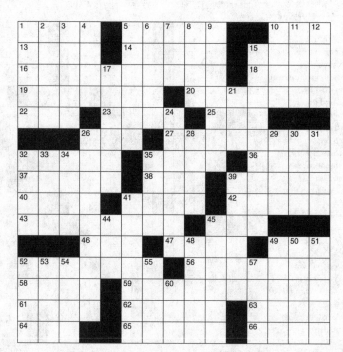

by Fred Piscop

ACROSS

1 "That ___ a close one!"
4 "Fingers crossed!"
9 Numbers for sports analysts
14 Everyone
15 A physicist or a fashion designer might work with one
16 Hall-of-Famer Banks a.k.a. "Mr. Cub"
17 ___ sauce (sushi condiment)
18 One reading secret messages
20 Edible casing in a stir-fry
22 Singer Carly ___ Jepsen
23 Narrow cut
24 Vends
26 Goddess who lent her name to the capital of Greece
28 Professional joke teller
32 Half-___ (java order)
33 Karl who co-wrote a manifesto
34 Home that may be made of logs
38 Pleasant smell
41 Collectible animation frame
42 Swiss Army ___
43 Point of connection
44 Revise, as text
46 Org. that might ask you to remove your shoes
47 Health professional who has your back?
51 Quick races
54 Title woman in songs by the Beatles and the Spinners
55 Brainstorming output
56 ___ Vegas
59 "Amen to that!"
62 Apt command to an 18-, 28- or 47-Across

65 Actress Mendes
66 Hilo hello
67 Home made of hides
68 1980s gaming console, in brief
69 Mortise's counterpart
70 Department store that once had a noted catalog
71 Like deserts and some humor

DOWN

1 The "murder hornet" is one
2 ___ vera (cream ingredient)
3 Quite cunning
4 "Brrr!"
5 Ruffian
6 Peculiar
7 Person equal to you
8 Idris of TV's "Luther"

9 "Believe me now?"
10 Item rolled to the curb for a pickup
11 Joint below the knee
12 Cross-promotion
13 Sealy competitor
19 500 sheets of paper
21 Farm enclosure
25 Orthodontic device
27 Target of a camper's scalp-to-toe inspection
28 Digitize, in a way
29 Set to zero, as a scale
30 Words to live by
31 Yellow flowers in the primrose family
35 Conclusion a die-hard might stay for
36 "Should that be the case . . ."
37 Close by
39 Hombre-to-be, perhaps

40 Tennis great Arthur
45 Fitness coach
48 Gran Canaria or Mallorca, por ejemplo
49 Wise sayings
50 Nicotine source, informally
51 Try to unearth
52 One-named singer of 2011's "Someone Like You"
53 New Jersey's ___ Hall University
57 Headings in a playbill
58 ___-Ball
60 Penultimate word in many fairy tales
61 "No sweat!"
63 Went on, as errands
64 Hoppy beer choice, briefly

by Eric Bornstein

148

ACROSS

1. Hacky ___ (game)
5. Loud, mocking call
9. Wash with vigor
14. Sound of a chuckle
15. Stare at, as a creep might
16. Principle to fight for
17. Z ___ zebra
18. Poetic foot with a short and a long syllable
19. Opposite of rural
20. Popular dog crossbreed
23. Common dog command
24. Coins in India
27. Have an invisible footprint
32. Whimper
35. ___ and tonic
36. Part of a test that may produce a hand cramp
37. Thurman of "Pulp Fiction"
38. Was gentle with
41. Before, in a poem
42. Tinker Bell, for one
44. Locale of the anvil and the stirrup
45. Vehicle that travels in only one direction
46. One version of poker
50. Actor Nielsen of "Airplane!"
51. Pants might burst at them
55. "S.N.L." offering
59. Commuting option
62. Grand achievement
63. Root used in making poi
64. "Party on, ___!" "Party on, Garth!"
65. Jane Austen novel
66. Lake that feeds into Lake Ontario
67. Newspaper opinion pieces
68. Optimistic
69. Ballpoint points

DOWN

1. Retrieves, as baseballs
2. "The Fox and the Grapes" author
3. Country along Argentina's entire western border
4. Model and reality star Jenner
5. Connect
6. "Holy moly!"
7. Furry red monster of children's TV
8. Having a new life
9. Made a bust?
10. Occupations
11. Massage
12. John Cougar Mellencamp's "R.O.C.K. in the ___"
13. "Big" name in London
21. Barely scrape (by)
22. Batman and Robin are a "dynamic" one
25. Artist's stand
26. Panic
28. Prior to now
29. YouTube clip, informally
30. Ceased
31. Green-___ monster
32. Botch, as a catch
33. Inbox accumulation
34. Relinquish, as one's rights
38. Tornadoes
39. "Wee" fella
40. Botch something
43. Take back, as an offer
45. Add sugar to
47. Skill of an archer
48. Marijuana cigarette, in old slang
49. Use a sentence with a "?"
52. Maker of Asteroids
53. Intermittently available fast-food sandwich
54. High heels, e.g.
56. Version that's just for show
57. Some Thanksgiving side dishes
58. Common dog command
59. Start of every ZIP code in Virginia
60. Genre for Megan Thee Stallion
61. Sailor's "yes"

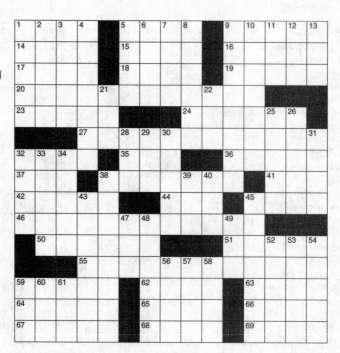

by Luke Vaughn

ACROSS

1 Thing with pads and claws
4 Wanders
9 Rod, reel, tackle box, etc., for a fisher
13 Olympic Dream Team inits.
14 Place in a mausoleum
16 ___ Tokarczuk, 2018 Literature Nobelist
17 Raiser of the dead?
19 Musk who founded SpaceX
20 Brainstorms
21 Go by, as time
23 Young Scottish lady
24 Financial aid for college that doesn't need to be repaid
27 Country whose name becomes another country if you change the last letter to a Q
29 Person with a basket or cart
31 Mixed-breed dog that's part spaniel
35 "Keen!"
36 "That's ___ from me" (refusal)
37 Arthropod that can roll into a ball
40 Melted chocolate, e.g.
41 Word before mall or poker
43 Right to cross someone else's land
45 Unlucky
48 Start of a newspaper article, in journalese
49 Busy person just before an election
51 Pledge drive giveaway
55 Fix, as a shoe
56 Insects that love wool
57 Appropriate initials of "stuff we all get"
59 Lures for magazine readers
62 Tiny bit
63 Minneapolis's twin city
64 Defining period
65 Banana leftover
66 Cosmetician Lauder
67 Singer Lana Del ___

DOWN

1 Necessity for a teacher
2 Carne ___ (grilled beef dish)
3 Home of Cardiff and Swansea
4 Yanks' foes
5 Number said just before "Liftoff!"
6 ___ snail's pace
7 Edible mushroom with a honeycomb cap
8 Gets a whiff of
9 Flips out
10 Best Actress nominee for "Juno"
11 "A long time ___ in a galaxy far, far away . . ." ("Star Wars" intro)
12 Tried to get elected
15 "Erin go ___!"
18 Elective eye surgery
22 Having tines
24 Big ___, nickname of baseball's David Ortiz
25 Unstable chemical compound
26 Grand ___ National Park
28 Comes down a mountain, in a way
30 Rummage (around)
31 Alternative to Venmo
32 Like some beer at a bar
33 Related to big business
34 Cry to a toreador
38 Hay unit
39 For whom a product designer designs
42 Against the law
44 Trending hashtag beginning in 2017
46 Dots on a transit map
47 What lieutenants do to captains
50 "Trees" in underwater forests
52 It's said to have the thickest fur of any mammal
53 When repeated, comforting words
54 Op-ed piece, e.g.
56 Farm animal that kicks
57 Sample a soda, say
58 Tribulation
60 Back muscle, for short
61 "What?," in Oaxaca

by Kate Hawkins

ACROSS

1 Tricked by doing something unexpectedly, with "out"
6 Original airer of "Doctor Who" and "Monty Python's Flying Circus"
9 Jitter-free jitter juice
14 Slicker, as winter highways
15 Writer Tolstoy
16 Speechify
17 Sweet item at a bakery
19 One streaming on Twitch, maybe
20 Wedding vow
21 "In memoriam" piece
22 Drinking mug
23 Keep watch while a homeowner's away
26 Drs.' co-workers
27 Categorize
30 Zippo
32 Not an original, informally
33 Bar-to-bar activity
37 Skater Lipinski
38 Heart chambers
39 What a smiley or frowny emoji indicates
41 What a speaker or musician may adjust before starting
43 Immature bug
44 Tidy
45 Wagered
46 Green item proffered by Sam-I-Am
48 Easy win
52 Tally mark
54 The "E" in PG&E: Abbr.
55 "___ unto them that call evil good, and good evil": Isaiah
58 In flames
59 Small advances . . . or the progression suggested by the ends of 17-, 23-, 33-, 41- and 48-Across
62 Police trainee
63 Convenience for withdrawing $$$

64 Appear out of nowhere
65 Maples and myrtles
66 Mattress's place
67 Nervous about what's ahead

DOWN

1 Island group whose name is a brand of water
2 Got an A on
3 Metric weight, informally
4 Slithery fish
5 Thirsty
6 Ill-defined shapes
7 Misrepresent
8 Fillies' counterparts
9 Sirius . . . or Lassie, for example?
10 It was: Lat.
11 Job for a cinematographer

12 Didn't go out to a restaurant
13 Some greenery on forest floors
18 Give a drubbing
23 Roman poet who wrote "Seize the day, put no trust in the morrow!"
24 Spanish gold
25 Member of an early Andean civilization
27 Field of Frida Kahlo or El Greco
28 Coal deposit
29 Shore phenomenon around the time of the new and full moons
31 Tablecloth fabric
33 School fund-raising org.
34 "Ode on a Grecian ___"
35 Action on eBay

36 Score before 15, in tennis
38 Lead-in to girl or boy
40 Family man
42 Scented bags
43 Rap's ___ Wayne
45 R-rated, say
46 Put into law
47 Succeed in life
49 Shish ___
50 Gladden
51 Popular health info source
53 First Nations group
55 Shed tears
56 Magnum ___
57 Catch sight of
60 Place to get a mani-pedi
61 Truckload unit

by Jennifer Nutt

ACROSS

1 Talon
5 Sign of a wound's healing
9 Wallace of Fox News
14 Smog, e.g.
15 "This is terrible!"
16 White gemstone
17 White gemstone
18 Australian wind instrument
20 "Hmm, good enough"
22 Way over there, quaintly
23 Minor fender damage
24 Fish eggs
25 Caller of balls and strikes
27 Kind of pudding
29 Hole-digging tool
31 U.S. president who was once president of the Harvard Law Review
33 Fleming who created 007
34 Third-largest city in Japan
36 Rubber gaskets
38 System of underwater mountains
41 Dine at a restaurant
42 Artist's stand
43 Two auto-racing Unsers
44 Exchange
46 City between Phoenix and Mesa
50 Horror film villain with a knife
52 Reggae relative
54 Atmosphere
55 Fraternity party costume made from a bedsheet
56 Forlorn
58 Belfast's province
60 Wedding attendant
63 Book after II Chronicles
64 Like the smell of burning rubber
65 ___-European languages
66 Threadbare
67 Sch. in New Haven, Conn.
68 Insolent talk
69 Place to store garden tools

DOWN

1 Church groups in robes
2 Take-it-with-you computer
3 Pink-flowering shrub
4 In good health
5 Wicked city in Genesis
6 Ho ___ Minh City
7 Tennis's Murray or Roddick
8 Capital of Colombia
9 Lifesaving subj. taught by the Red Cross
10 Longtime "Project Runway" host Klum
11 Communicating by wireless
12 Severe place of confinement
13 "Think" for IBM and "Think outside the bun" for Taco Bell
19 Fills with love
21 Exactly below, on a map
26 Jab
28 ___ lobe (part of the brain)
30 "Dumb" bird
32 Sounded like sheep
35 Tyne Daly or Keira Knightley
37 Not busy
38 Spanish resort island, to locals
39 Delivery room announcement
40 Scottish refusals
41 Locale of Oakland and Alameda
45 One of the Three Musketeers
47 Unleavened bread for Passover
48 Justin Trudeau's father
49 Quick trip to a store and back, e.g.
51 "Sexy ___" (Beatles song)
53 Words of praise
57 Comic Carvey once of "S.N.L."
59 Stitches
61 End of a school's email address
62 Two forms of them are found in 18-, 38- and 60-Across

by Stanley Newman

ACROSS

1 "Hell ___ no fury . . ."
5 Shout from Scrooge
8 Capital of 71-Across
14 Suffix with switch
15 Life is short and this is long, per Hippocrates
16 Places to sweat it out?
17 Painter Chagall
18 *Restaurant chain known for its coffee and doughnuts
20 Classic fund-raising event
22 1950s presidential inits.
23 Writer/illustrator Silverstein
24 Premium theater spot
28 Nobelist William Butler ___
32 Spy grp.
33 Word often following "best-case" or "worst-case"
36 Nobody special
40 Arizona tribe
41 Pepsi and Coke
43 ___ the Terrible
44 Conundrum
46 Estrange
48 Chick's mother
49 Corporate shuffle, for short
50 Early challenge overcome by Joe Biden
54 Actress Rae of "Insecure"
57 Container for a caterer
58 Some brandy fruits
62 *Pancake topping
66 Seized property, for short
68 Makes flush (with)
69 Greek "H"
70 Weather often associated with Vancouver

71 Place associated with the answers to the starred clues
72 Professor's deg.
73 Village People hit with a spelled-out title

DOWN

1 ___ and haw
2 Saudis, e.g.
3 Bar mitzvah text
4 *Leafs-watching time, maybe
5 Cave dwellers
6 "Salome" solo
7 Web designer's code
8 Bear, in un zoológico
9 Road goo
10 Pharaoh known as a "boy king," informally
11 Battery terminal
12 "A Fish Called ___"
13 Plus on the balance sheet
19 Lang. in which "peace" is "shalom"
21 Home of the ancient philosopher Zeno
25 Representative Alexandria ___-Cortez
26 Mark, as a ballot
27 *Important step after erring
29 Esoteric
30 Spanish uncle
31 Word before system or power
33 ___-crab soup
34 Opposite of pro
35 Commercial prefix with Pen
37 Eggs in a lab
38 D.C. player, formerly a Montreal Expo

39 Toronto-to-Montreal dir.
42 Pint at a pub
45 ___ Gala (big event in fashion)
47 Guitarist Clapton
50 Poison ___
51 Gaily sung syllables
52 Remove, as a brooch
53 Unit of sunshine
55 Cook, as mussels
56 Savory jelly
59 Elite sort of school, for short
60 The "R" of R.B.G.
61 Apple tablet
63 N.Y. airport with many flights to Toronto Pearson
64 Cease
65 Govt. agency for retirees
67 "Cat ___ Hot Tin Roof"

by Emma Craven-Matthews

ACROSS

1 Message to the office staff
5 Old South American empire
9 Mosquitoes and gnats
14 Grp. that sets oil benchmarks
15 Start a game of cards
16 American living abroad, e.g.
17 Traveled by subway?
20 Mexican mister
21 Seat at the bar
22 ___ v. Wade
23 Magnum ___ (greatest work)
25 Like a recovering hosp. patient, perhaps
27 "Would you call the elevator for me?"
32 Japanese sash
33 Piece of pizza
34 Foreordained
38 Chrissy of "This Is Us"
40 Pet peeves?
42 Wine region of California
43 Dickens's "___ House"
45 "Naughty" and "nice" things for Santa
47 Letters after nus
48 "Hand me a flashlight"?
51 Admits, as an offense
54 Pouty expression
55 "Well, lookee here!"
56 "Person" that speaks in beeps and boops
60 Home that might melt
63 Use French fries as legal tender?
66 Constellation with a "belt"
67 Good amount of land to build on
68 Golf ball stands
69 Insurance giant
70 Worker paid day by day, maybe
71 Hairstyle that may have a pick

DOWN

1 Cuts the grass
2 Fencing sword
3 Amish cousin
4 Tentacled sea creatures
5 Vow before a judge
6 The latest
7 Jargon
8 Cher, e.g., voicewise
9 Remove, as a sticker
10 Part of an office telephone no.
11 Period of rapid growth
12 It's a no-no
13 Like some ski slopes and prices
18 Pharmacy offerings
19 Certain pueblo dweller
24 ___-evaluation
26 Ending of seven Asian countries' names
27 Item in a purse
28 Whom Cain slew
29 Drawers for money
30 Nail the test
31 Dog walker's need
35 Reason some people move to the Cayman Islands
36 More than amazing
37 Dot's counterpart in Morse code
39 Microwaves
41 Long part of a rose
44 Hurricane that was the subject of 2006's "When the Levees Broke"
46 Keeping a stiff upper lip
49 Any minute now
50 Should, informally
51 Hot après-ski beverage
52 Alternative to Chicago's Midway
53 Put forward, as a theory
57 Dinghy or dory
58 First word of a fairy tale
59 Six years, for a U.S. senator
61 Abbr. on a 0 button
62 ___ buco
64 Sweetie pie
65 Leaf-turning time: Abbr.

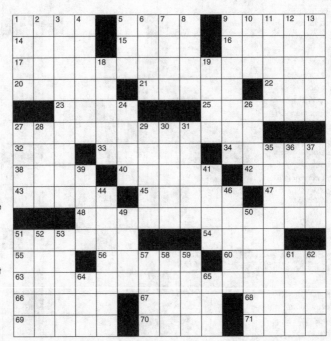

by Barbara Lin

ACROSS

1 Swedish group that once comprised two married couples
5 With skill
9 Opening to be filled
12 Sagan who hosted TV's "Cosmos"
13 Like calamari . . . or overloaded circuitry
15 Catches, as a crook
16 Game with Mrs. White and Professor Plum
17 Kendrick with 13 Grammys and a Pulitzer Prize
18 "The Little Rascals" assent
19 Model/TV host on a record five Sports Illustrated Swimsuit Issue covers
22 Envision
23 Top card
24 Skeeves (out)
26 Spirited horse
28 "Grey's Anatomy" actress
30 Snitch (on)
32 Rink surface
33 It has a double helix
34 "Full Frontal" host
38 Dem.'s counterpart
40 Prefix with -phyte or -lithic
41 Down Under hopper, informally
42 North Carolina senator who unseated Elizabeth Dole
45 Kind of tea from India
49 Highly decorative
50 Parts of the body that are "crunched"
52 Blue, e.g. . . . or a rhyme for "blue"
53 Female scholars . . . or a hint to 19-, 28-, 34- and 42-Across
57 Cher or Adele

58 Storehouse of valuables
59 "Pick me, pick me!"
60 Like, for-EV-er
61 See 64-Across
62 ___ mortals
63 Fashion monogram
64 With 61-Across, like some typefaces
65 Small wire nail

DOWN

1 Means of entering
2 "Swan Lake," for one
3 Crème ___ (dessert)
4 Downwind, at sea
5 Company with a spokesduck
6 Aid for a twisted knee or ankle
7 Result of a twisted ankle
8 Opposite of nah
9 Beverage with a lightning bolt in its logo
10 Leave in the lurch
11 "Gangnam Style" rapper
14 Got close
15 Negative reply to a general
20 ___ President
21 G.O.P. color on an election map
25 ___ Na Na
27 1970s measure that fell three states short of passing, in brief
28 Not publish yet, as a scoop
29 German's "Alas!"
31 Completely different lines of thought
34 Typical John le Carré work

35 Unionized teachers' grp.
36 Brag
37 Greek goddess of the dawn
38 Studio behind "It's a Wonderful Life"
39 Pincered insects
43 Gaza Strip governing group
44 Devoured
46 Common pronoun pairing
47 Roman goddess of the dawn
48 Intertwined
50 Choreographer Ailey
51 Fortifies, with "up"
54 Metal deposits
55 Places to hold discussions
56 Dead zone?
57 Temp's work unit

by Jessie Bullock and Ross Trudeau

155

ACROSS

1 Prattle
8 Public square
13 Like records stored for research
15 Popeye's profession
16 Browser's start-up point
17 Buses, as tables
18 Freshly
19 Nonsense
21 Second letter after epsilon
23 Tic-tac-toe win
24 Prohibit
25 Worthless talk
31 Fury
32 Financial claim
33 Hanker (for)
37 Neighs : horses :: ___ : sheep
39 Landscaper's tool
42 Raft for a polar bear
43 =
45 It's not odd
47 R.N.'s touch
48 Unintelligible jargon
52 "So that's it!"
55 Itinerary preposition
56 Inexperienced reporter
57 Twaddle
61 Line down the length of a skirt
65 Signing-on info
66 Sudden thought that makes you go "Wow!"
68 Poisons
69 Goes through hurriedly, as during a robbery
70 Jacket alternatives to buttons
71 "Huh?" . . . or a possible response to 1-, 19-, 25-, 48- and 57-Across

DOWN

1 ___ Men, group with the 2000 hit "Who Let the Dogs Out"
2 Scientology founder ___ Hubbard
3 Highest point
4 Where spiders get their information?
5 Way cool
6 Actress Saint of "North by Northwest"
7 Alternative to Prego
8 1957 title role for Frank Sinatra
9 In ___ of (replacing)
10 March goes out like this, as the expression goes
11 "___ the Greek"
12 Pyromaniac's crime
14 Old NASA moon-landing vehicle
15 Great Dane of cartoons, informally
20 Short hairstyle
22 ___ Aviv, Israel
25 Match up (with)
26 Baghdad's land
27 Boyfriend
28 Bartlet of "The West Wing" or Clampett of "The Beverly Hillbillies"
29 Figure made by lying in the snow and waving one's arms
30 Sports official, informally
34 Voice below soprano
35 Chocolate/caramel candy
36 Narrow part of a bottle
38 Droop
40 Christmas ___ (December 24)
41 Mao Zedong was its leader
44 1960s hippie gatherings
46 Big Apple sch.
49 Hawks and doves
50 Rebuke to a dog
51 "Pygmalion" playwright, for short
52 Borders
53 Wears, as clothes
54 Amazon's virtual assistant
58 Icicles and burning candles both do this
59 ___ Lingus
60 Mineral springs
62 Individually
63 Singer/lyricist Paul
64 Classic computer game set on an island
67 "Gangnam Style" singer

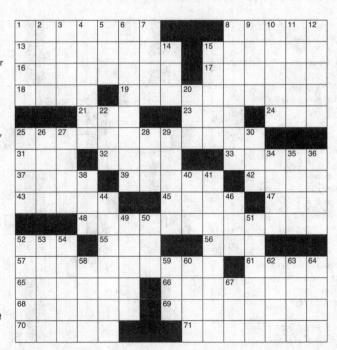

by Sarah Keller and Derek Bowman

ACROSS

1 Health resorts
5 Georgia fruit
10 Tuxedo shirt fastener
14 ___ and every
15 Person with a microphone
16 Finest-quality, informally
17 Word after pen or pet
18 Company behind Battlezone and Asteroids
19 "Wheel of Fortune" play
20 Late "Jeopardy!" host Alex
22 V.I.P.'s
24 Quibbles
26 Stack of papers
27 Stand-up comic Margaret
29 "___ whiz!"
30 Approx. when to get to the airport for a pickup
31 Unknown, on a sched.
34 German "mister"
36 "Gnarly, dude!"
38 Bold response to a threat
40 Ready for picking
41 Written material of no consequence
43 Flying: Prefix
44 Enthusiastic response to "Who wants candy?"
46 Internet image file, familiarly
47 Cyclops and Wolverine, for two
48 Title for Paul McCartney or Elton John
49 "The Lord of the Rings" baddie
51 ___ Castellaneta, voice of Homer Simpson
53 "To a Skylark," e.g.
54 Lure of a coffee shop
56 Grouchy Muppet
58 Be sociable

61 Like Satan and some owls
64 BBQ spoiler
65 Supermodel Campbell
67 DVR system
68 Shoestring woe
69 Trio or quartet
70 Rare blood type, for short
71 "The Brady Bunch" threesome
72 German industrial hub
73 Shrek, for one

DOWN

1 Email outbox folder
2 Jack who once hosted "The Tonight Show"
3 Wile E. Coyote's supplier
4 Biblical land with a queen
5 Athlete's goal in competition
6 911 call respondent, for short
7 Hail ___ (cry "Taxi!")
8 Cherry-colored
9 Absolute chicness
10 Malia Obama's sister
11 Quaint greeting
12 Quart, liter or gallon
13 Cozy retreats
21 Tiny bit of work
23 Brown, as a roast
25 One clapping at a circus?
27 Cuomo of CNN
28 Model and TV host Klum
32 Revealed, as one's soul
33 The devout do it on Yom Kippur
35 Big sporting goods retailer
37 Found groovy
39 Honeycomb stuff

42 Relative of Rex or Rover
45 Choice on "Let's Make a Deal"
50 Chocolate beans
52 Sgt., for one
55 Amounts on Monopoly cards
57 "Star Wars" droid, informally
58 Really bugs
59 Prefix meaning "super-tiny"
60 Male turkeys
62 Anytime at all
63 Onetime Venetian V.I.P.
66 U.K. medal accepted and then returned by John Lennon, in brief

by Alan Massengill and Andrea Carla Michaels

ACROSS

1 Has a long shelf life
6 The Lone Star State
11 Place to recover one's health
14 Native Alaskan
15 Vigilant
16 Arctic diving bird
17 Identity of 61-Across
19 "The X-Files" agcy.
20 Like some reactions and flights during storms
21 Blacktop
23 Opposite of WSW
24 Part of a needle
26 Something a diva may sing
27 Overhaul, as a show
30 Originator of 61-Across
34 Teacher's note accompanying a bad grade, maybe
35 Rapper Shakur
36 Television portrayer of 61-Across
40 Singers Bareilles and Evans
41 Steer clear of
44 Film portrayer of 61-Across
48 Contract stipulation
49 Lead-in to "man" in superhero-dom
50 Flow out, as the tide
52 Youngster
53 Pain in the lower back
57 "Just leave!"
60 Back talk
61 Co-founder of the Justice League
63 Bullring cheer
64 Humdingers
65 Plainly visible
66 Something to write on or crash in
67 Ocular inflammations
68 Smell or taste

DOWN

1 Corporate hierarchies, figuratively
2 Property recipient, in law
3 Rising concern?
4 ___ fish sandwich
5 Linger
6 Late in arriving
7 Inventor Whitney
8 "Hercules" character who got her own show
9 Rainbows, for example
10 Part of an assembly instruction
11 Mac browser
12 Go ___ (become listed on a stock exchange)
13 Japanese dogs
18 "I don't want to hear a ___ out of you!"
22 Meat in many an omelet
25 Teach
28 Adams who played Lois Lane in "Man of Steel"
29 Brainy bunch
31 Tax return pros
32 Batmobile, e.g.
33 Eight-related
35 Poi ingredient
37 Mid-June honoree
38 Longoria of "Desperate Housewives"
39 Some delivery people
42 Weather map lines
43 Easing of international tensions
44 Racehorse's gait
45 Eagle constellation
46 Thrown (together)
47 Shoot the breeze
48 Trucker who relays "bear traps"
51 Confer divine favor on
54 Leather-punching tools
55 Joint malady
56 Just
58 "Terrible" time for tykes
59 Relocate
62 Payment ___

by Kathy Wienberg

158

ACROSS

1 Periodically sold fast-food item
6 What melting ice cream cones do
10 Swindle
14 Actress Donovan of "Sabrina the Teenage Witch"
15 "Othello" villain
16 House in Mexico
17 Less risky
18 Cast celebration at the end of filming
20 Feelers
22 Frozen expanse
23 Olive ____ (Popeye's sweetie)
24 It can be used for welcoming or wrestling
25 Charged particle
26 Souvenirs from Havana
31 Loosen, as laces
32 CPR performer
33 Occupants of kennels
37 Subjects in which women have traditionally been underrepresented, for short
38 Letters between thetas and kappas
40 Human rights attorney Clooney
41 FX network's "____ of Anarchy"
42 Mediterranean, e.g.
43 Prenatal test, for short
44 Going from nightspot to nightspot
47 Soccer star Hamm
50 Buffoon
51 "____ you serious?"
52 Worker just for a summer, maybe
54 Source of healthful fat and fiber
59 Certain online board for discussion of a topic
61 Like an angle less than 90°

62 Old Russian ruler
63 Brontë's "Jane ____"
64 Ethical
65 Divisions of tennis matches
66 Rocker Lou
67 Popular vodka brand, for short

DOWN

1 Flat-topped hill
2 Extended family
3 Break in relations
4 "Understood"
5 Without exception . . . as in dry counties?
6 Hindu festival of lights
7 Hard to find
8 Supermarket chain that's big in small towns
9 Breakfast treats from a toaster
10 Read over
11 Rap's ____ B
12 Member of a major-league team with a name that's out of this world?
13 Like an early Central American civilization
19 "Nobody ____ Baby in a corner" (line from "Dirty Dancing")
21 Big Apple inits.
24 One of a baby's first words
26 Talk a blue streak?
27 "Do ____ others . . ."
28 Vitamin also known as PABA
29 Goals
30 Do better than average, gradewise
33 Like a just-used towel
34 Hilton alternative
35 Profit
36 Trudge

38 Bahamian or Fijian
39 Egg: Fr.
43 Ways to earn college credits while in H.S.
44 Part of a reactor
45 Stopped
46 60 minuti
47 Sprays
48 Occupied
49 Chance for a hit
53 Blunders
54 Command to a cannoneer
55 Edinburgh native
56 Continental currency
57 And others: Abbr.
58 Where you might find the starts of 18-, 26-, 44- and 59-Across
60 Easter egg colorer

by Martha Kimes

ACROSS

1 Get ready to hem, say
6 Hankering
10 Thomas Edison's middle name
14 Boxing venue
15 ___ Hari (W.W. I spy)
16 Russian "no"
17 City where you won't find the Eiffel Tower
19 Cotton processors
20 Not to mention . . .
21 Org. for which Jason Bourne works in "The Bourne Identity"
22 Author Charlotte, Emily or Anne
24 City where you won't find the Parthenon
28 1965 Alabama march site
30 Saintly "Mother"
31 Utopian
32 Plant on a trellis
33 1950s White House nickname
36 "Nuts!"
37 Gets ready, as for surgery
39 Insect flying in a cloud
40 CPR pro
41 Sound made by helicopter rotors
42 Rings, as a church bell
43 Yasir of the P.L.O.
45 What the back of a store might open onto
46 City where you won't find Virgil's Tomb
50 Pal of Jerry on "Seinfeld"
51 Driveway material
52 QB successes
55 Excessive drinking or gambling
56 City where you won't find the El Greco Museum
60 Neck and neck

61 Cousin of "Kapow!"
62 Refrigerator compound
63 Cincinnati squad
64 "Well, that was stupid of me!"
65 Commuter boat

DOWN

1 Owner of the first bed that Goldilocks tested
2 Tehran's land
3 "Here comes Poindexter!"
4 Prefix with lateral or cellular
5 Easter-related
6 "Let me rephrase that . . ."
7 Receipt line just above the total
8 Org. that runs Windy City trains
9 Fading stars
10 Kind of goat that's the source of mohair
11 Not upstanding, in either sense of the word
12 20-ounce size at Starbucks
13 Confounded
18 Bit of attire you might learn how to put on while using a mirror
23 Valentine's Day flower
25 I.R.S. agent, quaintly
26 More than a couple
27 Part of a golf club
28 Pro or con, in a debate
29 Dutch cheese
33 All riled up
34 Curly-leafed cabbage

35 Online market for craftspeople
37 What follows the initial part of a master plan
38 Repeated bit in jazz
39 Neuter, as a horse
41 Small, brown bird
42 Join in couples
43 1986 sci-fi sequel set in deep space
44 Venerated symbols
46 "Not a chance!"
47 Still surviving
48 Walked nervously back and forth
49 Far out
53 Designer Christian
54 ___ Pictures, one of Hollywood's Big Five studios
57 Cry of surprise
58 Drink like a cat
59 Bauxite, e.g.

by Jeff Stillman

ACROSS

1 Modern Persia
5 Arnaz who loved Lucy
9 Become acclimated
14 "Finding ___" (2003 Pixar film)
15 Alternative to a wood, in golf
16 Name said twice before "Wherefore art thou"
17 In vogue
18 Oscar the Grouch's home
20 International Court of Justice location, with "The"
22 Bulls in a bullfight
23 Old weapon in hand-to-hand combat
26 Place for a nest
30 Digital picture, maybe
31 Less fresh
33 Emergency call in Morse code
36 Wild guess
39 With 60-Across, one of two U.S. vice presidents to resign from office
40 Result of a football blitz, maybe
44 Completely anesthetized
45 Exercise that might be done on a mat
46 Cover gray, perhaps
47 Like vinegar
49 "Holy moly!"
52 English channel, informally, with "the"
53 Bit of fashionable footwear
58 Home in the shape of a dome
60 See 39-Across
62 Dreaded cry from a boss . . . or a hint to the ends of 18-, 23-, 40- and 53-Across
67 Listing in a travel guide
68 Texas ___ (school NW of Houston)
69 Dealer in futures?
70 It's a plot!
71 News media
72 Rival of Harvard
73 Wood for boat decks

DOWN

1 Not give an ___ (be stubborn)
2 Give a makeover, informally
3 Spanish girlfriend
4 "Hey, don't jump in front of me in the line!"
5 Insult
6 Time span sometimes named after a president
7 Rather, informally
8 Where work may pile up
9 Best Picture winner set in 1-Across
10 Swims at the Y, say
11 "The Walking Dead" network
12 Cause of a sleepless night for a princess, in a fairy tale
13 Whole bunch
19 Greek counterpart of Mars
21 Yadda, yadda, yadda
24 Zap with a light beam
25 Contest attempt
27 Classic work that's the basis for Shakespeare's "Troilus and Cressida"
28 "Goodness gracious!"
29 Not having two nickels to rub together
32 "For shame!"
33 Fledgling pigeon
34 Weight whose abbreviation ends in a "z," oddly
35 "Sexy" lady in a Beatles song
37 Blood grouping system
38 Hole-some breakfast food?
41 Nickname for the Cardinals, with "the"
42 Prefix with -pod or -partite
43 Zoo enclosure
48 Foal : mare :: ___ : cow
50 Lawyers' org.
51 Took care of someone else's pooch
54 Loud
55 Land with a demilitarized zone
56 Delayed
57 Four: Prefix
59 Insets in a crown
61 Line on a calendar
62 Talk, talk, talk
63 Regatta implement
64 French "a"
65 Wriggly fish
66 Dr. of hip-hop

by Kevin Christian and Andrea Carla Michaels

ACROSS

1 Entry in a doctor's calendar: Abbr.
5 Thanksgiving vegetable
8 100, gradewise
13 Rage
14 "Early in life, I had learned that if you want something, you had better ___ some noise": Malcolm X
15 Take care of
16 Journey
17 Jessica of "Fantastic Four"
18 Reeves of "The Matrix"
19 One on the front lines during a crisis
22 Do a new production of, as a recording
23 Alternative to carpeting
24 "You bet!"
25 Became a millionaire, say
29 "It's ___ of the times"
33 Finish first in a race
34 Factory-inspecting org.
35 Crown wearer at a fall football game
39 Bullets and such
40 Since, informally
41 Turn topsy-turvy
42 Tight embrace
44 Advanced deg. for a writer or musician
46 Hair tamer
47 ___ Trench (deepest point on earth)
52 Unmanned Dept. of Defense aircraft
56 Rob
57 With 58-Across, collective consciousness . . . or a hint to the ends of 19-, 35- and 52-Across
58 See 57-Across
59 "Beats me!"
60 Qatari leader
61 Lake bordering Cleveland
62 Kick up ___ (be unruly)
63 Web portal with a butterfly logo
64 Bucks and does

DOWN

1 ". . . happily ever ___"
2 Prize money
3 Light beam splitter
4 Like a go-go-go personality
5 Certain New Haven collegians
6 "Allahu ___!" (Muslim cry)
7 Brunch, e.g.
8 Invite on a date
9 One's equals
10 Faucet problem
11 ___ Reader (magazine with the slogan "Cure ignorance")
12 Like lemons
14 Dull photo finish
20 "Bye Bye Bye" boy band
21 Incorrect
25 ___ and tonic
26 "Understood"
27 Fifth-most-common family name in China
28 Round of applause
29 "Moby-Dick" captain
30 A few
31 "___ Be" (2010 #1 hit by the Black Eyed Peas)
32 Raphael Warnock and Jon Ossoff, for two
33 Rapper ___ Khalifa
36 Circular windows
37 Popular gift shop purchase
38 Actor Dennis
43 Greetings
44 Singer Gaye
45 Cooking device in a fast-food restaurant
47 Injures
48 Ready for battle
49 Bête ___
50 "Little Orphan ___"
51 Passover observance
52 ___-certified organic
53 Double ___ Oreos
54 DoorDash list
55 Not us

by Soleil Saint-Cyr

162

ACROSS

1 Actress/TV host ___ Pinkett Smith
5 The five weekdays, for short
10 33⅓ r.p.m. records
13 Satan's doings
14 One who's habitually afraid
16 Constitutional proposal supported by the National Woman's Party, for short
17 "Scenter" of the face
18 Musical key with three flats
19 ___ Man ("The Wizard of Oz" character)
20 "You did it!"
22 Wandered off
24 "Without further ___ . . ."
25 Harp-shaped constellation
27 Annual science fiction awards
28 China's Chairman ___
30 Snake in "Antony and Cleopatra"
32 Ballyhoos
34 Celestial bodies
36 Like the newest gadgetry, informally
38 No longer employed: Abbr.
39 Winnie-the-___
40 J'___ (Dior perfume)
41 Very
42 Banned pollutant, in brief
43 Lead-in to -stat
44 "Ant-Man and the ___" (2018 film)
45 Relative of a steam bath
47 Narrow inlet
48 Actor Mahershala
49 City NNW of Detroit
51 Times before eves, in ads
53 Deliverer of a noted speech upon the death of Martin Luther King Jr. (4/4/1968), in brief
56 February 29
58 Acquired lots of, as money
60 ___-country (music genre)
61 Music genre for Billie Eilish
63 Dog in Oz
64 Cry to a toreador
65 Monster slain by Perseus
66 Nincompoop
67 Unhappy
68 Tirades
69 St. ___ Bay, Jamaica

DOWN

1 Liz's best friend on "30 Rock"
2 Shun
3 Completely confused
4 Away from the wind, at sea
5 "Star Trek" doctor
6 Lara Croft, in film
7 Conflict in 2017's "Wonder Woman," in brief
8 Light browns
9 Foam
10 "Loosen up!" . . . or a hint to this puzzle's circled letters
11 "High" figure in a tarot deck
12 Beach composition
15 Noted sex therapist
21 Musical artist "from the block," familiarly
23 In the past
26 Queens neighborhood
29 What's left in a fireplace
31 Layer of soil that never thaws
33 Octagonal street sign
34 Antonyms: Abbr.
35 Record label co-founded by Jay-Z
36 "That'll be the day!"
37 Corp. V.I.P.
41 Messenger bird in the Harry Potter books
43 Bicycle built for two
46 Tiny bite
48 Question
50 Horse whisperer, e.g.
52 Patatas bravas, calamares and others
54 Naturally belong
55 They may be hard to untie
56 Vientiane's land
57 Who says "When you look at the dark side, careful you must be"
59 "At Last" singer James
62 Wordplay joke

by Portia Lundie

ACROSS

1 Dance at a Jewish wedding
5 Chemical that burns
9 Chevrolet muscle car
15 Home of Waikiki Beach
16 Capital of Italia
17 Brought (in), as a fish
18 Vittles
19 "What ___ goes!" (parent's pronouncement)
20 Task to "run"
21 "Rush Hour" and "21 Jump Street" [Clinton]
24 Handle with ___
25 Friends' opposite
26 TV deputy of Mayberry [Bush 43]
30 Leave out
34 Kind of port on a computer, in brief
35 Zig or zag
36 Anticipate
38 Dines
40 The Buddha is often depicted meditating under it [Obama]
43 Numerical information
44 Windsurfing locale NE of Honolulu
46 "Superfruit" berry
48 Cousin of "Kapow!"
49 Boxer Spinks who upset Muhammad Ali
50 C-D-E-F-G-A-B-C, e.g. [Biden]
53 Linguist Chomsky
55 Small amounts
56 What the starts of 21-, 26-, 40- and 50-Across are, for the presidents in their clues
63 Prayer beads
64 Shoe bottom
65 More than magnificent
68 Smitten
69 ___ of Arendelle (Disney queen)
70 Device that makes a TV "smart"
71 Combs to add volume, as a stylist might
72 Not the passive sort
73 Part of a stairway

DOWN

1 Go ___-wild
2 Means of propelling a boat
3 Baked dessert made with tart red stalks (and loads of sugar)
4 University that's also a color
5 Really dry
6 Cloth used to cover a teapot, to Brits
7 Apple on a desktop
8 Respite from work
9 ___ brûlée (French custard)
10 Spray can mist
11 ___ Griffin Enterprises
12 Jai ___
13 Actress Russo
14 Probability
22 Mosquito repellent ingredient
23 Author Edgar Allan ___
24 Like Friday attire in some offices
26 Play music in the subway, perhaps
27 Rhyming title character who plays the tuba in Cuba, in a Rudy Vallee song
28 Curly hairstyle, for short
29 1099-___ (bank-issued tax form)
31 Plenty steamed
32 Stuck, with no way out
33 Sums
36 Orchard fruit
37 Identify
39 ___-mo
41 Howard's best friend on "The Big Bang Theory"
42 "Green" prefix
45 Rattle
47 "What ___ be done?"
50 Founder of Communist China
51 Made smile
52 Basketball players, quaintly
54 "You got that right!"
56 Legal order
57 Sharpen
58 ___ Verde (locale of San Juan's airport)
59 Tourist town in northern New Mexico
60 By oneself
61 "If all ___ fails . . ."
62 Letter starter
66 Prez with the pooch Heidi
67 Saucer go-with

by Meconya Alford

ACROSS

1 Players in a play
5 In a while
9 One of thousands in a Rose Bowl float
14 Prussia's ___ von Bismarck
15 Fat-removing surgery, for short
16 Extreme pain
17 Caboose's location
18 Ode or sonnet
19 Shrink in fear
20 "Jeez, lighten up, will ya!"
23 Ram's mate
24 How extraterrestrials come, we hope
25 Think (over)
27 U.S. intelligence org.
28 Bombarded, as with questions
32 Ham it up
35 Score in hockey
36 Black-tie charity event, maybe
37 Sprinted
38 As expected
39 Long-running CBS drama
40 The "I" of I.M.F.: Abbr.
42 Abode in Aachen
43 Earns
45 Pieces of evidence in court
47 Grammy winner ___ Nas X
48 Replacement for the lira and mark
49 Faux fireplace items
53 U.S.S.R. intelligence org.
55 Like medical expenses you pay for yourself
58 Long (for)
60 What a wheel connects to
61 Author/journalist Quindlen
62 Cove
63 Order to someone holding a deck of cards

64 Game suggested by the ends of 20-, 38- and 55-Across and 11- and 34-Down
65 On/off device
66 Fare for aardvarks
67 Letters on love letters

DOWN

1 Welsh ___ (dog)
2 Had dinner at home
3 It may say "Forever"
4 Suffering
5 Andean animal valued for its wool
6 Mythical woman after whom element 41 is named
7 Abbr. below "0" on a phone
8 Iditarod terminus
9 Get stuff ready to go
10 Bigheadedness
11 Bar from the bathroom?
12 Once more
13 Muse's instrument
21 "At ___, soldier!"
22 Enough
26 Turkey drumstick, e.g.
28 Hocus-___
29 Évian and Perrier
30 Alternatively
31 Speaker's platform
32 Great Lake with the smallest volume
33 Tail-less cat
34 Alert
35 Insect you may swat away
38 State school SE of Columbus, in brief
41 Lucy of TV's "Elementary"
43 Kind of soup often served at a sushi bar

44 Sign of online shouting
46 Literary Emily or Charlotte
47 Places for tiny U.S. flags
49 Key for Debussy's "La fille aux cheveux de lin"
50 "All righty then . . ."
51 Italian city known for its salami
52 What holds up an ear of corn
53 Ukraine's capital, to Ukrainians
54 Actress Rowlands
56 "Look what I did!"
57 Animals in a yoke
59 Gun, as an engine

by Barbara Lin

165

ACROSS

1 Unruly throng
4 Houston team
10 Sound heard in a long hallway, maybe
14 "___ Father who art in heaven . . ."
15 Engages in thievery
16 Emotional state
17 Baton Rouge sch.
18 *Seattle, 1962
20 "And you?," to Caesar
22 Queries
23 Photos at the dentist's
24 Happen next
26 Pigs' digs
27 *Paris, 1889
31 Partook of a meal
34 Wake others up while you sleep, perhaps
35 Ostensible
37 100%
38 Theme park with an "Imagination!" pavilion
40 Mont Blanc and Matterhorn
41 "Why didn't I think of that!"
43 Laudable Lauder
44 Salt Lake City athlete
45 *Chicago, 1893
48 "___ appétit!"
49 More recent
50 Word before shell or mail
53 Rock band that electrifies audiences?
55 Dull-colored
58 Events for which the answers to the three starred clues were built
61 Jack Nicholson's weapon in "The Shining"
62 Burn soother
63 The "P" in UPS
64 "___ get you!"
65 Wanders (about)
66 Like some college bros
67 After tax

DOWN

1 Undercover operative
2 Remove from power
3 Inelegant problem-solving technique
4 Nincompoop
5 One of the Twin Cities
6 Cups, saucers, pot, etc.
7 Eight lamb chops, typically, or a frame for 15 pool balls
8 Cheers at a fútbol match
9 Nine-digit government ID
10 Manicurist's board
11 Musical finale
12 Sacred
13 Lyric poems
19 Like a 10th or 11th inning, in baseball
21 Not at liberty
25 Visualize
26 Sunni or Shia, in Islam
27 TV channel for college sports
28 Arctic native
29 ___ the Grouch
30 Ply with chocolates and roses, say
31 Kind of vehicle to take off-road
32 Shelter that might be made of buffalo skin
33 '50s Ford flop
36 Made a verbal attack, with "out"
38 Garden of earthly delights
39 Pay-___-view
42 Words spoken after a big raise?
43 "Yu-u-uck!"
46 Charge with a crime
47 Hush-hush
48 Gymnast Simone
50 Promotional goodies handed out at an event
51 The Big Easy, in brief
52 Three-time A.L. M.V.P. (2003, 2005 and 2007), informally
53 Miles away
54 Sweetheart, in Salerno
56 One of several on a tractor-trailer
57 Pants holder-upper
59 Tanning lotion stat
60 Sneaky

by Michael Lieberman

ACROSS

1 Schoolyard friend
9 Strolled
15 Abandon
16 Percussion item that's shaken
17 Manufacturing of factory goods, e.g.
18 Victimize
19 Ace of spades or queen of hearts
20 Biblical twin of Jacob
22 Existence
23 Before, poetically
24 "___ Beso" (1962 Paul Anka hit)
25 Shared with, as a story
27 Sandwich often served with mayo
28 Connector between levels of a fire station
29 "I'm shocked!," in a text
31 Religion based in Haifa, Israel
34 Sulk
35 Bothered state
36 "What goes up must come down," e.g.
37 NPR host Shapiro
38 Big name in transmission repair
39 Young lady
40 U.S. sports org. with many prominent Korean champions
41 Gown
42 The Monkees' "___ Believer"
43 Catch sight of
44 Org. in "Zero Dark Thirty"
45 Noted children's research hospital
47 Actor Philip with a star on the Hollywood Walk of Fame
48 Uncle ___ (patriotic figure)
51 Dragon in "The Hobbit"
52 Legendary queen and founder of Carthage
54 Change domiciles
55 Tasket's partner in a nursery rhyme
57 Hazards for offshore swimmers
59 Go to
60 Faucet attachments
61 Writings of Ph.D. candidates
62 X-axis

DOWN

1 Y-axis
2 Moon-related
3 Tennis's Agassi
4 "___ be surprised"
5 Greek M's
6 Swear (to)
7 Middle part of the body
8 One-named Irish singer
9 Bit of concert equipment
10 Stone for a statue
11 One of over 200 recognized by the American Kennel Club
12 "I'm listening"
13 Subject of this puzzle
14 "Nuts!"
21 Golden state?
24 "Night" memoirist Wiesel
26 Cheer at a bullfight
27 Sacks
28 "___ and Bess"
30 Classic Pontiac sports cars
31 Much-visited Indonesian isle
32 "Father" of 13-Down
33 Tries some food
34 Drew for an atlas
35 Singer Bareilles
38 Tennis score after deuce
40 '60s hallucinogen
43 Playwright O'Neill
44 Actress Priyanka who was 2000's Miss World
46 Fakes out of position, as in football
47 Farewell
48 "Me too"
49 Prevent, as disaster
50 Complicated, as a divorce
51 "A.S.A.P.!"
53 Baghdad's land
54 Baseball glove
56 Football scores, for short
58 Lie in the sun

by Eric Bornstein

ACROSS

1 Vehicles on snow-covered hills
6 Watering place for a camel
11 Indoor animal
14 "The Fox and the Grapes" storyteller
15 Trick-taking card game
16 Messenger ___
17 Large bird of prey with a brownish-yellow neck
19 Suffix with cynic or skeptic
20 Pleased
21 Hombre
22 Pool stick
23 Make excited, as a crowd
26 Smooshed into compact layers
28 ___ carte (ordered separately)
29 Blue race in "Avatar"
31 Kind of pickle
32 ___ for tat
33 Actor Kevin whose last name shares four letters with his first
35 Eric Clapton hit that's over seven minutes long
38 Light bulb unit
40 Butchers' offerings
42 Like tops and tales
43 Speak extemporaneously
45 Boringly proper
47 Conclude
48 Greek god of love
50 Away from the wind, nautically
51 It's just a number, they say
52 Single, double and triple, on the diamond
55 Shows mercy to
57 Plant bristle
58 Poet's "before"
59 Olla podrida, for one
60 Sheep's cry

61 Where you can find a 17-Across perched on an 11-Down devouring a 25-Down
66 Noah's construction
67 Opening remarks
68 One of the Allman Brothers
69 Envision
70 Valuable item
71 New York's Memorial ___ Kettering Cancer Center

DOWN

1 Droop
2 Zodiac sign before Virgo
3 Course for some immigrants, in brief
4 Historic Kansas fort name
5 Explore caves
6 Like debts
7 "Bingo!"
8 Letter after rho
9 Cuba or Aruba
10 Sign maker's pattern
11 Cactus with an edible fruit
12 Follow as a consequence
13 No longer feral
18 Incendiary bomb material
23 Formal ruling on a point of Islamic law
24 Trojan War epic poem
25 Venomous predator with a vibrating tail
26 They get smashed at parties
27 "Sadly . . ."
30 Strives for victory
34 And others: Abbr.
36 Sudden forward thrust

37 World's longest continental mountain range
39 Lose stamina
41 Afternoon nap
44 European region that lent its name to a nonconforming lifestyle
46 "Could be . . ."
49 Ambulance sounds
52 Rum-soaked desserts
53 In the loop
54 Messages that sometimes contain emojis
56 Really, really bad
59 Get off ___-free
62 Fury
63 Philosopher ___-tzu
64 Get ___ on (ace)
65 Four-star officer: Abbr.

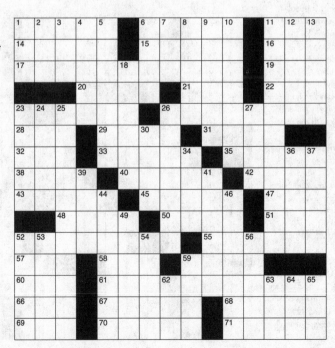

by Philip K. Chow

168

ACROSS

1 Quick punch
4 Submitted a résumé
11 Old-fashioned record collection, for short
14 Friend in France
15 Comedian Jimmy who joked of his "schnozzola"
16 The "A" of I.P.A.
17 Collectible toy vehicle
19 Long-bodied jazz instrument, for short
20 Mother hen's responsibility
21 Mil. branch with dress blues and dress whites
23 Couch
24 Bygone Swedish auto
27 Energy-efficient illumination sources, for short
29 Birthplace of General Motors
33 Nosy sort
34 Flowing, musically
35 Those who are not among us (or are they?)
38 Locale for the radius and ulna
39 Family
40 Use needle and thread
41 "Here, you'll like it!"
43 Prefix with red or structure
45 Certain online dating bio
48 No more than
49 Yanks' opponents in the Civil War
50 Plummet
53 Birdsong
56 Sierra ___ (African land)
57 Predicament
58 1980 Stephen King novel . . . or a hint to the beginnings of 17-, 29- and 45-Across
62 Preceding, poetically
63 Flipped (out)
64 Squid's defense
65 "You called?"

66 Glittery dress adornments
67 Investments with account nos.

DOWN

1 Door parts
2 Bitter Italian liqueur
3 Removed with the teeth
4 Condition that affects concentration, for short
5 Stop on a drinker's "crawl"
6 Expert
7 Not stringently enforcing the rules
8 Nighttime demons
9 Greek letters that rhyme with three other letters
10 Laura with an Oscar and an Emmy
11 So-called "Sin City"
12 Tots' time together
13 Health class subject
18 Classic eyes for Frosty
22 Prank interviewer who referred to Buzz Aldrin as "Buzz Lightyear"
24 Person who might bother a bedmate
25 Elemental part of an element
26 Band aid
28 Contents of some drifts
30 Imbecilic
31 White ___ of Dover
32 Artist Matisse
35 Famous almost-last words from Caesar
36 Security alarm trigger
37 They establish order in language classes
39 Door part
42 Skunk funk
43 Rageaholic's state

44 Tree in the birch family
46 Algebra, for calc, e.g.
47 Like art that might offend prudish sorts
51 Without interruption
52 Corner offices and prime parking spots, for company V.I.P.'s
54 Tightest of pals, in brief
55 Old Italian money
56 Blokes
57 Funny Tina
59 ___ de vie
60 Hit the slopes
61 Point value for a "Z" in Scrabble

by Daniel Grinberg

ACROSS

1 Fighting, as countries
6 Team sport with scrums
11 Naked ___ jaybird
14 Stage of development
15 Writer Zola
16 Fractional amt.
17 Equestrian outfit
19 Part of a chem class
20 Lie snugly
21 Perfect example
23 French friend
24 Take a lo-o-ong bath
26 Home plate officials, informally
27 Minor job at a body shop
29 Children's character who lives in a briar patch
33 Not bottled or canned, as beer
35 Word that might be "proper"
36 Hamlet's dilemma . . . with a phonetic hint for the last words of 17- and 29-Across and the first words of 45- and 63-Across
42 ___ vera
43 Wedding or parade
45 "E-G-B-D-F" musical symbol
51 Voice below mezzo-soprano
52 Schemer against Othello
53 What the Supremes said to do "in the name of love"
55 Test for an advanced deg. seeker
56 Requirement for sainthood
60 Peninsula with Oman and Yemen
62 Suffix with Sudan or Japan
63 California golf resort that has hosted six U.S. Opens
66 Tennis do-over
67 Garlicky sauce
68 Slow, musically
69 Units on a football field: Abbr.
70 One who laughs "Ho, ho, ho!"
71 Beginning

DOWN

1 Mo. with many (not so) happy returns?
2 Popular Girl Scout cookie
3 Undertake with gusto
4 Buyer's warning
5 Monopoly payments
6 Try, try again?
7 Actress Thurman
8 Taunt
9 Spot on a radar screen
10 Supposed source of mysterious footprints in the Himalayas
11 Self-assurance
12 Shrimp ___ (seafood dish)
13 Optimally
18 Amorphous lump
22 Place to take a bath
23 Kerfuffle
25 Shelters for shelties
28 Run one's mouth
30 Outback hopper, informally
31 Routine that one might get stuck in
32 Pay to play
34 Ring, as church bells
37 Mississippi's ___ Miss
38 Huge bird of lore
39 In vitro fertilization needs
40 Citizens of Brussels and Antwerp
41 Theatergoer's break
44 What a ballerina twirls on
45 At just the right moment
46 Made a higher poker bet
47 White wetlands birds
48 ___ constrictor
49 And others: Lat.
50 Shout after an errant drive
54 Artist Picasso
57 Tax pros, for short
58 "Star Wars" princess
59 Black, in poetry
61 Has-___
64 Toasted sandwich, familiarly
65 All the rage

by Lynn Lempel

170

ACROSS
1 Animal that barks
4 Bourbon barrel material
7 Tribal leader
12 Blunder
13 ___ colada
15 List for a meeting
16 *Certain psychedelic experience
18 Nintendo game featuring balance exercises
19 ___ of the game
20 Early auto engine's power source
22 Construction area, e.g.
23 Performs like Iggy Azalea
25 Social stratum
27 Provoke
30 Nevada city on the Truckee River
31 PC monitor type, in brief
34 *Hairstyle popularized by Lucille Ball
36 Hip-hop producer who founded Aftermath Entertainment
38 For two, in music
39 Jeans material
41 At the drop of ___ (instantly)
42 Drops in the mail
44 *Cheap neighborhood bar
46 Bygone Mach 1 breaker, for short
47 Major water line
49 Hang around idly
50 "Wanna join us?"
52 Fairy tale bear with a hard bed
53 Delivery room instruction
55 Put on hold
57 Religious sisters
61 Real lowlife

63 "So there!" . . . or what you can do to the ends of the answers to the starred clues?
65 Looks without blinking
66 Ship personnel
67 Number of Q tiles in Scrabble
68 Item that may be baked or mashed, informally
69 Caustic solution
70 Ingredient in a Denver omelet

DOWN
1 College faculty head
2 Whale that preys on octopuses
3 Worrisome, as news
4 Make a pick
5 Cockpit reading
6 Makes a scarf, say

7 FX in much sci-fi and fantasy
8 Bank holdup
9 *Bunt single, e.g.
10 Heading in a word processing menu
11 Destiny
14 Gibbon or gorilla
15 "Geez, that sucks!"
17 Expressed contempt for
21 Like vinegar
24 Falcons, on scoreboards
26 Roll for a greenskeeper
27 "No bid from me"
28 Connection points
29 *Home of many a courthouse
30 Talk too long
32 Yearn for
33 Scare off
35 Pop singer Dion

37 Visibly elated
40 Nonsense
43 Home of the George W. Bush Institute, in brief
45 Hack (off)
48 Capitol Hill staffers
51 Busiest airport in the Midwest
52 Oyster's creation
53 "Hey, over here!"
54 ___ Beauty (Sephora competitor)
56 Org. that monitors consumer scams
58 "Here comes trouble . . ."
59 Mama's mama
60 Part of a cherry you don't eat
62 Gen ___ (millennial's follower)
64 Ovine mother

by Zhouqin Burnikel

ACROSS

1 Things that justify the means, some say
5 Eight: Sp.
9 Rampaging groups
13 Hoedown locale
14 "Moby-Dick" captain
15 Feverish fit
16 Cinnamon buns and such
19 Community-maintained website
20 Person from Bangkok
21 Disney character loosely based on Hans Christian Andersen's "Snow Queen"
23 "Hmm, that's not good . . ."
25 Slight coloring
27 Slight downturn
28 Modern pet name
29 Cyclical paradox discussed in "Gödel, Escher, Bach"
32 Societal problems
34 Brain reading, for short
35 Touches one's chin and moves the hand down to say "Thank you," for example
36 Recipe amt.
38 ___ and crafts
40 "Shucks!"
43 Bar serving
44 The "A" of I.R.A.: Abbr.
48 Onetime TV political drama set in Washington
52 "Now I get it!"
53 Tit for ___
54 Mike of TV's "Dirty Jobs" and "Somebody's Gotta Do It"
55 Strategy
57 Yours: Fr.
59 Potato accompanier in soup
61 Shopping center
62 Sports metaphor used to describe esoteric knowledge . . . with a hint to the circled letters
66 Cinema showing
67 Amateur mag
68 1998 Sarah McLachlan hit
69 Ladder rung
70 Jazzy James
71 Forest feline

DOWN

1 Flow back, as the tide
2 Tusked marine animal
3 Spinning top with a Hebrew letter on each side
4 Type not to be trusted
5 Fumbler
6 Informal conversation
7 #, on social media
8 Procure
9 China's ___ Zedong
10 Eye creepily
11 Yale's Handsome Dan mascot, for one
12 Time spent with a psychiatrist, e.g.
17 Optimas and Souls, in the auto world
18 Good thing to have on hand at a wedding?
22 TikTok and Fitbit, for two
23 Kimono sash
24 GPS suggestions: Abbr.
26 Rorschach, for one
30 Street cred
31 Simpson who is a Buddhist and a vegetarian
33 Hearty bowlful
37 Bar serving
38 Heavyweight champ known as "The Greatest"
39 Figure in home economics?
40 Lead-in to boy or girl
41 Hypothetical musings
42 "Now, work!"
43 Slightly
45 Purr-son who loves her pets?
46 Doin' nothin'
47 Tic-___-toe
49 Last word at an auction
50 Pluck, as an eyebrow
51 Charades or dominoes
56 Scheming group
58 ___ of Skye
60 Philosopher Immanuel
63 Little troublemaker
64 South China ___
65 Opposite of strict

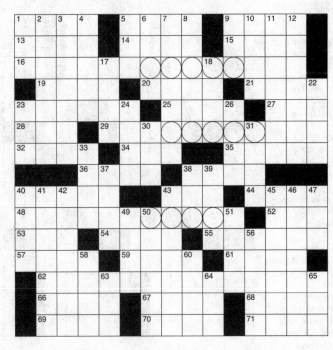

by Aimee Lucido and Ella Dershowitz

172

ACROSS

1 Opening made by a letter opener
5 Antifur org.
9 Wee bit
14 Old-fashioned fight club?
15 Wrinkle remover
16 Pacific Island group that was once a setting for "Survivor"
17 New couple, in a gossip column
18 Look after, as a fire, bar or flock
19 1940s nuclear event, for short
20 "I'm willing to pay that amount"
23 "___ Just Not That Into You" (2009 rom-com)
24 New newt
25 Get value from
26 "Law & Order" spinoff, informally
27 Longtime advertiser at the Indy 500
29 Oolong or Darjeeling
32 "If I can be honest here . . ."
37 Submarine device
38 The "A" of E.T.A.: Abbr.
39 Main line from the heart
40 "Absolutely! 100% positive!"
43 E.R. staffers
44 Snake symbolizing old Egyptian royalty
45 Gives a thumbs-up
46 Transmission by telephone
48 ___ alai
49 Pennies: Abbr.
52 20-, 32- or 40-Across
58 Boots from political office
59 Southwestern tribe with a snake dance
60 Start of every California ZIP code
61 How a ballerina often dances

62 Israeli statesman Abba ___
63 Historical novelist Seton
64 Jumped
65 Alternative to a drumstick
66 Historical

DOWN

1 Actress Dame Maggie
2 Woodworker's tool
3 Drinks akin to Slush Puppies
4 Work as a sub
5 Pathetic
6 Put up, as a monument
7 Muscular firmness
8 "___ Love Her" (Beatles ballad)
9 Practices jabs and hooks
10 TV journalist Couric
11 Fashion designer Cassini
12 Bit of attire that might say "MISS UNIVERSE"
13 Jabba the ___
21 Paul who went on a midnight ride
22 Building manager, for short
26 Wild guess
27 Razor sharpener at a barbershop
28 By way of, for short
29 Surf's partner, on menus
30 Suffix with Smurf
31 "So it's you!"
32 Bugs Bunny or Wile E. Coyote
33 Burden to bear
34 Potato chip brand
35 Walkie-___
36 Louis Treize, Louis Quatorze and others
37 Damascus's land: Abbr.

41 Something hailed on city streets
42 Wandering
46 Camera lens setting
47 Beauty, brawn or brains
48 Land east of the Yellow Sea
49 Land west of the Yellow Sea
50 Awards for Broadway's best
51 Blood, ___ & Tears
52 Hip
53 Debussy's "Clair de ___"
54 "The Thin Man" pooch
55 What a puppy likes to do to toys and socks
56 Mongolian desert
57 Jacket fastener

by Andrea Carla Michaels

ACROSS

1 Document for foreign travel
5 Spend much time in front of the mirror
10 "Omnia vincit ___" ("Love conquers all": Lat.)
14 "SportsCenter" channel
15 Rapper Kendrick
16 Designate as "commercial" or "residential," e.g.
17 Nonbinary pronoun
18 Best possible athletic performance
19 Very top
20 Figurative site of a 35-Down
23 Elevator brake inventor Elisha
24 Parched, as a desert
25 Abut
28 Close
32 Neigh : horse :: ___ : sheep
33 Emerge from the ocean, say
37 French "yes"
38 Alternative to Google
40 Michael who directed "Fahrenheit 9/11"
41 Starting point for a car sale negotiation: Abbr.
42 To the back
44 Auction unit
45 Feudal superior
46 Alma mater of five U.S. presidents
47 Singers Ames and Sheeran
48 Push to do something
49 Posse
50 %: Abbr.
51 Wolf Blitzer facial feature
53 Vienna's home: Abbr.
54 Nitpick, literally
57 Old rival of MGM
58 Prefix with stasis or tarsus
60 Summa cum ___
61 Tennis score after deuce
62 Sound much heard in traffic
63 Damascus's home
64 Nashville's home: Abbr.
65 Only daughter of Elizabeth II
66 Lady ___, first female member of Parliament
67 French celestial being

DOWN

1 Ex-G.I.
2 "About"
3 What a volcano might do
4 Informal segue
5 Shade of blond
6 Rants and raves
7 Certain Apple
8 Half of a 1960s folk-rock group
9 Something that might be felt at a séance
10 Spring bloomer
11 Sulk
12 Last number in a countdown
13 Former secretary of state Tillerson
21 "No lie!"
22 Apple or maple
25 Alphabetically first group in the Rock & Roll Hall of Fame
26 Figurative ruler of a 35-Down
27 "Pride and Prejudice" novelist
29 Locale of many White House photo ops
30 Figurative ruler of a 35-Down
31 "Eek!"
34 Isn't oneself?
35 Feature of many a mall . . . or a place for 20-Across and 26- and 30-Down?
36 Place to make a scene?
39 Soiree, say
41 Bog down
43 Chris of "S.N.L."
45 ___ job (bit of garage work)
49 Brazilian ballroom dance
52 John who wrote "No man is an island"
55 Disney's ___ of Arendelle
56 Singe
59 Mimic
61 Keep ___ distance

by Eric and Lori Bornstein

174

ACROSS

1 Surrounded by
5 Senator Mike of Idaho
10 Its state fair is much visited by politicians
14 Stream from a volcano
15 Any episode of "Parks and Recreation," now
16 Toot one's own horn
17 *Joe cool?
19 Taj Mahal locale
20 Wall Street average, with "the"
21 Backstabs
23 Annual TV awards
26 Island nation in the western Pacific
28 Opposite of yeses
29 Word before sauce or milk
30 *Amenity for jet-setters
33 Trail
35 Neither's partner
36 The first "X" of X-X-X
37 *What investigators really want to know
42 [It's c-c-cold!]
43 A-to-zed lexicon, in brief
44 Attire
46 *Aromatic fragrance with a French name
51 Color TV pioneer
52 Some investments, for short
53 Untagged, in a game of tag
54 What a red-faced emoji might mean
56 Relaxing soak after a long day, maybe
58 Bay Area hub, for short
59 Fit for military service
60 Fairy tale chant from a giant . . . or the ends of the answers to the starred clues
66 Make, as money
67 Not illuminated
68 Boston's ___-Farber Cancer Institute
69 Hockey puck, e.g.

70 Animals symbolizing innocence
71 Community facility that often has a gym and pool, in brief

DOWN

1 Mahershala of "Green Book"
2 PC alternative
3 "Now ___ heard everything!"
4 Papa
5 Bird that caws
6 Official with a whistle
7 Little dog's bark
8 Southwest tribe or one of its dwellings
9 Where meaningless words go in (and out the other)
10 Letter-shaped construction support
11 Natural food producer
12 On guard against
13 Tennis great Andre
18 ___ Nostra
22 ___-frutti
23 Telepath's "gift"
24 Means of defense that doesn't actually have alligators
25 Discovery Channel program that debunked popular beliefs
26 Amateurs no more
27 Kind of reasoning
31 Red Roof ___
32 Part of a bird or museum
34 What's rounded up in a roundup
38 "The Faerie Queene" woman
39 Adroit
40 University email ending

41 Apex predator of the ocean
45 Rebuke to Marmaduke
46 Bounced back, as a sound
47 God, in the Torah
48 Quantity of stew
49 Greek goddess of wisdom
50 Peeve
55 Full of emotional swings
57 Establishment that's usually closed on Sundays
58 Poses for a photo
61 Boston's Liberty Tree, e.g.
62 Whopper junior?
63 Kin, informally
64 Tar Heels' sch.
65 Goat's bleat

by Ross Trudeau

ACROSS

1 Desktop computer covered by AppleCare
5 Opposite of buys
10 PBS science show since 1974
14 ___ Raton, Fla.
15 Clothing crease
16 Like the climate of Death Valley
17 Easy-to-peel citrus fruits
20 Sherri's twin sister on "The Simpsons"
21 Stockpile
22 Main ingredients in meringue
26 Verbal shrug
29 Warmly welcome, as a new era
30 Whack on the head
33 "Do not ___" (blackboard words)
35 Variety
36 Big name in tractors
38 Shapes of Frisbees and tiddlywinks
39 Welcome gift upon arriving at Honolulu International Airport
40 Mascara mishap
41 Sore, as after a workout
42 NASCAR champion Hamlin
44 Apt name for a car mechanic?
45 Scientist's workplace
46 Facial expressions
48 "Do you ___ my drift?"
49 What many children begin to do in kindergarten
51 Practice for a bout
53 Website with trivia quizzes
56 "Medicine" that doesn't actually contain medicine
59 Axed
60 Love to pieces
62 Estate beneficiary

63 Coffeehouse dispensers
64 First episode in a TV series
65 Change for a five
66 Try out
67 Cherry throwaways
68 World capital where the Nobel Peace Prize is awarded

DOWN

1 Creator of Watson on "Jeopardy!"
2 Protective trench
3 Target of the skin cream Retin-A
4 Close-knit group
5 Bits of parsley
6 Man's name hidden in "reliableness"
7 Man's name hidden in "reliableness"
8 Language akin to Thai
9 Low-altitude clouds
10 Grannies
11 A.C.L.U. and others
12 Fights (for)
13 Commercials
18 Has a war of words
19 Changes, as the Constitution
23 Fritters (away), as time
24 Montana's capital
25 Peeving
26 Purple Heart, e.g.
27 TV journalist Hill
28 Crispy breakfast side dish
30 Salad base similar to Swiss chard
31 Speak from a podium, say

32 Two-time presidential candidate Ross
34 "The ___ is falling!" (Chicken Little's cry)
37 Angsty music genre
42 Worked out in a pool
43 "We should do that!"
46 Rug cleaner, informally
47 Spot for a mud facial
50 ___ & Young (accounting firm)
52 "Bless you!" elicitor
53 Closed
54 Father, in French
55 Make tweaks to
56 Dance with a king and queen
57 Actress Jessica of "Hitchcock"
58 Approximately
61 Fútbol cheer

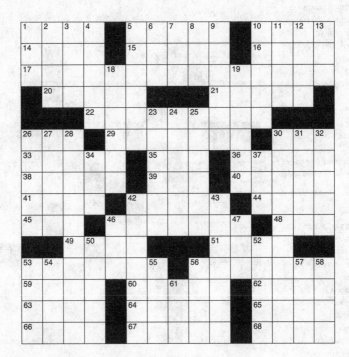

by Zhouqin Burnikel

ACROSS

1 ___ Newton (cookie)
4 Salty water
9 In ___ land (dreaming)
13 Many a craft brew, in brief
14 Just before the weekend
15 Big name in polo shirts
16 Alternative to Zumba
18 ___ pro quo
19 "Don't get any funny ___"
20 Ad ___ committee
21 Opportunities to play in games
22 Govt. org. with a classified budget
24 Chevy S.U.V.
26 Donated
29 Where to order a Blizzard
34 Poem of tribute
35 Trader ___ (restaurant eponym)
36 Break into with intent to steal
37 Illegally downloaded
40 Early offering, as of goods
41 More sunburned
42 Mai ___ (cocktail)
43 "Look what I ___!"
44 Supposed means of communication with the dead
46 Employs
47 When some local news airs
48 . . . ––– . . .
50 Construction details
53 Like many HDTVs, in brief
55 Change with the times
59 Interlaced threads
60 Biggest city in South Dakota
62 Like, with "to"
63 Noted portrait photographer Anne

64 Place to apply ChapStick
65 What ice cubes do in the hot sun
66 Lock of hair
67 What the circled letters all mean

DOWN

1 Country whose name is a brand of bottled water
2 Apple tablet
3 Fixed look
4 "I'm f-f-freezing!"
5 Like the 1%
6 Nonsensical
7 Daytona 500 acronym
8 CBS logo
9 Kahlúa and Sambuca
10 Côte d'___ (French Riviera)
11 Cut of a pork roast

12 Puts two and two together, say
14 Admit, with "up"
17 Grey who wrote "Riders of the Purple Sage"
21 Chef's hat
23 Most words ending in "-ly"
25 Cars with gas/electric engines
26 Lose one's amateur status
27 Fancy goodbye
28 Giuseppe who composed "Rigoletto"
30 Assistance
31 "Holy smokes!"
32 Singer Goulding
33 Food, water and air
38 Next (to)
39 Things milking machines attach to

40 Number on a miniature golf card
42 Some reading for an I.R.S. auditor
45 Slicker
46 Meat-inspecting org.
49 Ham-handed sorts
50 Participated in the first third of a triathlon
51 Rude touch
52 "Don't be ___" (Google motto)
54 Clothing, informally
56 Friend in a conflict
57 Ballet bend
58 Measures of salt and sugar: Abbr.
60 One crying "Hup, two, three, four!": Abbr.
61 Critical marks on treasure maps

by Wren Schultz

ACROSS

1 Library catalog listing after "author"
6 Ribbit : frog :: ___ : cat
10 Bit of land in the sea: Sp.
14 Author Asimov
15 Scrabble or Boggle
16 Challenging vegetables to eat with a fork
17 Harmonica
19 ___ and sciences
20 What "Yes, I'm willing!" signifies
21 Contend
22 Talks effusively
25 Place to get some barbecue
28 It might be confused with a termite
29 Tanning lotion fig.
31 Pointy-leaved desert plants
32 Lo-o-ong bath
34 ___ Asia (China, Japan and environs)
37 Poor grades
38 Dummy
41 Bog fuel
42 Brontë's "Jane ___"
43 Quick bite to eat
46 Tranquil
48 Grp. overseeing the World Series
50 Wildebeest
51 Negative repercussions
54 Individual
56 Capital of Georgia: Abbr.
57 "You don't have to take responsibility for the mistake"
59 Tidy
61 Stand-in during a film shoot . . . or a hint to 17-, 25-, 38- and 51-Across
65 Platform for a ceremony
66 Send off, as rays
67 Autumn bloom
68 Follower of hop and skip
69 "The lady ___ protest too much": "Hamlet"
70 More recent

DOWN

1 Dickens's Tiny ___
2 Prefix with -therm
3 Letter after sigma
4 Gate closer
5 Sounds heard in canyons
6 People in charge: Abbr.
7 Raring to go
8 Neighbor of a Saudi and Yemeni
9 Passed
10 Brewery letters
11 Ones leading the blind, maybe
12 Jennifer Lopez and Christina Aguilera, for two
13 Good things to have
18 Without assurance of purchase
22 Word after laughing or natural
23 Half of dos
24 Assert one's ownership, as to land
26 "Hey ___" (Beatles hit)
27 Roughly 71% of the earth's surface
30 Like many Rolex watches sold on the street
33 Natural ability
35 Apt letters missing from "_tea_th_"
36 Six years, for a U.S. senator
39 Electricity or water, e.g.: Abbr.
40 Assisted
41 Level off at a higher point
44 ___ Balls (chocolaty snack)
45 Attila the ___
46 Three-ingredient lunchbox staple, familiarly
47 Lightly touched, as with a handkerchief
49 Express sorrow over
52 Sports replay effect
53 Lost patience
55 Do something else with
58 George Washington's chopping down a cherry tree, e.g.
60 Small recipe amt.
62 "As an aside," in a text
63 Film director Spike
64 Flub

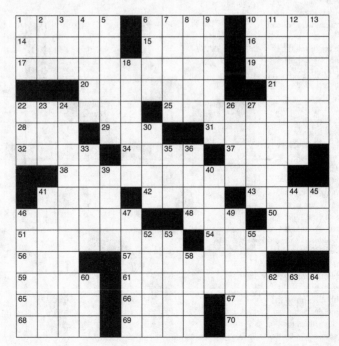

by Adrienne Atkins

178

ACROSS

1 ___-schmancy
6 Apple's digital assistant
10 Sandwiches that may use Skippy and Smuckers, informally
14 Regions
15 The "Odyssey," for one
16 ___ Canal, connector of the Hudson River to the Great Lakes
17 Arkansas's capital
19 "___ from New York, it's . . ."
20 Bonny young woman
21 Overhaul
22 "Superbad" co-star Seth
23 Loss offsetter
25 Derrière
26 Bicolor cookies also called half-moons
32 Hold responsible
33 Cause of some nose-wrinkling
34 "How was ___ know?"
35 Red, as a steak
36 Portmanteau for denim cutoffs
38 Condition treated by Adderall, for short
39 Corp. giant spelled backward inside "giant"
40 Something tried out for in a tryout
41 Follows, as orders
42 Final practice before the big show
46 Opening between mountains
47 Opening for a coin
48 One of a pair of a carnival entertainer
50 How many times the Washington Nationals have won the World Series
52 Chocolate candy with a caramel center
56 Rice-shaped pasta
57 Fashion designer associated with the item spelled out by the starts of 17-, 26- and 42-Across

59 Clown of renown
60 Prerevolution Russian leader
61 Had a role to play
62 Obsessive fan, in slang
63 Plane assignment
64 Feed, as a fire

DOWN

1 Leaf-changing season
2 Prima donna's big moment
3 Brooklyn basketball team
4 Tie in tic-tac-toe
5 Big inits. in fashion
6 Tennis star Williams
7 Cher holder?
8 Puerto ___
9 "Gross!"
10 House speaker Nancy
11 Flash of genius
12 "___ Talkin'," #1 hit for the Bee Gees

13 Observed
18 Composer Satie
22 German industrial valley
24 There's only one spot for this
25 Deuces
26 Former British P.M. Tony
27 Circular food item that may come in a 16" square box
28 Up, on a compass
29 Banned pesticide, for short
30 ___ alcohol (fuel source)
31 Installs, as a lawn
32 ___ Rutter, "Jeopardy!" contestant with the all-time highest winnings ($4.9+ million)
36 Places for tips
37 Valuable deposit

38 Existing in the mind only
40 "Hey, over here!"
41 Spanish gold
43 Place for a brawl in a western
44 Accompany on the red carpet, say
45 One of the Baldwin brothers
48 Bawls
49 Horse's gait
50 Slowly seep (out)
51 Org. with bowl games
53 "Hold ___ your hat!"
54 Vegetable paired with potato in a soup
55 Quaint shoppe descriptor
57 Adds to an email chain, in a way
58 Possesses

by Michael Lieberman

ACROSS

1 Come ___ with (accompany)
6 Cover for a smartphone
10 Lines at the cash register, for short?
14 ___ Day (September observance)
15 Vizio or Panasonic product
16 Snow clearer
17 Sleuth for hire
19 ___ chips (Hawaiian snack)
20 Poem of praise
21 Angel's instrument
22 Entrance hall
23 Perform an act of kindness, in a way
26 Kind of seeds on a bagel
29 Musk of SpaceX
30 Actor Wilson of "Wedding Crashers"
31 ___ Peninsula, area above Singapore
33 Gorilla
36 1977 #1 Eagles hit
40 Gives the go-ahead
41 Desi of "I Love Lucy"
42 George Washington bills
43 Popular berry
44 What loves company, in a saying
46 It might catch a thief or a speeder
51 President after Washington
52 Library item
53 Dance style for Bill Robinson or Gregory Hines
56 Jeans maker Strauss
57 Be willing to accept whatever . . . or a hint to the ends of 17-, 23-, 36- and 46-Across
60 Bear's retreat
61 Skating leap

62 Crunchy, colorful commercial candies
63 Otherwise
64 Bloody
65 Stuck (to)

DOWN

1 Brand for Rover
2 Cooking grease
3 Annual drama award
4 Election mo.
5 Kind of cracker needed for a proper s'more
6 Paris sweetheart
7 Thoroughly proficient
8 Mudhole
9 Garden of Eden woman
10 Train direction from Manhattan to the Bronx
11 Spanish beach

12 Tool for preparing apples
13 Weapon in a scabbard
18 Actor Diggs
22 Cold treat with a rhyming name
23 Window square
24 "___ Navidad"
25 Snowman in "Frozen"
26 London theater district
27 Furry "Star Wars" creature
28 6–1, 4–6 and 7–6, in tennis
31 Frenzied
32 Montgomery's state: Abbr.
33 Hathaway of "The Devil Wears Prada"
34 Where boats tie up
35 "Piece of cake!"
37 Shoestrings

38 Commercial lead-in to Apple
39 Parks of Montgomery
43 Idolize, say
44 ___ Mix, brand for Whiskers
45 Bothering
46 Popular Berry
47 Perfect
48 Tennis's ___ Cup
49 More up to the task
50 "Good Golly, Miss ___"
53 Kind of traffic, familiarly
54 Helper
55 Possible condition for a war vet, for short
57 Cloth for cleaning
58 Kitchen utensil brand
59 Abbr. on a business card

by Erika Ettin

180

ACROSS

1. Fills with wonderment
5. Rating for "Supergirl" or "Gilmore Girls"
9. Piece of the pie
14. The ___ of one's existence
15. Get wind of
16. Prop for a painter
17. Abbr. for routing of mail
18. Spooky-sounding lake?
19. Format for old computer games
20. Food for Little Miss Muffet
23. "___ the Force, Luke"
24. Drink in a tavern
25. Increases, as the pot
29. ___ Madre (Western range)
31. Chinese dissident artist
33. Like Shakespeare's feet?
35. Common injury locale for an athlete, in brief
36. U.S. Naval Academy anthem
41. Lyric poem
42. Pacific weather phenomenon
43. Neighbor of Botswana
47. Driver's license, e.g., in brief
51. Grab 40 winks
52. Music genre for Weezer or Fall Out Boy
53. Follower of Red or Dead
54. Breakup song by Fleetwood Mac
58. Energy alternative to wind
61. Shoelace annoyance
62. Snooty manners
63. In the loop
64. Tilt-a-Whirl, e.g.
65. Get ready, as for surgery
66. Messages that may include emojis
67. x and y, on a graph
68. "M*A*S*H" co-star Alan

DOWN

1. Something you can always count on
2. 1960s dance craze
3. Main dish
4. Email button
5. 1836 site to "remember"
6. Science fiction pioneer Jules
7. Stamp on an invoice
8. Increased, as the pot
9. Withdraw formally
10. Mom of Princes William and Harry
11. Home of Tel Aviv: Abbr.
12. Bigwig hired by a board
13. Street frequented by Freddy Krueger
21. Actress ___ Jessica Parker
22. Hem and ___
26. Freebies at a corporate event
27. Field for many Silicon Valley jobs
28. Shipment from Alaska's North Slope
30. Rocker Ocasek of the Cars
31. What a bride walks down
32. The Who's "___ See for Miles"
34. Batch of beer
36. Tennis score after deuce
37. 6-Down's submarine captain
38. Nintendo controllers
39. Fund, as a fellowship
40. Org. with Summer and Winter Games
41. Parts of lbs.
44. Bergman's "Casablanca" co-star
45. Islands west of Lisbon
46. Queen ___ (pop nickname)
48. Eddying
49. Stood on its hind legs, as a horse
50. Place to be pampered
52. Wear down bit by bit
55. Southern soup ingredient
56. Operating system developed at Bell Labs
57. California vineyard valley
58. Took a rest . . . or a test?
59. Be in debt
60. Not strict

by Andrea Carla Michaels and Doug Peterson

ACROSS

1 Make sense
6 Many a get-rich-quick scheme
10 Meal cooked in a Crock-Pot
14 Atlanta train system
15 Wife of Zeus
16 Domesticated
17 Moolah
18 Distance between belt holes, maybe
19 Sign at a highway interchange
20 Capable of floating, as a balloon
23 Low-ranking "Star Trek" officer: Abbr.
24 Sombrero, e.g.
25 Smidgen
26 Neon or xenon
27 Soul singer Thomas
29 Wail
32 Sanctimonious
36 Ken, to Barbie
37 "Rocks," in a drink
38 Captain's place on a ship
39 Imposing and then some
44 Units on a football field: Abbr.
45 ___ Susan (dining table centerpiece)
46 How long it might take for a mountain to form
47 Word before "bite" or "go"
48 Rapper ___-Z
49 Word sometimes confused with "lie"
52 "Let's put things in perspective" . . . or a title for this puzzle
57 Martin Luther King's "Letter From Birmingham ___"
58 Debtors' notes
59 Brain divisions
60 Gawk at
61 ___ menu (where to find Cut, Copy and Paste)

62 Longtime Yankees manager Joe
63 Runner Usain
64 Where bears hibernate
65 Gives a thumbs-up

DOWN

1 Saunter
2 1950s–'60s singer Bobby
3 Bottom of the barrel
4 Salt Lake City's home
5 Stir-fried noodle dish
6 Jersey
7 Penny
8 Feature over many a doorway
9 Honorific for Gandhi
10 Ending with farm or home
11 Move from the gate to the runway, say

12 Mideast bigwig
13 "Caution—___ paint" (sign)
21 Simplicity
22 Vindaloo accompaniment
26 When repeated, water cooler sound
27 Like a poison ivy rash
28 Mother of Zeus (and an anagram of 15-Across)
29 "Give my compliments to the ___"
30 Part to play
31 "De-e-elish!"
32 Chairperson, e.g.
33 Cousins of paddles
34 Cracker brand with a yellow-and-blue logo
35 Like Girl Scout "Mints"
36 Pioneering journalist Nellie

40 Woman's name that's also a Spanish pronoun
41 Made a comeback
42 1963 Best Actress Patricia
43 Never betraying
47 Speck of land in the sea
48 Kids around
49 The Scales
50 Big office supply brand
51 Positive responses
52 Shakespeare villain who says "Virtue? A fig!"
53 Cash register drawer
54 Rich vein of ore
55 Pompeii or Machu Picchu
56 Nabbed
57 What you're hired to do

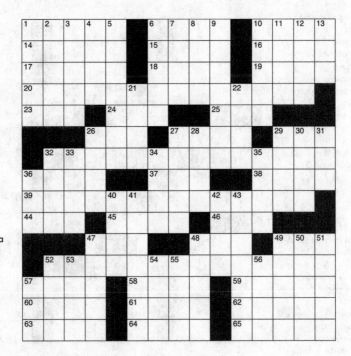

by Jacob Stulberg

182

ACROSS
1 Potato, informally
5 Desert succulent
10 Net material
14 ... approximately
15 ___ Heights (Syria/Israel border area)
16 Reverberation
17 "So, this red thing, Mom? This is not good."
19 Ending with church or party
20 Wild time at the mall
21 Assesses visually
23 Lounge around
26 Amend a tax return, perhaps
27 "The French one is my favorite. Wait, no, the pretzel one."
32 Lamb's mother
33 Gaze intently
34 Get out of ___ (leave town)
38 Boring
40 Mexican marinade made with chili pepper
42 Sonnet or ode
43 Request from
45 Blissful spots
47 Printer malfunction
48 "Eww, mollusks . . . I don't know, didn't this make me sick last time?"
51 Actress Meryl with nine Golden Globe Awards
54 "Buona ___" (Italian greeting)
55 Render impossible
58 Fumble (for)
62 It's a crime to lie under it
63 "Wow, Mom, this is like at a restaurant! Dibs on the chocolate pudding!"
66 Garfield's canine pal
67 Energy giant synonymous with corporate scandal
68 "I get it now"

69 Ecosystem built by corals
70 Seat at a counter
71 Has an evening meal

DOWN
1 Weeps loudly
2 Get ready for a test, say
3 ___ name and password
4 "Ooh, spill the tea!"
5 "___ before beauty"
6 Republicans, for short
7 ___ vera
8 Change into different forms
9 Walks in
10 Epic failure
11 Culprit in some food poisoning cases
12 Conch, e.g.
13 Animal in a stable
18 Rises up on its hind legs, as a 13-Down

22 Item strung on a necklace
24 Actress Catherine ___-Jones
25 Manages to elude
27 Singer McEntire
28 You can't say they won't give a hoot!
29 Reveal, as confidential information
30 Gradually wear away, as soil
31 Rises up in protest
35 Training place for martial arts
36 One of 10 on a 10-speed
37 Award won multiple times by "Modern Family" and "All in the Family"
39 Popular meal kit company (or the mother of the food critic featured in this puzzle?)

41 "You can count ___"
44 Gas or coal
46 Twilled fabric for suits
49 Sea foams
50 Former Philippine president Ferdinand
51 Scent of an animal
52 Exchange
53 Fix, as a knot
56 Journey's "___ Stop Believin'"
57 Continental currency
59 Honolulu's home
60 Sound of sitting down heavily
61 Fraternal order
64 Phillipa ___, Tony nominee for "Hamilton"
65 NBC sketch show, in brief

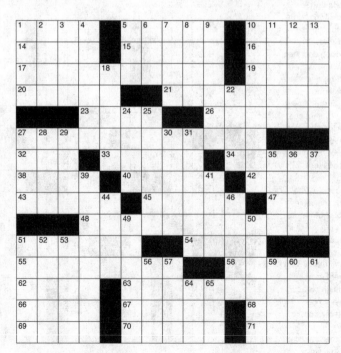

by Pamela F. Davis

183

ACROSS

1 Negative media coverage, in brief
6 Undergraduate's declaration
11 Consumer protection org.
14 Open-air rooms
15 Olio di ___ (bread dip at a trattoria)
16 Water: Fr.
17 Marine inhabitant that's an animal, not a plant, despite what it's called
19 ___ de Triomphe
20 Tiny drink
21 Org. with missions to Mars
22 Put back in the suitcase
24 43,560 square feet
26 Nightclub
27 Angry shout to a miscreant
29 Prince who married Meghan Markle
32 Swollen mark
33 Garden tool with a long handle
34 Heed
35 Top Olympic prizes
37 Many a sacrifice play in baseball
38 Padre's sister
39 Make do
40 Bar mitzvah reading
41 Sobriquet for Simón Bolívar
45 Actress Lohan of "Mean Girls"
46 Camrys and Corollas
50 Challenges for dry cleaners
51 Ares and Apollo, to Zeus
52 Insect that can carry up to 50 times its body weight

53 "Ready, ___, fire!"
54 Observation satellite
57 Service charge
58 Fictional detective Nero
59 Wide receiver ___ Beckham Jr.
60 Shape on a winding road
61 Peeved states
62 Blender setting

DOWN

1 Low opera voice
2 Had a home-cooked meal
3 Curtain
4 Snapchat transmission, for short
5 Vulgar, as some humor
6 Dull brown, as hair
7 ___ mater
8 Triangular sail
9 Attire for the Mario Bros. or the Minions
10 Cheese-on-toast dish
11 Co-star of TV's "Maude"
12 Only Spanish city to host the Olympics
13 Facial feature of Disney's Goofy
18 Actor Elwes
23 Butter unit
25 Out of kilter
26 Fed a line to
28 What can barely give a hoot?
29 Place to store valuables when traveling
30 Skills
31 Shawn Carter for Jay-Z and Tracy Morrow for Ice-T

35 Be lenient with
36 Grand Ole ___
37 The Bronx or Brooklyn, informally
39 Employer of Norah O'Donnell
40 Place to buy gifts for kids
42 Ugandan tyrant ___ Amin
43 Makes amends (for)
44 "___ mention it!"
47 Electrified weapon
48 What a maxi dress reaches
49 Fashion
51 De-clump, as flour
55 Yale collegian
56 Yale URL ender

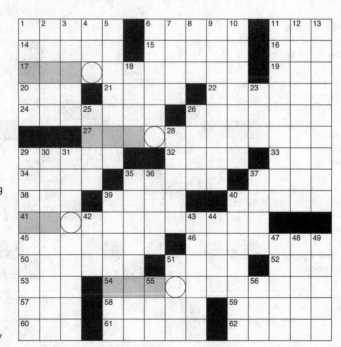

by Peter Gordon

184

ACROSS

1. Hard to understand
7. Vegan protein source
11. Electric guitarist's need
14. It makes an auto shine
15. Spirited horse
16. Luau finger food
17. Song lyric before "short and stout"
20. Turn down, as lights
21. "Check this out!"
22. Out of practice
23. "The Simpsons" character voiced by Nancy Cartwright
24. ___ to the throne
26. Attorney general under George W. Bush
33. Sully
34. 1960s Ron Howard TV role
35. Eggs in a fertility lab
36. End of a cigarette or rifle
37. Were in accord
39. Nephew of Donald Duck
40. Number that never goes down
41. Morrison who said "A writer's life and work are not a gift to mankind; they are its necessity"
42. Some pork cuts
43. Appeasing, idiomatically
47. Writes
48. Gape
49. What designated drivers should be
52. Taurus symbol
53. Give silent approval
56. Grilled Japanese dish on skewers
60. What a dipstick measures the level of
61. Prep for publication
62. Where this puzzle's circled letters can be found
63. Part of the body that's stubbed
64. Trick
65. ___ network

DOWN

1. The "A" of DNA
2. Oscar-winning Malek
3. Do some last-minute studying
4. Leatherworker's pointed tool
5. Fancy work from a manicurist
6. Squeeze money from
7. Format of much AM radio
8. Metal in a mine
9. What Jack Sprat couldn't eat, in a nursery rhyme
10. Transform using mobile technology, as a market
11. TikTok and Zoom, for two
12. Not worth debating
13. Feel sorry for
18. Band with the 1983 #1 hit "62-Across"
19. Surrounding glow
23. Like the wire in paper clips
24. "Cross my heart and ___ to die"
25. Oklahoma city
26. Facing the pitcher
27. Ha-ha
28. Dog to avoid
29. Pull out all the stops
30. Nephew of Donald Duck
31. 100- or 200-meter, e.g.
32. Final authority
37. Enlist
38. Quaint lodgings
39. Sound of a car or goose
41. Brought up the rear?
42. Disreputable sort
44. International grp. with a 1970s U.S. embargo
45. Water: Sp.
46. Southeast Europe's ___ Peninsula
49. Person who may speak with a brogue
50. Home of Cincinnati
51. Ill humor
52. Unit that may be preceded by kilo-, mega- or giga-
53. Black: Fr.
54. Killer whale
55. Telephone
57. Univ. URL ending
58. ___ in the bud
59. ___TV (cable channel with "Impractical Jokers")

by Kevin Christian

ACROSS

1 Printer paper problems
5 Respected person in a tribe
10 Included in an email, in brief
14 Wax-wrapped cheese
15 Way overcharge
16 "O ___ Night" (Christmas song)
17 Summery quip, part 1
19 Relaxation
20 Love or hate
21 Pinnacles
23 Decorates with bathroom tissue, as in a Halloween prank
24 Musical note that's a step and a half below A
26 Trio of Greek goddesses
29 Auto
30 Grandmothers, informally
34 Pizazz
35 Quip, part 2
37 Vice president Gore and others
38 Venture to declare
39 Opus ___
40 Quip, part 3
42 Liqueur flavor
43 Total bargain
44 Clean air and water org.
45 What balloons do when you prick them with something 46-Across
46 Pointed, say
48 Little bit, as of ointment
49 Computer whiz
52 JetBlue or Delta
56 Native of Glasgow, e.g.
57 End of the quip
60 Opera solo
61 Tanker from the Mideast
62 Opening on a schedule
63 Step on a ladder
64 Oneness
65 Scarce as ___ teeth

DOWN

1 Ballet leap
2 "Madam, I'm ___" (palindromic greeting)
3 Relative of a great white
4 In love
5 Breakfast items in a toaster
6 Money you have to pay back
7 Total flop
8 What's all about me, me, me
9 Kingly or queenly
10 Large cat you shouldn't trust on a test?
11 Encourage with sweet talk
12 "What ___ is new?"
13 Easter egg colorers
18 Puppy bites
22 Showy garden flower
24 Words With Friends, for one
25 Coca-Cola soft drink brand
26 Outstanding accomplishments
27 Apportion
28 Aesthetic judgment
29 ___ counseling (aid for job-hunters)
31 Consumer advocate Ralph
32 Geometric calculations
33 Garment below a blouse
35 Catch in the act
36 "Zip-a-Dee-Doo-___"
38 Indian megacity
41 #, in social media
42 Issue a book or magazine
45 The ___ of Avon (Shakespeare)
47 Group of five to which is added "and sometimes y"
48 Writing you might keep away from prying eyes
49 Old Russian ruler
50 Sandy hue
51 Penny or nickel
52 Help in wrongdoing
53 Keep an engine running without moving
54 Like some advertising lights
55 Has dinner
58 Break one of the Ten Commandments
59 Boxer who floated like a butterfly, stung like a bee

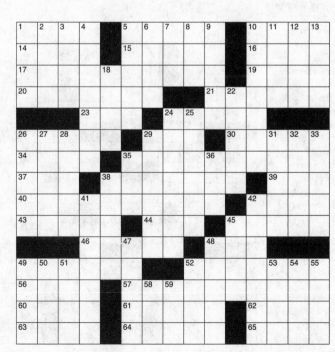

by Stephanie Lesser

186

ACROSS

1. With 68-Across, what the trio in this puzzle's clues is trying to promote
5. Enthusiasts
9. Cries of pain
14. Fencing blade
15. Israeli airline
16. Bothered, as one's conscience
17. Tax IDs
18. Past the deadline
19. Full of gristle, say
20. The first member of the trio said he'd . . .
23. Like a ship on an ocean floor
24. The "I" of FWIW
25. Lead-in to gender
28. Ability to keep one's balance on a ship
31. Companion of Frodo in "The Lord of the Rings"
34. Move stealthily
36. Sorta
37. T. rex, e.g.
38. The second member of the trio said he'd . . .
42. What sleeves hold
43. Witch
44. Make giggle, say
45. Org. that funds PBS
46. "Way to go!"
49. Lines on an urban map: Abbr.
50. Rock's ___ Fighters
51. First group with a #1 Billboard hit, alphabetically
53. The third member of the trio said she'd . . .
60. What a bouquet emits
61. Rational
62. ___ Devers, three-time Olympic track gold medalist
63. Attired like Batman or Superman
64. ___ and sciences

65. The Bruins of the N.C.A.A.
66. Chasm
67. Thomas Hardy's "___ of the D'Urbervilles"
68. See 1-Across

DOWN

1. Jokey comment
2. Lhasa ___ (dog)
3. Greek philosopher known for paradoxes
4. Twists of lemon or lime
5. Catlike
6. Home of 17 of the 20 highest peaks in the U.S.
7. Post-W.W. II alliance
8. Whole lot
9. Leisure boats
10. Community spirit
11. Unwelcome look
12. One of 16 in a chess set
13. Pigpen
21. Coverings on ears of corn
22. When to stargaze
25. Network for watching Congress
26. Accustom
27. 2014 film starring David Oyelowo as Martin Luther King Jr.
29. Feudal sovereign
30. Serpentine letter
31. Nasal cavity
32. Emotional turmoil
33. Leader of the Israelites across the Red Sea
35. Lou Gehrig's disease, for short
37. Faint, as light
39. State sch. southeast of Columbus

40. Apple computer, for short
41. Torah teacher
46. Wanderers
47. Short excursions
48. Focus single-mindedly on something
50. Risky things for a car to run on
52. Cattle breed
53. Dull-colored
54. Fibrous
55. Exam for many a 10th grader, for short
56. Naked
57. Apiece
58. Large grain container
59. Common side dish at a barbecue
60. Signature Obama legislation, for short

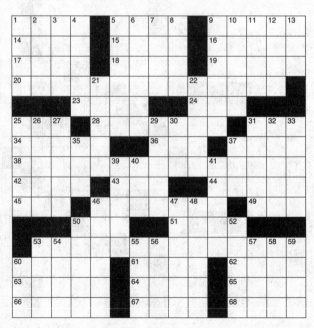

by Tommy Pauly

187

ACROSS

1 "Hey, over here!"
5 Just manage, with "by"
8 Bits of rain or dew
13 Where Honolulu is
14 Egg to be fertilized
16 New York's ___ City Music Hall
17 Laugh ___ (something very funny)
18 Roman emperor who said before dying "What an artist the world is losing in me!"
19 "Well, ___ we all?"
20 Service offered by Dropbox
23 F.D.R.'s successor
24 Computer for Apple pickers?
25 Kitchenware brand
26 A megalomaniac has a big one
29 Firefly
32 Place to play roulette
35 That guy's
36 Train travel
37 "Can't we all just get ___?"
38 Jean-___ Picard, Starfleet commander
39 Get the shampoo out
40 What's pulled through a pulley
41 May honoree
42 Less cooked in the center, say
43 Classic Corvette alternatives
46 Maple product
47 GPS option: Abbr.
48 Sticky stuff
49 Word after school or party
52 What precedes a storm . . . or a hint to 20-, 29- or 43-Across
55 TV, newspapers, etc.
58 "Goodbye, my friend!"
59 Lead-in to girl
60 Glass that refracts light
61 Came down, as to earth
62 To ___ a phrase
63 Sorry! and Trouble, for two
64 Summer: Fr.
65 Past partners

DOWN

1 Place to hang wind chimes
2 Goes by ship, say
3 "Dang it!"
4 Ballerina wear
5 Wa-a-a-ay in the past
6 Gripe
7 Deutsche mark replacer
8 Figure seen during Chinese New Year
9 Happening once in a blue moon
10 Tribute poem
11 What you have to remember to use an A.T.M.
12 Drunkard
15 Completely stupid
21 Contacting privately via Twitter or Instagram
22 x, y or z, in geometry
26 Manage one's account via the internet
27 Outward appearance
28 Gawker
29 Napkins, tablecloths, etc.
30 A green one is helpful in a garden
31 Smiles
32 Grocery conveniences
33 Greeting in Hawaii
34 Absorb, as gravy
38 Country singer Lynn
39 Free from
41 Self-referential
42 Apportion, as costs
44 Night visions
45 "You've said that already! Jeez!"
49 Injection that conceals wrinkles
50 Loosen, as laces
51 Is a huge fan of, in modern slang
52 Like an owl, in a simile
53 Patriot Nathan
54 10K or marathon
55 Fuel efficiency stat
56 Victorian ___
57 Not bright

by Kyra Wilson

188

ACROSS

1 Places where surgeries are performed, for short
4 Not in any way, in dialect
9 Composition of many reefs
14 Sneaky laugh
15 Practice piano piece
16 "The Phantom of the ___"
17 Gets past, as an obstacle
19 Say
20 Spiral shapes
21 Private eye, quaintly
23 Tattoos, informally
24 In that case
25 Where pirates roam
27 Vogue competitor
28 Period in human history after bronze was supplanted in toolmaking
30 ___ Lilly & Co.
31 Website for techies
32 Zaps, in a way
35 Omitted
37 Opposite of 35-Across?
39 Worrisome directive from a boss
40 Divisions of a subdivision
41 ___ Bird, many-time W.N.B.A. All-Star
42 Child's play
44 It rhymes with fire, appropriately
45 Opposite of 25-Across?
48 Frisbee, e.g.
49 Flexible blackjack card
50 Male cat
51 Hyundai compact
54 2014 Ava DuVernay drama
56 Opposite of 17-Across?
58 Place to go for the highlights?
59 Wham or bam

60 Pig follower in the Chinese zodiac
61 Beginning
62 Gown
63 Moody genre of music or fashion

DOWN

1 "Pick me! Pick me!"
2 Wake-up calls played on bugles
3 Twinkies have a long one
4 Classic wafer brand
5 Nebraska native
6 Carries a tune, in a way
7 Poem of praise
8 Hilton competitor
9 Visual jokes in openings of "The Simpsons" (a tradition since the first episode)
10 Make a choice
11 Knot again
12 Venue with tiered seating
13 Birds that do things just for the fun of it?
18 What good soufflés do
22 "Liberté, ___, fraternité" (Haiti's motto)
25 Spicy
26 Informal get-together
27 Sinuous swimmer
28 Raging blaze
29 One tweeting about football?
31 Warrior
33 Place to sell homemade crafts online
34 Enchilada topping, maybe
36 Blue-green shade

37 The New Yorker cartoonist Chast
38 Jill Biden ___ Jacobs
40 ___ États-Unis
43 Hillary who climbed Mount Everest with Tenzing Norgay
44 Radar sound
45 Dogie catcher
46 Atlantic or Pacific
47 Wishing sites
48 Induces to pull a prank, maybe
51 Actress Falco
52 Not so much
53 Regarding
55 Leader of the Three Stooges
57 Oslo's country: Abbr.

by Alex Eaton-Salners

ACROSS

1 What a plumber might fix a leak in
5 Artist Vincent van ___
9 Feathered Outback runners
13 Baghdad's land
14 Visually challenged "Mr." of cartoons
15 Steady look
16 Universal code of ethics
18 Stick-to-itiveness
19 More gray in appearance
20 Active Sicilian volcano
22 ". . . or thereabouts"
23 Midwife's instruction
25 Phrase starting a legal memo
27 Xmas mo.
30 Quick-minded sort
35 Put pen to paper
37 Desire for a contestant on "The Bachelor"
38 ___ Blanc
39 Packing heat
40 What wolves do at the moon
41 Language group of southern Africa
42 Need for tug of war
43 Long-necked pear
44 Finished
45 One who says that you're not on the ball?
48 Flamenco dancer's cry
49 At the home of: Fr.
50 Pizzeria fixture
52 Toward the stern
54 Finish second, say
57 "Please allow me . . ."
61 Civil rights pioneer Parks
63 Speaking of which . . . or where the starts of 16-, 30- and 45-Across can be found?
65 Pivotal point
66 Singer Carpenter or actress Gillan
67 Button at the start of a Zoom call
68 Possess
69 King Kong and others
70 The "A" in B.A.

DOWN

1 ___ colada
2 Cousins of 401(k)s
3 Trail
4 Gear up
5 Participant in a square dance
6 Eye lewdly
7 Bearded farm animal
8 "What a kind gesture!"
9 Nog ingredient
10 Organizing guru who asks "Does it spark joy?"
11 Israeli submachine guns
12 Late-night host Meyers
14 Boggy tract
17 Got some extra life out of
21 365 días
24 Where ships arrive and depart
26 Like I, for one?
27 ___ planet (designation for Pluto)
28 Swashbuckling Flynn
29 Kia Sportage or Ford Escape
31 Make fun of mercilessly
32 Hitchcock film with a classic shower scene
33 Info from a spy
34 One of 27 Chopin piano pieces
36 Things that gears and crocodiles share
41 Lacking, with "of"
43 Brand of bubble gum
46 Conger, for one
47 Brand of water named after a town on Lake Geneva
51 Assassin of old Japan
52 One half of the McDonald's logo
53 "It's ___ good cause"
55 Jacket fastener that's not a button
56 Raison d'___
58 Heathland
59 Squabbling
60 Longs (for)
62 Cancel, as a show
64 "___ dead, Jim" (much-parodied "Star Trek" line)

by Freddie Cheng

190

ACROSS

1 Molten rock in a volcano
6 Opposite of tight-fitting, as jeans
11 Does needlework
15 Native Americans originally of the Plains
16 State one's views
17 Welsh "John"
18 "Siskel & Ebert & the Movies" catchphrase
20 Designer Wang
21 "There! I did it!"
22 Grp. with a Most Wanted list
23 Typographical flourish
24 Alternative to .com and .edu
25 "Seinfeld" catchphrase
29 Manipulates
31 Break down grammatically
32 Lofty ambition
34 Headdress for the archbishop of Canterbury
36 Relatives, informally
39 "Columbo" catchphrase
43 Ave. crossers
44 The fact that the Bible is the most shoplifted book in America, e.g.
45 Brings in, as a salary
46 Vowel sound heard twice in "true blue"
48 What aspirin helps alleviate
49 "The Jackie Gleason Show" catchphrase
54 West Coast winter hrs.
57 Battery terminal
58 Scoundrel
59 Tiny bit
60 Pond amphibian
61 "Who Wants to Be a Millionaire" catchphrase
65 Largest city in the Palestinian territory

66 Aged Grimm character
67 Opposite of drowsy
68 Thick slice
69 The "99" in $2.99, e.g.
70 Shore birds

DOWN

1 "Be Prepared," for Boy Scouts
2 Battling
3 "You were close with that response"
4 Self-referential, in modern lingo
5 Campfire waste
6 Gets an F on a test, say
7 Tough H.S. science course
8 Ones with A.P.O. addresses
9 Wildebeest
10 Slangy affirmative
11 Harsh, as a storm or criticism

12 Each and ___
13 Nintendo antagonist with a "W" on his cap
14 Mess of a mistake
19 Interplanetary craft, for short
23 "Help!"
25 Verne captain
26 Model Kate
27 Ward off, as a sword
28 Gratis
30 Took a chair
32 Record spinners, in brief
33 Groove it's hard to get out of
34 Sign at the end of an entrance ramp
35 "See ya!"
36 Military muscle
37 ___ Arbor, Mich.
38 Classic British sports cars

40 The sum of the digits of any multiple of ___ is a multiple of ___ (arithmetic curiosity)
41 Sleuths, in old slang
42 "Fat chance!"
46 '60s drug dose
47 Have debts
48 Verdi opera
49 Is suspended
50 Shaquille of the N.B.A.
51 "Surprisingly impressive!"
52 Words from one who's defeated
53 Many works of Edgar Allan Poe
55 Back of a ship
56 Fruit desserts
59 Castaway's site
61 TV-monitoring agcy.
62 Ill temper
63 Parisian denial
64 ___ King Cole

by Bruce Haight

ACROSS

1 Mongolian desert
5 Eggplant ___ (cheesy dish, informally)
9 ___ vera
13 Either separately ___ combination
14 Plagued
16 Wander
17 Leave in a hurry
18 Doesn't have fortitude
20 Winged cupids in art
22 Enter, as a foyer
23 Home of the University of Kentucky
25 Longtime name on "Wheel of Fortune"
29 "Why are you telling me this?"
30 Fury
32 Big part of a dachshund
33 Coach Parseghian in Notre Dame history
34 The "A" of A-K-Q-J
35 Sorority's counterpart, informally
36 Finishes eating ice cream or soup, say
40 Word before language or temperature
41 One running for office, for short
42 "Xanadu" grp.
43 End of a shoe
44 Means of communication in "A Quiet Place," in brief
45 Voyage by boat
49 Escargot
51 Rescuer for when you've lost your key
53 Jose ___ (tequila brand)
55 Mix of coffee and chocolate
56 Tiny neighbor of France
60 Performs
61 Buffalo's lake
62 Seats at a hoedown
63 She: Fr.
64 Deliver a burn to
65 "Wild" actress Laura
66 Units in track or swimming

DOWN

1 Develop a chrome dome
2 Start of a Juliet soliloquy
3 Mississippi city on the Gulf of Mexico
4 Complexity
5 Friend
6 Barely any, as food or drink
7 Right-hand page of a book
8 Show friendliness, despite ill feeling
9 Setting for a rock concert
10 Hawaii's Mauna ___
11 Rower's implement
12 CPR pro
15 1/48 of a cup: Abbr.
19 Where everything's abuzz?
21 Sarcastic criticism
24 Gets hold of
26 Roman emperor who succeeded his adoptive father
27 Tandoor bread
28 Grade school class with crayons
31 Hunt for again
34 Calder Cup rink org.
35 One who might have a contract with a sandal manufacturer
36 Bird on the Canadian dollar
37 Something that might pop into your head
38 Opposite of a freeway
39 Suffix with cyto- or proto-
40 First K-pop group to have a #1 Billboard hit
44 Grad
45 Player making a basket or goal
46 Swiss cough drop brand
47 Need after a computer crash, informally
48 New moon, full moon and others
50 Some frozen drinks
52 Female flower part
54 Flow out
56 Headed
57 New England state sch.
58 Letters between nus and omicrons
59 Airer of "Family Feud" reruns

by Brooke Husic

ACROSS

1 Combat sport on pay-per-view, in brief
4 On the ___ of the moment
8 Like oversize clothes
13 ___ milk (nondairy choice)
14 On the up-and-up
16 Match in opinion
17 *Chinese-born director who became only the second woman to win the Oscar for Best Director
19 Shrek's love
20 Listened to
21 Penthouse or attic
23 Rear end, to Brits
24 *Runway model famous for her work as a Victoria's Secret Angel
26 Agcy. dealing with workplace accidents
28 Animals around the house
29 Elvis's wife
34 Jewish community center, for short
37 D.C. "Squad" member
38 Fashionable . . . or where you might find the starts of the answers to the starred clues
41 Command between "ready" and "fire"
42 Like a basso's voice
44 Vegetables in traditional moussaka
46 Did a sketch
49 Disturb, as sediment
50 *Longest resident performer at the Colosseum at Caesars Palace
54 Have ___ in one's belfry
58 Response to a stimulus
59 Baked pudding of potatoes or noodles in Jewish cooking
60 Loosen, as laces
61 *Atlanta rapper featured on Lizzo's Grammy-nominated "Exactly How I Feel"
64 Bishop's hat
65 Stop and Yield
66 AOL, for one
67 Budweiser and Beck's
68 Altoids containers
69 Tennis court divider

DOWN

1 Chocolate-flavored coffee
2 HBO's "Real Time With Bill ___"
3 Book of maps
4 Transport down a winter hill
5 Dispenser candy
6 "That tastes bad!"
7 Cowboy's rope
8 Perplex
9 Nimbleness
10 Bachelor party attendee
11 Italian city where Columbus was born
12 Ache (for)
15 Saturday morning TV character
18 Dunkable cookies
22 Vitality
24 Place for a goatee
25 Split in two
27 Biol. or chem.
29 Increase unnecessarily, as an expense report
30 ___ v. Wade
31 Cold drink with caffeine
32 Something to throw on a fire
33 Belligerent, in London
35 Runaway success
36 Mornings, informally
39 "Once ___ a time"
40 Inventor Whitney
43 More costly
45 Collection of songs
47 Goes in
48 One of ancient China's Three Kingdoms
50 Bit of bread
51 Start of a playground rhyme
52 Kennel occupants
53 Arctic dweller
55 Once more
56 All wound up
57 Got some shut-eye
59 Candy item in foil
62 Some movie f/x
63 MSNBC competitor

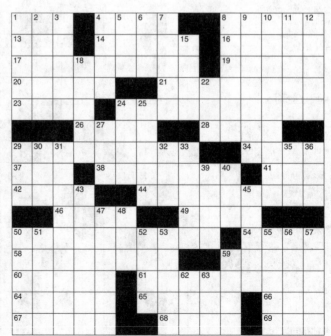

by Joshua Rosenblatt

193

ACROSS

1 Walk heavily
6 Face ___ (app that creates bizarre photos)
10 Successors of VHS tapes
14 Deed holder
15 Leonardo da Vinci's "___ Lisa"
16 Collect, as profits
17 Group of Washington politicians?
19 Turkish title of honor
20 C.I.A. forerunner
21 Old MacDonald had one
22 Bakery items that may come with lox and cream cheese
24 Lemon twists, e.g.
25 Border on
26 Bit of attire that may have a slogan on it
29 Group of diamond jewelry wearers?
32 Hilarious person
33 State whose flag, with eight gold stars in the shape of the Big Dipper, was designed by a 13-year-old
36 Title word sung 52 times in a 2000 hit by 'N Sync
37 Nonmainstream, as music
39 De-squeak
40 Italian city known as a fashion hub
42 Sunny-side-up item
43 Coastlines
46 Millennials, informally
47 Group of profoundly insightful people?
49 Major Ukrainian port known as the "Pearl of the Black Sea"
51 Urgent request
52 Cruise ship
54 About
56 "You lose"
57 Modeled, as for a portrait
60 Fishing sticks

61 Group of big rig haulers?
64 Artist Vincent van ___
65 Baseball officials, for short
66 Subside
67 "___ doke!"
68 Instruction on a door
69 Vehicles that might have bars and minifridges inside

DOWN

1 Manhattan neighborhood above Canal Street
2 Lowest pair in poker
3 Burden
4 ___ amis (my friends: Fr.)
5 Rather have
6 Intelligent
7 Rewards for early birds

8 Tiny hill dweller
9 Revenge
10 Bring back, as a bad memory
11 "Eat your ___!" (parent's order)
12 Roald who wrote "James and the Giant Peach"
13 Pampering places
18 Angel hair or penne
23 Crosswise, to a sailor
24 Baked Italian dish
26 Made an attempt
27 Lightly burn
28 Mixed bag
29 Spot of land in the ocean
30 Shades of blue used in print cartridges
31 Country that celebrated Obama Day in 2008
34 Pirate's treasure

35 Broadcast
38 German city in the Ruhr Valley
41 Longtime Disney chief Bob
44 "Careful!"
45 ___ boom (plane effect)
48 Soft toy
50 Turndown
52 Walks with some difficulty
53 "If only that were true . . ."
54 Jason's ship, in Greek myth
55 Corner chess piece
57 Con job
58 Intermediate choir voice
59 Golfer's bagful
62 Relative of an ostrich
63 Slugger's stat

by A. Tariq

ACROSS

1 What lava becomes after an eruption
6 The "S" of L.S.U.
11 Number of provinces in Canada
14 Relative by marriage
15 "This ___ to do the trick"
16 Pub brew
17 Pizza feature for a specialized diet
20 Nay's opposite
21 College official
22 Gossiping types
23 Products of Pilot and Bic
24 Lead-in to girl or boy
25 River beneath 37 Parisian bridges
27 Pain
28 Lucy of "Charlie's Angels"
31 Five, in French
32 Classic arcade game set in outer space
34 Take on a position, along with its responsibilities
37 Cleaned, as a window
38 Storage for garden tools
39 Sticky part of a gecko
40 Dress like, for a costume party, say
41 Contemptuous look
43 Soccer great Mia
44 Iota
45 Eastern place of worship
48 James who played Sonny Corleone
49 Letters on a bottle of tanning lotion
52 Lacking any moral compass
55 Year, in Spain
56 "Cleanup on ___ 5!"
57 ___ noir (wine)
58 "Affirmative!"
59 Los Angeles N.B.A. player
60 What lava is before an eruption

DOWN

1 Latvia's capital
2 Solitary
3 Aid in solving a mystery
4 Dennings of "2 Broke Girls"
5 Land between Norway and Finland
6 Couches
7 Word before "the tables" or "the tide"
8 Grow older
9 Nonbinary pronoun pair
10 ". . . and the list goes on"
11 Opposite of loose
12 Disney princess voiced by Idina Menzel
13 Safeguards for tightrope walkers
18 Official bird of Hawaii
19 Genetic "messenger"
23 Excite, as curiosity
24 Played a part on stage
25 One-named R&B singer with the 1999 6x platinum album "Unleash the Dragon"
26 Follow shortly thereafter
27 Volcanic emissions
28 Thin and graceful
29 One just passing time
30 Secondhand
31 Group in a playbill
32 Starting squad
33 Arrival
35 Business announcement involving billions of dollars
36 It's all about me, me, me
41 Former Iranian leader
42 Prime-time hour
43 Sweltering
44 One piece of evidence of a planet's habitability
45 Address God
46 Top-notch
47 Classic Pontiac muscle cars
48 Rapper J. ___
49 Serenade, e.g.
50 Big night for a high schooler
51 Crumbly salad cheese
53 Chastising syllable
54 "Zero Dark Thirty" org.

by Pao Roy

ACROSS

1 Org. exploring Mars
5 Paul who sang "Diana" and "Lonely Boy"
9 "Tsk!"
14 Highest point
15 One of 10 on a ten-speed
16 Hulk in a wrestling ring
17 Olympic event for which the world record stands at a little over 20 feet
19 Obvious
20 Tanning lotion spec
21 Broadcast
22 One of Haiti's two official languages, along with French
23 Magic duo with a 20+ year act in Las Vegas
27 Explorer Ericson
29 San ___ Obispo, Calif.
30 Prefix with function
31 ___ the Hun
34 Tex-Mex items associated with Tuesdays
37 "Spring forward" and "fall back" plan
42 Writer ___ Allan Poe
43 Like some food for dieters
44 Areas for hosp. surgeons
47 Mexican poet Juana ___ de la Cruz
49 Any member of NATO to any other
50 Added cost of buying soda
55 Keeps watching . . . and watching
56 "Rocks" in a drink
57 "I"-strain?
60 Completely fail
61 Guaranteed . . . or where you can find the ends of 17-, 23-, 37- and 50-Across

64 Basketball great Curry
65 It's a bad look
66 Relatives of ostriches
67 Taste or touch
68 Ore locale
69 Canadian gas brand

DOWN

1 Quick time outs?
2 Each . . . as in the price of balloons?
3 "Woe is me" feeling
4 Lumberjack's tool
5 Once more
6 ___ network
7 ___ Kan (dog food brand)
8 Paintings and sculptures
9 Where the land meets the sea
10 Rude dwelling
11 Seemingly timeless
12 Bob who sang "One love, one heart / Let's get together and feel all right"
13 Goes in
18 Airport shuttle, typically
22 M.R.I. alternative
24 Modern tax option
25 Almond or pecan
26 "Buenos ___"
27 Young fellow
28 I ___ Pi (punny fraternity name)
32 Jar topper
33 Longhorns : Texas :: ___ : Texas A&M
35 Egg: Prefix
36 Peninsula in the Six-Day War
38 Round of applause
39 Two of them meet every year in the Super Bowl
40 Gadot of "Wonder Woman"
41 Pigs' digs
44 Dwell (on)
45 What blades on windmills do
46 ___ Island (part of New York City)
48 Treated maliciously
51 Stumbles
52 River of forgetfulness, in myth
53 Earth tone
54 "Get what I'm saying?"
58 Wildebeests
59 "Then here's what happened . . ."
61 Sick
62 Prefix with natal
63 "Busy" insect

by Zachary David Levy

196

ACROSS

1 Head of a monastery
6 ___ Carlo (gambling mecca)
11 Corn on the ___
14 Dry heat bath
15 Accessory for a witch
16 Serve up a whopper
17 Traditional end of summer
20 Alternative to Beano
21 Corner pieces in chess
22 Things bullfighters wave
25 "Othello" villain
27 Dare to exceed normal limits
33 Swing clarinetist Shaw
34 Salvador who painted melting watches
35 Most emails offering life insurance policies, say
36 Word after bumper or cable
37 Stray from a topic
40 Brian who was once with Roxy Music
41 Airport guesses, for short
43 Alternative to suspenders
44 Frankly admit something
46 FedEx or DHL
49 Parts of i's and j's
50 Tilts
51 Hot dog topping
54 Extreme happiness
56 1967 hit by the Tremeloes suggested by the starts of 17-, 27- and 46-Across
63 Setting for a couples cruise?
64 ___ Gay (W.W. II bomber)
65 Bird on the Mexican flag
66 U.S. airer of "Downton Abbey"
67 Believer in a nonintervening God
68 Many vaccinations

DOWN

1 Handy way of communicating, in brief?
2 Sound heard in a herd
3 "Listen, ___!"
4 Musical Yoko
5 Aimed at
6 Degrees for C.E.O.s
7 "___ and Crake" (Margaret Atwood novel)
8 This very instant
9 Little piggy
10 Come into view
11 Queen of the Nile, informally
12 Sound from a piggy
13 Places for flowers and oysters
18 Sprinkle, as of salt
19 Some menthol cigarettes
22 Organize, as an exhibition
23 Of the stars
24 ___ Beta Kappa
25 Coves and fjords
26 "We try harder" auto rental company
27 Walked nervously back and forth
28 Lawn-cutting tools
29 Before the due date, say
30 What screen doors usually don't do
31 Freaks out
32 Be overdramatic
38 "Yeah, right!"
39 Recipients of a welcome sight, proverbially
42 Move crabwise
45 State with the words "Wild Wonderful" on its license plates: Abbr.
47 Said aloud
48 Like the first through fifth grades: Abbr.
51 Crack and redden, as lips
52 Basil or dill
53 Ruffles the feathers of
54 Some toothpastes and hair goops
55 Aspiring atty.'s exam
57 "We're number ___!"
58 Me, to Miss Piggy
59 Scrooge's "Phooey!"
60 In the past
61 Diner sandwich, for short
62 "Definitely"

by Christina Iverson and Andrea Carla Michaels

ACROSS

1 Large seashell
6 "Uncle ___ Wants You"
9 Social influence
14 Director Kurosawa
15 Uncle: Sp.
16 Reddish-brown dye
17 "This is my final offer"
20 What may have the solution to your vision problems?
21 Sign up
22 Attire for Caesar
24 Next-___ technology
25 Like something that's polarizing
32 Licoricelike flavoring
33 Mentions by name, in a tweet
34 Word after "That's my" or "right on"
36 Opening of an article, in journalism lingo
37 Put off until later, as a motion
39 Lip service?
40 King Kong or Donkey Kong
41 Forbidden action
42 Official language of Iran
43 "Get out of the way!"
47 Bird in a barn
48 Tip (over)
49 D.C. mayor Muriel
52 Not-quite-in-shape male physiques
57 Having no middle ground between success and failure
59 Country singer Steve
60 Try to win over romantically
61 German river to the North Sea
62 Material for Cinderella's slipper
63 "On the Basis of ___" (film about Ruth Bader Ginsburg)
64 Like some hills and prices

DOWN

1 Actress Blanchett
2 "Sure, why not"
3 Brand with a swoosh logo
4 Good reputation, in slang
5 Ponytail necessity
6 Halting, as rush-hour traffic
7 Put on TV
8 Small mammal that lives mostly underground
9 Homes in the Alps
10 Adam ___, longtime panelist on "The Voice"
11 Half of the digits in binary code
12 Cubit or karat
13 Pic that might use 16-Across
18 Play a trumpet, e.g.
19 Command to the helmsman from Jean-Luc Picard
23 Purchase at the Met museum, maybe
25 In ___ land
26 Time in New York when it's noon in Chicago
27 Feature introduced to the iPhone in 2009
28 Opposite of WNW
29 Rogue computer in "2001: A Space Odyssey"
30 "You have my sympathy"
31 Former Hawaii representative Gabbard
35 Send off, as rays
37 W.C.
38 Tiny builder of tunnels and hills
39 Some college grads, for short
41 Hit 2012 musical about paperboys
42 Documents, Downloads, Desktop, etc.
44 A, E, I, O, U . . . and sometimes Y
45 Big name in DVD rental kiosks
46 Titular Shakespearean king
49 Biblical false god
50 Vegetable used to thicken stews
51 Counterpart of columns
53 Thai currency
54 1930s migrant
55 Have a nice meal
56 Any rung on a ladder
57 Actress Ryan
58 ___ v. Wade

by Ben Pall

198

ACROSS

1 State known for lobsters and pine trees
6 Laziest of the deadly sins
11 Pal
14 St. ___ fire
15 Outdoor lounging area
16 Actress Gasteyer of "Saturday Night Live" fame
17 Athlete who rarely gets sacked or has a pass intercepted
20 Pig
21 Stereotypical name for a dog
22 Like neon gas
23 Classic cinema name
26 It's inhaled on an ocean cruise
27 Frenzies
29 Run-down places
31 2, 4, 6 and 8, but not 1, 3, 5 and 7
32 ___ latte
33 Figure to aim for, according to personal trainers
40 Moistens
41 Bar mitzvah dances
42 Pastry made with an orchard fruit
47 Start, as a computer
48 Coins of India
49 Stuff of little substance
50 Woman's name derived from the Greek for "peace"
51 Angel's overhead?
53 "That's really nice!"
56 Political group symbolized by a donkey
60 ___ out a living
61 Not with the times
62 Handmade sign held up by a kid in the bleachers

63 ___ Andreas fault
64 Histories that may be checkered or sordid
65 Twin Mary-Kate or Ashley

DOWN

1 Fine lattice
2 Kind of sax
3 "It's curtains for me!"
4 Conjunction used in logic
5 Abbr. after a lawyer's name
6 Ferdinand and Isabella's land
7 Nonvegan shortening
8 Germany's von Bismarck
9 Classic Father's Day gift
10 Charlotte hoopster
11 Start of a nursery rhyme about bags of wool

12 Detach, as a seatbelt
13 Bread makers
18 Causes of some mysterious radar blips, in brief
19 Pig in the wild
24 Microwave notification
25 Simplicity
26 Mix with a spoon
27 Ran across
28 Director DuVernay
29 Butler of "Gone With the Wind"
30 Penlight batteries
32 One-named pop diva
34 "___ the night before Christmas . . ."
35 Holier-than-___
36 Housetop
37 Various creative mediums . . . or a hint to variations found in the shaded squares
38 Sigma's follower

39 Telepathic letters
42 Lion packs
43 Shout accompanying a brilliant realization
44 Prehistoric human relations?
45 Nevada slots city
46 Super-miniature dog breed size
47 Voting group
49 Tosses, as a coin
51 Disbelieving laughs
52 "Look ___ this way . . ."
54 Siouan people
55 "Amazing Grace," for one
57 Messenger molecule
58 Noodle soup in Hanoi
59 Feel sick

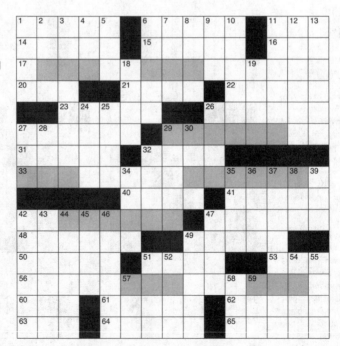

by Freddie Cheng

ACROSS

1 Wood strip
5 Circus animal balancing a ball on its nose
9 Cook, as vegetables
14 Farmland measure
15 ___ Major (the Big Dipper)
16 Issue to discuss
17 Former CNN anchor with a true-crime series on the Investigation Discovery channel
19 Apple tablets
20 Shrimp dish
21 On the ocean
23 German article
24 Places where kids can feed goats and sheep
30 College entrance exams
32 "Approximately speaking"
33 Obsolescent TV hookup
34 Annoying
37 Round trips?
40 Classic Nintendo character named after F. Scott Fitzgerald's wife
43 Like Mr. Spock's ears
44 Failed epically
45 Hoppy quaff, in brief
46 Body part that a Manx cat lacks
48 Western lily
52 Warsaw currency
57 Neighbor of Syria: Abbr.
58 ___ (the Jet) Walker, Basketball Hall-of-Famer
59 Long-haired, pot-smoking 1960s stereotype
61 Eyelashes
64 So simple . . . like 17-, 24-, 40- and 52-Across?
67 Ballpark purchase in a bun
68 Study, study, study
69 Tennis great Arthur
70 Overhang
71 Eyelid affliction
72 Warty fly-catcher

DOWN

1 Unwanted gaps
2 Thorny tree
3 School skipper
4 Captain's post
5 "The World of ___ Wong"
6 Timeline segment
7 Wood for a baseball bat
8 Hawaiian porches
9 Larsson who wrote the "Millennium" trilogy
10 November birthstone
11 Smog-monitoring org.
12 Lend a hand
13 Ones making introductions, in brief
18 TikTok, Instagram or Google's Find My Device
22 Kind of alarm often activated in the morning
25 Puff from a pipe or cigarette
26 It's hoisted on a brig in high winds
27 "Ars Amatoria" poet
28 Twice tetra-
29 Many takers of 30-Across: Abbr.
31 Whirl or twirl
35 Sinus doc
36 Grim Reaper's implement
38 Big retailer of outdoor gear
39 Three-ingredient sandwiches, for short
40 Law officers, in slang
41 Iranian money
42 Normandy battle site in W.W. II
43 Backup singer for Gladys Knight
47 Montezuma's people
49 Only major Texas city on Mountain Time
50 Performer in a kimono
51 Did as directed
53 Sweet cake topper
54 Malted, e.g.
55 Spice whose name consists of two consecutive pronouns
56 Bark like a lap dog
60 Fuel from a bog
61 North-of-the-border sports org.
62 Fury
63 Young fellow
65 Good name for a museum curator?
66 "___ what?"

by Damon Gulczynski

200

ACROSS

1 "No need to say it again"
6 Group of criminals
10 Father on a stud farm
14 Tennis star Osaka
15 Cookie whose packaging shows a splash of milk
16 What might give "caws" for concern for a farmer?
17 "Cómo ____?" ("How are you?": Sp.)
18 Droplet of happiness or sadness
19 Assistant
20 Things modern travelers pack
23 Woodman's makeup in "The Wizard of Oz"
24 Auto tankful
25 Dickens's Oliver Twist or Kipling's Mowgli
28 In the year of ____ Lord
29 Decrease in size, as the moon
31 NNW's opposite
32 Forms of some kids' multivitamins
36 Direction after adding sugar
37 Stockpile
38 ____-tac-toe
39 Road Work ____ (highway sign)
40 Ice hockey venue
41 Breakfast side at a diner
43 "____, humbug!"
44 Exam
45 One who cries "Yer out!"
46 Ice hockey player
48 Ironically humorous
49 Score 100% on
52 Government-backed investments
56 B sharp or B flat
58 The Cowboys' five-pointed star or the Colts' horseshoe
59 Listings on an actor's IMDb page
60 Melee
61 Idiot
62 Cognizant (of)
63 Camera's "eye"
64 Ocular swelling
65 Items on a to-do list

DOWN

1 Like a butterfingers
2 Healthful Kellogg's cereal brand
3 Off, palindromically
4 "Toe" of the Arabian Peninsula
5 Smart alecks
6 High schoolers who dress in black, maybe
7 Calculation in calculus
8 In the neighborhood
9 Mythological monsters with snakes for hair
10 Steep embankment
11 Traditional St. Patrick's Day dish
12 Support for a shower curtain
13 Farm animal that sounds like a letter of the alphabet
21 Low-____ diet
22 "Able was I ____ I saw Elba"
26 Like Russia, east of the Urals
27 Jocks' counterparts, stereotypically
28 Southern Siberian city
29 Dress part that may be taken in
30 St. Louis landmark
32 Clothes
33 Inuit boat
34 Whiskey cocktail . . . or where it was invented
35 When planes are due in, for short
36 Engage in some "retail therapy"
39 Kid with military parents
41 Some angels . . . or some newspapers
42 Hide in a hard-to-find spot
44 Prop for a football kickoff
47 Three-point shots, informally
48 Jotted down
49 Star student's report card, maybe
50 Worker for a Supreme Court justice
51 Twisty curves
53 Chimney buildup
54 Pretty ____ (oxymoron)
55 Hawkeye State
56 Org. that's home to the ends of 20-, 32-, 41- and 52-Across
57 Mineral-bearing rock

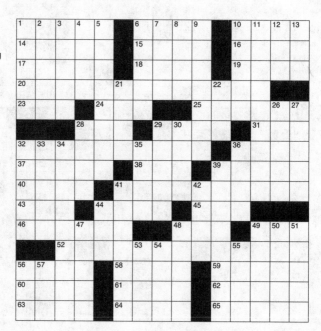

by Fiona Taylor

ANSWERS

1

```
M A R C O . M O A T S . M I G
O W N U P . V A N D A L . A C A
B L A Z E O F G L O R Y . K E G
. . C R A W . O N T . P E C S
P T B O A T . A A A A . A N A T
F E E . B U R N I N G L O V E .
C A L A M A R I . . P O S E R
. E T E R N A L F L A M E .
S P A T E . . O I L S A N D S
L I G H T M Y F I R E . S H H
A Q U A . R O A N . W I S E L Y
S U E T . P U T . S Y N C .
H A R . D I S C O I N F E R N O
E N E . I B E A M S . E N V O Y
S T D . A B E T S . R E S T S
```

2

```
D O T E . G O A D . E L K S
E T E S . H O R S E . M A L A
A H A S . I S T H A T O K A Y
R E C . U H O H . N Y J E T S
G L A S S O F O J . C I R C A
O L D W E S T . I D O . S H H
D O D O . . F L U B S .
. Y O U W I L L O B E Y .
. P R I C Y . L E T O
R A S . B I B . S T C L A I R
A V E D A . M I L O O S H E A
S I L E N T . P E R M . F I N
C A F E A U L A I T . Z I N G
A R I D . L O D G E . A N T E
L Y E S . L U S H . C E O S
```

3

```
S T P . C I T G O . O D O R
I H O P . O N I O N . L E N O
N E W R E L E A S E . I N T O
. O D E S . P R O . A V I A S
. E L K . T A X E X E M P T
M E R L I N . . L E O .
I C K . M E M O R Y . I R K S
T H E C O A S T I S C L E A R
T O G O . R U B B E R . A L A
. S E E . E A G L E S
B E G P A R D O N . V I D
E X A L T . A R I . A R E A
G I L A . F R E E A T L A S T
A L L Y . R I C C I . S L A B
N E S S . I N K E D . S P A
```

4

```
S C A M S . D A M E . A F T S
O H F U N . R I A L . C L A P
X A C T O . E M M A S T O N E
. L E E R S . A B I T . O L E
Q U A R T E R T O N E . R I D
V P S . S T E . E L N I N O
C A T O . A T M S . M A T E S
. M E T R I C T O N .
O C T A D . O D O R . A S E A
B L O N D E . R I G . P R Y
L A S . I M E A N C O M E O N
A P T . E A R N . E P I C S .
S T A N D I N G O . A N T I C
T O D O . L I L A . S C R O D
S N A G . S E E K . T E E N S
```

5

```
G O S S I P . T G I . M E S S
L A M A R R . R E D D I W I P
E T A L I I . A L I E N A T E
N H L . S N O W . A G N E W
. S L Y . T E L L A L L .
. W E B M D . A T T E M P T
S H O P P E . T I L . R U L E
T A R . A D M I R A L . M I A
E L L S . I O N . R O B B E R
M O D E L U N . I G L O O
. V A M O O S E . P J S
E S S E S . P A R K . U P C
D O W N S I Z E . A N E M I A
N A U T I C A L . C O M B E D
A R M Y . U P S . E X T O L S
```

6

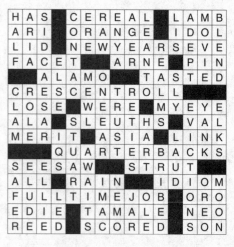

```
H A S . C E R E A L . L A M B
A R I . O R A N G E . I D O L
L I D . N E W Y E A R S E V E
F A C E T . A R N E . P I N
. A L A M O . T A S T E D
C R E S C E N T R O L L .
L O S E . W E R E . M Y E Y E
A L A . S L E U T H S . V A L
M E R I T . A S I A . L I N K
. Q U A R T E R B A C K S
S E E S A W . S T R U T .
A L L . R A I N . I D I O M
F U L L T I M E J O B . O R O
E D I E . T A M A L E . N E O
R E E D . S C O R E D . S O N
```

7

S	A	W	I	I	■	E	C	H	O	■	V	A	N	S
P	L	A	N	T	■	D	A	M	P	■	O	B	I	E
E	L	V	I	S	A	N	D	M	E	■	R	U	L	E
W	I	E	■	O	J	A	Y	■	R	I	T	T	E	R
S	E	D	A	K	A	■	■	M	A	C	E	■	■	■
■	■	O	A	X	A	C	A	M	E	X	I	C	O	■
S	P	I	N	Y	■	D	R	Y	A	D	■	T	A	Z
P	A	N	E	■	D	E	I	O	N	■	G	E	T	Z
U	P	N	■	W	A	X	E	R	■	C	O	N	E	Y
D	I	S	C	O	V	E	R	S	I	O	N	■	■	■
■	■	E	R	I	C	■	■	T	O	G	A	E	D	■
U	N	J	A	M	S	■	B	A	C	K	■	U	V	A
C	O	O	S	■	C	A	R	D	H	O	L	D	E	R
L	I	N	E	■	U	T	A	H	■	F	A	I	N	T
A	R	I	D	■	P	E	N	D	■	F	O	O	T	S

8

H	E	M	S	■	E	L	M	O	■	B	A	L	D	S
A	V	E	C	■	M	E	A	L	■	C	L	A	R	K
L	I	F	E	G	U	A	R	D	■	C	A	S	E	Y
F	L	I	N	T	■	P	L	E	A	■	C	A	L	■
W	E	R	E	O	N	■	A	N	D	S	O	A	M	I
A	Y	S	■	S	E	A	■	S	A	D	L	O	T	■
Y	E	T	I	■	L	I	E	S	■	L	O	A	N	■
■	■	■	F	I	L	M	L	O	V	E	R	■	■	■
■	S	H	O	D	■	S	I	R	I	■	S	H	E	L
G	O	A	L	I	E	■	■	T	E	M	■	O	V	A
H	A	N	D	G	R	I	P	■	W	E	S	L	E	Y
O	K	S	■	■	A	M	O	S	■	R	H	I	N	E
U	S	O	F	A	■	P	O	L	I	C	E	D	O	G
L	U	L	U	S	■	E	L	A	N	■	B	A	N	G
S	P	O	R	K	■	I	S	M	S	■	A	Y	E	S

9

A	R	F	■	S	A	A	B	S	■	P	H	O	T	O
M	A	O	■	M	I	L	L	I	■	L	E	T	I	N
A	I	L	■	O	R	L	O	N	■	A	I	S	L	E
S	T	I	L	L	K	I	C	K	I	N	G	■	■	■
S	T	O	O	D	I	N	■	■	V	E	L	C	R	O
■	■	■	W	E	S	■	C	O	A	T	■	L	O	U
W	A	T	E	R	S	D	O	W	N	■	D	E	U	S
H	E	A	R	S	■	O	U	I	■	G	I	A	N	T
A	I	M	S	■	R	U	N	E	R	R	A	N	D	S
R	O	E	■	K	U	R	T	■	E	E	L	■	■	■
F	U	R	I	E	S	■	■	O	R	W	O	R	S	E
■	■	■	D	E	E	P	T	H	O	U	G	H	T	S
M	A	S	O	N	■	L	E	G	U	P	■	Y	R	S
S	T	A	L	L	■	U	S	E	T	O	■	M	A	E
N	E	W	S	Y	■	S	H	E	E	N	■	E	P	S

10

C	O	B	R	A	■	B	R	A	S	H	■	C	O	Y
A	R	I	E	S	■	R	O	U	T	E	■	H	M	O
C	I	T	Y	S	L	I	C	K	E	R	■	R	I	G
H	O	E	■	A	I	D	S	■	T	O	Y	O	T	A
E	N	S	U	I	N	G	■	A	S	I	A	N	■	■
■	■	■	B	L	U	E	S	T	O	C	K	I	N	G
E	M	C	E	E	S	■	W	O	N	■	C	E	O	■
B	O	A	R	D	■	J	A	M	■	P	A	L	E	D
B	O	P	■	B	U	Y	■	L	O	N	E	R	S	■
S	T	U	F	F	E	D	S	H	I	R	T	■	■	■
■	C	U	R	R	Y	■	U	N	K	E	M	P	T	■
G	E	H	R	I	G	■	A	N	D	Y	■	A	A	A
A	M	I	■	S	M	A	R	T	Y	P	A	N	T	S
G	U	N	■	K	A	T	I	E	■	I	N	L	E	T
A	S	S	■	S	N	E	A	D	■	G	A	Y	L	E

11

A	R	M	S	■	A	G	O	R	A	■	S	H	E	D
B	E	A	U	■	P	L	I	E	S	■	E	E	R	O
C	A	R	P	■	P	O	L	Y	P	H	E	M	U	S
S	P	E	E	D	E	R	S	■	■	A	G	A	P	E
■	■	■	R	A	N	I	■	M	O	D	E	L	T	S
S	A	M	M	Y	D	A	V	I	S	J	R	■	■	■
U	V	E	A	S	■	■	E	S	A	I	■	E	Y	E
M	O	R	N	■	D	I	R	T	Y	■	I	G	O	R
O	N	E	■	S	E	C	S	■	■	S	C	A	R	E
■	■	J	A	C	K	O	F	S	P	A	D	E	S	■
R	A	C	E	W	A	Y	■	A	T	E	N	■	■	■
A	B	O	R	T	■	■	A	N	E	W	H	O	P	E
B	A	Z	O	O	K	A	J	O	E	■	E	V	I	L
I	T	E	M	■	F	R	A	U	D	■	L	A	P	S
N	E	N	E	■	C	E	R	T	S	■	P	L	E	A

12

A	B	B	I	E	■	Z	I	N	G	■	B	L	O	W
R	O	L	F	E	■	A	S	E	A	■	L	I	V	E
O	R	A	N	G	E	P	E	E	L	■	U	S	E	S
A	N	N	O	■	S	P	E	D	■	H	E	A	R	T
R	E	D	T	A	P	E	■	■	P	U	B	■	■	■
■	■	■	I	N	D	I	G	O	G	I	R	L	S	■
O	N	D	V	D	■	■	M	O	N	O	R	A	I	L
L	I	I	I	■	P	A	P	P	Y	■	D	U	M	A
A	L	L	O	C	A	T	E	■	■	I	S	L	E	T
Y	E	L	L	O	W	L	I	G	H	T	■	■	■	■
■	■	■	E	O	N	■	R	A	I	N	B	O	W	■
M	A	L	T	S	■	F	W	I	W	■	O	U	Z	O
A	C	E	R	■	G	R	E	E	N	A	R	R	O	W
T	I	N	A	■	R	E	E	F	■	C	A	R	N	E
E	D	D	Y	■	R	E	P	S	■	S	H	O	E	D

13

```
P E R T █ A D D A M S █ U S E
A V O N █ C R E D I T █ N A G
V I C T O R Y L A N E █ T U G
E L K █ N E A T █ █ A M I N O
█ █ C U R █ D A V I D L E A N
P E A N U T S █ E D Y S █ █
E L V I S H █ C E O █ █ C I G
T O E T H E P A R T Y L I N E
S I S █ █ N E W █ O E U V R E
█ █ O F F S █ S O R T I E S
M I C R O L O A N █ T E C █
O T H E R █ G O A L █ D A B
M A O █ C L A I R D E L U N E
M L K █ E A G L E D █ E T N A
A Y E █ S P E E D S █ D Y E D
```

14

```
D E S I █ K E B A B S █ K F C
O M A N █ A N O D E S █ I L L
E I F F E L T O W E R █ R O Y
S T E R N E █ T E T █ F O O D
█ █ T O R █ T H E L O U V R E
S A Y N O T O █ K E R R █ █
P O N T N E U F █ A S K M E
E N E █ A R E N A █ I E D
D E T O O █ S O R B O N N E
█ █ G R I P █ N E R F G U N
N O T R E D A M E █ I A M █
A L O E █ E T A █ B A N I S H
K I N █ P A R I S F R A N C E
E V E █ A T O N O F █ G O A L
D E S █ R E N E W S █ E S T D
```

15

```
U R L █ A M A █ A P P L E T
L E A H █ C A T █ T H R I V E
T A K E A C U T █ H A I L E D
A L E C G U I N N E S S █ █
█ █ K O R █ O N E M O R E
A N D Y G A R C I A █ S H E A
D I R E █ C U L █ █ I M S
A G E S █ Y E A R S █ F O O T
P I X █ █ R A W █ E A V E
T R E S █ A V A G A R D N E R
S I L E N T I █ G E E █ █
█ █ S I L V E R S C R E E N
I T H A C A █ R E U S A B L E
C H I M E S █ O A R █ L A S S
E X P E R T █ S P F █ Y E T
```

16

```
L E W D █ A M B E R █ R A S H
I D E A █ L O I R E █ E L M O
S U N N I I S L A M █ A L O U
A C T █ N B A █ I G L O O S
█ █ S E T I I N S T I T U T E
B L O T █ C O M █ M Y T H S
R E F U S E █ W O M B █ █
A N T I I M M I G R A T I O N
█ █ M O O S █ S L I C E R
A S T R O █ L E M █ T Y R A
S K I I N S T R U C T O R █
S A D D E N █ S O N █ O N O
U T I L █ E Y E C O N T A C T
R E N E █ E A G L E █ E D I T
E D G Y █ R O G E R █ E S S O
```

17

```
A T W A R █ S T E P █ M Y T H
L I E T O █ T H A I █ C O H O
(S C A T) T E R R U G █ Q U I P
O K R A █ R O O █ D U N N E
█ █ (S C R A M) B L E D E G G S
M A T H I S █ A L E E █ █
A S H E N █ A L U M █ N I C E
W I I █ G O F I R S T █ N A Y
S A N D █ P I T A █ H A S T E
█ █ E V E R █ D E B I T S
(L E A V E N) E D B R E A D
I N B O X █ I R A █ L I S A
E D I T █ (S H O O T) H O O P S
N U D E █ A U D I █ I N U I T
S P E D █ P E E L █ P E S T O
```

18

```
S H O T S █ T I P S Y █ I T D
T O R S O █ E L O P E █ N O R
L E G A L B R I E F S █ A L E
█ █ A R I A N A █ █ E N D S
O W N █ D I S C J O C K E Y S
T H I R S T █ A S H G R A Y
S O S O █ H A M L E T █ █
█ A M A T E U R B O X E R S
█ █ D R A M A S █ S E L F
A N T W E R P █ S E T F E E
M O V I E S H O R T S █ E W W
D O W N █ S U I T O R █ █
I D I █ C A S H D R A W E R S
A L F █ F A K E D █ T E E N A
L E E █ O H Y A Y █ E S S A Y
```

19

```
M T F U J I   D A T A   G A L
P O L L E N   O W E N   O L E
G R O U N D S C R E W   R V S
  E E L   E A S Y   A E G I S
    A W E D     O R L O N
  E A T A P E A C H   S N A P
A S S E T     P A N E   Z I T
S P H   T O O L B O X   O L A
T A B   S U P E     P A L E S
I D L E   S T A Y S A W A Y
  R O G E T     E T T A
R I N G S   S O A R   S K A
O L D   T U N A S A S H I M I
A L E   E M I T   T A I L O R
D E S   R A P S   I G N O R E
```

20

```
L E E R   O B L A   P O U L T
A R T E   F U E L   L U C I E
B I T E V A L V E   A T L A S
S C U B A   K I C K S T A R T
    O R B S     E M O
L I L K I M   D I Y   W A I L
A N O   E O S I N   T I N N Y
S C R A T C H A N D S N I F F
S U R L Y   E L S I E   S E T
O R E L   P A S   E L D E R S
    O T C     A M I E
P U N C H B O W L   O U G H T
A R O A R   F I G H T C L U B
P L U T O   F R A U   E E L S
A S N E W   S E E M   S N A P
```

21

```
J E A N   P A L M   H A S N T
O R B S   I P S O   O C H O A
B A B Y A L B U M   T R A M S
S T A N C E     A F I R S T
    C H I L D P R O D I G Y
E B B   T O R I N O
T E E N V O G U E   T O A S T
C A R E E N     S I M I L E
H U M O R   A D U L T S W I M
    M O D U L E     A P P
S E N I O R M O M E N T
A C O R N S     P E E W E E
G O T A T   G H O S T T O W N
E L A T E   T E R I   R O O D
S I X E R   O X E N   A S K S
```

22

```
  T R A M P S   C H A R T S
A R A M A I C   A I L E R O N
P U T O N A H A P P Y F A C E
H E R S   N O T I T   S U L U
I D A   P O O L T O Y   M O T
D A C H A   L A O   A B A S E
S T E A L   D S L   W I S E R
    D A T A   D A N G
B R E A K I N T O A S M I L E
R E A M   S C A M S   O N E S
A C R E S   E R E   R U F F S
  O C A L A   P E T I T
F U L L O F G O O D C H E E R
E P I   G R O W L A T   L Y E
E S P   S O A N D S O   D E B
```

23

```
T O D D   L S D   B A S R A
O D O R   A C A I   A N T I C
T E N D   B A L D E R D A S H
  T O P   M I A M I   B E E
A R B O R S   H U S K
D E L M O N I C O S T E A K
U F O   P A L O   A R M E D
L E W D   G L A D S   R E N O
T R I E S   C I A O   N N E
  S T E A L T H F I G H T E R
  T R I O   D R O O L S
E S C   A V O I D   E A T
D O U B L E T R E E   R H E A
I S S U E   S I L L   D A R N
T A S T E   S I S   S T A Y
```

24

```
H U T   R A T   S I R   V O W
E P I T A P H   A M A T E U R
S I D E C A R   G A V O T T E
  E M E R I L   M I M O S A
B R O     L O S S   M E E K
R A V E   B L O T   C Y S T S
A N E M I A   K I L O
  D R I N K S A R E O N M E
    N E I L   F L A C K S
S A R I S   L I S T   G E E K
I R I S   A L V A   N S A
G I M L E T   E L D E S T
N A M E T A G   M A R T I N I
O N E Y A R D   O N M E R I T
R A D   L I P   N E A   E P S
```

25

```
A S A P ▪ T A R T ▪ ▪ C U R B
M A C A D A M I A ▪ T A N I A
P H O N E J A C K ▪ E M I T S
S A R G E ▪ T E E M S ▪ C U E
U R N ▪ ▪ ▪ D I A L S O A P
P A S T I M E ▪ ▪ P A E L L A
▪ ▪ E L I T E S ▪ ▪ R O S Y
▪ C A L L T O O R D E R ▪ ▪
S W A B ▪ ▪ A S S O O N ▪ ▪
C A N A A N ▪ ▪ O N W A T C H
R I N G P O P S ▪ ▪ E R A
I K E ▪ I S A A C ▪ A C H E S
B I D O N ▪ B U Z Z W O R D S
E K I N G ▪ S N A I L M A I L
S I T E ▪ ▪ T A R P ▪ A N T E
```

26

```
F I F I ▪ Q T I P ▪ O S C A R
E B O N ▪ T A C O ▪ H E A T H
T E A G A R D E N ▪ M A P L E
A X L E S ▪ ▪ U Z I ▪ P R A T
▪ ▪ S H O P P I N G L I S T
P A S T E U R ▪ ▪ S L A P ▪
O N O ▪ Z O O S ▪ U N A G I
G O L F T O U R N A M E N T S
O N A I R ▪ D E A R ▪ T O E
▪ R E E D ▪ F I N E S S E
A P P L E S T R U D E L ▪ ▪
R E A D ▪ T R A ▪ M I F F S
R E N E E ▪ A D D T O C A R T
O V E R T ▪ M A Y O ▪ I K E A
W E L S H ▪ P R E Y ▪ T E E N
```

27

```
H A Z E S ▪ A C T ▪ B O A R
O C E A N ▪ A L O E ▪ A M M O
P A S T A S H E L L ▪ Y A P S
S I T ▪ P E A S A N T A R M Y
▪ ▪ H A N ▪ E A R ▪ ▪
▪ W H A T A G E N T L E M A N
M A A M ▪ T A R O ▪ C A R G O
A N T ▪ E V I T A ▪ B A G
I D E S T ▪ E C I G ▪ V I P S
M A R K U P L A N G U A G E
▪ ▪ I N A ▪ I N N ▪ ▪
P R I M E N U M B E R ▪ C H E
H O D A ▪ I T S A S E C R E T
E V E S ▪ N E R D ▪ S P A R S
W E A K ▪ I S P ▪ T A B B Y
```

28

```
T O O L ▪ I D T A G S ▪ S P A
E A V E ▪ S E R I E S ▪ P O T
C H E E S E C U R L S ▪ O I L
H U R ▪ P E A R ▪ K O N A
▪ S H E ▪ F O R K L I F T S
D E T A C H ▪ H O O T S A T
I V E S ▪ A S C O T S ▪ ▪
P E P P E R M I N T T W I S T
▪ ▪ A P O G E E ▪ A R E A
S T I R R E R ▪ R E N O W N
W I N E P R E S S ▪ Y E N ▪
E D D Y ▪ E A S E ▪ R B I
A B E ▪ D I D D L Y S Q U A T
T I E ▪ A D A G E S ▪ E L S E
S T P ▪ M O D E S T ▪ D E E M
```

29

```
O P A L ▪ S W A G ▪ P E R M A
P A C E ▪ T A L E ▪ I M O U T
E L L A ▪ O X E N ▪ L O O M S
C O U N T R Y C O D E ▪ F B I
▪ ▪ I I I ▪ M R I ▪ T A G
C O U N T E R F E I T C O I N
C N N ▪ S I R ▪ P O O P
S O F A S ▪ G A P ▪ N O B E L
▪ A M E N ▪ M I C ▪ A G O
C O M P L E T E C O N T R O L
O U I ▪ F Y I ▪ R O E
A T L ▪ C O M E C O R R E C T
R A I T A ▪ E T O N ▪ E V E R
S T A R R ▪ R A C E ▪ S I L O
E E R I E ▪ S L O T ▪ A L L Y
```

30

```
E M C E E ▪ I S I S ▪ M I C E
L A R A M ▪ N O S E ▪ E B O N
S P U R O F T H E M O M E N T
E S S ▪ T A H O E ▪ N E R V E
▪ A D E L E ▪ I V E ▪ I E R
O R D E R S O F T H E D A Y
L I E N ▪ E R A ▪ F Y I
A P R I L ▪ Y I N ▪ E D G A R
▪ R I B ▪ N O B ▪ T U N A
▪ B O O K O F T H E M O N T H
L O S ▪ E W E ▪ I N Y O U
A L I A S ▪ L A T C H ▪ S M U
P E R S O N O F T H E Y E A R
E R I K ▪ A N T E ▪ R E R U N
L O S S ▪ T S A R ▪ O A S I S
```

31

```
V A S E   R A K E   A S C A P
E S P N   E V E R   S P A D E
S T A T E F A I R   K I R I N
T A C I T     R O S   F L E A
    E C O   P A R T Y F O U L
C A D E N C E   S E A U
E L O     O R B   A L P H A S
S T U   G U M B A L L   O R E
T O T I N G   C O T   T E E
    N A A N   N H L T E A M
A I R S T R I K E   U R L
C H I P   S E E   B A S S O
T O P I C   C L O S E C A L L
O P E R A   E S A U   T F A L
R E N E W   S O R E   S E G A
```

32

```
T O P   O R A L   P R A W N
E P A   S N A K E   R O M P S
E R R   L E T I N   O B A M A
M A K E I T S N A P P Y
S H A M P O O   E U N I C E
    B U G   S T E P   O H M
L O V E P O T I O N   S N I P
A P E R S   O F T   C L I N T
T E N S   N O T S O L U C K Y
C R U   P E N S   T E D
H A S S L E   S T A G G E R
    W A R O N P O V E R T Y
6 I R O N   T O R M E   A H A
0 C A R B   I D E A S   D E N
S E N D S   S E E N   E L S
```

33

```
B O S C   F A C T   L L A M A
O H I O   A R E A   P O L O S
G O D O W N I N H I S T O R Y
    E L I   E T O N   T H E E
M A K E P A S S E S   E A S T
I B I S E S     T A R
T A C T   H E M P   N Y P D
T S K   G E T A R U N   R I B
    E S P N   C R O C   A I D E
    I C E   L A T V I A
V A M P   D R A W A B L A N K
A L O E   G A T E   E A T
G O O D N E W S B A D N E W S
U N D U E   L E E K   T E A R
E G Y P T   S A R A   A R G O
```

34

```
S H E E T   C A M E L   U S A
E A R N S   I N A N E   N A B
C H I C K E N K I E V   S N L
T A C O   L E A N   E T U D E
    R O A M   S T E R N
    V I E N N A S A U S A G E S
S E N S E   T I N   P H A T
A R F   S A R A L E E   E T A
A S I A   B E L   D A R E R
B E E F W E L L I N G T O N
    L A H T I   N O E L
H Y D R A   A U T O   A L D A
O O F   L O N D O N B R O I L
O Y L   E P C O T   A G R E E
T O Y   S T E N O   D E E D S
```

35

```
B L U R B   S H I M   H E A L
R U N T O   P U Z O   A C R E
I N D E X   A N O N   G O Y A
T K O   K I R K D O U G L A S
    F I T S   S P L I N T
A E R A T E   P E K O E
S T E V E M A R T I N   S A X
K A L E   C I A   H I V E
S T Y   J A M E S T A Y L O R
    B E N E S   E N D O W S
A M B I E N   R A T E
B I L L R U S S E L L   S L O
A M O K   I H O P   E Q U A L
B I K E   T O D O   R U M B A
A C E D   Y E A S   S A S S Y
```

36

```
C H A S E   S T O R M   A P P
A E S O P   I O N I A   W A R
S I T T I N G D U C K   K E A
E R A   S E N D S   E L W A Y
    S O H O   A S I A N S
S T A N D I N G O R D E R
A E R I E S   R I C O   D A B
A A R P   A O L   T A M E
B R O   A U R A   S P I G O T
    W A L K I N G P A P E R S
I N H A L E   E A R S
G E E S E   S O N I A   P A W
L E A   R U N N I N G J O K E
O D D   G R A C E   O L L I E
O S S   Y I P E S   N O E N D
```

37

```
I D T A G . A B S . R A S T A
F O R C E . M E W . E A T O N
F R E E T R A D E . F R O N T
Y A K . B O S S E S . P O S H
. . B U D S . T H E . D I E .
C H E E S E . D E A D C A L M
C O M F Y . T O N G U E S . .
S O B E . N A M E S . L I F E
. A L R O K E R . S E D A N .
B U R L I V E S . S P R E A D
I N K . G A S . P L A Y . . .
A W E D . S A V I O R . L E O
N O D U H . B I L G E P U M P
C R O N E . O N E . M E R I T
A N N E X . W E D . E W E R S
```

38

```
S P E W . P I T S . B O S S Y
L A V A . O P E N . I R A T E
A C I D . T R E E . F A U L T
T E L E P H O N E P O L E . .
. . D O O M . Z A C . R A T .
N E G . S L I D E T A C K L E
E X A M . E S O . L O R A X .
A C N E . S E N D S . E A S T
R E D D I . O I L . D U K E .
B L O O P E R R E E L . T A D
Y S L . A G E . T E E S . . .
. F I D G E T S P I N N E R .
C H I R P . D U O S . I O N A
T E N O R . E N D O . F R O S
R H I N O . D E A N . F I S H
```

39

```
A G E G A P . D R I P . S N O
P I N A T A . R E B A . E O N
U N C L I P . J E O P A R D Y
. . A L E S . S O A P B O X .
A L E X T R E B E K . T I N E
F U R Y . M R I S . M E A T S
E S L . C O I N . G A S . . .
W H E E L O F . F O R T U N E
. . F A N . F A D E . G E D .
S T R I P . Q U I P . S L A G
A R A L . V A N N A W H I T E
W E G E T I T . T R I O . . .
P A T S A J A K . E S P I E S
I T O . L A R A . N E P A L I
T S P . L Y I N . T R E M O R
```

40

```
L A P D . . A F L A C . S W A B
A R E A S . M I A M I . M I C E
D R A M A T I S P E R S O N A E
E A R . H I G H . C O R G I S .
S U L T A N O F B R U N E I . .
. . I R T . R O O S . S N U B .
S U N D A E . Y A W . . G R O .
T H E E N D . . I S N I G H .
A N A . D O H . N E A T E R .
G O R P . S O B A . L X I . .
. F I G H T I N G I L L I N I .
A S A S E T . G E N E . X E R .
B A T T L E O F T H E S I N A I
L M A O . T R U E R . S O A R S
Y E L L . L E N N Y . . N Y S E
```

41

```
E L B O W . F R O M . T W I T
B E E N E . R A V E . R I T A
B A T T E R Y T E R M I N A L
S H A H . E I S N E R . E L K
. . E R I N . . T A C I T
G O L D E N G A T E . C O C O
I W I L L . S O A S T O . . .
G E M . A I R P O R T . L P S
. P R Y N N E . A D E L E
T C B Y . C A N N E R Y R O W
I L I E D . O P E N . . . .
P E Z . I L L I N I . A M P S
T A K I N G A B A C K S E A T
O V I D . B R I M . A T A R I
P E T S . T A S E . T Y L E R
```

42

```
I N C U B U S . A K I T A .
M O O N I N G . S I D E B E T
A P R I C O T . A N A T O L E
C E N S E . I N D . M I A
. . O P T I C A L F I B E R
S C A N . U T E . Y A M .
P U G . S T A G E . K I O S K
A R E Y O U K I D D I N G M E
S E D A N . E A G E R . R O Y
. . R I C . N A V . B E G S
J O H N C O L T R A N E .
A C E . N Y S . Y E A S T
W H A T A M I . E L M T R E E
S O D A C A N . R E P L I E S
. Y O U N G . A T H E A R T
```

43

H	O	M	E		E	B	B	S		C	U	B	E	S
U	N	I	T		T	R	O	N		A	S	A	N	A
M	E	R	C	U	R	I	A	L		M	E	R	C	I
O	R	A		G	A	G	S		V	E	N	I	A	L
R	O	N	A	L	D		T	O	O		E	S	S	O
M	U	D	P	I	E	S		P	L	A	T	T	E	R
E	S	A	U		C	I	T	G	O		A	D	S	
		M	A	R	T	I	A	L						
I	M	P		P	R	I	S	M		Y	E	L	P	
W	O	R	S	H	I	P		A	P	P	A	R	E	L
O	N	I	T		E	T	S		L	A	K	O	T	A
J	O	V	I	A	L		P	O	O	R		S	S	N
I	M	A	L	L		S	A	T	U	R	N	I	N	E
M	E	T	E	S		E	C	I	G		B	O	O	T
A	R	E	S	O		T	E	S	H		A	N	T	S

44

G	R	A	B		A	C	A	D	S		T	E	S	T	Y
L	E	N	A		S	O	B	E	R		A	L	T	A	R
O	M	I	T		P	U	F	F	I	N	B	O	O	K	S
S	A	M	O	A		G	A	I		A	L	I	C	E	
S	K	U	N	K	C	A	B	B	A	G	E		K	O	D
Y	E	S		B	A	R			A	S	T	R	I	D	E
		A	A	S		A	S	H			A	N	D	Y	
	Z	E	B	R	A	C	R	O	S	S	I	N	G	S	
B	A	L	E		A	M	Y		T	N	T				
O	N	E	L	U	M	P		R	Y	E		M	B	A	
A	I	M		P	A	N	D	A	E	X	P	R	E	S	S
	N	E	A	T	H		I	L	L		T	A	X	I	S
P	E	N	G	U	I	N	S	U	I	T		B	I	D	E
O	S	T	E	R		A	C	M	E	S		A	C	E	S
E	S	S	E	N		P	O	S	S	E		T	O	S	S

45

T	H	R	O	B		S	T	O	P		B	O	W	L
A	M	I	N	O		H	A	H	A		U	V	E	A
T	O	O	T	S	I	E	P	O	P		R	E	A	M
		H	O	M	E	S		E	T	E	R	N	E	
G	A	T	E	M	A	N		A	R	E	A			
A	R	I	D		C	A	P	N	C	R	U	N	C	H
S	M	E	L	T		R	O	U	E			A	L	I
B	A	S		A	C	C	E	N	T	S		P	A	P
A	N	O		K	A	Y	E			A	B	A	S	H
G	I	N	G	E	R	S	N	A	P		A	L	S	O
		R	I	O	T		R	O	A	D	M	A	P	
I	N	S	I	T	U		R	E	N	T	S			
C	O	N	N		S	O	U	N	D	B	I	T	E	S
E	P	I	C		E	D	N	A		A	D	O	R	E
S	E	T	H		L	E	G	S		T	E	N	E	T

46

W	A	D	E		W	N	B	A		S	C	R	A	P
O	P	E	L		H	O	E	R		U	H	U	R	A
K	E	E	L	S	O	V	E	R		C	A	N	T	S
	S	T	I	C	K	A	F	O	R	K	I	N	I	T
		S	O	N			W	E	E		Y	E	S	
A	L	I		P	E	L	E		B	R	O			
G	A	G	M	E	W	I	T	H	A	S	P	O	O	N
O	G	L	E		A	A	A			E	B	A	Y	
G	O	U	N	D	E	R	T	H	E	K	N	I	F	E
		S	O	U		S	A	D	E		S	S	T	
A	T	E		N	R	A		I	N	T				
C	O	M	E	T	O	T	H	E	T	A	B	L	E	
E	N	O	L	A		P	U	T	O	N	A	I	R	S
R	A	J	A	S		A	L	O	U		L	E	G	O
B	L	I	N	K		R	U	N	T		L	U	S	T

47

W	E	B	B		G	O	N	G		A	B	E	T	S
H	A	R	I		R	H	E	A		N	O	V	A	K
E	C	I	G		I	B	E	T		I	T	A	L	Y
T	H	E	C	O	L	O	R	O	F	M	O	N	E	Y
		H	O	L	Y		L	A	X					
M	A	K	E	M	E		P	A	U	L		S	P	A
A	D	R	E	P		S	E	L	F		B	A	R	R
T	H	E	S	H	A	P	E	O	F	W	A	T	E	R
R	O	M	E		D	I	V	E		H	B	O	G	O
I	C	E		F	I	N	E		H	E	Y	N	O	W
		A	L	E		B	U	L	B					
T	H	E	S	O	U	N	D	O	F	M	U	S	I	C
W	I	D	O	W		O	R	F	F		G	Y	R	O
O	V	I	N	E		R	I	F	E		G	N	A	W
D	E	T	E	R		I	P	O	D		Y	E	N	S

48

W	O	K	E		E	L	B	A		C	H	A	S	M
O	H	N	O		R	A	I	N		L	O	C	K	E
W	I	E	N	E	R	D	O	G		E	A	T	I	T
S	O	W		S	O	L		S	A	R	I			
		S	C	R	E	E	N	E	R	D	V	D	S	
	H	A	S	H		T	O	V		S	E	E	N	
D	I	N	N	E	R	D	A	T	E			P	L	O
O	D	D		R	O	W		I	R	A		L	A	W
L	E	I		B	A	N	N	E	R	D	A	Y	S	
E	M	T	S		I	D	O		G	U	Y	S		
D	E	S	I	G	N	E	R	D	R	U	G			
		G	M	O	S		E	V	E		B	A	G	
C	R	O	O	N		I	N	N	E	R	N	E	R	D
B	O	O	N	E		P	A	I	R		A	L	I	A
S	E	D	E	R		A	T	M	S		S	T	A	Y

49

```
GASPS _ AWE _ BALKS
ASTRO _ DOG _ EVENT
SCOOBYDOO _ RECUR
EONS _ ATE _ FINITE
STEP _ MORNINGDEW
_ TEAS _ INGE _
ACORN _ SINE _ RSVP
MOO _ NOCANDO _ TAR
POLO _ MANY _ ABATE
_ USER _ BRIT _
POSTAGEDUE _ MEAT
AMELIA _ INN _ ORZO
BATIN _ PASDEDEUX
SHUNT _ ONE _ CAPRI
TAPES _ PAR _ OLSEN
```

50

```
LACES _ FRY _ PABST
SLATE _ LIE _ ALOHA
DIRTCHEAP _ SAFES
_ PUTOUT _ ATMFEE
TAO _ GRASSROOTS
ELOPES _ ICY _
APLUS _ MAGI _ SWAT
THEPLOTTHICKENS
SARA _ TIES _ PINTA
_ PHD _ BUSTER
BUSHLEAGUE _ RDS
ONTOUR _ LAREDO _
ODIUM _ JUNGLEGYM
SENSE _ IED _ KAUAI
TREES _ FYI _ SLEPT
```

51

```
CAL _ SCORES _ ABIT
ALA _ ISRAEL _ TROY
BAT _ SPARROWHAWK
AMIE _ ALE _ ALGAE
LONDONBRIDGE _
_ LIU _ MUSTERS
SCOTCH _ ZAC _ EXIT
TOV _ HIJACKS _ TSA
EKES _ JUG _ SURREY
PERUSAL _ MIA _
_ RUBYSLIPPERS
ASHEN _ PAN _ EXEC
BLACKFRIDAY _ THE
LAVA _ RECENT _ RAN
EVEN _ OPENED _ ABE
```

52

```
BESO _ ALICE _ WHEW
LAIN _ VENOM _ HOLE
ASTA _ IVANA _ ERIE
HYBRIDENGINES _
SAYOK _ REALIZES
_ LET _ TEMPE
_ KALAHARIDESERT
FEN _ ALIKE _ AAA
GENDERIDENTITY _
SLIER _ YUM _
_ SESSIONS _ NAVAL
_ HITCHINGARIDE
AJAR _ BYCAR _ EMMA
DALE _ MOORE _ TEEN
OWLS _ SULKY _ SONS
```

53

```
CABO _ GAB _ LABRAT
ALES _ ERA _ ENOUGH
PATRILEY _ NATGEO
_ AIM _ SONG _ TENT
PETCAT _ NETWORTH
ONE _ CUREDHAM
MDS _ GET _ FUJI
PITBOSS _ NITPICK
_ TSAR _ AIR _ MAI
_ TEENBEAT _ MRT
POTHOLES _ NOTYET
OVER _ SEEM _ MUD
PUTOUT _ NUTBREAD
ELROPO _ CSI _ BABY
SEAMAN _ ESP _ ONCE
```

54

```
TAPER _ PAPA _ ABCS
ILLBE _ EDEN _ SLOT
DOU(B)LE(C)(H)IN _ SINE
YES _ ORTO _ KINDA
_ MAG(I)(C)(K)INGDOM
TREADON _ NOEND
ROMP _ SETA _ ARM
AMP _ (J)(U)(G)HEAD _ TOE
PAL _ ELLE _ EELS
_ ORFEO _ GUESSES
SAYAF(E)(W)(W)ORDS
TUMMY _ AUDI _ WOO
AREA _ DISGUSTING
LAND _ ACNE _ OWNER
ESTA _ BETS _ NOOSE
```

55

```
PASHA · · OSLO · SON
FREED · CAROM · UZI
FITFORAKING · PAX
TAO · ABEL · MERE
· NATIONALPARKS
SCHMIDT · NEAR ·
HEAPS · SKETCHUP
URL · TREAD · INO
TALKSHOW · LOTUS
· ICED · ABOUTME
THEWHOLETRUTH ·
HEMI · AMOR · ECO
ELM · CIVILRIGHTS
FLY · ODELL · TIARA
TAS · DORY · SLYLY
```

56

```
ANKLE · NICHE · DAS
TANYA · USHER · OCT
FREECYCLING · ETA
IRE · HULA · SOPSUP
RABE · KENT · ANAL
STOP · SIDEHUSTLE
TONIC · SEEST
· RELOAD · SHALOM
· EASES · FILAS
DROPTHEMIC · FINE
EONS · PINE · EVAN
NOTYET · REND · EGO
TMI · KICKSTARTER
AIM · ELIAS · TETRA
LEE · STATE · AMISS
```

57

```
PAIR · SILOS · WASP
ULNA · KNAVE · AUTO
TINFOILHAT · TROD
· ATBAT · REINS
SOP · OUTINFORCE
WRITEME · EASY
ANNA · IRIS · AGO
YOUREINFORITNOW
STP · ACES · HIDE
· STAR · SPIESON
· BRAINFOODS · ETS
PLAIN · AVILA
RIND · INSIDEINFO
INKS · TRIED · MILD
MISO · TASTY · SPUD
```

58

```
SHUTS · NASAL · BYOB
HADAT · OVINE · IOWA
IHOPE · TILDE · GREY
VANILLASKY · UBERS
· OMIT · ETTA
CHOCOLATETHUNDER
LEIA · LIN · ARGYLE
IAL · CALMDOWN · LAN
PREFAB · EEL · MANE
STRAWBERRYBLONDE
· REAL · MOAN
SOSAD · NEAPOLITAN
AVOW · MIAMI · AKITA
TADA · ANTIC · LEDON
SLAY · POSES · ARENA
```

59

```
TAROT · AWED · ROPE
UNION · MATA · OBEY
NIGHTNIGHT · ANNE
EMU · ODE · ALMOND
REPOSTS · ESSEX
· WHITEWEDDING
PASEO · PET · OIL
ELUDE · USS · SAUCE
RON · CFO · IBSEN
MUSHROOMBALL
· COOPS · ATTESTS
PARODY · SNO · TOE
AGED · CAPANDGOWN
TREE · ALAN · NAMES
HAND · TINA · APPLE
```

60

```
STL · ASP · CHARM
HOOD · UNTO · DALEY
ADNAUSEAM · SWIPE
GOINGSWIMMINGLY
· ALT · REIN · NYE
WET · YES · LAGS
OPAL · EKE · LISZT
RECYCLINGCENTER
METRO · DUO · SURE
· ELBA · SEA · BOX
SOS · DUSK · QUI
OUTOFTHERUNNING
USAGE · TRIATHLON
STYLE · ORAL · DIVA
ASSET · NIL · EAT
```

61

```
L A Y E R   W R A P   M I F F
A L E V E   H O R A   A S E A
M U T E D   O N E S   T A R T
B M I N O R M A S S   H A M S
      S N A P   A F L C I O
D E M O E D   H O W I E
A D O   B E A A R T H U R
U G L I   G O D R Y   E A S E
B E E S T I N G S   T E D
    T I N G E   L O N E R S
T I T H E S   P O N E
I D E A   B E Y O U R S E L F
P A N T   U R A L   U T T E R
S H O O   R I L E   S L A T E
Y O R K   G E E S   H E S S E
```

62

```
C O L I C   S A S S   N E W S
O H A R E   A L T O   O L I N
L I V I N G D E A D   D I N E
T O A S T E D   T A P I O C A
      E L L I E   A C T E D
R E C O R D E D L I V E
O D O R   S A D E   L I L
L I P B A L M   W A R H E R O
L E E   R O O F   A V O N
    F O U N D M I S S I N G
A P L U S   E R O D E
C R U D E L Y   A E R I A L S
R I N G   O P E N S E C R E T
E D G E   T I M E   N O O N E
S E E D   S T U D   E N D O W
```

63

```
S A I N T   K E D S   I C E D
A P N E A   T A I L   M A R A
P L A I N T O S E E   P R I M
S I N G   E W E   U S O P E N
  T E H R A N   S T A L E
      S A M   L A H D I D A H
L T S   G O B A G S   T I N A
O H A R E   E R A   D E E T S
L A N E   P I C N I C   M E H
A I M S H I G H   D O T
    A C U T E   F A N A R T
S P R I G S   D O H   M O O D
O L I N   T H E R O Y A L W E
F O N D   O U S T   E L L E N
T W O S   P E K E   S E E D S
```

64

```
T A L C   P E S O   Y O W Z A
I G O R   A R T S   E N R O N
L A T I N P E R C U S S I O N
    T S E   I A N   I T S O
L E O P A R D P R I N T
A L P   P A R   E E L S
P O R   M A M M A S   A E R
U P I   L O W P O S T   T R A
P E Z   U N S H O D   E B B
  S E E N   C O O   X I I
  L A U N C H I N G P A D
A S A P   M E H   M A A
L E G A L P R O C E E D I N G
G R A S P   V I S E   O N E A
A F R O S   E R I K   T T O P
```

65

```
L A P E L   T A L C   S T A R
O B A M A   O L G A   O H I O
F I N I S   M O B S   R E N O
T T T T T T T T T T T T T T T
      S A O   F L U S H
E A R W O R M   L I T   I D A
G R A I N   P A N   A N O N
G G G G G G G G G G G G G G G
O U I S   I R A   A R I E L
S E N   U N A   E N M A S S E
    G A S S Y   B A E
B B B B B B B B B B B B B B B
L O U D   U L E E   A E I O U
A C L U   R U S T   L A N D S
H A L L   G E T S   L U G E S
```

66

```
Z I N G   T A U   Z A P S
A C R E   G O T H S   E X I T
G U A C   I N O U T   S E X Y
    K E V I N H A R T
M O R O S E   G A Y B A R
I M O   P A N P I P E   R U E
N E W T   H O O H A   W I N S
A G A R   O T T E R   H A T E
J A N E D O E   A T F I R S T
    B E T S   R Y A N
  M A L E   W E B B
D I V E R S E   H I N D L E G
A L E   X E D   A D O   O A R
V A R Y I N G   D A V I N C I
I N T E N S E   A H E A D O F
D O S A G E S   T O R M E N T
```

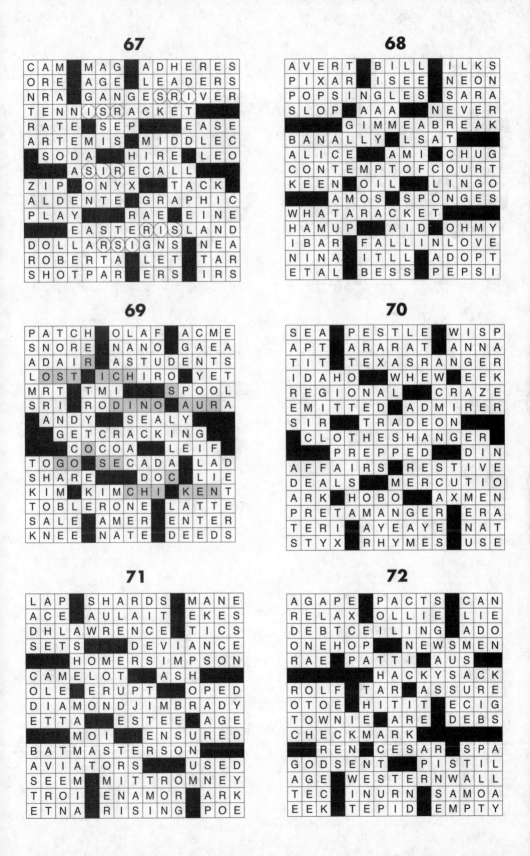

67

```
C A M _ M A G _ A D H E R E S
O R E _ A G E _ L E A D E R S
N R A _ G A N G E S R I V E R
T E N N I S R A C K E T _ _ _
R A T E _ S E P _ _ E A S E
A R T E M I S _ M I D D L E C
_ S O D A _ H I R E _ L E O
_ A S I R E C A L L _ _ _
Z I P _ O N Y X _ T A C K
A L D E N T E _ G R A P H I C
P L A Y _ _ R A E _ E I N E
_ E A S T E R I S L A N D
D O L L A R S I G N S _ N E A
R O B E R T A _ L E T _ T A R
S H O T P A R _ E R S _ I R S
```

68

```
A V E R T _ B I L L _ I L K S
P I X A R _ I S E E _ N E O N
P O P S I N G L E S _ S A R A
S L O P _ A A A _ N E V E R
_ G I M M E A B R E A K
B A N A L L Y _ L S A T _
A L I C E _ A M I _ C H U G
C O N T E M P T O F C O U R T
K E E N _ O I L _ L I N G O
_ A M O S _ S P O N G E S
W H A T A R A C K E T _
H A M U P _ A I D _ O H M Y
I B A R _ F A L L I N L O V E
N I N A _ I T L L _ A D O P T
E T A L _ B E S S _ P E P S I
```

69

```
P A T C H _ O L A F _ A C M E
S N O R E _ N A N O _ G A E A
A D A I R _ A S T U D E N T S
L O S T _ I C H I R O _ Y E T
M R T _ T M I _ S P O O L
S R I _ R O D I N O _ A U R A
_ A N D Y _ S E A L Y _
_ G E T C R A C K I N G _
_ C O C O A _ L E I F
T O G O _ S E C A D A _ L A D
S H A R E _ D O C _ L I E
K I M _ K I M C H I _ K E N T
T O B L E R O N E _ L A T T E
S A L E _ A M E R _ E N T E R
K N E E _ N A T E _ D E E D S
```

70

```
S E A _ P E S T L E _ W I S P
A P T _ A R A R A T _ A N N A
T I T _ T E X A S R A N G E R
I D A H O _ W H E W _ E E K
R E G I O N A L _ C R A Z E
E M I T T E D _ A D M I R E R
S I R _ T R A D E O N _
_ C L O T H E S H A N G E R _
_ P R E P P E D _ D I N
A F F A I R S _ R E S T I V E
D E A L S _ M E R C U T I O
A R K _ H O B O _ A X M E N
P R E T A M A N G E R _ E R A
T E R I _ A Y E A Y E _ N A T
S T Y X _ R H Y M E S _ U S E
```

71

```
L A P _ S H A R D S _ M A N E
A C E _ A U L A I T _ E K E S
D H L A W R E N C E _ T I C S
S E T S _ D E V I A N C E
_ H O M E R S I M P S O N
C A M E L O T _ A S H _
O L E _ E R U P T _ O P E D
D I A M O N D J I M B R A D Y
E T T A _ E S T E E _ A G E
_ M O I _ E N S U R E D
B A T M A S T E R S O N _
A V I A T O R S _ _ U S E D
S E E M _ M I T T R O M N E Y
T R O I _ E N A M O R _ A R K
E T N A _ R I S I N G _ P O E
```

72

```
A G A P E _ P A C T S _ C A N
R E L A X _ O L L I E _ L I E
D E B T C E I L I N G _ A D O
O N E H O P _ N E W S M E N
R A E _ P A T T I _ A U S _
_ H A C K Y S A C K
R O L F _ T A R _ A S S U R E
O T O E _ H I T I T _ E C I G
T O W N I E _ A R E _ D E B S
C H E C K M A R K _
_ R E N _ C E S A R _ S P A
G O D S E N T _ P I S T I L
A G E _ W E S T E R N W A L L
T E C _ I N U R N _ S A M O A
E E K _ T E P I D _ E M P T Y
```

73

```
J I M . H O B O S . S T A B
A R E . B E A U T . A U D I
C O R P O R A T E W O R L D
K N E E . . O N O . B E E .
. W O R D F O R W O R D . .
L E T S D I E . N A B . . .
E C O . O O M P H . L O F T
T O R O N T O R A P T O R S
O N C D . S N O R E . S E A
. H O G . S P A T T E R . .
H O R R O R S T O R Y . . .
E V E . B O A . . . P S S T
M U L T I P L E C H O I C E
A L A S . E E R I E . T A R
N E Y O . S M E A R . H M M
```

74

```
L P S . A L T O . . R E F E R
I R K . B A R N . S O M A L I
M A I N S T A Y . E G O I S M
I D E E . K I X . M E T R E S
T A R H E E L . F I R E S . .
. . . R L S . L O P . S H E D
A R G U E . B E R R A . A V E
R O O . G O O D D O G . K E N
I D O . Y U R T S . L E E R Y
D E S K . T A O . C O M . . .
. . E N A C T . H O W C O M E
M E D I N A . P O L . E R A S
C L O V I S . H O U S E S I T
A L W E S T . D E M I . O N E
T E N S E . . S Y N C . N E E
```

75

```
S E W S . T A X I . E C L A T
O A H U . I V A N . S H A P E
D R A M A T I C L I C E N S E
A T M . T A S T E D . E D E N
S H O O I N . O T T E R . . .
. . . A L I T . A N Y H O W
S H I F T C H A N G E . O N O
L I D S . E P A . O S L O . .
U R L . F L O R I D A K E Y S
E E Y O R E . R O L E . . . .
. . . F O A L S . G O D E E P
P I A F . V A N I S H . G R U
S A N D I E G O C H A R G E R
A G O A T . O R E O . D O C S
T O N Y S . S T E W . A N T E
```

76

```
S C R U B . S L A M . M O S
P R U N E S . L O B E . A A H
F U N I N T H E S U N . C S I
S E T . G O O D S . O N A I R
. . . M A L T . A R O U S E
I C I C L E . S P L A T . . .
M A D E I N T H E S H A D E .
O R E S . I O N . C R A W
. B A C K I N T H E B L A C K
. . H I R E S . L A U G H S
T E R E S A . B E N E . . .
U S E R S . E P I C S . O O H
P I C . E Y E I N T H E S K Y
A G O . R E N T . S E A L E D
C N N . S A Y S . E R O D E
```

77

```
R A S P S . S C R E W . W I T
E L T O N . E L U D E . H M O
B E A T L E M A N I A . A P U
E X I T . M I D . T V S T A R
L A D Y D I . W E A N S . .
. M A R C H M A D N E S S
M I N O R . L A I R . T R I O
I S O U T . E R S . S A V O R
F L I T . J A D E . I L E N E
F A S H I O N C R A Z E . .
. M E E T S . G E T S A T
B A L D I E . M O O . T A R A
A B A . S P R I N G F E V E R
J A W . S H I N E . D R E S S
A D S . O S A K A . A S D O I
```

78

```
H D T V S . U S O F A . N I L
A E I O U . L E A S T . O R E
H A R U M S C A R U M . S O D
A L E C . H E M . F L I N G
. . H E A R Y E H E A R Y E
C A L . D Q S . L O E W E .
A S A D A . D S L . F E E L
M A K E M I N E A D O U B L E
O P E L . O O F . G L O M S
. G U S T O . C A R . B O T
A L E X V A N H A L E N
D O N E E . O V A . A G A R
O N E . L O G G I N G I N T O
R E V . T R E A T . A V A I L
E R A . E B O N Y . B E T T E
```

79

```
C A P P . I M I N G . S C A M
L U L U . N O L I E . T O G A
A R A B . P O I N T G U A R D
P A Y G R A D E . G O A L I E
S E A A I R . . B O O R . . .
. . M D T . P A I N T G U N
H O S E S . B E N N Y . R N A
A R T S . P A N D G . P A I N
S E E . P R I U S . S A N T A
P O P G R O U P . F U N . . .
. . H I L L . E N G E L S
S A F E C O . P E A G R E E N
P A R T Y G I R L S . A N N A
A B E T . U B O L T . V I D I
M A Y O . E M M Y S . Y E L L
```

80

```
C A L F . R O S Y . R A I D S
A R I E . O P I E . E P C O T
B U Z Z W O R D S . P R E G O
. G A Z A . Y E N T A . A B U
P U R E S T . B O B S A G E T
O L D S A W S . . S T B E D E
W A S . B I L G E . U S S R
. . P I X I E D U S T . .
O A T H . T O A S T . F U M
R E H E A T . M E R G I N G
C R E W N E C K . R E E S E S
H A M . G L O A T . E L S A
A T A L L . S H O R T C U T S
R O G U E . E L I E . A R E A
D R I V E . C O L A . P E N D
```

81

```
C A P . D E E R . D O D G E D
R I O . I D L E . O R I O L E
E S P . R U M M A G E S A L E
E L U D E . U R N . C L A P
P E L I C A N S T A T E . .
. A E T N A . . P E R I L S
R A T S . A D O S . E N D O W
A L I . S T I L T O N . I R A
S T O V E . R E U P . P O E M
P O N I E D . D E B I T .
. S K I N N Y D I P P E R
A U D I . S A O . S E R T A
W H A T S M Y N A M E . O U T
E U R O P A . O P E C . O D E
S H E R Y L . S E N T . F E D
```

82

```
B I G I F . S K I N . W E S T
A R E S O . T A C O . E X P O
B A L L P L A Y E R . R E I N
A N T E . E R A . T E R R E
. . P A R K V I S I T O R
G E T B U S Y . E B A N . .
A T A L L . H E E . L E A K
T R I A L C O U R T J U D G E
E E L S . A S H . I C A R E
. . T O N S . M I L K M A N
J A Z Z P I A N I S T . .
A D I O S . U S E . B A A S
P E N N . O N T H E B E N C H
A L E E . R O S A . B A N T U
N E S S . S T O P . Q U E S T
```

83

```
C A S T . L A T H . C L A S P
A S H E . A C H Y . H U M O R
S T A N . T E E M . E M P T Y
H U D D L E . G N O M E . .
I T O . A R G O . W I N D U P
N E W T S . R O S E S . O N E
. . B A E . O D I S T . W I G
S C O U R . U S E . R U N T S
P O X . P A T H S . Y A W
A R E . O N S E T . L E A F S
S P R A I N . P A P A . R E A
. . G N A S H . A B I D E S
C A R A T . H E W N . O D D S
P R I M E . O R E S . T O M E
A M B E R . E D D Y . A G E D
```

84

```
F L A T . L O C A . S A G A S
L U S H . O V I D . A L I B I
O B I E A W A R D . P I T O N
P E N P A L . C O S . E M M A
. . O B I W A N K E N O B I
A C T U A T E . I L S . .
T U R N . E S T E E . T L C
O B E D I E N C E S C H O O L
M A X . C R Y I N . O R S O
. . B O O . E M I T T E D
O B G Y N D O C T O R S . .
S L A G . E C O . P A T E N T
C A P O N . O H B E Q U I E T
A R E N A . M E A D . F R A Y
R E S E T . E N D S . F E L L
```

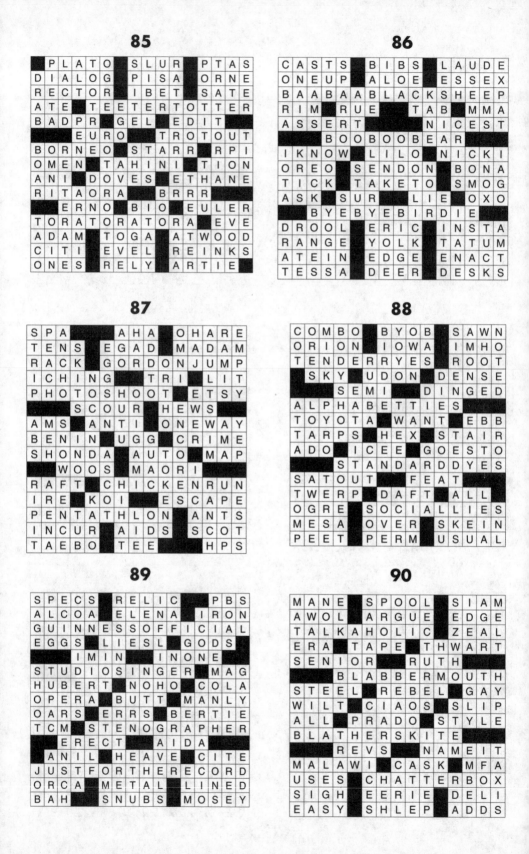

85

P	L	A	T	O		S	L	U	R		P	T	A	S
D	I	A	L	O	G		P	I	S	A		O	R	N	E
R	E	C	T	O	R		I	B	E	T		S	A	T	E
A	T	E		T	E	E	T	E	R	T	O	T	T	E	R
B	A	D	P	R		G	E	L		E	D	I	T		
	E	U	R	O			T	R	O	T	O	U	T	
B	O	R	N	E	O		S	T	A	R	R		R	P	I
O	M	E	N		T	A	H	I	N	I		T	I	O	N
A	N	I		D	O	V	E	S		E	T	H	A	N	E
R	I	T	A	O	R	A			B	R	R	R	
	E	R	N	O		B	I	O		E	U	L	E	R
T	O	R	A	T	O	R	A	T	O	R	A		E	V	E
A	D	A	M		T	O	G	A		A	T	W	O	O	D
C	I	T	I		E	V	E	L		R	E	I	N	K	S
O	N	E	S		R	E	L	Y		A	R	T	I	E

86

C	A	S	T	S		B	I	B	S		L	A	U	D	E
O	N	E	U	P		A	L	O	E		E	S	S	E	X
B	A	A	B	A	A	B	L	A	C	K	S	H	E	E	P
R	I	M		R	U	E			T	A	B		M	M	A
A	S	S	E	R	T					N	I	C	E	S	T
		B	O	O	B	O	O	B	E	A	R			
I	K	N	O	W		L	I	L	O		N	I	C	K	I
O	R	E	O		S	E	N	D	O	N		B	O	N	A
T	I	C	K		T	A	K	E	T	O		S	M	O	G
A	S	K		S	U	R			L	I	E		O	X	O
		B	Y	E	B	Y	E	B	I	R	D	I	E		
D	R	O	O	L		E	R	I	C		I	N	S	T	A
R	A	N	G	E		Y	O	L	K		T	A	T	U	M
A	T	E	I	N		E	D	G	E		E	N	A	C	T
T	E	S	S	A		D	E	E	R		D	E	S	K	S

87

S	P	A			A	H	A		O	H	A	R	E
T	E	N	S		E	G	A	D		M	A	D	A	M
R	A	C	K		G	O	R	D	O	N	J	U	M	P
I	C	H	I	N	G			T	R	I		L	I	T
P	H	O	T	O	S	H	O	O	T		E	T	S	Y
		S	C	O	U	R		H	E	W	S	
A	M	S		A	N	T	I		O	N	E	W	A	Y
B	E	N	I	N		U	G	G		C	R	I	M	E
S	H	O	N	D	A		A	U	T	O		M	A	P
	W	O	O	S		M	A	O	R	I			
R	A	F	T		C	H	I	C	K	E	N	R	U	N
I	R	E		K	O	I		E	S	C	A	P	E
P	E	N	T	A	T	H	L	O	N		A	N	T	S
I	N	C	U	R		A	I	D	S		S	C	O	T
T	A	E	B	O		T	E	E			H	P	S

88

C	O	M	B	O		B	Y	O	B		S	A	W	N
O	R	I	O	N		I	O	W	A		I	M	H	O
T	E	N	D	E	R	R	Y	E	S		R	O	O	T
	S	K	Y		U	D	O	N		D	E	N	S	E
		S	E	M	I				D	I	N	G	E	D
A	L	P	H	A	B	E	T	T	I	E	S		
T	O	Y	O	T	A		W	A	N	T		E	B	B
T	A	R	P	S		H	E	X		S	T	A	I	R
A	D	O		I	C	E	E		G	O	E	S	T	O
		S	T	A	N	D	A	R	D	D	Y	E	S	
S	A	T	O	U	T			F	E	A	T		
T	W	E	R	P		D	A	F	T		A	L	L
O	G	R	E		S	O	C	I	A	L	L	I	E	S
M	E	S	A		O	V	E	R		S	K	E	I	N
P	E	E	T		P	E	R	M		U	S	U	A	L

89

S	P	E	C	S		R	E	L	I	C			P	B	S
A	L	C	O	A		E	L	E	N	A		I	R	O	N
G	U	I	N	N	E	S	S	O	F	F	I	C	I	A	L
E	G	G	S		L	I	E	S	L		G	O	D	S
			I	M	I	N			I	N	O	N	E	
S	T	U	D	I	O	S	I	N	G	E	R		M	A	G
H	U	B	E	R	T		N	O	H	O		C	O	L	A
O	P	E	R	A		B	U	T	T		M	A	N	L	Y
O	A	R	S		E	R	R	S		B	E	R	T	I	E
T	C	M		S	T	E	N	O	G	R	A	P	H	E	R
			E	R	E	C	T		A	I	D	A		
	A	N	I	L		H	E	A	V	E		C	I	T	E
J	U	S	T	F	O	R	T	H	E	R	E	C	O	R	D
O	R	C	A		M	E	T	A	L		L	I	N	E	D
B	A	H			S	N	U	B	S		M	O	S	E	Y

90

M	A	N	E		S	P	O	O	L		S	I	A	M
A	W	O	L		A	R	G	U	E		E	D	G	E
T	A	L	K	A	H	O	L	I	C		Z	E	A	L
E	R	A		T	A	P	E		T	H	W	A	R	T
S	E	N	I	O	R			R	U	T	H		
		B	L	A	B	B	E	R	M	O	U	T	H	
S	T	E	E	L		R	E	B	E	L		G	A	Y
W	I	L	T		C	I	A	O	S		S	L	I	P
A	L	L		P	R	A	D	O		S	T	Y	L	E
B	L	A	T	H	E	R	S	K	I	T	E		
			R	E	V	S		N	A	M	E	I	T
M	A	L	A	W	I		C	A	S	K		M	F	A
U	S	E	S		C	H	A	T	T	E	R	B	O	X
S	I	G	H		E	E	R	I	E		D	E	L	I
E	A	S	Y		S	H	L	E	P		A	D	D	S

91

```
L A I R . P C S . . C A P E S
A L O E . A H A . O R I O L E
P A N P I P E S . M O R T O N
. . . T R A S H P I C K U P S
C L A I M . S A L T . I S E E
D O L L A R . . U S E S . .
R O D E . B U R G . V S I G N
O N E . R I P T I D E . R O O
M S N B C . T E N S . T O R T
. . O A H U . . T B O N E S
S C A B . E R A S . L A S S O
P U T D O W N R O O T S . .
O T O O L E . B L A S T O F F
T I L L E D . Y A K . E R I E
S E L E S . . S R S . D E N Y
```

92

```
. . . O P T . T V S . . S G T
P R A N C E . O W I E . H U H
F O R E S T F L O O R . A R R
F T S . . R O D . L E A G U E
T H O R E A U . F I N E S S E
. . N O W . R E I N E R . .
C H I M E S . A V I . O D E S
P I S A . O O Z E S . S I R I
A T T N . L A Y . T H O R A X
. . T R I K E S . A L E . .
S E R I A L S . L E N S C A P
E X A C T O . O U R . . T U E
V I N . S Q U A R E R O O T S
E S C . O U S T . C A R R O T
N I H . N Y C . . T E E . .
```

93

```
C A R D S . D E F Y . M E S S
A V A I L . O R E O . O T T O
P E R S I A N R U G . M E A N
I R E . E M T . D I V E R T .
T A B . R A G S . E N N U I .
A G I N . H O T M U S T A R D
L E T O N . A I N T . L E O .
. . . V O C A L C O R D . . .
C B S . S A I L . Y A C H T .
F L I G H T D E C K . P A I R
C A D R E . D U N E . P R O .
. T E A S E T . T O T . E S T
S H A M . M A K E T H E C U T
P E R M . I R I S . E M O T E
A R M Y . T O N Y . R U D E R
```

94

```
E S P N . A S A P . H A I K U
L U R E . G O G O D A N C E R
K N O W S O N E S O N I O N S
. . . D O G S . E N G . N S A
. N O A H . . D U N S T . .
L O N D O N M A R A T H O N .
I C E S . T A R . . E X C E L
F A N . T H R E E O N . T R Y
E R I C A . . N O R . P A U L
. B L O N D E O N B L O N D E
. . P L A I T . . I K E A .
I R A . I N G . A B L E . .
S E C O N D H O N E Y M O O N
T U R K E Y T R O T . O N L Y
O P E D S . Y E N S . N O D E
```

95

```
O S C A R . . C A R B . O T S
P H O T O . T O N Y A . N I T
T A K E A G A N D E R . I M O
S H E . D A T A . . B R O I L
. . . A R I A N A G R A N D E
K A P L A N . . P L A N B . .
I S A A C . S A N E . G A L L
N E V . E S T R E E T . G O O
G A L A . P U M A . I N E R T
. . O R I O N . . A M U L E T
C O V E N T G A R D E N . . .
I M S A D . . D A H L . I M P
T E D . O U T O F D A N G E R
E G O . O P A R T . G O O S E
S A G . R I P E . . S T R A Y
```

96

```
B E A R D . K N E E . . E A R S
A R R A Y . A B E L . A T O P
N I C K E L B A C K . G O Y A
A C H E . O U T . . A L L A N
. . . . S I L V E R B E L L S
C O S T A S . . B I A S . .
A S T O R . T E E S . C O O S
P L A T I N U M R E C O R D S
N O N E . A L O T . L U Z O N
. . . M B A S . . M O T O R S
T I N P A N A L L E Y . . .
A F O O T . . A L A . J E D I
M I L L . M E T A L M U S I C
P L I E . I T E M . I N A N E
A L E S . T A R A . R E U S E
```

97

```
A S H   C H E S T   B A S I S
P H O   Y U C C A   A D E P T
P O O L S H A R K   A S A H I
S T P A T   R U E S     T O N
      W I N D M I L L D U N K
S T A N C E       Y O U R E
U R L S   N A P E   B O T C H
M A G   T E A R G A S   L A M
O M A N I   H O O D   P E S O
  P L A N E       A R I S E S
B O B B Y S H E R M A N
A L L   P A T H   C O O K S
K I O S K   T H I N K T A N K
E N O K I   E E N I E   F E E
R E M I X   D R E A D   S E W
```

98

```
M O L D   A B E L   O M E G A
O R E O   B O R E   L Y R I C
D O G G Y B A G S   D I N A H
E N A M O R S   L A S T O N E
M O L A R     P E S O S
        B U L L Y P U L P I T
T A S M A N I A   E L A I N E
A G E E   L E C A R   T E R N
L U A N D A   A N S W E R E D
C A T T Y C O R N E R
      O N E N D   Y A P A T
C H A R A D E   S E L L E R S
A E G I S   P I G G Y B A N K
G A U N T   I N T O   E R I E
E L E G Y   N E S S   E Y E D
```

99

```
N A D I R   G A S P   N E S
O N E N O   O R C A S   A T A
S N A C K A T T A C K   S C I
    L A U G H   L E A S H E D
D A M N   R I A L   A U T O
R U E   B A C K O N T R A C K
I D I N A   A P A R T
P I N E T A R   S P U R S O N
    W I N E D   N E A T O
C R A C K I S W A C K   B I S
H O L A   P I T H   G O S H
A V E R A G E   H A D A T
R E X   Y A C K E T Y Y A C K
M R I   E L T O N   A L G A E
S S S   A S I S   N E E D Y
```

100

```
L A B O R   A L P S   H E M S
E V A D E   B I T E   U R G E
G O R E D   B O A R D G A M E
O W E   B U R N   M O E
S A M B A S   E G O S   L A P
  L I A R S   L O N E S O M E
  N G O   M B A S   E W E S
F E I G N   Y A P   C R E S T
A C M E   O G R E   A I R
S T U D Y F O R   A B E T S
T O M   A N D Y   D A S H E S
    H M O   M O O R   E L I
R E A D S U P O N   E B B E D
N E A T   S O R E   T R A C E
S L A V   E X E S   S O R T S
```

101

```
M A S T S   N I L S   E P I C
A L O H A   O P E C   L A V A
V A L E N C I A O R A N G E S
S N O W   A D D   I C I E S T
      A B L E   E B A N
C L E V E L A N D B R O W N S
L A C E D   A I L   S H O P
E T O   S M I T T E N   I S U
A C N E   A A A   A C T E D
R H O D E I S L A N D R E D S
      H O N K   B E A U
A S P E N S   P B S   E L S A
H I L L S T R E E T B L U E S
E D A M   A I R Y   A L L A H
M E N S   Y A K S   R A L L Y
```

102

```
Y O U T H   G O O F   R E B A
A R N I E   O M A R   E V I L
M A D E A   L I T E   M A N E
  L O R D O F T H E R I N G S
        D R S     W A X
B A D G E R   J O I N   D D T
A R I E S   P O O F   A U R A
R I C E K R I S P I E S B O X
B A E Z   O T I S   N E A L E
S L Y   A C H E   A V A I L S
      O A K     T R I
S A N T A S W O R K S H O P
P L O T   T O B E   A I L E Y
R O V E   A V O N   G L A R E
Y E A R   R E E D   E L V E S
```

103

```
MAYANS■■DOTCOM
EXOTIC■■EUROPA
MIDDLERELIEVER
ESAU■NOAH■XENA
■■■SLEDRIDE■■■
AWAKE■■■■ISLAM
RIG■STAMOS■EWE
CFOS■OPAL■AVOW
HIGHSPEEDDRILL
■■■EAT■■■SOL■■
■REDDELICIOUS■
TUX■■NINO■■PTA
SPINTHEDREIDEL
PETERI■■ELROND
SESTET■■SIESTA
```

104

```
ASH■ATWAR■CIGAR
ICE■LAINE■ANOSE
MARGARINE■ROOTS
STEAM■■DOORDIE■
■■HONORSTUDENT■
ORCA■APE■TSE■■■
DEAN■ARCS■ERASE
DAM■ONAROLL■RIA
SPEAR■HONE■RAPS
■RBI■OON■ELSE
ALUMINUMFOIL■■
DENOTES■■DIALS
ZAIRE■MONEYCLIP
ESTER■ARIAL■BOA
SHEDS■PEARL■ANT
```

105

```
VACATE■GENT■GEM
ARABIA■ELIA■ANY
RUBIES■EMERALDS
■GAT■TUNIC■GLUT
SUN■SNARE■TORE
ELASTIC■ASA■PER
WASHEDUP■FUSSY
■■AMETHYSTS■■
SCAMP■DECREASE
COG■EEG■SHADIER
ACID■ALLEN■LAG
NATO■RAISA■RES
DIAMONDS■PEARLS
ANT■WELT■PANOUT
LEE■EDYS■STINGY
```

106

```
MEATY■PUMA■DAIS
ALPHA■IRAS■ONTO
PIPEWRENCH■CYST
■EELER■NEN■WAH
SPA■COMESOFAGE
ALLOT■GAI■TRYON
DUTCHAIRLINE■■
EMOTED■■BESTED
■ALOTTOMANAGE
PIANO■ASP■ROMAN
ITSTOOLATE■EDY
LAW■POL■ELFIN
OLEO■MIDDLESEAT
TILL■PEDI■ELSIE
SALE■ADEN■TESLA
```

107

```
GOBIG■GAME■ACTS
UMAMI■AMEN■WORE
SATAN■GILD■ONYX
SNICKERDOODLE■
YIN■GRE■DRE■SAT
■COMEDYSKETCH
PAPA■ALI■EEYORE
SEARS■SAN■DIGIT
AIRACE■NET■NADA
LOTTODRAWING■
MUY■TIE■SKA■PBJ
■GETTHEPICTURE
LEON■WIRE■HURON
BRED■ARIA■ONION
JARS■REEK■SAMMY
```

108

```
APPS■MEALS■ARTS
TRIP■AGLOW■NOEL
BOLA■DRFUMANCHU
AVEC■LEI■LAKER
YOSEMITESAM■YEP
■■CABS■ONAIR■
ADWAR■OPT■DOES
SNIDELYWHIPLASH
PANE■EEL■LEDTO
■ETAIL■STAT
HAS■CAPTAINHOOK
IMAPC■AVE■RUNE
MOUSTACHES■ETTA
ORCS■NAOMI■ATON
MEET■TWEEN■TAPE
```

109

F	E	T	A	■	P	I	B	B	■	B	A	H	A	I
L	A	R	D	■	E	T	R	E	■	A	L	E	R	T
U	S	E	R	■	A	C	E	S	■	N	E	A	T	O
E	Y	E	O	F	T	H	E	T	I	G	E	R	■	■
S	A	D	I	E	■	■	Z	I	N	■	■	M	M	A
■	■	■	T	H	E	B	E	E	S	K	N	E	E	S
I	B	M	■	P	A	D	■	■	P	E	O	N	S	■
D	R	Y	H	E	A	T	■	I	N	H	O	U	S	E
A	I	M	E	E	■	■	S	R	O	■	■	T	A	T
H	A	I	R	O	F	T	H	E	D	O	G	■	■	■
O	R	S	■	A	H	A	■	■	R	O	A	M	S	■
■	■	T	H	E	M	O	N	K	E	Y	S	P	A	W
K	R	A	U	T	■	■	M	A	I	N	■	O	R	C	A
O	A	K	E	N	■	A	N	N	O	■	L	O	A	N
S	E	E	Y	A	■	S	A	G	S	■	O	N	U	S

110

A	D	F	E	E	■	T	H	U	G	■	B	C	U	P
I	C	E	A	X	■	V	I	N	E	■	I	O	N	A
W	O	R	T	H	A	S	H	O	T	■	L	U	G	S
A	N	N	■	A	R	E	A	■	■	M	O	N	E	T
■	■	■	A	L	I	T	T	L	E	E	X	T	R	A
J	A	B	B	E	D	■	■	U	S	A	I	N	■	■
A	C	R	E	■	■	S	A	R	A	N	■	O	U	T
C	H	I	■	C	R	E	W	C	U	T	■	S	H	O
K	E	G	■	H	A	R	S	H	■	■	P	E	O	N
■	■	H	E	A	R	T	■	■	M	A	R	S	H	Y
S	E	T	T	L	E	A	S	C	O	R	E	■	■	■
I	T	S	O	K	■	■	H	A	I	R	■	F	E	Z
G	A	I	N	■	D	O	U	B	L	E	T	A	K	E
M	I	D	I	■	A	N	T	I	■	S	K	I	E	R
A	L	E	C	■	B	E	S	T	■	T	O	R	S	O

111

P	U	P	■	A	N	G	E	R	■	O	V	E	N	S
A	S	L	■	T	U	L	S	A	■	P	E	K	O	E
L	A	U	R	A	B	U	S	H	■	E	L	E	N	A
S	I	T	U	■	B	E	E	■	A	R	C	■	■	■
■	■	R	O	S	A	L	Y	N	N	C	A	R	T	E	R
■	■	■	T	R	Y	■	■	O	H	S	O	R	R	Y
E	P	I	C	■	■	G	O	T	O	■	■	A	M	E
■	■	M	I	C	H	E	L	L	E	O	B	A	M	A
F	O	X	■	■	M	O	D	S	■	A	L	P	S	■
E	J	E	C	T	O	R	■	■	S	R	O	■	■	■
H	I	L	L	A	R	Y	C	L	I	N	T	O	N	■
■	■	A	N	Y	■	L	O	X	■	O	V	U	M	■
A	G	I	N	G	■	B	E	T	T	Y	F	O	R	D
G	E	C	K	O	■	B	A	T	H	E	■	I	S	S
A	M	E	S	S	■	C	R	O	S	S	■	D	E	E

112

S	H	O	D	■	S	I	C	K	O	■	■	B	O	A
L	E	V	I	■	A	M	A	I	N	■	R	U	M	P
I	R	A	N	■	V	E	R	N	E	■	A	R	E	S
P	O	L	I	C	E	D	O	G	■	H	I	N	G	E
■	■	■	N	A	M	■	B	A	R	I	S	T	A	S
M	O	N	G	R	E	L	■	L	O	C	I	■	■	■
U	B	O	A	T	■	E	F	F	S	■	N	A	S	H
S	O	I	L	■	A	G	O	R	A	■	G	L	U	E
S	E	R	F	■	S	A	G	E	■	U	T	T	E	R
■	■	■	R	O	I	L	■	D	O	S	H	O	T	S
F	A	C	E	O	F	F	S	■	W	E	E	■	■	■
A	W	A	S	H	■	O	P	E	N	S	F	I	R	E
N	A	R	C	■	C	R	A	T	E	■	L	O	O	M
T	I	V	O	■	A	C	T	O	R	■	A	T	O	M
A	T	E	■	T	E	E	N	S	■	G	A	M	Y	■

113

C	B	A	■	E	T	C	H	■	B	S	I	D	E
H	I	N	T	■	L	O	R	I	■	R	A	T	I	O
E	B	A	Y	■	A	R	A	P	■	I	B	S	E	N
Z	I	P	P	O	L	I	G	H	T	E	R	■	■	■
■	■	O	E	R	■	■	O	A	F	I	S	H	■
S	Q	U	A	T	J	U	M	P	S	■	N	Y	E	T
K	A	T	■	E	R	M	A	■	L	A	M	A	R
I	T	O	■	G	R	A	N	I	T	E	■	P	R	O
M	A	F	I	A	■	O	D	O	M	■	A	S	L
P	R	I	M	■	Z	E	R	O	M	O	S	T	E	L
■	I	T	A	L	I	C	■	■	N	T	H	■
■	■	N	O	T	H	I	N	G	D	O	I	N	G
D	E	L	A	Y	■	O	D	O	R	■	C	Z	A	R
O	M	E	G	A	■	E	L	S	A	■	K	E	N	O
M	O	D	E	L	■	D	Y	E	D	■	R	A	W

114

B	A	R	■	H	A	R	E	■	F	O	R	A	G	E
A	W	E	■	O	P	E	L	■	R	O	U	T	E	S
L	A	D	■	G	R	A	I	N	O	F	S	A	L	T
M	Y	H	A	T	■	P	T	A	■	■	T	R	E	E
■	■	A	R	I	D	■	I	T	S	A	L	I	E	■
O	U	N	C	E	O	F	S	E	N	S	E	■	■	■
O	L	D	S	■	L	E	T	■	A	T	S	T	U	D
P	E	E	■	P	L	Y	■	G	P	A	■	A	S	A
S	E	D	E	R	S	■	C	O	O	■	E	K	E	S
■	■	■	P	O	U	N	D	O	F	F	L	E	S	H
■	D	R	I	P	P	E	D	■	F	E	M	A	■	■
A	R	E	S	■	■	A	R	E	■	A	S	P	E	N
T	O	N	O	F	B	R	I	C	K	S	■	E	R	E
R	O	A	D	I	E	■	V	O	I	T	■	E	L	O
A	L	L	E	G	E	■	E	N	D	S	■	K	E	N

115

```
P A W S   W O R E   A G I T A
A L O E   A P E X   K U D O S
S C R A P H E A P   C L E R K
T A R S I   N C A A   F A T E
A N I   S E A T T L E S L E W
  S T A R R   S E A T
P O O H   I M P   S A M M Y
I T M E A N S A L O T T O M E
S T E N S   Y E P   E T A T
  A H E M   G E S S O
B A T T E R Y P A C K   R Y E
E C R U   R O L L   O G R E S
S C A R S   P A P A L M A S S
T R I A L   E T A L   A C N E
S A L L Y   S O D A   N E O N
```

116

```
A M O K   H G T V   S K I F F
B O R E   E R I E   C A S I O
E T S Y   A I N T   R H I N O
  H O P E L E S S C A U S E
    A N T S   O W N
H O L D T H E A P P L A U S E
E R A S E   S A T   S H A M
A T L   R A Y K R O C   U N C
T H A I   Q U E   H O R D E
H O W C O U L D I R E F U S E
  E P A   S E R F
  A H O U S E D I V I D E D
S L A V S   M I N I   U Z I S
T E H E E   T E T E   T R O U
Y E A R S   S T O W   Y A R N
```

117

```
A L P S   A J A R   R E A C T
W O O L   P O L O   A L L A H
N O N O   B L O O D Y M A R Y
S K Y P E   L E S A G E
  P R A Y S   Z U R I C H
G E Y S E R   S E N   T A I
H A D J   R O A N   S L A N T
E R G O   O G L E S   A L T O
A R I E S   E S A U   Z I O N
L E E   A P R   K E N Y A N
S T R A T A   G Y R O S
  M I S H A P   D U T C H
E V E N S T E V E N   S A L E
S E R I F   R I T A   A X I S
L E R O Y   O N E G   N I P S
```

118

```
A C L U   A G O   A P A R T
L O O N   H E N S   D E L H I
M R S C R A T C H   V R O O M
A D E L E   R E E L   M O N O
  S A Y H I   L U C I F E R
C O L D   O D E   T O T
D O E   L O L   H E M A N
S P E A K O F T H E D E V I L
  S P E E D   O A R   A C E
  O R E   N B A   V I E D
O L D N I C K   A N S E L
P O O F   K O L N   E N A C T
E C O L E   B E E L Z E B U B
R A N U P   E A R S   E L B A
A L E X A   P O D   R E A R
```

119

```
D R O P S   R E S T   S H A M
V E N T I   A R I A   L E N O
R E L A X   D I L L   I D E A
S K Y   T R I C K L E D O W N
  M E N U   O X E N
  S T R E A M L I N E   I C K
S T E I N   A C E S   S H E
E R R S   H A T E S   S T O P
W A R   B A T H   H O I S T
S P A   R I V E R D A N C E
  C Z A R   E O N S
F L O O D L I G H T S   A H A
A S T O   O K R A   O P I U M
D A T E   S E A S   L A D L E
S T A Y   S A S H   O C E A N
```

120

```
L A P   E L M O   J O S T L E
I C U   D E E D   U N T I E D
B A L L G A M E   M O U N D S
I D S A Y S O   B F F
D I E T   H I G H O F F I C E
O A S E S   R O U T   S L A T
  E L S   T A R A   I R A
B A D N E W S   C O W B E L L
A L I   W A L L   N O R
N E S T   L O O P   L E A K Y
S C H O O L P L A Y   E D I E
  O H O   R O M C O M S
O U T L A W   B O Y O H B O Y
A S S U R E   I D O L   E N O
R A P P E D   N Y S E   S O U
```

121

S	W	A	B		A	S	I	A		S	T	A	R	T
W	I	R	E		A	P	S	E		T	H	R	O	B
A	N	G	E	L	H	A	I	R		P	R	O	V	O
N	O	O	S	E		R	A	I	D		O	M	E	N
			A	C	E	H	A	R	D	W	A	R	E	
S	C	L	E	R	A			L	E	A	S			
C	O	U	P		M	A	G	I		D	O	G	M	A
A	C	C	I	D	E	N	T	S	H	A	P	P	E	N
R	O	Y	C	E		C	O	T	E		E	A	R	N
		H	A	S	H		L	E	N	S	E	S		
A	R	S	E	N	I	O	H	A	L	L				
L	A	H	R		P	R	O	P		M	I	D	A	S
I	D	I	O	M		A	H	A	M	O	M	E	N	T
S	A	N	E	R		G	U	R	U		I	K	E	A
T	R	E	S	S		E	M	T	S		N	E	W	T

122

J	E	S	T	S		C	O	P		R	I	C	C	I
A	D	H	O	C		A	D	O		I	N	E	R	T
P	E	E	P	H	O	L	E	S		A	R	L	E	S
E	N	D		O	R	E	L	S	E		A	L	D	O
		G	O	B	B	L	E	D	Y	G	O	O	K	
T	W	I	R	L	S			W	A	S	P			
R	I	C	A		E	A	T	I	N		H	I	P	
U	S	E	F	O	W	L	L	A	N	G	U	A	G	E
E	P	S		N	A	K	E	D		S	N	O	W	
		K	E	E	N			C	A	P	E	R	S	
Q	U	A	C	K	D	O	C	T	O	R	S			
U	N	T	O		S	T	R	O	N	G		Z	O	E
A	D	E	L	E		H	O	N	K	Y	T	O	N	K
S	U	R	E	R		E	W	E		L	A	N	C	E
H	E	S	S	E		R	E	D		E	P	E	E	S

123

A	P	S	E		B	L	A	B			T	U	T	
B	O	O	T	Y		T	A	I	L		B	U	N	S
S	E	R	T	A		W	I	D	E		E	R	I	K
C	H	E	E	K	S		R	E	A	R	E	N	D	
O	L	A		S	E	Z		D	R	A	F	T	E	D
N	E	R	F		X	E	S		I	T	S	W	A	R
D	R	M	O	M		S	H	O	E	S		O	L	E
		B	O	T	T	O	M	R	O	W				
P	S	S		R	A	Y	O	N		N	E	I	G	H
O	K	T	H	E	N		T	I	E		A	S	I	A
M	I	R	A	N	D	A		A	B	S		A	N	N
	C	A	B	O	O	S	E		B	E	H	I	N	D
A	L	I	I		O	K	R	A		R	E	D	I	D
B	U	T	T		R	U	M	P		F	A	N	N	Y
C	B	S			I	P	A	S		L	O	G	E	

124

B	A	R	D		G	A	S			U	S	M	A	P
O	H	I	O		P	R	O		I	N	H	A	L	E
B	O	O	T	C	A	M	P		D	I	A	L	E	R
S	Y	S	C	O			H	A	T	T	R	I	C	K
			O	W	E	N		M	A	S	K			
T	H	I	M	B	L	E	R	I	G		O	S	L	O
O	E	R		O	M	N	I		S	N	I	P	E	D
G	A	U	D	Y		A	N	N		O	L	I	V	E
A	T	L	A	S	T		G	U	A	C		E	E	O
S	H	E	D		I	R	O	N	M	A	I	D	E	N
		S	W	A	Y		S	Y	N	C				
D	O	G	T	I	R	E	D			D	E	L	V	E
A	U	R	O	R	A		M	O	N	O	P	O	L	Y
T	R	I	B	E	S		V	W	S		O	B	O	E
E	S	T	E	S		S	E	A		P	E	G	S	

125

S	T	A	B		B	A	R	S		C	A	S	T	E
A	R	I	E		I	C	A	L		A	L	P	H	A
M	I	D	N	I	G	H	T	I	N	P	A	R	I	S
E	M	A	I	L	M	E		P	O	I		I	R	E
			G	E	O		M	U	S	T		T	D	S
	F	I	N	D	M	Y	I	P	H	O	N	E		
E	A	R		E	M	T	S			L	A	Z	E	D
G	I	R	L		A	D	M	I	N		M	E	S	A
G	R	E	E	N		A	T	O	Z		R	P	M	
	L	E	O	N	A	R	D	N	I	M	O	Y		
E	Y	E		S	I	C	K		E	N	E			
L	A	V		E	L	I		A	V	E	R	A	G	E
C	H	A	N	G	E	D	O	N	E	S	M	I	N	D
I	O	N	I	A		I	R	O	N		A	D	A	Y
D	O	T	T	Y		C	E	N	T		N	E	W	S

126

S	T	O	W		A	B	B	A		A	J	A	R	
L	A	V	A		F	L	O	A	T		V	E	R	A
A	P	E	X		R	U	M	B	A		O	M	E	N
W	E	R	E	N	U	M	B	E	R	O	N	E		
		S	C	I		S	L	I	P		L	I	E	
A	S	S		I	T	T			A	M	E	N	S	
N	T	H		S	H	E	S	A	L	L	T	H	A	T
D	R	O	P		A	C	U	T	E		V	I	D	A
Y	O	U	R	E	T	H	E	T	O	P		L	A	T
E	N	T	E	R			A	P	E		L	Y	E	
T	G	I		I	T	C	H		A	A	A			
	T	H	E	Y	R	E	G	R	R	R	E	A	T	
W	H	O	A		P	A	L	E	D		M	A	X	I
H	A	U	L		E	V	I	L	S		O	S	L	O
O	N	T	O		S	E	X	T		R	Y	E	S	

127

```
HUE . BEAR . ALIKE
ENDS . ISLE . PESOS
CLICKBAIT . TAROT
TITANS . BAM . ALA
ANIME . TIGERBEAT
REN . ECO . STOOLIE
EDGE . LEO . LURID
. FROSTBITE .
. MALES . CAF . STAR
SOFALEG . REF . ELO
PARTYBOAT . URALS
ANO . YEN . EMERGE
REPEL . ANKLEBOOT
TROVE . SIAM . AUNT
ASPEN . YEAS . TEA
```

128

```
BRIT . PASS . GASPS
OATH . RICH . RANAT
SCOOBYDOO . ASANA
SEOUL . WREN . PEG
. GOOGLEDOODLE
CASHBAR . SLUR .
FACT . HALF . ARAIL
ORR . AUPAIRS . GMO
SPAWN . HAVE . LOAD
. PENN . ENHANCE
BAMBOOSHOOTS .
AGE . TRIO . TESLA
LOTSA . FOOLPROOF
KRAUT . THAI . ELLA
SALVE . SAKE . DEAR
```

129

```
NADA . HOOP . AHEM
OXEN . ADMIT . LAVA
DESKPHONES . FLED
. DELI . RISKPRONE
. REEL . ERE .
CATTREAT . DADBOD
RBI . CAMEO . YOURE
ABS . ESCAPEE . FDR
SOLID . STARR . FEB
STEREO . SLOBBERY
. EAU . SOAR .
ASKPRICES . ORZO
KANE . JAMESKPOLK
IKEA . ARIEL . INGA
NEWT . ETSY . NEAT
```

130

```
STAR . ATBAT . GOLD
LICE . BEANO . ARIA
ANTI . SENATESEAT
MAINMAN . ALGORE
. EEL . SELMA .
. SURROUNDSOUND
OWN . IMPEI . GOOD
RESET . TET . HEDGE
BEEP . AROSE . OIL
. PRITZKERPRIZE
. LAYER . LON .
AFIELD . BESTBET
SAMPLESALE . ELLE
IRAS . COLON . NASA
SEXY . OBITS . THEM
```

131

```
NADAL . MICA . SLID
OBAMA . OPAL . TYNE
SALTY . VANGUARDS
ELL . SAID . ATTIRE
JOYRIDES . OSCAR
ONIONS . PUP . SGT
BEND . PEORIA .
. GINGERSNAPS .
. NOMORE . RIPA
GEL . DAN . MAIDEN
ALAMO . BOBSLEDS
MODIFY . ALAS . LAW
BILLFOLDS . EMILE
ISEE . RAGE . TONER
TESS . EDEN . SEEDS
```

132

```
CHER . AREAS . TOTS
RUTH . MANGO . BURP
ALTO . UDDER . STAR
PLUMBLOSSOM . TIE
. BEEN . REBATE
AUGUST . TWISTS .
FROST . NORTHWIND
AGO . HIDEY . GEE
REDDRAGON . LOHAN
. FROTHS . PANTRY
BOOYAH . NANA .
ERR . MAHJONGTILE
ENYA . WEAVE . EDIT
FOOD . ARIEL . ALMA
STUD . YELLS . REES
```

133

```
N A S H   A S I A   H A H A S
A M I E   V A N S   E N A C T
R I G H T O N T H E M O N E Y
W A N   U N D R E S S   D H L
H B O M B     U S C   E V I E
A L F A   G O T     D R A G S
L E F T I N T H E L U R C H
    O A T   T E N
  F R O N T O F T H E L I N E
J E E P S   L E I   I C O N
A R F S   I O U   E L E C T
B R O   I W A S H A D   C A R
B A C K T O T H E F U T U R E
E R U P T   H O R A   A B B A
D I S H Y   S T A R   B E S T
```

134

```
S A R A   S L I P S   J O C K
A R A L   H E N R I   A V I A
Y O D A   H I K I N G G E A R
A M I S S     J A K E   R O T
H A I K U P O E M   M S N
    A D O P T       W I N D
C P A   D R E S S   T I G E R
H I G H E N D   H E I G H H O
A P R O N   S T A G E   T I P
P E E R     E R A S E
    E A T   H E I D I K L U M
S P A   M I E N   N E A T O
H Y B R I D C A R S   O N T O
E L L E   O H G E E   U K E S
D E E P   S E E Y A   T Y R E
```

135

```
S A M O A   A B S   S I G H
A L A R M B E L L S   O T R O
G A S S T A T I O N   S H E A
A S T O   C A B O   B O O E R
    S O L I D G R O U N D
I M D O W N     L A N G
M A R D I   O L M E C   H O P
P L A S M A S C R E E N T V S
S I M   S T U D S   L O S E S
    A G U A     R E T O R T
L I Q U I D A S S E T
A D U L T   Q U I P   O N I T
N O E L   J U S T A P H A S E
A L E E   D A I S Y C H A I N
I S N T   S S E   P I N T S
```

136

```
C U B A   B O A S     H A M
A H A B   H O R D E   C O L A
R O B E   O R G A N D O N O R
S H Y   M U G   G A R R E T S
    B A R N   T I T A N
F L O R I D A R O O M   G M T
R A N G   S R O   R A H R A H
O W N U P   F I G   S U E D E
S N E E R S   K I A   N E R F
H S T   A T L A S R O C K E T
    C Y R U S   M O H S
C I C A D A S   D O H   A R K
L O C K O F H A I R   C L U E
A N N E   E L W A Y   E A S Y
P S Y   D Y E S   O D E S
```

137

```
W O O S   P A L S   A D L I B
A U N T   A V O W   A I O L I
L I E U   W A V E S H E L L O
L O A F S     I D E S T
S U R F T H E N E T   S E L F
T I M   R A Y     T O N E R
    P O L E S   S A D D A Y
  S H E L L S O U T C A S H
B E E T L E   S N I T S
T A R T S     U R I   B A E
U S E R   P A L M S C A R D S
    I S D U E   S C O O P
B E A C H F R O N T   H O R A
L A T K E   A N E W   O M E N
T R E S S   S E G O   O S S A
```

138

```
S N I T   B O O R   G E S S O
W I N E   A N T E   A G A I N
E X T E N S I O N   B O R N E
D E O   E S T H E R   C A P
E D W A R D   E X C L A I M
    N O R T H   S H E S
P A S T   U R I S   I N T W O
E X C O M M U N I C A T I O N
R E U N E   E T C H   I C E S
    L I S T   S K I L L
E X P O S E S   C O S M O S
P E T   A L A S K A   A R I
I N U S E   E X P E N D I N G
C O R E R   E L A N   A N O N
S N E E R   K E Y S   B E T S
```

139

```
D I S █ C D R O M █ A B Y S S
A R E █ A R O M A █ L O O P Y
T I L █ R O D E S H O T G U N
A S L E E P █ N A O H █ A R C
█ █ B E T S Y █ D U A L █ █
A L Y R A I S M A N █ M B A S
L A D █ K N E E █ D I A L I N
I N A N E █ R R S █ N O O S E
A C T O R S █ G O O D █ O L E
S E E D █ W H E Y P O W D E R
█ █ E R I E █ A U N T Y █ █
U S B █ A N A L █ L E S M I Z
C H A N G E L A N E S █ A K A
L U N G E █ E V E N I █ R E C
A N D O R █ R A S T A █ Y A K
```

140

```
L I P █ M A T T E R █ V A V A
A V A █ E R R A T A █ E R I N
M A R B L E A R C H █ N E R D
A N T E █ A C S █ █ L I N E R
█ █ H A W █ T I C T A C T O E
A G E L E S S █ R A G E █ █
H O N E S T █ D E L A █ S O B
O N O █ T A R H E E L █ E P A
Y E N █ B I E L █ S A S S E S
█ █ L A R D █ S E X T A L K
L E M O N S O L E █ Y A M █
A B A C K █ I C E █ F E T A
W O R K █ A B O U T A F O O T
N O D E █ C O N R A D █ I R A
S K I T █ E A S E L S █ L I D
```

141

```
W A S P █ R E S T S █ G N P
O P I E █ A L L O W █ F U E L
R I F E █ D I A N A █ E N V Y
D E T R O I T T I G E R S █
I C E █ D O E █ A M I S S
S E R V E █ S I T T I G H T
█ I L K █ E C O █ H E Y
█ S P L I T T I C K E T █
O W L █ W I T █ K E G
W A I T T I M E █ I O T A S
E D G E D █ S A T █ R N A
█ H A S I T B O T H W A Y S
B O T S █ S H I L L █ I D O S
F R E E █ L A R V A █ R E N O
F E D █ A I D E S █ E D E N
```

142

```
S O L O S █ K E E N █ E M I T
A L I C E █ O R C A █ M A M A
F I G H T N I G H T █ U R N S
E V E R S O █ O O H █ D O T
R A R E █ A T E █ E V I T E
█ W H I T E K N I G H T
B O T C H █ N A M E █ B R E E
U P R O O T S █ E N D E A R S
B E A N █ N E A R █ A S S E T
B R I G H T L I G H T █
L A N A I █ L E I █ F E E L
E T S █ P A T █ K A R A T E
T O T E █ Q U I T E R I G H T
E R O S █ U G L I █ A T E A M
A S P S █ A S K S █ B O R N E
```

143

```
V E R D I █ A S A P █ J O A N
A D O R N █ M E M O █ U N T O
L U A U S █ P R O P A G A T E
█ D I E T █ U S E R █ P I X
C A R D A M O M █ A T A R I
A T A █ M I R █ C A B A R E T
B O G S █ C L E R I C █
█ M E T A P H Y S I C I A N
█ E D D I E S █ T B A R
C R A W D A D █ N A S █ U M A
H O R S E █ C A S T A N E T
A T E █ R I G A █ K I N D
P A N A S O N I C █ G N A T S
E T A L █ T A R A █ M I N O R
L E S T █ A W O L █ A E T N A
```

144

```
P I N █ P A T E N T █ F D I C
E S E █ O L I V E R █ T E R I
R A W F O O T A G E █ M B A S
P I E R R E █ A S P E R █
S A R I █ M I T █ R A I M I
█ H A L F B A K E D I D E A S
█ L I E G E █ W O E F U L
A N G █ T M I █ H E R █ S I A
C O R O N A █ P O E T S █
C O O K E D T H E B O O K S
T R U S S █ E D S █ D I C E
█ P I S A N █ S O O T H E
P R I G █ B U R N T U M B E R
E D E N █ B R E Y E R █ A M I
P A S S █ R E N E W S █ G E E
```

145

B	E	S	T		F	R	A	N		B	A	N	A	L
A	V	E	R		L	E	G	O		A	L	I	B	I
B	A	R	I	T	O	N	E	S		N	A	C	H	O
E	N	V		O	W	E		E	T	D		H	O	N
		E	L	L	E		B	R	O	I	L	E	R	S
R	A	T	E	D	R		A	I	N	T	I			
A	M	I	T	Y		B	I	N	G		A	C	D	C
M	M	M		A	M	A	L	G	A	M		R	U	E
P	O	E	T		A	L	E	S		A	M	I	N	O
		A	C	I	D	Y		G	R	A	T	E	S	
E	N	D	Z	O	N	E	S		A	G	R	I		
K	I	A		A	S	A		B	R	O		C	O	E
E	V	I	L	S		G	O	O	D	T	H	I	N	G
B	E	R	E	T		L	A	N	E		I	S	T	O
Y	A	Y	A	S		E	T	O	N		D	M	V	S

146

B	U	S	H		C	A	I	R	O		S	A	M
A	N	T	E		A	L	D	E	R		W	I	N	E
S	T	O	R	M	C	L	O	U	D		A	R	T	S
A	I	R	D	A	T	E		P	E	E	V	I	S	H
L	E	E		R	U	N	S		R	A	Y			
			L	A	S		O	V	E	R	L	O	A	D
C	I	V	I	C		S	A	I	D		I	D	L	E
O	M	E	G	A		C	N	N		S	N	I	P	E
M	A	T	H		F	A	D	E		T	E	N	O	R
E	M	O	T	I	O	N	S		S	O	S			
			B	A	R		O	P	E	L		G	A	P
L	E	G	U	M	E	S		E	P	I	T	O	M	E
O	V	A	L		S	W	E	A	T	D	R	O	P	S
L	I	M	B		E	A	R	L	E		O	S	L	O
A	L	E		E	G	R	E	T		T	E	E	S	

147

W	A	S		I	H	O	P	E		S	T	A	T	S
A	L	L		M	O	D	E	L		E	R	N	I	E
S	O	Y		C	O	D	E	B	R	E	A	K	E	R
P	E	A	P	O	D		R	A	E		S	L	I	T
		S	E	L	L	S		A	T	H	E	N	A	
S	T	A	N	D	U	P	C	O	M	I	C			
C	A	F		M	A	R	X		C	A	B	I	N
A	R	O	M	A		C	E	L		K	N	I	F	E
N	E	X	U	S		E	D	I	T		T	S	A	
		C	H	I	R	O	P	R	A	C	T	O	R	
D	A	S	H	E	S		S	A	D	I	E			
I	D	E	A		L	A	S		I	A	G	R	E	E
G	E	T	C	R	A	C	K	I	N	G		E	V	A
A	L	O	H	A		T	E	P	E	E		N	E	S
T	E	N	O	N		S	E	A	R	S		D	R	Y

148

S	A	C	K		J	E	E	R		S	C	R	U	B
H	E	H	E		O	G	L	E		C	A	U	S	E
A	S	I	N		I	A	M	B		U	R	B	A	N
G	O	L	D	E	N	D	O	O	D	L	E			
S	P	E	A	K		R	U	P	E	E	S			
		L	E	A	V	E	N	O	T	R	A	C	E	
M	E	W	L		G	I	N		E	S	S	A	Y
U	M	A		C	O	D	D	L	E	D		E	R	E
F	A	I	R	Y		E	A	R		S	L	E	D
F	I	V	E	C	A	R	D	D	R	A	W			
	L	E	S	L	I	E		S	E	A	M	S		
	C	O	M	E	D	Y	S	K	E	T	C	H		
T	R	A	I	N		F	E	A	T		T	A	R	O
W	A	Y	N	E		E	M	M	A		E	R	I	E
O	P	E	D	S		R	O	S	Y		N	I	B	S

149

P	A	W		R	O	A	M	S			G	E	A	R
U	S	A		E	N	T	O	M	B		O	L	G	A
P	A	L	L	B	E	A	R	E	R		E	L	O	N
I	D	E	A	S		E	L	A	P	S	E			
L	A	S	S		P	E	L	L	G	R	A	N	T	
		I	R	A	N		S	H	O	P	P	E	R	
C	O	C	K	A	P	O	O		N	E	A	T	O
A	N	O		P	I	L	L	B	U	G		G	O	O
S	T	R	I	P		E	A	S	E	M	E	N	T
H	A	P	L	E	S	S		L	E	D	E			
	P	O	L	L	T	A	K	E	R		T	O	T	E
	R	E	S	O	L	E			M	O	T	H	S
S	W	A	G		P	U	L	L	Q	U	O	T	E	S
I	O	T	A		S	T	P	A	U	L		E	R	A
P	E	E	L		E	S	T	E	E		R	E	Y	

150

F	A	K	E	D		B	B	C		D	E	C	A	F
I	C	I	E	R		L	E	O		O	R	A	T	E
J	E	L	L	Y	R	O	L	L		G	A	M	E	R
I	D	O		O	B	I	T		S	T	E	I	N
		H	O	U	S	E	S	I	T		R	N	S	
A	S	S	O	R	T		N	A	D	A				
R	E	P	R	O		P	U	B	C	R	A	W	L
T	A	R	A		A	T	R	I	A		M	O	O	D
	M	I	C	S	T	A	N	D		L	A	R	V	A
	N	E	A	T		R	I	S	K	E	D			
E	G	G		C	A	K	E	W	A	L	K			
N	O	T	C	H		E	L	E	C		W	O	E	
A	F	I	R	E		B	A	B	Y	S	T	E	P	S
C	A	D	E	T		A	T	M		P	O	P	U	P
T	R	E	E	S		B	E	D		A	N	T	S	Y

151

```
C L A W   S C A B   C H R I S
H A Z E   O H N O   P E A R L
O P A L   D I D G E R I D O O
I T L L D O   Y O N   D I N G
R O E   U M P   T A P I O C A
S P A D E   O B A M A   I A N
    O S A K A   O R I N G S
  M I D O C E A N R I D G E
E A T O U T   E A S E L
A L S   T R A D E   T E M P E
S L A S H E R   S K A   A I R
T O G A   S A D   U L S T E R
B R I D E S M A I D   E Z R A
A C R I D   I N D O   W O R N
Y A L E U   S A S S   S H E D
```

152

```
H A T H   B A H   O T T A W A
E R O O   A R T   S A U N A S
M A R C   T I M H O R T O N S
  B A K E S A L E     D D E
  S H E L     B O X S E A T
    Y E A T S   C I A
S C E N A R I O   A N Y O N E
H O P I   C O L A S   I V A N
E N I G M A   A L I E N A T E
    H E N   R E O R G
S T U T T E R     I S S A
U R N   A P R I C O T S
M A P L E S Y R U P   R E P O
A L I G N S   E T A   R A I N
C A N A D A   P H D   Y M C A
```

153

```
M E M O   I N C A   P E S T S
O P E C   D E A L   E X P A T
W E N T D O W N T H E T U B E
S E N O R   S T O O L   R O E
    O P U S     P O S T O P
C A N I G E T A L I F T
O B I   S L I C E   F A T E D
M E T Z   F L E A S   N A P A
B L E A K   L I S T S   X I S
    P A S S T H E T O R C H
C O P S T O     M O U E
O H O   R O B O T   I G L O O
C A S H I N O N E S C H I P S
O R I O N   A C R E   T E E S
A E T N A   T E M P   A F R O
```

154

```
A B B A   A B L Y       G A P
C A R L   F R I E D   N A B S
C L U E   L A M A R   O T A Y
E L L E M A C P H E R S O N
S E E   A C E   W E I R D S
S T E E D   S A N D R A O H
    R A T   I C E   D N A
  S A M A N T H A B E E
R E P   N E O   R O O
K A Y H A G A N   A S S A M
O R N A T E   A B S   H U E
  W O M E N O F L E T T E R S
D I V A   T R O V E   O H O H
A G E S   S E R I F   M E R E
Y S L     S A N S   B R A D
```

155

```
B L A T H E R     P L A Z A
A R C H I V A L   S A I L O R
H O M E P A G E   C L E A R S
A N E W   M U M B O J U M B O
    E T A     O O O   B A N
J I B B E R J A B B E R
I R E   L I E N   Y E A R N
B A A S   E D G E R   F L O E
E Q U A L   E V E N   T L C
    G O B B L E D Y G O O K
A H A   V I A   C U B
B A L D E R D A S H   S E A M
U S E R I D   E P I P H A N Y
T O X I N S   R A N S A C K S
S N A P S   S A Y W H A T
```

156

```
S P A S   P E A C H   S T U D
E A C H   E M C E E   A O N E
N A M E   A T A R I   S P I N
T R E B E K   B I G S H O T S
  C A R P S   S H E A F
C H O   G E E   E T A   T B A
H E R R   R A D   O R W H A T
R I P E   F L U F F   A E R O
I D O I D O   G I F   X M E N
S I R   O R C   D A N   O D E
  A R O M A   O S C A R
I N T E R A C T   H O R N E D
R A I N   N A O M I   T I V O
K N O T   C O M B O   O N E G
S O N S   E S S E N   O G R E
```

157

L	A	S	T	S	■	T	E	X	A	S	■	S	P	A
A	L	E	U	T	■	A	L	E	R	T	■	A	U	K
D	I	A	N	A	P	R	I	N	C	E	■	F	B	I
D	E	L	A	Y	E	D	■	A	S	P	H	A	L	T
E	N	E	■	E	Y	E	■	■	A	R	I	A	■	■
R	E	V	A	M	P	■	D	C	C	O	M	I	C	S
S	E	E	M	E	■	T	U	P	A	C	■	■	■	■
■	■	L	Y	N	D	A	C	A	R	T	E	R	■	■
■	■	S	A	R	A	S	■	A	V	O	I	D	■	■
G	A	L	G	A	D	O	T	■	C	L	A	U	S	E
A	Q	U	A	■	■	E	B	B	■	■	T	O	T	■
L	U	M	B	A	G	O	■	L	E	T	M	E	B	E
L	I	P	■	W	O	N	D	E	R	W	O	M	A	N
O	L	E	■	L	U	L	U	S	■	O	V	E	R	T
P	A	D	■	S	T	Y	E	S	■	S	E	N	S	E

158

M	C	R	I	B	■	D	R	I	P	■	S	C	A	M
E	L	I	S	A	■	I	A	G	O	■	C	A	S	A
S	A	F	E	R	■	W	R	A	P	P	A	R	T	Y
A	N	T	E	N	N	A	E	■	T	U	N	D	R	A
■	■	■	O	Y	L	■	M	A	T	■	I	O	N	■
C	U	B	A	N	C	I	G	A	R	S	■	■	■	■
U	N	T	I	E	■	E	M	T	■	D	O	G	S	■
S	T	E	M	■	I	O	T	A	S	■	A	M	A	L
S	O	N	S	■	S	E	A	■	A	M	N	I	O	■
■	■	■	C	L	U	B	H	O	P	P	I	N	G	■
M	I	A	■	O	A	F	■	A	R	E	■	■	■	■
I	N	T	E	R	N	■	F	L	A	X	S	E	E	D
S	U	B	R	E	D	D	I	T	■	A	C	U	T	E
T	S	A	R	■	E	Y	R	E	■	M	O	R	A	L
S	E	T	S	■	R	E	E	D	■	S	T	O	L	I

159

P	I	N	U	P	■	I	T	C	H	■	A	L	V	A
A	R	E	N	A	■	M	A	T	A	■	N	Y	E	T
P	A	R	I	S	T	E	X	A	S	■	G	I	N	S
A	N	D	■	C	I	A	■	B	R	O	N	T	E	■
■	■	A	T	H	E	N	S	G	E	O	R	G	I	A
S	E	L	M	A	■	T	E	R	E	S	A	■	■	■
I	D	E	A	L	■	V	I	N	E	■	I	K	E	■
D	A	R	N	■	P	R	E	P	S	■	G	N	A	T
E	M	T	■	W	H	I	R	■	P	E	A	L	S	■
■	■	A	R	A	F	A	T	■	A	L	L	E	Y	■
N	A	P	L	E	S	F	L	O	R	I	D	A	■	■
E	L	A	I	N	E	■	T	A	R	■	T	D	S	■
V	I	C	E	■	T	O	L	E	D	O	O	H	I	O
E	V	E	N	■	W	H	A	M	■	F	R	E	O	N
R	E	D	S	■	O	O	P	S	■	F	E	R	R	Y

160

I	R	A	N	■	D	E	S	I	■	A	D	A	P	T
N	E	M	O	■	I	R	O	N	■	R	O	M	E	O
C	H	I	C	■	G	A	R	B	A	G	E	C	A	N
H	A	G	U	E	■	■	T	O	R	O	S	■	■	■
■	B	A	T	T	L	E	A	X	E	■	L	I	M	B
■	■	■	S	C	A	N	■	■	S	T	A	L	E	R
S	O	S	■	S	T	A	B	■	S	P	I	R	O	■
Q	U	A	R	T	E	R	B	A	C	K	S	A	C	K
U	N	D	E	R	■	Y	O	G	A	■	■	D	Y	E
A	C	I	D	I	C	■	E	G	A	D	■	■	■	■
B	E	E	B	■	A	N	K	L	E	B	O	O	T	■
■	■	■	I	G	L	O	O	■	■	A	G	N	E	W
Y	O	U	R	E	F	I	R	E	D	■	S	I	T	E
A	A	N	D	M	■	S	E	E	R	■	A	C	R	E
P	R	E	S	S	■	Y	A	L	E	■	T	E	A	K

161

A	P	P	T	■	Y	A	M	■	A	P	L	U	S	■
F	U	R	Y	■	M	A	K	E	■	S	E	E	T	O
T	R	I	P	■	A	L	B	A	■	K	E	A	N	U
E	S	S	E	N	T	I	A	L	W	O	R	K	E	R
R	E	M	A	S	T	E	R	■	R	U	G	■	■	■
■	■	■	Y	E	S	■	G	O	T	R	I	C	H	■
A	S	I	G	N	■	W	I	N	■	O	S	H	A	■
H	O	M	E	C	O	M	I	N	G	Q	U	E	E	N
A	M	M	O	■	C	U	Z	■	U	P	E	N	D	■
B	E	A	R	H	U	G	■	M	F	A	■	■	■	■
■	■	■	G	E	L	■	M	A	R	I	A	N	A	S
U	S	M	I	L	I	T	A	R	Y	D	R	O	N	E
S	T	E	A	L	■	H	I	V	E	■	M	I	N	D
D	U	N	N	O	■	E	M	I	R	■	E	R	I	E
A	F	U	S	S	■	M	S	N	■	D	E	E	R	■

162

J	A	D	A	■	M	T	W	T	F	■	■	L	P	S
E	V	I	L	■	C	O	W	A	R	D	■	E	R	A
N	O	S	E	■	C	M	I	N	O	R	■	T	I	N
N	I	C	E	J	O	(B)	■	S	T	R	A	Y	E	D
A	D	O	■	L	Y	R	(A)	■	H	U	G	O	S	■
■	■	M	A	O	■	(A)	S	P	■	T	O	U	T	S
O	R	(B)	S	■	H	I	T	E	C	H	■	R	E	T
P	O	O	H	■	A	D	O	R	E	■	O	H	S	O
P	C	(B)	■	T	H	E	R	M	O	■	W	A	S	P
S	A	U	N	A	■	R	I	(A)	■	A	L	I	■	■
■	F	L	I	N	T	■	A	(F)	T	S	■	R	F	K
L	E	A	P	D	A	Y	■	(R)	A	K	E	D	I	N
A	L	T	■	E	M	O	P	(O)	P	■	T	O	T	O
O	L	E	■	M	E	D	U	S	A	■	T	W	I	T
S	A	D	■	R	A	N	T	S	■	A	N	N	S	■

163

H	O	R	A		A	C	I	D		C	A	M	A	R	O
O	A	H	U		R	O	M	A		R	E	E	L	E	D
G	R	U	B		I	S	A	Y		E	R	R	A	N	D
	B	U	D	D	Y	C	O	P	M	O	V	I	E	S	
	C	A	R	E				F	O	E	S				
B	A	R	N	E	Y	F	I	F	E		O	M	I	T	
U	S	B		T	U	R	N			P	L	A	N	O	N
S	U	P	S		B	O	T	R	E	E		D	A	T	A
K	A	I	L	U	A		A	C	A	I		B	A	M	
	L	E	O	N		M	A	J	O	R	S	C	A	L	E
	N	O	A	M				T	A	D	S				
W	H	I	T	E	H	O	U	S	E	D	O	G	S		
R	O	S	A	R	Y		S	O	L	E		E	P	I	C
I	N	L	O	V	E		E	L	S	A		R	O	K	U
T	E	A	S	E	S		D	O	E	R		S	T	E	P

164

C	A	S	T		A	N	O	N		P	E	T	A	L
O	T	T	O		L	I	P	O		A	G	O	N	Y
R	E	A	R		P	O	E	M		C	O	W	E	R
G	I	M	M	E	A	B	R	E	A	K		E	W	E
I	N	P	E	A	C	E		M	U	L	L			
			N	S	A		P	E	P	P	E	R	E	D
E	M	O	T	E		G	O	A	L		G	A	L	A
R	A	N		O	N	C	U	E		C	S	I		
I	N	T	L		H	A	U	S		M	A	K	E	S
E	X	H	I	B	I	T	S		L	I	L			
	E	U	R	O		G	A	S	L	O	G	S		
K	G	B		O	U	T	O	F	P	O	C	K	E	T
Y	E	A	R	N		A	X	L	E		A	N	N	A
I	N	L	E	T		D	E	A	L		P	O	O	L
V	A	L	V	E		A	N	T	S		S	W	A	K

165

M	O	B		A	S	T	R	O	S		E	C	H	O
O	U	R		S	T	E	A	L	S		M	O	O	D
L	S	U		S	P	A	C	E	N	E	E	D	L	E
E	T	T	U		A	S	K	S		X	R	A	Y	S
	E	N	S	U	E			S	T	Y				
E	I	F	F	E	L	T	O	W	E	R		A	T	E
S	N	O	R	E		S	O	C	A	L	L	E	D	
P	U	R	E		E	P	C	O	T		A	L	P	S
N	I	C	E	I	D	E	A		E	S	T	E	E	
U	T	E		F	E	R	R	I	S	W	H	E	E	L
	B	O	N			N	E	W	E	R				
S	N	A	I	L		A	C	D	C		D	R	A	B
W	O	R	L	D	S	F	A	I	R	S		A	X	E
A	L	O	E		P	A	R	C	E	L		I	L	L
G	A	D	S		F	R	A	T	T	Y		N	E	T

166

P	L	A	Y	M	A	T	E		A	M	B	L	E	D
R	U	N	O	U	T	O	N		M	A	R	A	C	A
I	N	D	U	S	T	R	Y		P	R	E	Y	O	N
C	A	R	D		E	S	A	U		B	E	I	N	G
E	R	E		E	S	O		T	O	L	D	T	O	
	B	L	T			P	O	L	E		O	M	G	
B	A	H	A	I		M	O	P	E		S	N	I	T
A	D	A	G	E		A	R	I		A	A	M	C	O
L	A	S	S		L	P	G	A		D	R	E	S	S
I	M	A		E	S	P	Y		C	I	A			
	S	T	J	U	D	E		A	H	N		S	A	M
S	M	A	U	G		D	I	D	O		M	O	V	E
T	I	S	K	E	T		R	I	P	T	I	D	E	S
A	T	T	E	N	D		A	E	R	A	T	O	R	S
T	H	E	S	E	S		Q	U	A	N	T	I	T	Y

167

S	L	E	D	S		O	A	S	I	S		P	E	T
A	E	S	O	P		W	H	I	S	T		R	N	A
G	O	L	D	E	N	E	A	G	L	E		I	S	M
		G	L	A	D		M	A	N		C	U	E	
F	I	R	E	U	P		P	A	N	C	A	K	E	D
A	L	A		N	A	V	I		D	I	L	L		
T	I	T		K	L	I	N	E		L	A	Y	L	A
W	A	T	T		M	E	A	T	S		S	P	U	N
A	D	L	I	B		S	T	A	I	D		E	N	D
	E	R	O	S		A	L	E	E		A	G	E	
B	A	S	E	H	I	T	S		S	P	A	R	E	S
A	W	N		E	R	E		S	T	E	W			
B	A	A		M	E	X	I	C	A	N	F	L	A	G
A	R	K		I	N	T	R	O		D	U	A	N	E
S	E	E		A	S	S	E	T		S	L	O	A	N

168

J	A	B		A	P	P	L	I	E	D		L	P	S
A	M	I		D	U	R	A	N	T	E		A	L	E
M	A	T	C	H	B	O	X	C	A	R		S	A	X
B	R	O	O	D			U	S	N	A	V	Y		
S	O	F	A		S	A	A	B			L	E	D	S
	F	L	I	N	T	M	I	C	H	I	G	A	N	
		S	N	O	O	P		L	E	G	A	T	O	
E	T	S		A	R	M		K	I	N		S	E	W
T	R	Y	O	N	E		I	N	F	R	A			
T	I	N	D	E	R	P	R	O	F	I	L	E		
U	P	T	O		R	E	B	S		D	R	O	P	
	W	A	R	B	L	E			L	E	O	N	E	
F	I	X		F	I	R	E	S	T	A	R	T	E	R
E	R	E		F	R	E	A	K	E	D		I	N	K
Y	E	S		S	E	Q	U	I	N	S		C	D	S

169

```
A T W A R ■ R U G B Y ■ ■ A S A
P H A S E ■ E M I L E ■ ■ P C T
R I D I N G H A B I T ■ ■ L A B
■ N E S T L E ■ E P I T O M E
A M I ■ S O A K ■ ■ U M P S ■
D I N G ■ ■ B R E R R A B B I T
O N T A P ■ ■ N O U N ■ ■ ■ ■
■ ■ T O B E O R N O T T O B E
■ ■ A L O E ■ ■ E V E N T ■ ■
T R E B L E C L E F ■ A L T O
I A G O ■ ■ S T O P ■ G R E ■
M I R A C L E ■ A R A B I A ■
E S E ■ P E B B L E B E A C H
L E T ■ A I O L I ■ L E N T O
Y D S ■ S A N T A ■ O N S E T
```

170

```
D O G ■ O A K ■ ■ ■ C H I E F
E R R ■ P I N A ■ A G E N D A
A C I D T R I P ■ W I I F I T
N A M E ■ S T E A M ■ S I T E
■ ■ R A P S ■ C A S T E ■ ■
I N C I T E ■ R E N O ■ L C D
P O O D L E C U T ■ D R D R E
A D U E ■ D E N I M ■ A H A T
S E N D S ■ L O C A L D I V E
S S T ■ M A I N ■ L O I T E R
■ ■ Y O U I N ■ P A P A ■ ■
P U S H ■ D E F E R ■ N U N S
S L E A Z E ■ T A K E T H A T
S T A R E S ■ C R E W ■ O N E
T A T E R ■ ■ L Y E ■ H A M
```

171

```
E N D S ■ O C H O ■ M O B S
B A R N ■ A H A B ■ A G U E
B R E A K F A S T R O L L S
■ W I K I ■ T H A I ■ E L S A
O H D E A R ■ T I N T ■ D I P
B A E ■ S T R A N G E L O O P
I L L S ■ E E G ■ S I G N S
■ ■ T B S P ■ A R T S ■ ■
A W G E E ■ A L E ■ A C C T
T H E W E S T W I N G ■ A H A
T A T ■ R O W E ■ T A C T I C
A T O I ■ L E E K ■ M A L L
■ I N S I D E B A S E B A L L
■ F I L M ■ Z I N E ■ A D I A
■ S T E P ■ E T T A ■ L Y N X
```

172

```
S L I T ■ P E T A ■ S K O S H
M A C E ■ I R O N ■ P A L A U
I T E M ■ T E N D ■ A T E S T
T H E P R I C E I S R I G H T
H E S ■ E F T ■ ■ U S E ■ ■
■ ■ S V U ■ S T P ■ ■ T E A
■ T O T E L L T H E T R U T H
S O N A R ■ A R R ■ A O R T A
Y O U B E T Y O U R L I F E ■
R N S ■ A S P ■ O K S ■ ■ ■
■ ■ F A X ■ J A I ■ C T S
C L A S S I C G A M E S H O W
O U S T S ■ H O P I ■ N I N E
O N T O E ■ E B A N ■ A N Y A
L E A P T ■ W I N G ■ P A S T
```

173

```
V I S A ■ P R I M P ■ A M O R
E S P N ■ L A M A R ■ Z O N E
T H E Y ■ A G A M E ■ A P E X
■ W H I T E C A S T L E ■ ■
■ O T I S ■ S E R E ■ ■
A D J O I N ■ ■ N E A R B Y
B A A ■ S U R F A C E ■ O U I
B I N G ■ M O O R E ■ M S R P
A R E A R ■ L O T ■ L I E G E
■ Y A L E ■ E D S ■ U R G E
S Q U A D ■ P C T ■ B E A R D
A U S ■ D E L O U S E ■ R K O
M E T A ■ L A U D E ■ A D I N
B E E P ■ S Y R I A ■ T E N N
A N N E ■ A S T O R ■ A N G E
```

174

```
A M I D ■ C R A P O ■ I O W A
L A V A ■ R E R U N ■ B R A G
I C E D C O F F E E ■ A G R A
■ ■ ■ D O W ■ B E T R A Y S
E M M Y S ■ P A L A U ■ N O S
S O Y ■ A I R P O R T W I F I
P A T H ■ N O R ■ T I C ■ ■
■ T H E I N S I D E I N F O
■ B R R ■ O E D ■ G A R B
E A U D E P A R F U M ■ R C A
C D S ■ N O T I T ■ I M M A D
H O T B A T H ■ S F O ■ ■
O N E A ■ F E E F I F O F U M
E A R N ■ U N L I T ■ D A N A
D I S K ■ L A M B S ■ Y M C A
```

175

```
I M A C   S E L L S   N O V A
B O C A   P L E A T   A R I D
M A N D A R I N O R A N G E S
  T E R R I       A M A S S
      E G G W H I T E S
M E H   U S H E R I N   B O P
E R A S E   I L K   D E E R E
D I S K S   L E I   S M E A R
A C H Y   D E N N Y   O T T O
L A B   V I S A G E S   G E T
    R E A D       S P A R
S P O R C L E   P L A C E B O
H E W N   A D O R E   H E I R
U R N S   P I L O T   O N E S
T E S T   S T E M S   O S L O
```

176

```
F I G   B R I N E   L A L A
I P A   F R I D A Y   I Z O D
J A Z Z E R C I S E   Q U I D
I D E A S   H O C   T U R N S
    N S A   T A H O E
G A V E   D A I R Y Q U E E N
O D E   V I C   B U R G L E
P I R A T E D   P R E S A L E
R E D D E R   T A I   D I D
O U I J A B O A R D   U S E S
  A T S I X   S O S
S P E C S   L C D   A D A P T
W O V E   S I O U X F A L L S
A K I N   G E D D E S   L I P
M E L T   T R E S S   Y E S
```

177

```
T I T L E   M E O W   I S L A
I S A A C   G A M E   P E A S
M O U T H O R G A N   A R T S
  C O N S E N T   V I E
G U S H E S   R I B J O I N T
A N T   S P F   Y U C C A S
S O A K   E A S T   D E E S
  K N U C K L E H E A D
  P E A T   E Y R E   N O S H
P L A C I D   M L B   G N U
B A C K L A S H   P E R S O N
A T L   B L A M E M E
N E A T   B O D Y D O U B L E
D A I S   E M I T   A S T E R
J U M P   D O T H   N E W E R
```

178

```
F A N C Y   S I R I   P B J S
A R E A S   E P I C   E R I E
L I T T L E R O C K   L I V E
L A S S   R E D O   R O G E N
    G A I N   T U S H
  B L A C K A N D W H I T E S
B L A M E   O D O R   I T O
R A R E   J O R T S   A D H D
A I G   P A R T   O B E Y S
D R E S S R E H E A R S A L
  P A S S   S L O T
S T I L T   O N C E   R O L O
O R Z O   C O C O C H A N E L
B O Z O   C Z A R   A C T E D
S T A N   S E A T   S T O K E
```

179

```
A L O N G   C A S E   U P C S
L A B O R   H D T V   P L O W
P R I V A T E E Y E   T A R O
O D E   H A R P   F O Y E R
  P A Y I T F O R W A R D
S E S A M E     E L O N
O W E N   M A L A Y   A P E
H O T E L C A L I F O R N I A
O K S   A R N A Z   O N E S
  A C A I   M I S E R Y
H I D D E N C A M E R A
A D A M S   B O O K   T A P
L E V I   R O L L W I T H I T
L A I R   A X E L   N E R D S
E L S E   G O R Y   G L U E D
```

180

```
A W E S   T V P G   S L I C E
B A N E   H E A R   E A S E L
A T T N   E R I E   C D R O M
C U R D S A N D W H E Y
U S E   A L E   A D D S T O
S I E R R A   A I W E I W E I
  I A M B I C   A C L
  A N C H O R S A W E I G H
O D E   E L N I N O
Z I M B A B W E   I D C A R D
S N O O Z E   E M O   S E A
  G O Y O U R O W N W A Y
S O L A R   K N O T   A I R S
A W A R E   R I D E   P R E P
T E X T S   A X E S   A L D A
```

181

```
A D D U P ■ S C A M ■ S T E W
M A R T A ■ H E R A ■ T A M E
B R E A D ■ I N C H ■ E X I T
L I G H T E R T H A N A I R ■
E N S ■ H A T ■ ■ T A D ■ ■ ■
■ ■ ■ G A S ■ I R M A ■ C R Y
■ H O L I E R T H A N T H O U
B E A U ■ I C E ■ ■ H E L M ■
L A R G E R T H A N L I F E ■
Y D S ■ L A Z Y ■ E O N ■ ■ ■
■ ■ ■ I L L ■ J A Y ■ L A Y ■
■ I T S A L L R E L A T I V E
J A I L ■ I O U S ■ L O B E S
O G L E ■ E D I T ■ T O R R E
B O L T ■ D E N S ■ O K A Y S
```

182

```
S P U D ■ A G A V E ■ M E S H
O R S O ■ G O L A N ■ E C H O
B E E T R E P O R T ■ G O E R
S P R E E ■ E Y E B A L L S
■ ■ ■ L A Z E ■ ■ R E F I L E
R O L L R E V E R S A L ■ ■ ■
E W E ■ S T A R E ■ D O D G E
B L A H ■ A D O B O ■ P O E M
A S K O F ■ E D E N S ■ J A M
■ ■ ■ M U S S E L M E M O R Y
S T R E E P ■ ■ S E R A ■ ■ ■
P R E C L U D E ■ ■ G R O P E
O A T H ■ M O U S S E C A L L
O D I E ■ E N R O N ■ O H O K
R E E F ■ S T O O L ■ S U P S
```

183

```
B A D P R ■ M A J O R ■ B B B
A T R I A ■ O L I V A ■ E A U
S E A C U C U M B E R ■ A R C
S I P ■ N A S A ■ R E P A C K
O N E A C R E ■ C A B A R E T
■ ■ ■ W H Y Y O U L I T T L E
H A R R Y ■ ■ W E L T ■ H O E
O B E Y ■ G O L D S ■ B U N T
T I A ■ C O P E ■ ■ T O R A H
E L L I B E R T A D O R ■ ■ ■
L I N D S A Y ■ T O Y O T A S
S T A I N S ■ S O N S ■ A N T
A I M ■ E Y E I N T H E S K Y
F E E ■ W O L F E ■ O D E L L
E S S ■ S N I T S ■ P U R E E
```

184

```
A R C A N E ■ T O F U ■ A M P
C A R W A X ■ A R A B ■ P O I
I M A L I T T L E T E A P O T
D I M ■ L O O K ■ ■ R U S T Y
■ ■ ■ B A R T ■ H E I R ■ ■ ■
A L B E R T O G O N Z A L E S
T A I N T ■ O P I E ■ O V A
B U T T ■ J I B E D ■ H U E Y
A G E ■ T O N I ■ L O I N S
T H R O W I N G A B O N E T O
■ ■ ■ P E N S ■ G A W K ■ ■ ■
S O B E R ■ B U L L ■ N O D
C H I C K E N Y A K I T O R I
O I L ■ E D I T ■ A F R I C A
T O E ■ D U P E ■ N E U R A L
```

185

```
J A M S ■ E L D E R ■ C C E D
E D A M ■ G O U G E ■ H O L Y
T A K I N G A D O G ■ E A S E
E M O T I O N ■ ■ A P E X E S
■ ■ ■ T P S ■ G F L A T ■ ■ ■
F A T E S ■ C A R ■ N A N A S
E L A N ■ N A M E D S H A R K
A L S ■ D A R E S A Y ■ D E I
T O T H E B E A C H ■ P E A R
S T E A L ■ E P A ■ B U R S T
■ ■ ■ S H A R P ■ D A B ■ ■ ■
T E C H I E ■ ■ A I R L I N E
S C O T ■ I S A B A D I D E A
A R I A ■ O I L E R ■ S L O T
R U N G ■ U N I T Y ■ H E N S
```

186

```
J A Z Z ■ F A N S ■ Y E L P S
E P E E ■ E L A L ■ A T E A T
S S N S ■ L A T E ■ C H E W Y
T O O T H I S O W N H O R N
■ ■ ■ S U N K ■ ■ I T S ■ ■ ■
C I S ■ S E A L E G S ■ S A M
S N E A K ■ ■ I S H ■ D I N O
P U L L S O M E S T R I N G S
A R M S ■ H A G ■ A M U S E
N E A ■ N I C E J O B ■ S T S
■ ■ ■ F O O ■ ■ A B B A ■ ■ ■
■ D R U M U P B U S I N E S S
A R O M A ■ S A N E ■ G A I L
C A P E D ■ A R T S ■ U C L A
A B Y S S ■ T E S S ■ S H O W
```

187

```
P S S T . E K E . . D R O P S
O A H U . O V U M . R A D I O
R I O T . N E R O . A R E N T
C L O U D S T O R A G E . . .
H S T . M A C . O X O . E G O
. . L I G H T N I N G B U G
C A S I N O . H I S . R A I L
A L O N G . L U C . R I N S E
R O P E . M O M . P I N K E R
T H U N D E R B I R D S . . .
S A P . R T E . G O O . B U S
. W E A T H E R F R O N T
M E D I A . T A T A . A T T A
P R I S M . A L I T . C O I N
G A M E S . . E T E . E X E S
```

188

```
O R S . N O H O W . C O R A L
H E H . E T U D E . O P E R A
O V E R C O M E S . U T T E R
H E L I C E S . T E C . I N K
. I F S O . . H I G H S E A S
E L L E . I R O N A G E . .
E L I . C N E T . L A S E S
L E F T O F F . R I G H T O N
. S E E M E . L O T S . S U E
. . A B R E E Z E . P Y R E
L O W L A N D S . D I S C
A C E . T O M . E L A N T R A
S E L M A . U N D E R G O E S
S A L O N . N O I S E . R A T
O N S E T . D R E S S . E M O
```

189

```
P I P E . G O G H . E M U S
I R A Q . M A G O O . G A Z E
N A T U R A L L A W . G R I T
A S H I E R . E T N A . I S H
. . P U S H . I N R E . .
D E C . S H A R P C O O K I E
W R O T E . R O S E . M O N T
A R M E D . B A Y . B A N T U
R O P E . B O S C . E N D E D
F L A T E A R T H E R . O L E
. C H E Z . O V E N . .
A F T . L O S E . I F I M A Y
R O S A . O N T H A T N O T E
C R U X . K A R E N . J O I N
H A V E . A P E S . A R T S
```

190

```
M A G M A . B A G G Y . S E W S
O T O E S . O P I N E . E V A N
T W O T H U M B S U P . V E R A
T A D A . F B I . . S E R I F
O R G . N O S O U P F O R Y O U
. U S E S . P A R S E . .
D R E A M . M I T R E . . F A M
J U S T O N E M O R E T H I N G
S T S . I R O N Y . E A R N S
. . L O N G U . A C H E . .
H O W S W E E T I T I S . P S T
A N O D E . C A D . I O T A
N E W T . F I N A L A N S W E R
G A Z A . C R O N E . A L E R T
S L A B . C E N T S . T E R N S
```

191

```
G O B I . P A R M . A L O E
O R I N . A T E A T . R O A M
B O L T . L A C K S H E A R T
A M O R S . S T E P I N . .
L E X I N G T O N . V A N N A
D O I C A R E . I R E . E A R
. . A R A . A C E . F R A T
. L I C K S T H E S P O O N
B O D Y . P O L . E L O
T O E . A S L . S E A T R I P
S N A I L . L O C K S M I T H
. . C U E R V O . M O C H A
L U X E M B O U R G . D O E S
E R I E . B A L E S . E L L E
D I S S . D E R N . L A P S
```

192

```
M M A . S P U R . . B A G G Y
O A T . L E G I T . A G R E E
C H L O E Z H A O . F I O N A
H E A R D . T O P F L O O R
A R S E . C H A N E L I M A N
. . O S H A . P E T S .
P R I S C I L L A . Y M H A
A O C . I N V O G U E . A I M
D E E P . E G G P L A N T S
. . D R E W . R O I L .
C E L I N E D I O N . B A T S
R E A C T I O N . K U G E L
U N T I E . G U C C I M A N E
M I T E R . S I G N S . I S P
B E E R S . T I N S . N E T
```

193

```
S T O M P . S W A P . D V D S
O W N E R . M O N A . R E A P
H O U S E P A R T Y . A G H A
O S S . F A R M . B A G E L S
. . Z E S T S . A B U T . .
T S H I R T . I C E P A C K
R I O T . A L A S K A . B Y E
I N D I E . O I L . M I L A N
E G G . S H O R E S . G E N Y
D E E P S E T . O D E S S A
. P L E A . L I N E R . .
A R O U N D . I W I N . S A T
R O D S . S E M I C I R C L E
G O G H . U M P S . A B A T E
O K E Y . P U S H . L I M O S
```

194

```
R O C K S . S T A T E . T E N
I N L A W . O U G H T . A L E
G L U T E N F R E E C R U S T
A Y E . D E A N . Y E N T A S
. . P E N S . A T T A . .
. S E I N E . A C H E . L I U
C I N Q . A S T E R O I D S
A S S U M E T H E M A N T L E
S Q U E E G E E D . S H E D
T O E . G O A S . S N E E R
. . H A M M . W H I T . .
P A G O D A . C A A N . S P F
R O T T E N T O T H E C O R E
A N O . A I S L E . P I N O T
Y E S . L A K E R . M A G M A
```

195

```
N A S A . A N K A . S H A M E
A P E X . G E A R . H O G A N
P O L E V A U L T . O V E R T
S P F . A I R . C R E O L E
. P E N N A N D T E L L E R
L E I F . L U I S . D Y S
A T T I L A . T A C O S .
D A Y L I G H T S A V I N G S
. E D G A R . N O N F A T
O R S . I N E S . A L L Y
B O T T L E D E P O S I T
S T A R E S . I C E . E G O
E A T I T . I N T H E B A N K
S T E P H . L E E R . E M U S
S E N S E . L O D E . E S S O
```

196

```
A B B O T . M O N T E . C O B
S A U N A . B R O O M . L I E
L A B O R D A Y W E E K E N D
. . G A S X . R O O K S
. C A P E S . I A G O .
P U S H T H E E N V E L O P E
A R T I E . D A L I . S P A M
C A R . D I G R E S S . E N O
E T A S . B E L T . O W N I T
D E L I V E R Y S E R V I C E
. D O T S . L E A N S
C H I L I . G L E E .
H E R E C O M E S M Y B A B Y
A R K . E N O L A . E A G L E
P B S . D E I S T . S H O T S
```

197

```
C O N C H . S A M . C L O U T
A K I R A . T I O . H E N N A
T A K E I T O R L E A V E I T
E Y E D R O P . E N L I S T
. . T O G A . G E N .
L O V E I T O R H A T E I T
A N I S E . T A G S . C U E
L E D E . T A B L E . B A L M
A P E . N O N O . F A R S I
. M O V E I T O R L O S E I T
. O W L . K E E L .
. B O W S E R . D A D B O D S
M A K E I T O R B R E A K I T
E A R L E . W O O . R H I N E
G L A S S . S E X . S T E E P
```

198

```
M A I N E . S L O T H . B U B
E L M O S . P A T I O . A N A
S T A R Q U A R T E R B A C K
H O G . F I D O . N O B L E
. O D E O N . S E A A I R
M A N I A S . R A T T R A P S
E V E N S . C H A I .
T A R G E T H E A R T R A T E
. W E T S . H O R A S
P E A R T A R T . B O O T U P
R U P E E S . F L U F F .
I R E N A . H A L O . O O H
D E M O C R A T I C P A R T Y
E K E . U N H I P . H I M O N
S A N . P A S T S . O L S E N
```

199

```
L A T H   S E A L   S T E A M
A C R E   U R S A   T O P I C
P A U L A Z A H N   I P A D S
S C A M P I   A S E A
E I N   P E T T I N G Z O O S
S A T S   O R S O     V C R
    P E S K Y   O R B I T S
  P R I N C E S S Z E L D A
P O I N T Y   A T E I T
I P A   T A I L   S E G O
P O L I S H Z L O T Y   L E B
    C H E T   H I P P I E
C I L I A   E A S Y P E A S Y
F R A N K   C R A M   A S H E
L E D G E   S T Y E   T O A D
```

200

```
I K N O W   G A N G   S I R E
N A O M I   O R E O   C R O W
E S T A S   T E A R   A I D E
P H O N E C H A R G E R S
T I N   G A S     O R P H A N
    O U R   W A N E   S S E
G U M M Y B E A R S   S T I R
A M A S S   T I C   A H E A D
R I N K   H A S H B R O W N S
B A H   T E S T   U M P
S K A T E R   W R Y   A C E
  T R E A S U R Y B I L L S
N O T E   L O G O   R O L E S
F R A Y   D O L T   A W A R E
L E N S   S T Y E   T A S K S
```

The New York Times

SMART PUZZLES

Presented with Style

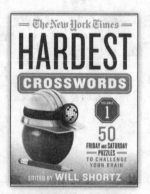